AN
INTRODUCTION
TO
COMPUTING

AN INTRODUCTION TO COMPUTING

Problem-Solving, Algorithms, and Data Structures

DANIEL U. WILDE
University of Connecticut

PRENTICE-HALL, INC.
ENGLEWOOD CLIFFS, NEW JERSEY

Library of Congress Cataloging in Publication Data

WILDE, DANIEL U.
    An introduction to computing.

    Includes bibliographies.
      1. Electronic digital computers—Programming.
2. Algorithms. I. Title.
QA76.6.W54   001.6'42   72-5754
ISBN 0-13-479519-9

10 9 8 7 6 5 4 3 2 1

PRENTICE-HALL INTERNATIONAL, INC., *London*
PRENTICE-HALL OF AUSTRALIA, PTY. LTD., *Sydney*
PRENTICE-HALL OF CANADA, LTD., *Toronto*
PRENTICE-HALL OF INDIA PRIVATE LIMITED, *New Delhi*
PRENTICE-HALL OF JAPAN, INC., *Tokyo*

Printed in the United States of America

Contents

Preface

The primary purpose of this book is to help the reader learn how to use a computer as a problem-solving tool.

    Problem solving is an acquired skill. Like any skill, it must be developed by imitation and practice. Swimming is a good example of an acquired skill. In the beginning, when you learned to swim, you imitated the arm and foot movements of those you saw swimming. At first you were barely able to keep your head above water, but with practice and coaching from more experienced swimmers you were able to improve your performance. Learning to solve problems is similar to learning to swim. In the beginning you observe and imitate what other people do when they solve problems. You start by solving small problems and then gradually advance to larger ones. If you want to refine your swimming ability, you practice swimming; likewise, if you want to develop your problem-solving ability, you practice problem solving.

    To the beginner, problem solving is difficult because he does not understand what to do. He does not know where to begin, and, once started, he does not know how to continue. This book introduces a procedure that should help the beginner learn to use a computer as a problem-solving tool. This procedure incorporates a *systems approach* and covers the total process of using a computer. It is *not* limited to just one part of the solution process, such as learning the grammar rules of a particular language. Rather, it starts by encouraging the beginner to define and understand his problem so that he realizes what is required. It then continues through a series of steps designed to guide him to a successful solution.

Organization of the Book

Chapter 1 introduces man as a problem solver and discusses how computers are being used to solve some of man's most pressing problems, such as those in the fields of education, medicine, pollution control, and crime prevention. Chapter 2 briefly summarizes the major innovations that preceded the development of the stored-program digital computer and then describes the major components of such systems.

Chapter 3 introduces a simplified but realistic model of a computer. Its operation is explained and then analyzed in order to predict the problems of using a computer.

Chapter 4 presents a six-step problem-solving procedure designed to help the beginner learn to use a computer. Four graphical techniques are introduced as problem-solving aids. The *input list* and *output list* are used to specify input and output data. The *data chart* is used to specify data interrelationships (data structures) of data sets. Finally, the *flow chart* is used to specify calculation procedures (algorithms).

Chapter 5 introduces a *simple* flow-chart language that allows the beginner to concentrate upon his algorithm without concerning himself with the details of a particular programming language. Once produced, he can use his flow chart to verify that his algorithm is valid and complete.

Chapter 6 introduces the simplest of all data structures—the single cell. It begins by describing the characteristics of data sets which have a single-cell structure and then uses this structure to solve sample problems. Chapter 7 begins by attempting to solve a problem whose data do not fit single cells, thus showing the need for additional data structures. The single-dimension or linear list data structure is introduced and then used to solve problems. Similarly, Chapter 8 repeats this process for multidimension or array data structures.

Chapter 9 introduces the function and subroutine as program structures that can be used for problem subdivision and easier problem solving and then uses them to solve a series of problems.

Chapter 10 introduces the concepts of sequential and random files and describes how they are stored via tape and disk. Techniques for sequential and random processing are presented and then sequential and random files are used to solve problems.

Finally, Chapter 11 introduces the list structure. It begins by illustrating the limitations of earlier data structures and then shows how list structures can overcome such drawbacks. Techniques for using list structures are presented and then example problems are solved.

Using the Book This book is arranged such that the reader can begin with Chapter 1 and work through the book chapter by chapter. Great care has been taken to ensure that when new material is presented, it builds upon earlier material. For example, each new data structure is introduced by attempting a problem which is best solved with a data structure that is more complex than those used previously. Furthermore, exercises are solved in order of increasing difficulty and have been selected because they introduce widely applicable computer techniques.

Problem solving as presented here is independent of programming language and machine configuration. For this reason, the details of a particular programing language have been omitted. This allows the reader to concentrate upon the more creative activities of problem definition, input and output specification, data structure selection, and algorithm development. Nevertheless, it is important for a beginning problem solver to test some of his solutions on an actual computer using some programming language.

Presently, many fine programming language manuals are available, and any of these is appropriate for use with this text. Furthermore, it is possible to use more than one programming language at once. In fact, the author has class tested this book with students using one or more of the following languages simultaneously: PL/I, PL/C, FORTRAN IV, WATFOR, and IBM 1130 FORTRAN. This allows students to compare different languages and to evaluate their effectiveness and usefulness for different types of problems.

This book is designed for a 14- or 15-week semester course, and the sample class schedule below shows general assignments by class meeting and indicates the appropriate language manual assignment. This book can be cut back to a quarter course by stopping at the end of Chapter 9, Functions and Subroutines. On the other hand, it can be expanded to a full year by increasing the number of assigned problems. The instructor's manual which accompanies this text shows detailed assignment sheets for various languages and language manuals.

The text of each chapter is followed by a list of selected references which guide the reader to expanded discussions of the various topics presented in that chapter. Since practice is the best method of improving problem-solving skills, each chapter contains a wealth of problems arranged in order of increasing difficulty. Earlier problems are adaptations of simpler examples discussed in the chapter while the later ones will challenge even the experienced student. The instructor's manual contains detailed solutions to all problems and expanded discussion of text material.

Finally, if a computer is available for student use, it is important that it be introduced as early as possible; a computer center tour should be arranged soon after the first class. Once the student is familiar with the *computer environment*, key-punch or on-line terminal exercises can be assigned. The author has found that this is best done in two steps. *First*, the student simply key punches a small set of cards or types a small number of input lines at his console from a prepared assignment sheet. This allows the instructor the opportunity to check for errors common to beginners. *Second*, the student produces a second set, but this time he submits his cards for processing or executes his program on-line. By this time he is ready to use the computer to test his text assignments and will have already learned how to use his computer center or on-line terminal.

SAMPLE CLASS SCHEDULE

Class	Topic	Text	Assignments Language Manual
1	Introduction	Ch. 1	Computer Center Tour
2	Background	Ch. 2	Key Punch No. 1
3–5	Problems of Using a Computer	Ch. 3	
6–7	A Problem Solving Procedure	Ch. 4	Key Punch No. 2
8–10	A Flow-Chart Language	Ch. 5	Introduction
11–12	Single-Cell Data Structures	Ch. 6	Nonsubscripted Variables
13–15	Problem Solving		
16–17	Coding		
18	First Exam		
19–20	Single-Dimension Data Structures	Ch. 7	Single-Subscripted Variables
21–23	Problem Solving		
24–25	Coding		
26	Multidimension Data Structures	Ch. 8	Multi-Subscripted Variables
27	Problem Solving		
28	Coding		
29	Functions and Subroutines	Ch. 9	Functions and Subroutines
30–31	Problem Solving		
32	Coding		
33	Second Exam		
34	Sequential and Random Files	Ch. 10	Tapes and Disks
35	Problem Solving		
36	Coding		
37–38	List Structures	Ch. 11	
39–40	Problem Solving		
41	Coding		
42	Review		

Acknowledge-ments   It is with great pleasure that I acknowledge the invaluable assistance that I have received from so many people, for without them, this book would not have been possible. In particular, I would like to thank the many students who used preliminary drafts of this text for their infinite patience and constant willingness to offer suggestions. I am most grateful to the many anonymous reviewers for their most valuable comments and insights that helped refine the organization and content of this text. My colleagues Professors Donald Klett and Marvin Rothstein class tested drafts, while Professor Ellis Page contributed his thoughts on problem solving. Jay Tunkel, Warren Sargent, Keith Gregory, Parthasarathy Sonty, and Stuart Harris assisted in class testing while Richard Smith co-authored the instructor's manual.

There could not have been a book without the support provided by R. O. Harvey. Dover Ford, Jane Conley, Mary Speltz, and Susan Mandeville typed drafts, while Susan Abramson did an outstanding job in typing final copy and drawing art work. I would like to thank the late Professor George Forsythe of Stanford University for his interest and advice and Karl Karlstrom and Rennie Rieger of Prentice-Hall, Inc., for their enthusiastic support of my problem-solving approach and for keeping production ahead of schedule.

Finally, Marylin Wilde provided the encouragement that was needed to write the manuscript. Only she knows how much she sacrificed; in reality, this book is as much hers as mine.

D. U. WILDE
Storrs, Connecticut

1 Introduction

1.1 Man—The Problem Solver

Since the beginning of time, man has been a problem solver. This ability has made him the dominant species on earth. While solving problems, he has invented tools that have enabled him to change his environment and overcome his physical limitations and human frailties, whereas other species have merely existed as best they can.

No doubt it was by chance that early man learned to use fire to make his life easier and more comfortable. Perhaps he came across the carcass of an animal that had been killed in a forest fire. Being desperately hungry, he ate some and found it better than raw meat. In time, man learned to start his own fire and was able to enjoy cooked meat whenever he desired. Eventually, he further refined his control of fire and used it as a tool to overcome his physical limitations. He discovered that other animals were afraid of fire and that it could be used as a weapon to compensate for his lack of physical strength. He also learned that fire could provide him with warmth and could make up for his lack of heavy fur. In modern times, man found that fire could be used in a variety of manufacturing processes, such as in the production of iron and steel, and as a means of waste disposal.

One can only guess how the first wheel was invented. Maybe it all began when someone noticed that it was easier to move a block of stone over a rolling log than to push it directly on the ground. Undoubtedly, such an observation led to a series of logs, where the load was pushed from one log to the next. Somehow, someone found a way to attach the rolling surface directly to the load via axle and wheels. In time, man learned to use the wheel as a tool to enhance his abilities and to overcome his physical limitations. He built carts and wagons and trained other animals to pull them so that he could move heavier loads over greater distances. Not satisfied, he invented engines that could power his vehicles so that they could carry more and travel faster. The most notable wheeled vehicle, the gasoline-powered automobile, provides man with a convenient and rapid means of ground travel.

Man's success in problem solving has also brought him unpredicted side effects and unanticipated problems. His amazing manufacturing processes generate by-products and wastes that contaminate his air, earth, and water. His modern automobiles with their internal combustion engines threaten to strangle his larger cities through smog and traffic jams. His modern jet airplanes with their ever-increasing airspeeds and passenger capacities dangerously clog airlanes and jam passenger and baggage handling facilities. Even his miracle medical discoveries produce cruel paradoxes. In some parts of the world, children who are saved by newly discovered medical techniques are in danger of starving to death from lack of food caused by the population explosion.

1.2 The Computer— A Problem-Solving Tool

Today, the computer holds enormous potential for people determined to find solutions to mankind's most pressing problems, such as education, the urban crisis, environmental pollution, exploding world population, hunger, natural disaster, and crime.

Presently, city planners are just beginning to use computers to meet the urban crisis. Traffic control projects have been initiated to study the ability of computers to expedite heavy traffic flows and to clear streets ahead of emergency vehicles. Large parking lots are computer controlled, with a computer not only calculating parking fees but also directing individual cars to open parking spaces. Police departments are using a centralized computer to store information on unpaid traffic tickets and stolen cars. With only a radio call, any patrolman in the city can determine within seconds whether an automobile is stolen or whether its driver is wanted for unpaid tickets. Interest is now being shown in using the computer for total city planning. For example, attempts are being made to use a computer to predict how, when, and where a city will expand. With such information, more effective and efficient plans can be developed for city services, such as water distribution and sewage collection, fire and police protection, and street layout and traffic control. In addition, the computer is beginning to be used to solve the problems of the inner city, such as air and water pollution and urban renewal planning.

The battle against hunger and starvation has just begun to enlist the power of a computer. For example, corn, one of the world's most important food crops, has 20 pairs of chromosomes, each of which has hundreds of genes that influence a plant's growth rate, yield, and disease resistance. In addition, production yields are affected by soil type, plowing, and local growing conditions. Test data from planting experiments from many parts of the world are being fed into a central computer for analysis. Hopefully, the results will reveal how an individual planter can increase his corn production by matching the best available variety of hybrid seed to his own particular growing conditions.

The effects of the application of computers in medicine are beginning to emerge. Computerized hospital information systems are transmitting patient data between wards and laboratories, relieving doctors, nurses, and laboratory technicians of time-consuming and error-prone paper work. Computerized intensive care units are being developed, which automatically call attention to potentially serious patient conditions even before the ever-present nurse can sense such changes. Radiologists are using computers to determine radiation dosages likely to be the most effective treatment for cancer patients. Physicians are using computers to analyze electrocardiograms and to diagnose heart ailments.

Work is just beginning on the control of the natural environment through computers. Meteorologists are improving their weather predictions by using computers to analyze vast amounts of weather data collected by meteorological satellites. Sensors transmit rainfall data from remote unmanned locations to a central computer, which watches for unusual conditions, such as potential flooding. Using a computer, scientists are simulating earthquakes and tidal waves in hope of learning how to predict the occurrence of such devastating natural phenomena.

Perhaps education is the field in which computers will have their greatest social impact. As population increases, it will be almost impossible to provide enough highly trained teachers. Elementary and high schools must instruct more students and yet insure that each student receives more individual attention—enough to guarantee that his performance matches his ability. Junior colleges, universities, and graduate schools must be able to admit and educate all students whose intellect and motivation make them suitable for additional education. The disadvantaged student at all levels must be given additional attention and training so that he can reach his full potential without distracting other students. Workers whose skills are no longer needed must be retained so that they can continue to make a contribution to their families and society. These educational problems are challenges not easily solved. Much still needs to be discovered about the learning process itself. Pilot projects indicate that a computer can be a student's personal tutor, guiding him through his lesson, testing him for complete comprehension, and automatically repeating improperly understood material before beginning the next lesson.

The application of the computer to man's most pressing problems will prove its real worth. However, you, the reader, will soon realize that a computer is not an almighty electronic brain. It is a tool—a tool that can help you overcome your human inability to perform rapid mental calculations and to digest masses of information. As with any tool, a computer needs an intelligent human being who knows how to apply it to his problem in the most effective manner.

1.3
Learning
to Use a
Computer
to Solve
Problems
Perhaps you know or have heard that you must write a computer program before you can use a computer to solve a problem. Figure 1.1 shows examples of computer programs that solve the same problem in two different programming

```
        READ(5,10)  PRIN,RATE,NYEARS
10      FORMAT(F7.2,1X,F4.3,1X,I3)
        BAL=PRIN
        DO 20 I=1,NYEARS
        BAL=BAL*(1+RATE)
20      WRITE(6,30) I,RATE,PRIN,BAL
30      FORMAT(1H ,I3,3X,F4.3,3X,F7.2,3X,F7.2)
        STOP
        END
```
(a)

```
INTEREST:   PROCEDURE OPTIONS (MAIN);
            GET DATA (PRIN,RATE,NYEARS);
            BAL=PRIN;
L1:         DO I=1 TO NYEARS;
            BAL=BAL*(1+RATE);
            PUT DATA (I,RATE,PRIN,BAL);
            END L1;
            END INTEREST;
```
(b)

Figure 1.1 *Examples of programming languages. (a) FORTRAN. (b) PL/I.*

languages. Both programs calculate the growth of a savings account balance (BAL) starting with an initial principal (PRIN) compounded yearly at an interest rate (RATE) for a given number of years (NYEARS). Each program is made up of a sequence of statements with individual statements written on separate lines. Each program statement must satisfy the rules of its own language just as the sentences of this book must comply with the rules of English grammar. For example, the fourth line of the FORTRAN program in Figure 1.1a is known as a *DO statement*. A DO statement in FORTRAN must always begin with the letters DO, followed by a positive integer that also appears to the left of some other statement below the DO. Figure 1.1b shows the same problem solution written in the PL/I programming language. Notice that there are similarities and correspondences between lines of the two programs even though they are written in different languages.

There is more to learning to use a computer for problem solving than memorizing grammar rules of some programming language. Before a computer can solve your problem, you must give it explicit instructions on how it is to perform its calculations. Not only must your instructions or program statements be written in correct grammar, but they must also be arranged in proper sequence. It is one thing to know how to write a DO statement, but it is a different matter to know when to use one. This situation is very similar to when you first began to study a foreign language. You were probably able to learn the grammar rules of the language quickly but found it very difficult to apply them. For example, it was easy to remember that every sentence must have a subject and a verb and must end with a punctuation mark; however, it was difficult to learn how to synthesize individual words into correct sentences and sentences into clear and meaningful paragraphs. You will find the same is true with programming languages, i.e., the rules are simple but their application is often difficult.

The purpose of this book is to help you overcome these difficulties. It assumes that you want to learn how to use a computer to solve problems and that later you will have problems of your own to solve. It will introduce you to problem-solving techniques that should help you produce computer programs having correct statements in proper sequence. These techniques are machine and language independent, and should help you solve problems no matter which computer or programming language you use.

SELECTED REFERENCES

1. Desmonde, William H., *Computers and Their Uses*, Prentice-Hall, Inc., Englewood Cliffs, N. J., 1964.

2. Greenberger, Martin, *Management and the Computer of the Future*, Massachusetts Institute of Technology Press, Cambridge, Mass., 1962.

3. Martin, James, and Adrian Norman, *The Computerized Society*, Prentice-Hall, Inc., Englewood Cliffs, N. J., 1970.

4. Scientific American, *Information*, W. H. Freeman and Co., Publishers, Philadelphia, 1966.

5. Sedelow, Sally Y., "The Computer in the Humanities and Fine Arts," *Computing Surveys*, Vol. 2, No. 2, June 1970, pp. 89–110.

2 Background

Man has solved problems and invented tools because he has wanted to overcome his human limitations. In Chapter 1, the probable development and use of fire and the wheel as tools were briefly outlined. A closer examinaton would show that their development was actually a sequence of events where one innovation led to the next or made the next one possible. The same is true for today's modern computer. Its development began long ago when men became frustrated by their inability to perform mental calculations. In time, one innovation after another led to what is now known as the *stored program digital computer*.

Before we begin our study of the use of a computer as a problem-solving tool, let us review the sequence of events that led to today's computer. Our brief review will demonstrate that the computer is just the latest innovation in a long sequence of events and is not a completely new concept. Once this development has been outlined, we shall describe a modern computer system. This commentary is intended to give an overview of how a computer is constructed and how its individual components are combined to form a system. Furthermore, this discussion should provide a general background so that you will be better able to understand both the operation and the operational problems of a computer, as presented in Chapter 3.

Only within recent times has man realized the value of on-the-spot recording of historical events. Because the history of mechanized computation began several thousand years ago, it is impossible to report accurately the series of events that led to the development of a digital computer. In addition, the author freely admits that the historical summary that follows contains his own interpretation of the importance of individual events.

2.1.1 Numbers

Probably, the history of mechanized computation began several thousand years ago with the development of numbers. The most popular, known today as *Arabic* or *Hindu* notation, uses 10 symbols, 0 to 9, and a _position system_, which makes it possible to form a number of any size from only 10 symbols. Each numerical position represents an increasing power of 10 beginning with 10^0 at the far right. For example, in the number 423, the 3 represents 3 times 10^0; the 2 represents 2 times 10^1; and the 4 represents 4 times 10^2.

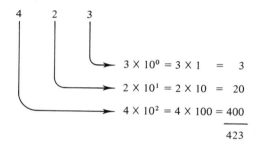

Because numbers in this system are composed of powers of 10, it is called a _base ten system_. Other bases are known to have been employed, but the decimal system proved most useful. In time, it replaced *Roman numerals* because calculations and counting were easier in a decimal system.

2.1.2 The abacus

The _abacus_ represents another significant event that led to the stored program digital computer. Developed in Asia, it is based upon a position system and was used by early Greeks and Romans to perform additions and subtractions. Today, it is still widely used in Russia and the Orient.

Usually, an abacus is composed of parallel wires with two beads above a crossbar and five beads below. Decimal numbers are represented by bead position where each bead against the bar from above counts five and those against the bar from below count one. Each parallel wire corresponds to a power of 10; thus, the number of bead rows determines the maximum value that can be represented. The abacus in Figure 2.1 illustrates the number 10,725, and since it has six wires, it can display any number up to and including 999,999.

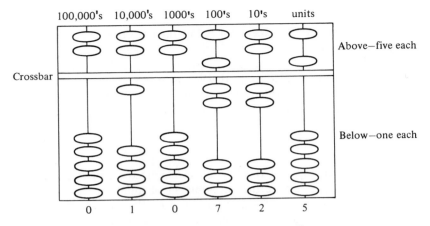

Figure 2.1   *The number 10,725 on an Abacus.*

Additions and subtractions are performed by manually shifting various beads back and forth in proper sequence. The abacus gained acceptance and use because it helped man overcome his inability to remember large numbers and to perform mental calculations.

2.1.3 Rotating wheel calculators

During the mid-seventeenth century, Blaise Pascal, a French religious philosopher and mathematician, invented the forerunner of today's mechanical desk calculator. Instead of representing numbers by beads, he used rotating wheels, as shown in Figure 2.2. Each wheel had ten positions, one for each of ten digits, and there was one such wheel for each numerical position or power of 10. Arithmetic carries from one position to the next were achieved through special gears such that when a wheel rotated from position 9 to 0, the wheel on its left advanced 1. Pascal's calculator could only add and subtract.

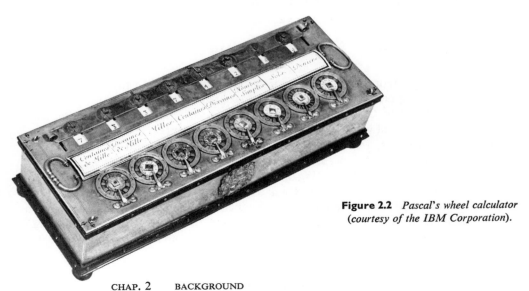

Figure 2.2   *Pascal's wheel calculator (courtesy of the IBM Corporation).*

But since multiplication can be performed by repeated additions and division by repeated subtractions, his calculator can be used for all four arithmetic operations. Near the end of the seventeenth century, Gottfried von Leibnitz advanced Pascal's rotating wheel concept and built a calculator that could multiply and divide directly. Because a wheel calculator could perform its arithmetic operations without human intervention, it proved to be more convenient and accurate than an abacus.

2.1.4 Difference and analytical engines

In the early nineteenth century, Charles Babbage, professor of mathematics at Cambridge University, conceived of a machine which he called a _difference engine_. Babbage used rotating wheels, as shown in Figure 2.3, but designed his machine to perform a sequence of arithmetic operations without human intervention. In particular, his machine was built to accelerate the computation of

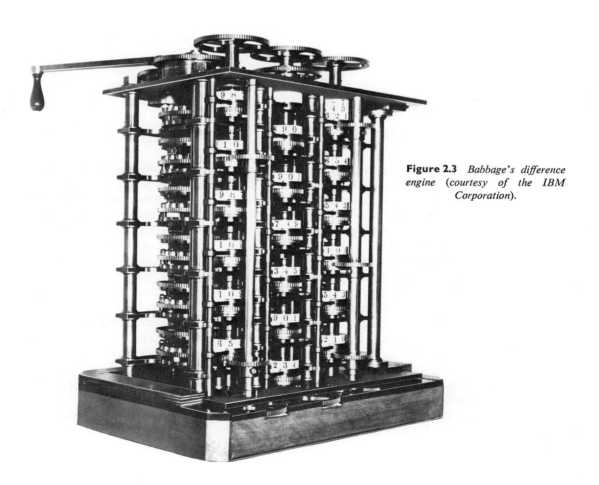

Figure 2.3 _Babbage's difference engine (courtesy of the IBM Corporation)._

mathematical values, such as logarithmic and trigonometric tables. The calculation procedure was based upon the fact that the values of an nth order polynomial can be calculated from its n differences and that the value of the nth difference is constant. The table in Figure 2.4 shows values of y and the first and second differences for the second-order polynomial, $y = x^2 + 2x - 1$. The first differences are calculated by subtracting adjacent values of y, whereas the second differences are calculated by subtracting adjacent first differences. Once the initial values of y and the first and second differences are known, all succeeding values of y can be calculated. For example, the first difference, 9, is calculated as the sum of the previous first difference, 7, and the constant second difference, 2. Once this first difference is known, the next value of y, 23, is simply the sum of the latest first difference, 9, and the previous value of y, 14. These new values can then be used to calculate the next value of y.

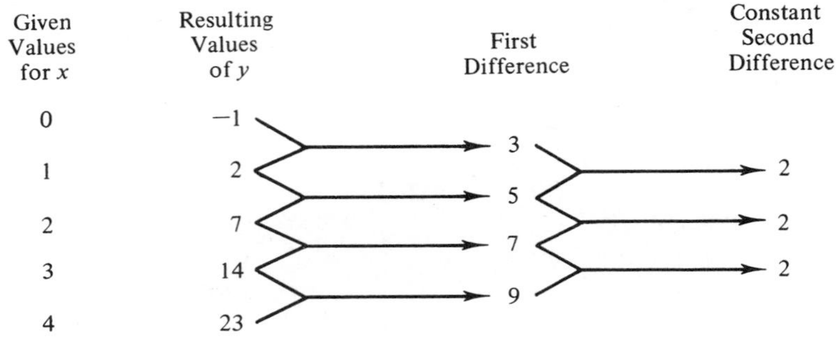

Given Values for x	Resulting Values of y	First Difference	Constant Second Difference
0	−1		
1	2	3	2
2	7	5	2
3	14	7	2
4	23	9	

Figure 2.4 *First and second differences for $y = x^2 + 2x - 1$.*

Babbage designed and built a difference engine that could evaluate second-order polynomials. His work showed that a mechanical device could perform a sequence of arithmetic operations without human intervention. Since the calculation procedure just described applies to any second-order polynomial, his machine could evaluate all such functions. But once his machine was built, it could only perform second-order sequences. It could not be used to evaluate higher order polynomials without adding additional gears and wheels to handle higher order numerical differences. Babbage realized this never-ending process and turned his attention toward the design of a generalized device that could perform any sequence of arithmetic calculations.

Babbage envisaged an *analytical engine*, the arithmetic sequence of which could be changed depending upon the problem. This time his engine would not only use rotating gears to represent decimal numbers, but it would also use them to control its arithmetic sequence. It would save numbers in its *store* while its *mill* would control and perform arithmetic operations. Babbage was never able to produce a working model because his craftsmen were simply unable to build enough precision components. Even though Babbage was ahead of the technology of his day, his ideas pointed the way for those who followed.

2.1.5 Punched cards

During the 1880's, Dr. Herman Hollerith, a statistician, was engaged by the U.S. Census Bureau as a special consultant to speed the processing of census data. Data obtained from the 1880 census took nearly eight years to analyze by hand, and it was clear that processing the 1890 data would take even longer and probably would not be completed before the start of the 1900 census. Something had to be done to accelerate analysis so that results would not be obsolete before they were finished.

Hollerith, setting out to mechanize the analysis, probably realized the impossibility of constructing a machine that could simultaneously process all his data. Instead, it would be necessary to build a device that would analyze small portions of data at a time. Therefore, he developed a means of data representation so that data could be fed into a machine over and over without significant additional human effort.

In the early 1800's, Joseph Marie Jacquard had invented a weaving machine that could produce intricate designs by following a set of instruction holes that had been punched into a paper card. The weaving pattern could be changed by simply shifting hole positions in an instruction card. Hollerith took Jacquard's idea and developed a coding system that represented decimal digits and alphabetical characters by different hole combinations.

Hollerith designed a set of card punches which were used to punch census data into paper cards. When the punching was completed, these cards were fed into a mechanical tabulating machine that could sense hole combinations and determine their data values. Once cards were punched, they could be fed repeatedly into the tabulator for analysis without additional punching. Hollerith's use of punched cards was successful, and results of the 1890 census were ready in less than three years.

In 1896, Hollerith left the Census Bureau to start the Tabulating Machine Company. After a series of mergers, it became part of the International Business Machines Corporation, maker of IBM digital computers. Hollerith was succeeded at the Bureau by John Powers, who remained there, improving upon Hollerith's early work, until 1911 when he, too, left to form the Powers Accounting Machine Company. Eventually, it became part of Sperry Rand Corporation's Univac Division, maker of UNIVAC computers. Thus, the punched card is the foundation of two of today's largest computer manufacturers.

2.1.6 Electromechanical calculators

In 1937, George Stibitz at Bell Telephone Laboratories observed similarities between circuit paths through telephone switching relays and binary numbers. In his spare time, using relays, a battery, and flashlight bulbs, Stibitz built an electromechanical device, called an *adder*, that could determine the sum of two numbers represented in the binary number system. The *binary digits*, 0 and 1, were represented inside the adder by the position of relay contacts, either open or closed. Once he had built a successful binary adder, Stibitz combined a number of adders and produced a device that could also subtract, multiply, and divide. After his initial success, Bell Laboratories asked Stibitz to generalize his machine so that it could perform calculations upon complex numbers, numbers composed of both real and imaginary parts. This device, called the *Complex Calculator*, received its input data and printed its results via a standard teletype keyboard. Stibitz went so far as to construct a special telegraph connection into his calculator so that it could receive input data from and transmit results to a remote teletype.

Once Stibitz had a calculator that could perform all four arithmetic operations, he turned his attention to a device that could perform an arbitrary sequence of such operations. His next machine, completed in 1940, received its instructions by reading holes that had been punched into paper tape. This machine could interpret hole combinations and determine its next operation. Thus, its instruction sequence could be altered by merely repunching its instruction tape.

Stibitz had succeeded in building the first *variable sequence calculator*. By using electromechanical relays as his main building component, he had prevailed where technology had defeated Babbage. In operating speed, his calculator greatly surpassed even the most advanced rotating wheel calculators. Furthermore, electromechanical relays do not wear as rapidly as gears, and thus are more reliable. Finally, a general purpose device had been built that could be used to solve a variety of problems.

Simultaneously, in 1937, Howard Aiken at Harvard University had begun to design a machine that could perform sequences of arithmetic operations. Completed in 1944, the *MARK I*, shown in Figure 2.5, contained 72 adding accumulators and was given its instructions through a combination of punched paper tape, switches and buttons, and plug boards. Although the MARK I was still electromechanical, its design ideas were carried over into electronic calculators.

2.1.7 Electronic calculators

In 1943, Professor John W. Eckert and J. Presper Mauchly from the Moore School of Electrical Engineering at the University of Pennsylvania proposed to the Ballistic Research Laboratories of the U.S. Army that it sponsor the development of an all-electronic calculator. This laboratory was responsible for the production of ballistic tables and was actively sponsoring the construction of electromechanical calculators. It was very willing to support any project that might increase arithmetic speeds of current calculators and thus reduce computation times required to produce its tables.

The *Electronic Numerical Integrator and Calculator* (ENIAC), shown in Figure 2.6, built by Eckert and Mauchly was the first large-scale electronic calculator. Instead of electromechanical relays, it used high-speed electronic vacuum tubes, which had been known for some time and were widely used in radios and electronic amplifiers. Binary digits, 0 and 1, were represented inside ENIAC by electrical voltages across vacuum tubes. ENIAC had no moving

Figure 2.5 *MARK I calculator (courtesy of the IBM Corporation).*

Figure 2.6 *ENIAC (courtesy of Sperry Rand Corporation).*

internal parts but still received its sequence of instructions from outside by means of boards and switches that were used to rewire connections between its components. Only data were retained inside its storage facility. Nevertheless, it was much faster than any electromechanical calculator, and it set the stage for a proposal that led to the stored program digital computer.

2.1.8 The stored program digital computer

In 1945, Dr. John von Neumann, a consultant to the ENIAC project from the Institute for Advanced Study (IAS) at Princeton University, wrote a proposal on behalf of the project for the first general purpose, *stored program digital computer*. ENIAC and all electromechanical calculators had saved only data in their storage facilities and received their instructions one at a time in sequence from outside. Von Neumann proposed that both data and instruction be stored in the computer with each different instruction, such as add or subtract, being represented by a different combination of 0's and 1's.

In the late 1940's, von Neumann supervised the construction of the IAS computer, a machine that incorporated his earlier proposals. This design was incorporated into a number of early computers: WHIRLWIND I at the Massachusetts Institute of Technology, MANIAC I at Los Alamos, ILLIAC I at the University of Illinois, and JOHNNIAC at Rand Corporation. The Electronic Delay Storage Automatic Calculator (EDSAC), built at Cambridge University, was the first *stored program* digital computer completed, and it went into operation in May, 1949. Eckert and Mauchly, who had formed their own company in 1946, built the Universal Automatic Computer. This machine, UNIVAC I, shown in Figure 2.7, became the first commercially available computer.

The von Neumann stored program concept greatly increases the flexibility and versatility of a computer. First, its instruction sequence can be changed without manually rewiring connections. All that is necessary is to load a new instruction sequence into its storage facility before processing is initiated. Second, because instructions are stored as numbers, a computer can process its instructions just as if they were data. Consequently, it can modify its instructions and alter its instruction sequence as it proceeds with computations.

2.2 Stored Program Computer Systems

Since the early work of von Neumann, Eckert, and Mauchly, a variety of digital computers have been built incorporating their basic ideas. Probably no one knows exactly how many different computers have been built. However, it is significant that they have all incorporated the same basic ideas that germinated in the ENIAC project, and it is, therefore, worthwhile to discuss the characteristics and features that are common to all. Once again, our study is not exhaustive and is meant as a prelude to Chapter 3, which describes how computers operate.

The *block diagram* in Figure 2.8 represents the physical components of a simplified computer system by blocks and indicates their interconnections

Figure 2.7 *UNIVAC I (courtesy of Sperry Rand Corporation).*

Figure 2.8 *The block diagram of a simplified computer system.*

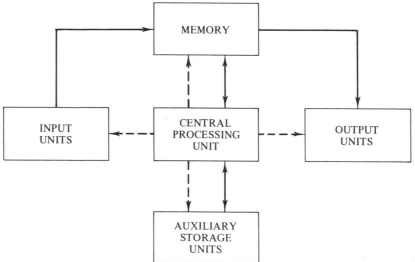

by directed arrows. Each block in the diagram corresponds to a specific unit or function that is usually present in a computer system. The solid arrows specify paths of information flow whereas dashed arrows indicate paths of control flow. The diagram shows that a computer system normally contains five components: *a central processing unit, input units, output units, memory, and auxiliary storage units.* Notice that there is a control path from the central processing unit (CPU) to each component; that information flows out of input units and flows into output units; and that it flows both ways between the CPU and the memory and auxiliary storage units. With these general comments in mind, let us turn our attention to the individual components.

2.2.1 Central processing unit

The *central processing unit* (CPU) performs the role of supervisor and manager of a computer system. It is responsible for determining which operations are to be performed and for directing system components to carry out those operations. It also controls and oversees the transmission of information between components.

A CPU contains no moving mechanical parts as one finds in ordinary desk calculators. All operations are performed electronically. Both data and instructions are represented inside a CPU by the presence or absence of electrical pulses, which are transmitted and processed by special electronic circuits known as *logic* or *switching* circuits. Logic circuits in early stored program computers built in the 1950's were constructed from individual electronic components, such as vacuum tubes, capacitors, and resistors. Today, these early vacuum tube machines are referred to as *first generation* computers. In the late 1950's, vacuum tubes were replaced by transistors, but logic circuits were still assembled by hand from individual components. Computers with transistorized circuits are classified as *second generation*. By the mid-1960's, techniques had been developed for automatic production of complete logic circuits and even groups of interconnected circuits. Such configurations are referred to as integrated and hybrid circuits, and computers containing these circuits are known as *third generation*. Computers with features that might be termed as *fourth generation* are beginning to appear. However, these do not include the dramatic technological changes characterizing the first three generations.

The replacement of vacuum tubes by transistors and transistors by integrated and hybrid circuits was motivated by a desire to improve the operating speed and reliability of a computer and thus increase its computational power. The operating speed of a computer is dependent upon the speed of its logic circuits and the distance that electrical pulses must travel between circuit components. Each generation of equipment saw faster circuits and smaller components packed closer together. In general, first generation operating speeds were measured in *milliseconds* (thousandths of a second); second generation speeds were expressed in *microseconds* (millionths of a second); and third generation equipment has internal speeds measured in *nanoseconds* (billionths of a second). Figure 2.9 shows sample circuits from these generations.

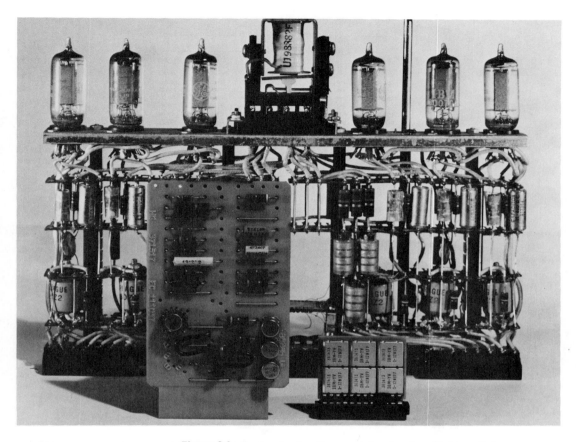

Figure 2.9 *Logic circuits, Vacuum tubes (rear), transistors (left front), and hybrid (right front), (courtesy of the IBM Corporation).*

2.2.2 Input units

Input units are channels of communication into a computer system, which provide it with operating instructions and data. A computer system can have any number of input units of different types, but every system must have at least one. Let us briefly review a variety of such units and the media that they use.

Today, *punched cards* are by far the most prevalent form of input media. Except for special, limited applications, the IBM design shown in Figure 2.10 is the standard and is an outgrowth of the card developed by Herman Hollerith. It is approximately $3\frac{1}{4}$ inches (in.) wide and $7\frac{3}{8}$ in. long and contains 80 columns and 12 rows. The columns are numbered from left to right, starting with 1 and ending with 80. By convention, the top 2 rows are numbered 12 and 11, starting from the top, whereas the bottom 10 are numbered 0 through 9. The

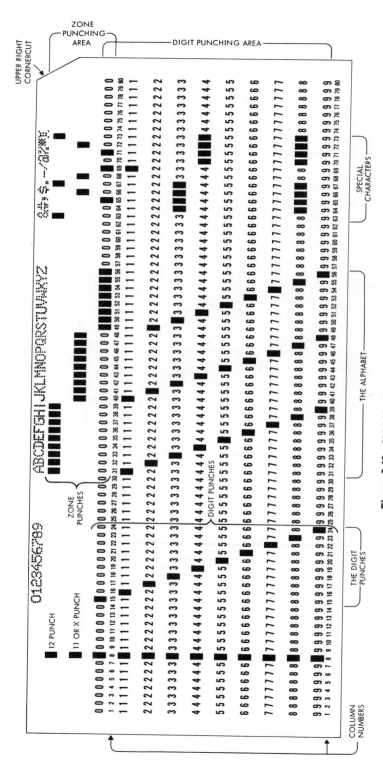

Figure 2.10 *IBM 80-column punched card and Hollerith code.*

18

top 3 rows, 12, 11, and 0, are known as *zone* rows, whereas the bottom 10 are referred to as digit rows. Notice that 0 is both a zone and a digit row. The top of a card is known as the *twelve edge* because it is nearest the 12 row, and similarly, the bottom is the *nine edge*. Finally, the front of a card is known as its *face*.

Information is represented on a Hollerith card one character per column. Each different character has its own unique combination of holes, as shown in Figure 2.10. Digits are represented by a single hole in the appropriate digit row. Thus, 0 is a single punch in row 0. Alphabetic characters are represented by a combination of a single zone and digit punch. For example, the letter A is coded as a 12 and 1 punch, a 12-1 code. Special characters, such as &, $, and %, are represented by combinations of either one, two, or three holes. Notice that even though the digit 0 and the letter O look identical when hand-written, the two characters have different hole combinations. The digit 0 is coded as a 0 punch, whereas the letter O is an 11-6 code. Because each card column can contain only one character, a Hollerith card can store up to 80 characters.

In 1969, IBM introduced a new 96-column small card in connection with its System/3 computer. By using smaller holes, this card is divided into three sets of rows of 32 columns each, as shown in Figure 2.11. Thus, even though it is about one-third the size of a Hollerith card, it can store up to 96 characters.

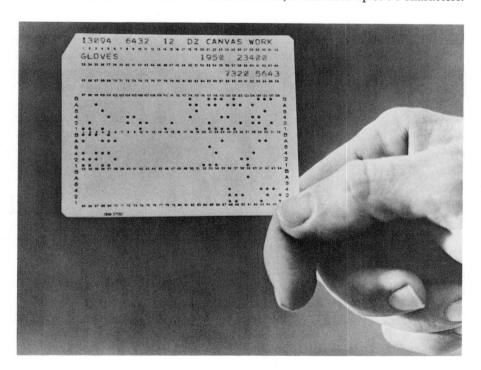

Figure 2.11 *IBM 96-column punched card (courtesy of the IBM Corporation).*

Generally, information is punched into cards by the use of a *keypunch*, a device similar to a typewriter. Each time a key or button is depressed, the proper combination of holes is punched into the card; the character is printed at the top of the card above the proper column; and the card is automatically advanced to the next column. Figure 2.12 shows an IBM 029 keypunch used to prepare Hollerith cards.

Information that has been punched into cards is read into a computer via an input unit known as a *card reader*. After cards have been prepared, they are placed together one after another in the *input hopper* of a card reader. The CPU then asks its reader to read one card at a time. As each card is read, it passes through the reader and stops in the *output stacker*. Once a card has been read, it cannot be reread until a computer operator removes it from the stacker and places it back into the hopper.

Card readers have maximum reading speeds that vary from 5 to 2000 cards per minute. Some readers sense the presence or absence of holes in each card via small wire brushes. When a hole is present, a brush makes contact through the hole with a metal roller below the card and completes an electrical circuit. An electrical current flows in this circuit, telling the reader that a hole has been found. If a hole is not present, the card keeps the brush from completing the circuit and no current flows. Other card readers use lights and light-sensitive photoelectric cells. When a hole is present, light rays shine through the hole, hitting a photoelectric cell which produces an electric current. If there is no hole, the card blocks the light and stops the current.

Card readers are built so that they read cards along either their columns or their rows. If a reader reads by columns, it reads one character at a time. A column reader must have 12 sensing circuits and must read 80 lines of holes per card. If a reader reads by rows, it reads one row of every character at a time. A row reader must have 80 sensing circuits but need read only 12 lines of holes per card. A column reader can decode each character as it reads each column, but a row reader must read a complete card and remember all hole positions before it can decode any characters. In general, row readers are faster than column readers, but they are more expensive because of extra sensors and decoding circuits.

Punched cards are the most popular input media because of their convenience. Usually, one piece of information requires 80 characters or less and, therefore, can fit onto a single card. If a mistake is made in punching a card, it can be thrown away and a new one punched for its place. Also, it is very easy to make corrections by replacing incorrect cards and to make additions by inserting new ones.

Paper tape is a second form of input media. It originally comes in blank rolls up to 1000 feet (ft) in length and in widths of up to 1 in. Figure 2.13 shows a strip of 1-in. tape punched with sample characters. As with punched cards, each character is punched in a separate column. A paper tape row is referred to as a *channel*, and there are eight channels in a standard 1-in tape. The 1, 2, 4, and 8 channels are used to represent digits, but in the case of paper tape, digits are coded as the sum of digit punches. For example, a 1 is a channel

Figure 2.12
IBM 029 keypunch (courtesy of the IBM Corporation).

Figure 2.13 *Paper tape, 8-channel code.*

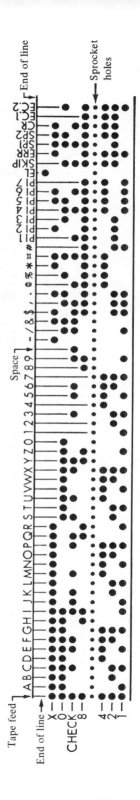

1 punch, whereas a 3 is a combined channel 1 and 2 punch $(1+2 = 3)$. The X and 0 channels are equivalent to the zone rows of a punched card. They are used in combination with digit channels to represent alphabetic and special characters. The check channel is used to insure that a tape has been read or punched correctly. Each column or character must always contain an odd number of holes. If a character code contains an even number, a check punch is added to its code. This method of error detection is referred to as *parity*; and since the number of holes must always be odd, it is said to be *odd* parity. Finally, the end-of-line channel is used to indicate the end of a line or the end of one piece of information and start of the next.

Information is punched into a paper tape by a *paper tape punch*, a typewriterlike device that punches proper hole combinations each time a key is depressed. At the same time, smaller holes are punched along the center of the tape. These *sprocket holes* move and synchronize the tape. Once information has been punched onto tape, it can be read into a computer one character at a time via an input unit known as a *paper tape reader*.

As an input media, paper tape does have several advantages over punched cards. It is cheaper and comes in blank rolls that do not require prior printing. Once a paper tape is punched, it cannot get out of order if dropped. However, the disadvantages of paper tape usually outweigh its advantages. Once a tape is punched, errors are hard to locate and identify because a tape shows only holes without printing. If a mistake is discovered when made, the incorrect character can be deleted by overpunching it with a tape feed code. However, once a tape has been completed, mistakes can only be corrected by duplicating the correct characters and repunching the incorrect ones. Finally, information on a paper tape cannot be altered except by punching another tape.

Some systems have a typewriter located near and attached directly to the CPU, as shown in Figure 2.14. Such a device, known as a *console typewriter*, is used by a computer operator to input operating instructions directly to the CPU. The CPU can also use a console typewriter to transmit messages to its operator. As such, a console typewriter is also an output unit. Because a console typewriter is attached directly to a computer, it is referred to as being *on line*. In contrast, a keypunch used for punching cards is *off line* because it is not connected to a machine. Some computer systems have a number of typewriters or teletypes attached on-line from remote locations via telephone lines. Both data and instructions are entered directly to the CPU from these remote locations. Because a CPU is so much faster than a typewriter, it can simultaneously receive and process information from and transmit results to a number of remote typewriters. Such a procedure is sometimes referred to as *time sharing*, because the CPU divides and shares its time among a number of different users.

As the use of computers has increased, generation of input data has begun to tax input preparation facilities. For example, the Federal Reserve check processing system clears billions of checks each year. In the late 1950's, the American Banking Association realized that it would be impossible to keep

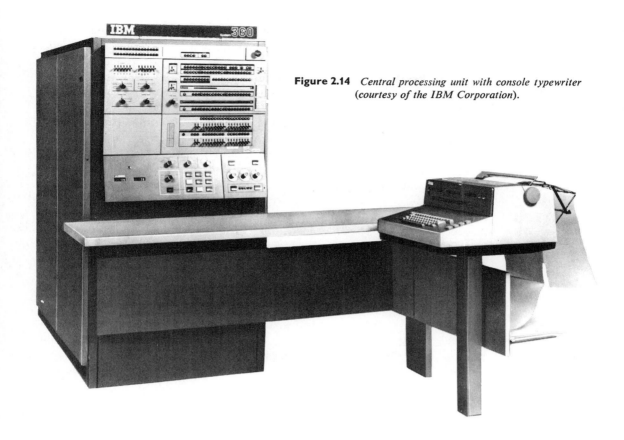

Figure 2.14 *Central processing unit with console typewriter (courtesy of the IBM Corporation).*

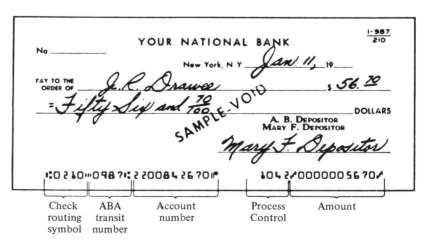

Figure 2.15 *Check encoded with magnetic ink characters (courtesy of the IBM Corporation).*

up with this volume by hand. The association encouraged computer manufacturers to develop an automated check processing method known as *Magnetic Ink Character Recognition* (MICR). Now, checks are imprinted with the bank's number and the customer's account number before being issued. After a check is cashed, the bank cashing it imprints on it, in specially shaped characters, the amount paid, as shown in Figure 2.15. This information can then be read into a computer via a magnetic character reader. Once a check has been prepared at the first bank, it can be rapidly processed at other banks along its clearing route without further human preparation.

A similar situation has developed in the gasoline industry. Each day, millions of automobile drivers purchase gasoline and charge their purchases to their credit card accounts. Initially, information from each credit slip had to be individually keypunched. This hand preparation has been eliminated by the development of *optical readers*, which can interpret special symbols and type fonts. When a gasoline service station attendant records a credit sale, he places his customer's credit card into a special imprinter which automatically transfers that customer's account number and the amount of his charge directly onto a credit slip in machine-readable form. These slips can then be processed by a computer without further human intervention.

Enter partial payment below	MUNICIPAL WATER WORKS			
0 0 0 0 0	Account Number	Gross Amount	Net Amount	Last Day To Pay Net
1 1 1 1 1				
2 2 2 2 2	RL 45332	56 01	45 98	4 30 6-
3 3 3 3 3				
4 4 4 4 4				
5 5 5 5 5	Present Reading	Previous Reading	Consumption Gals.	E D JONES
6 6 6 6 6				745 CHESTNUT ST
7 7 7 7 7	3255886	2369014	887	ANYTOWN USA
8 8 8 8 8				
9 9 9 9 9	PLEASE RETURN THIS WITH YOUR PAYMENT			

Figure 2.16 *Optically readable characters (courtesy of the IBM Corporation).*

Finally, optical readers can perform an additional operation know as *mark sensing*, the reading of ordinary pen or pencil markings. These marks, when placed in a specified location on a document, can represent specific information. This feature has many applications, such as recording partial payments directly onto a customer's bill that was previously printed in optically readable characters, as shown in Figure 2.16. Such preparation of data in computer-usable form at a data source is referred to as *source data automation* and greatly reduces the cost and increases the accuracy of data preparation for later computer processing.

2.2.3 Output units

Output units are outward channels of communication of a computer system and are used by it to transmit its computational results to the outside world. Each output unit receives its information as electrical pulses, converting them into a form that is readily understood by human beings. Output units also inform an operator that his machine needs attention. For example, he may need to clear a card jam in a reader or give a computer its next set of instructions. As with input units, a computer can have any number of output units of different types, but every system must have at least one. Let us briefly review a variety of such units and the media they employ.

The most popular form of output media is the *printed page*, and the most common printing technique depends upon the impact of a die or metal character against an inked ribbon. The impact of a die striking a ribbon transfers ink to paper as in a standard desk typewriter. Several *nonimpact* printing methods currently under development employ electronic techniques and do not depend upon mechanical impact. Office copy machines, such as Xerox, are examples of nonimpact printing.

Output printers are also classified by whether they print complete lines or whether they must print each line one character at a time. A typewriter under the control of a computer is an example of a *character* printer. Such an output device prints each character separately, one character at a time at about 15 to 30 characters per second. Because of its slow printing speed, typewriters are usually limited to short messages, such as those between a computer and its operator.

Faster output printers can print complete lines at a time and are known as *line* printers. They have a maximum printing speed that ranges from 100 to 2500 lines per minute. One type of line printer uses a rapidly rotating character *chain* composed of linked print dies, as shown in Figure 2.17a. As the chain rotates at a constant speed along the print line, electrically controlled hammers push the paper against a ribbon and the moving print dies. Accurate coordination and timing are required to insure that each hammer strikes at the proper instant so that the paper is knocked against the correct character at the desired line position. Print speeds are further increased by adding extra character sets to the print chain, thus reducing the time that each hammer must wait for the arrival of any given character.

A second type of line printer uses a rapidly rotating *drum*. As shown in Figure 2.17b, the drum is made up of a set of bands, each of which contains one complete character set. As the drum rotates at a constant speed, electrically controlled hammers opposite each band push the paper against the drum. When the A row appears in front of the print line, hammers fire in those positions requiring A's. Shortly thereafter, hammers fire where B's are required. This process continues until all characters for a complete line are printed. Consequently, it takes one drum revolution to print each line. Once again, great timing accuracy is required to insure that the correct character dies are selected from each band.

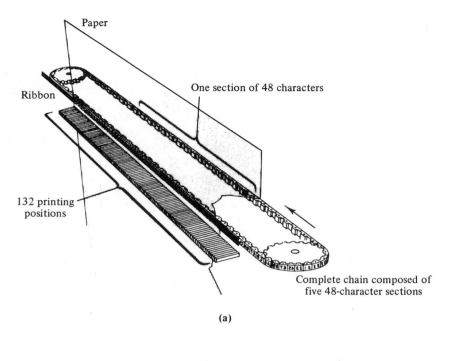

Paper

Ribbon

One section of 48 characters

132 printing
positions

Complete chain composed of
five 48-character sections

(a)

The number of bands corresponds
to the number of printing positions

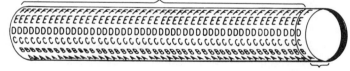

One band consists
of all printing
characters used

(b)

Figure 2.17 *Line printers: (a) chain printer; (b) drum printer.*

Punched cards are a second form of output media. Here again, characters are represented by combinations of punched holes. Blank cards are punched one card at a time by a *card punch* that operates in a manner similar to a card reader. Normally, card punches operate in the range of 100 to 300 cards per minute and usually produce cards without printing characters across the top of each card. However, there is a device, designated an *interpreter*, that reads these cards and prints characters along their tops. This operation is called *interpreting*. Even though card punches are slower than line printers, they do produce their output in a form that can be used as input to a card reader for later processing without further preparation. Likewise, a *paper tape punch* can be used as an output device.

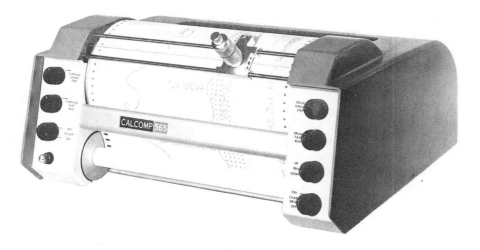

Figure 2.18 *(above) Plotter; (below) Drawing produced by plotter (courtesy of California Computer Products).*

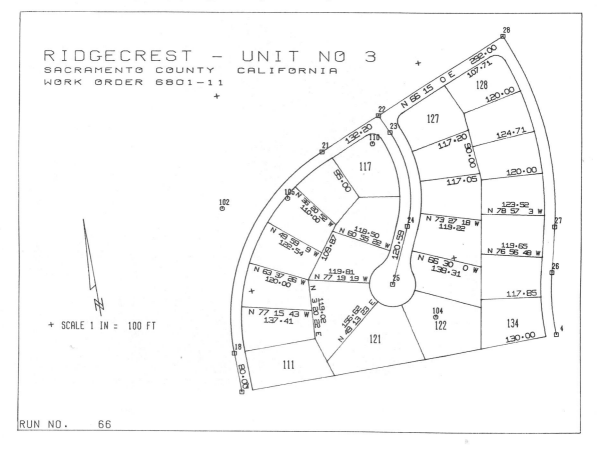

Sometimes the results of a calculation can best be understood and visualized when displayed in graphical form. Special output units have been designed that can display or draw graphs and line drawings under direct, on-line control of a computer. Figure 2.18 shows an example of such a device, known as a *plotter*, which operates by combination of horizontal movements of a pen and vertical movements of paper under that pen. Lettering, labels, and scales can be added to the drawings by the plotter to identify the results and to make the output more meaningful.

Visual display units produce another form of graphical output. Figure 2.19 shows a visual display unit in combination with an input keyboard. The output information is displayed on the face of a *cathode ray tube* (CRT), which resembles a television tube, and its output can be a combination of character and graphical information.

Figure 2.19 *Visual display unit (courtesy of the IBM Corporation).*

2.2.4 The memory unit

The *memory unit* of a computer system serves as storage for the CPU. The CPU directs input units to send their input information to memory. The CPU retrieves its operating instructions and data from memory and returns its results to memory. Finally, the CPU requests memory to send those results to output units.

The *magnetic core* is the most widely used device for constructing memories. A core is formed by molding *ferromagnetic* powder into doughnuts about the size of a pinhead. Aside from its compact size, the most important characteristic of a core is that it can be magnetized in a few millionths of a second. And, unless deliberately changed, it retains its magnetism indefinitely.

If cores are strung on a wire like beads and a strong enough electrical current is sent through the wires, the cores become magnetized, as shown in Figure 2.20a. The direction of current determines the polarity or magnetic state of the cores. Once a core has been magnetized in a given direction, it remains in that direction after current is removed, as shown in Figure 2.20b. By reversing the direction of current, the magnetic state of a core is changed (see Figure 2.20c). These two states or polarities can be used to store information. For example, the clockwise direction can represent a 1, whereas counterclockwise indicates a 0.

Individual cores are arranged in horizontal layers called *core planes*. In each plane, two *write wires* run through each core at right angles to each other, as shown in Figure 2.20d. A magnetic field is established in an individual core by applying one-half the current required to magnetize a core to each of the write wires that passes through the selected core. The magnitude of the current in each wire is carefully regulated so that it alone is not strong enough to change or *flip* the direction of magnetism in the cores along its path. However, the total current passing through the core at the intersection of the two wires is strong enough to flip the selected core. This wiring arrangement is known as a *coincident-current* core memory.

We read or access a core by attempting to magnetize it in a particular direction. If the core is already set in that direction, nothing happens; however, if the core is magnetized in the opposite direction, it flips, causing a current in a *sense wire* (Figure 2.20e). This current can be detected and used to determine whether the core originally contained a 1 or a 0. For example, if current is sent to write a 0 into the selected core and that core contains a 1, the core flips to a 0, causing current in the sense wire. On the other hand, if the core already contains a 0, the core remains at 0 and there is no current in the sense wire. Here, current in the sense wire indicates a 1, whereas no current indicates a 0. Only one sense wire is needed for an entire core plane, because only one core at a time in any plane is tested for its magnetic state. Consequently, this wire is strung through all cores in a plane, as shown in Figure 2.20f.

Note, that this read procedure is *destructive*, i.e. whenever a one is read, it becomes a zero. Therefore, in order to retain correct data in memory, it is necessary to immediately rewrite those cores that were changed during readout.

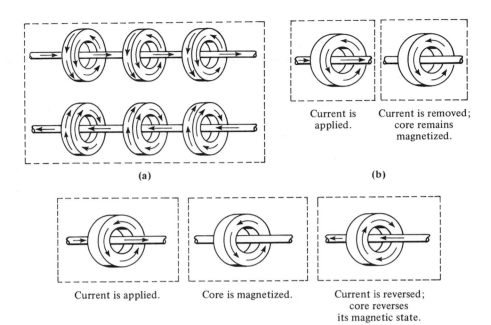

(a)

Current is
applied.

Current is removed;
core remains
magnetized.

(b)

Current is applied.

Core is magnetized.

Current is reversed;
core reverses
its magnetic state.

(c)

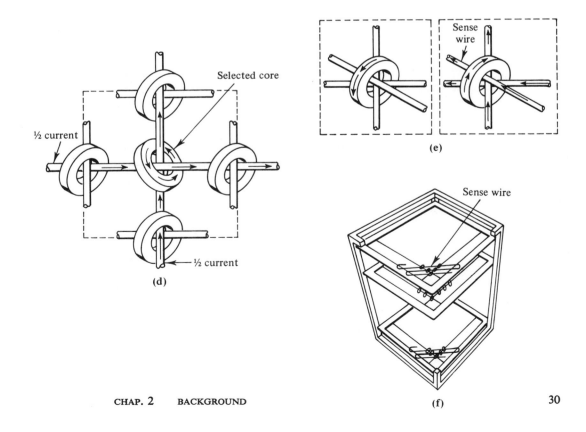

Selected core

½ current

½ current

(d)

Sense
wire

(e)

Sense wire

(f)

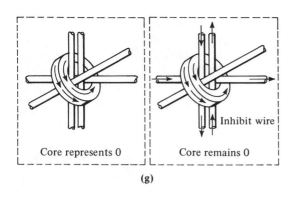

Core represents 0 | Core remains 0   Inhibit wire

(g)

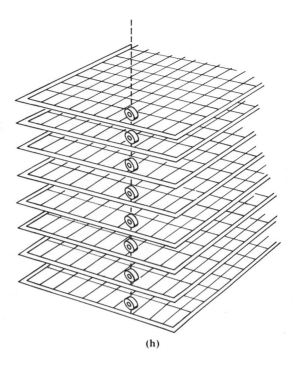

(h)

Figure 2.20 *Magnetic core memory: (a) polarities or magnetic states; (b) magnetizing a core; (c) reversing a core; (d) selecting a core; (e) core sense wire; (f) sense wire in core plane; (g) core inhibit wire; (h) sequence of bits.*

This is accomplished via a fourth wire, known as an *inhibit wire* shown in Figure 2.20g. Like the sense wire, there is one inhibit wire per core plane, and it runs through every core in that plane.

To regenerate the missing ones, ones are written into *all* cores that were just read. Simultaneously, current is sent through the inhibit wire of those cores that are to *remain* zero. This *inhibit current* cancels the effect of the current in one write wire. Consequently, the total current passing through such a core is not strong enough to flip it, and its real zero remains zero. In contrast, a core with an incorrect zero receives no inhibit current, and its two write currents are strong enough to flip it back to its correct one state.

The information represented by the direction of magnetism of a core is the smallest unit of information that can be stored in memory. A single core can store either a 0 or a 1, which is referred to as a *binary digit* or *bit*, for short. Larger numbers are stored in the binary number system as a sequence of bits where each bit is in a separate memory plane, as illustrated in Figure 2.20h. Thus, all bits in one number can be accessed simultaneously.

The time interval between the instant at which data are called from or sent to memory and the instant delivery is completed is referred to as *memory-access* or *memory-cycle* time. Generally, access times have ranged from as slow as 50 microseconds (μs) to as fast as 750 nanoseconds (ns). The magnetic core has proven very successful because of its high reliability and reasonable cost. However, access times, which have been reduced by making cores smaller and write currents larger, seem to be approaching a lower limit. Computers are now being built with wholly electronic memories without magnetic cores,

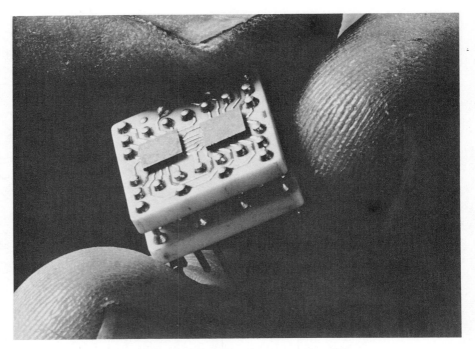

Figure 2.21 *Electronic memory storage module.*

as shown in Figure 2.21. Here, two silicon chips are mounted on a memory module held between two fingers for size comparison. Each $\frac{1}{8}$-in-square chip contains 1400 circuit elements with a storage capacity of 128 bits. Access times of these memories are now as low as 200 ns and undoubtedly will go even lower.

2.2.5 Auxiliary storage units

Auxiliary storage units provide a computer system with additional on-line storage. Generally, these units have higher storage capacity than primary memory, but, in contrast, they have slower or longer access times. Furthermore, these units have faster read-write rates than the common input-output devices we have already discussed. Consequently, if large amounts of data must be processed, it is faster and more convenient to use auxiliary storage units. Let us briefly review a variety of such units and the media they employ.

Magnetic tape is one of the most popular forms of auxiliary storage media. The tape, which is similar to that used in home tape recorders, is a strip of tough flexible plastic, such as Mylar, coated on one side with a thin layer of ferromagnetic material similar to that used in memory cores. The tape is usually $\frac{1}{2}$ in wide and comes in reels 50 to 2400 ft long. Because the coating is ferromagnetic, a magnetic field can be induced into the tape. Once a field is established in one direction, it retains that direction until flipped by a sufficiently large external field. Consequently, as in a memory core, bits of information can be stored on tape via the direction of a magnetic field—i.e., one direction represents a 0 whereas the opposite signifies a 1.

Magnetic tape is divided horizontally into *channels* or *tracks* and vertically into columns or frames, in a fashion similar to paper tape. Generally, most computer systems use magnetic tape in either a *seven-* or *nine-*channel format. One bit of information can be stored in each channel at each column position. Thus, a seven-channel tape has seven bits in each column, and a nine-channel has nine. These seven or nine bits are combined to code one character, as shown in Figure 2.22. Individual characters are packed quite closely together. In fact, *tape densities* range from 200 to 1600 characters per inch, and a 2400-ft reel can store from 2 to 40 million characters. Because each channel contains one bit in each column position, tape densities are usually stated in *bits per inch* (bpi).

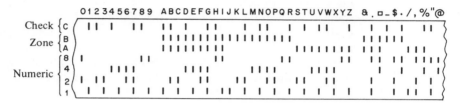

Figure 2.22 *Seven-channel magnetic tape codes.*

Information is written onto and read from magnetic tape by *tape drives* or *transports*. These units read and write information via a *read-write head*, shown in Figure 2.23, which contains two small electromagnets, one for reading and the other for writing, at *each* of the channel positions. During a write operation, a drive moves tape across its read-write head while current flows through its write coils. This current produces a magnetic field across the *write gap*, which is induced into the magnetic coating on the tape. The direction of current in the write coils determines the direction of the magnetic fields induced into the tape. Similarly, in a read operation, tape is moved across the read-write head. The motion of the magnetic fields causes current to flow in the read coils. The direction of this current is determined by the relative direction of the magnetic fields on the tape.

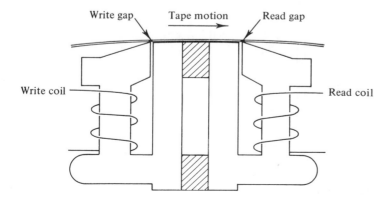

Figure 2.23 *Read-write head.*

The tape drive illustrated in Figure 2.24 shows that tape is mounted onto a drive in a manner similar to a sound recorder or movie projector. During processing, tape is taken from the feed reel past the read-write heads at speeds from 15 to 200 in. per second. *Vacuum columns* and *drive* and *stop capstans* permit tape drives to reach maximum tape speed within a few milliseconds without damaging or breaking tape. The *information transfer rate* between a tape drive and its CPU is measured in characters per second, which is calculated by multiplying the recording density of the tape times the tape speed of the drive. Information transfer rates of tape drives range from 3000 to over 320,000 characters per second.

A magnetic tape drive is a *sequential storage* device in that it records information onto tape in series. If a CPU needs specific information that is located in the middle of a reel, it must direct a drive to read tape until it finds the desired information. In this respect, tape drives are similar to home recorders. If you want to listen to the middle of a tape, you must listen or at least scan from the beginning. In addition, magnetic tape does have the advantage that once a reel has been filled, it can be removed and replaced by an empty one. Thus, a tape drive can provide on-line access to an unlimited amount of information. All that is required is a computer operator to change reels.

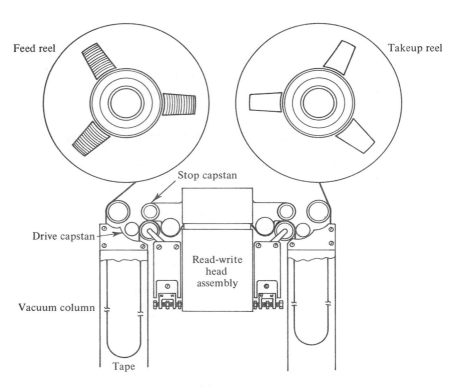

Figure 2.24 *Tape drive.*

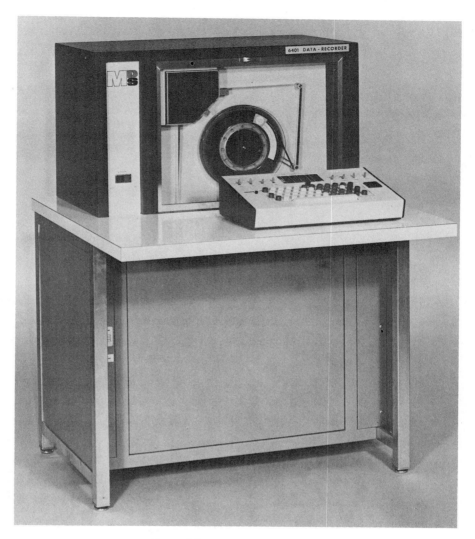

Figure 2.25 *Magnetic keyrecorder (courtesy of Mohawk Data Sciences Corporation).*

Originally, magnetic tape was designed as an auxiliary storage media. Information was first punched off-line into cards or paper tape and then read into memory via a card or paper tape. After the information was in memory, it was then written onto magnetic tape via a tape drive. Once information was on tape, it could be reread whenever necessary back into memory at speeds up to 100 times faster than from cards or paper tape. A typewriterlike device is now available which eliminates this intermediate card-to-tape operation. Figure 2.25 shows a *magnetic keyrecorder*, which transfers information one character at a time from keyboard to magnetic tape. Now tape drives can be thought of as both input and auxiliary storage units.

(a)

Figure 2.26 *Magnetic disks: (a) disk drive; (b) disk drive showing access arms and read-write heads; (c) schematic of disk drive; (d) nonremovable disk.*

(b)

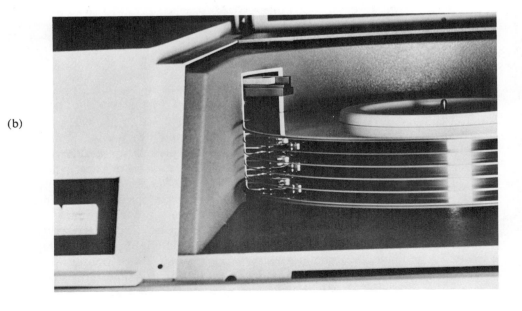

Magnetic disks are a second form of auxiliary storage media. A magnetic disk is a flat circular plate coated on both sides with ferromagnetic material. Each disk is divided into concentric circles called *tracks,* each of which stores information as bits in a manner similar to magnetic tape. A number of these disks are mounted on a vertical center rod and rotated at a high, constant speed by a *disk drive*, as shown in Figure 2.26a. The individual disk surfaces are separated by sufficient space to allow a set of read-write heads to move between them and access any particular track on any disk surface (Figures 2.26b and 2.26c).

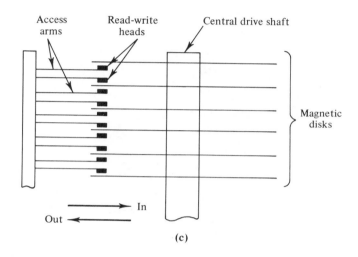

(c)

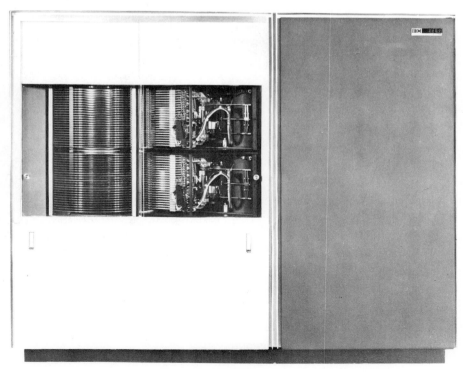

(d)

Disk drives are constructed with two types of disk surfaces. Older drives, such as the one shown in Figure 2.26d, were built with rigid, nonremovable disk surfaces. Drives are now being built with retractable _access arms_; once these arms are drawn back, the disk surfaces can be removed, as illustrated in Figure 2.26e. These removable surfaces, shown in Figure 2.26f, are called _disk packs_. A disk drive using packs has the advantages of both disk and tape; because its pack can be changed, it can store an unlimited amount of information, yet it can access that information at random.

Figure 2.26 _Magnetic disks: (e) removable disk._

Figure 2.26 *Magnetic disks: (f) disk pack.*

Typically, disk drives take from 20 to 600 milliseconds (ms) to move their read-write heads from one track to another. This head movement is referred to as *seeking,* and it results in an access delay known as *seek time*. Once its heads are in position, a disk can transfer at rates from 70,000 to 800,000 characters per second. Finally, disks have storage capacities that vary from 500,000 to 200 million characters on-line. Of course, there is no limit to the number of disk packs that can be stored off-line.

A magnetic disk drive is a *random-* or *direct-access* storage device in that it can record information at any track location. If a CPU needs specific information that is located in the middle of a disk, it need only direct a drive to seek that position. In this respect, a disk drive is similar to a home phonograph. If you want to listen to the middle of a record, you simply position the phonograph arm to the proper position. You do not have to start at the beginning of the record as you do with tape.

Magnetic drums are a third auxiliary storage device. Initially, they were used as main storage before the coincident-current core memory was invented. A magnetic drum is a cylinder having its outer surface coated with ferromagnetic material. Like a disk, the surface of a drum is divided into circular bands called *tracks*. Information is stored onto a drum by read-write heads. Some drums have fixed or stationary heads located over each track, as shown in Figure 2.27a, whereas other drums have fewer heads which are movable and must be positioned over the desired track, as shown in Figure 2.27b.

A drum can access any track by waiting for the start of that track to reach a read-write head. This access time is a function of the number of read-write heads and the rotational speed of a particular drum. Generally, access times average in the neighborhood of 5 to 10 ms; thus, drums are faster than disks. On the other hand, drums are usually limited in storage capacity from 5000 to 10 million characters. Consequently, drums are used to store small amounts of information that must be accessed quickly.

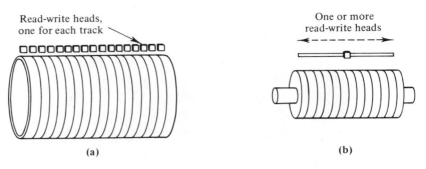

Read-write heads, one for each track

One or more read-write heads

(a)

(b)

Figure 2.27 *Magnetic drums: (a) fixed head; (b) movable head.*

Other auxiliary storage devices have been designed that provide large amounts of inexpensive, on-line storage capacity. In general, these devices have sacrificed access speed for higher storage capacity and lower storage cost. Two such units are the *Card Random Access Unit* (CRAM), built by National Cash Register (NCR), and the *Data Cell*, built by IBM. Basically, the CRAM and Data Cell work on the same principle of storing information on ferromagnetic coated plastic strips. Upon CPU command, these storage units identify the strip containing the desired information and position it under a read-write head. Once the desired information is read, the strip is returned to its original position. The strips themselves are removable in a manner similar to disk packs.

All auxiliary storage units discussed in this section use ferromagnetic material and magnetic fields for information storage. Such devices have proven very successful and highly reliable; however, other storage techniques are under development. For example, light-sensitive photographic material shows promise of storage densities measured in trillions of bits per inch. Once information is stored onto such photographic media, it cannot be changed, erased, or rewritten, as with magnetic material. Such media provide *read-only* storage (ROS) and should greatly reduce the costs of providing on-line access to great quantities of permanent information.

2.2.6 Programming languages

So far, our discussion has been limited to the physical components of a computer system. These include mechanical, magnetic, electrical, and electronic devices, generally referred to as *hardware*. Earlier, we said that a CPU performs the role of system manager. It does so by following a set of instructions, one instruction at a time in sequence. Since a computer cannot function without instructions, let us stop and consider how individual instructions are written.

According to the von Neumann concept of a stored program digital computer, both instructions and data are represented inside a computer as numbers. Since a computer memory stores numbers in binary, instructions appear as sequences of ones and zeros. Such instructions are said to be in machine language and are the only form that a computer can perform. Because the particular combinations of ones and zeros used for each instruction are inherent in the design of a computer, each machine has its own language. For example, the instruction

$$01011000010000000110000000010110$$

directs the CPU of an IBM 370 computer to ask its memory for the contents of some memory location.

In general, each machine instruction consists of two parts. The first part, known as the *operation code*, directs the computer to perform a specific operation. Each computer has its own limited number of built-in operations that it can execute. The second part of a machine instruction, referred to as the *operand*, specifies the object of the operation. Usually, the operand tells a computer where in memory to find the data to be processed or where to store the results. In the preceding example, the first 8 bits specify the operation code and the last 24 represent the operand.

Early computer users quickly found that writing programs in machine language was very tedious and time consuming and was thus quite expensive and prone to errors. Locating a mistake in a recently written program was very difficult because even an experienced programmer quickly forgot the meaning and function of individual instructions. For the same reason, even a slight modification to an existing program took almost as long as writing the original. The difficulties of machine language programming were further compounded by the fact that new machines were being developed at a rapid pace. To take advantage of the increased capabilities and greater computational power of these latest computers, existing programs had to be converted to new machine languages.

To reduce programming effort, *mnemonic* operation codes were assigned to each machine instruction. Now, rather than having to remember binary sequences, a programmer could use simple names, such as ADD or A for addition and SUB or S for subtraction. On the other hand, programs using mnemonics were no longer machine language and could not be executed by a computer. This problem was solved by writing a special machine language program that would read each mnemonic code and then replace it by its equivalent binary sequence. This translation procedure was so successful that it was reasoned that a computer could be used to perform other clerical functions, such as assigning memory locations to data. This led to *symbolic addressing*, where a programmer referenced his data by symbols while the computer kept track of where it had stored the actual data. (Programs that use mnemonics for operation codes and symbols for data locations are said to be written in *assembly language*, and the machine language program that converts assembly language programs into machine language is called an *assembler*.) Figure 2.28 lists an assembly language program that evaluates the algebraic equation

$$y = ax + b$$

in four statements, and illustrates how it might appear after it has been assembled into machine language. The original program is referred to as a *source program*, whereas the program resulting from its translation is known as an *object program*.

Machine	Assembly	Procedural
0101100001000000011000000010110	L 4,A	Y=A*X+B
0101110001000000011000000011010	M 4,X	
0101101001000000011000000011110	A 4,B	
0101000001000000011000000100010	ST 4,Y	

Figure 2.28 *Programming languages.*

Writing assembly language programs was still found to be time consuming. In general, a programmer still had to write one assembly language statement for each desired machine instruction. Even though he did not have to worry about such details as writing correct sequences of ones and zeros, he still had to have an understanding of the internal operation of his particular computer. Thus, assembly languages were still *machine oriented*, i.e., each one was developed for a specific machine. Therefore, programs written in assembly language, like those in machine language, had to be reprogrammed every time a different machine was used.

The success of the assembly language concept with its machine translation of mnemonic operation codes and symbolic addresses led to the development of *procedure-oriented* languages. Such languages are designed to help a computer user solve his problem without concerning himself about the details of his particular computer. In other words, a class of similar problems is identified, and a language is designed to process such problems. For example, FORTRAN (which stands for FORmula TRANslation) was developed for those users whose problems can best be solved by formulas and equations. Of course, a program written in such a language must be translated into machine language. In this case, the translating program is called a *compiler*. Usually, the translation of a procedural language statement generates more than one machine instruction. As an example, Figure 2.28 shows a single procedural statement that specifies the evaluation of an algebraic equation. When translated or compiled, this statement produces four machine instructions.

The first compiler, called the *A–2*, was developed by Dr. Grace M. Hopper of the Univac Division of Sperry Rand Corporation in 1952. Since then, many such languages have been developed. In fact, there have been so many that they are sometimes displayed as a tower of BABEL. FORTRAN is by far the most popular language for scientific users, whereas COBOL (COmmon Business Oriented Language) is the most widely used for business applications. In fact, these languages, as well as others, have been so widely adopted that computer manufacturers have written FORTRAN and COBOL compilers for their own machines. Now, for example, we can run a program written in FORTRAN on many different machines without completely rewriting the program. The FORTRAN compiler takes care of making the necessary changes when it generates the machine language program for the new machine. Thus, through their compilers, procedure-oriented languages have greatly reduced the reprogramming problem. Furthermore, they are easier to learn and require less time to write. Finally, they make it possible for a user to learn a single language that can be used on many different computers without knowing the internal working of each machine.

As computer systems have become more sophisticated and as the number of programming languages has increased, the job of operating a computer system has become extremely involved. This problem has been further compounded by the fact that computer systems have become very expensive, and it is necessary, therefore, that they be in operation at all times. As further illustration, a large computer system can have a purchase price of over $10,000,000 and can cost $1000 per hour to operate. At such prices, an unused minute of computer time can waste $15. To overcome this problem, researchers have developed special programs, referred to as *operating systems, supervisors,* or *monitors,* to take over the moment-to-moment control of a computer system. These programs perform such duties as reading user programs to discover which programming language was used, retrieving the desired compiler from auxiliary storage, telling the compiler to translate the user's program, and then directing the CPU to execute the resulting machine language program. When a computer system is under the control of a monitor or operating system, the computer operator loads programs into the card reader, mounts tape reels onto tape drives, and removes results from the printer while the monitor schedules the work flow and keeps the CPU busy.

The term, *software,* is used to refer to all programs associated with a computer system. In general, a computer manufacturer supplies a basic set of software at the same time he delivers his hardware. Usually, the software includes an operating system, an assembler, and one or more compilers. Thus, individual users are spared the expense and effort of developing such programming aids and are free to concentrate upon their own particular problems.

2.3 Summary

The computer is not a completely new concept, but rather is just the latest innovation in a series of related developments that probably began with positional number systems, such as our decimal notation. The abacus incorporated a positional feature, represented digits by bead location, and replaced involved arithmetic by simpler mental and mechanical operations. Rotating wheel calculators represented numbers by wheel position and eliminated the need for even simple mental arithmetic. The difference engine showed that machines could execute fixed arithmetic sequences while electromechanical calculators proved that variable sequences could be performed. Electronic calculators were faster and more reliable and set the stage for stored program digital computers, which saved *both* instructions and data in memory as *numbers.*

The stored program computer system is normally composed of five components. The CPU acts as system manager or supervisor. It contains no moving parts and performs all its operations electronically. Early CPU's were built from individual electronic components, such as vacuum tubes. In the second generation, vacuum tubes were replaced by transistors, which in the third generation were replaced by integrated and hybrid circuits.

Input and output units serve as channels of communication into and out of a computer system. Punched cards are the most popular input media, and a keypunch prepares them for input by a card reader. Paper tape readers, typewriter keyboards, and magnetic and optical character readers are examples of other input units. On the other hand, the printed page is the most common output media. Most printers depend upon the impact of metal dies against inked ribbons to transfer characters to paper. Some printers, such as the typewriter, print one character at a time, whereas others produce complete lines. The card punch, plotter, and visual display are examples of other output units.

Memory provides storage, and magnetic cores are the most popular memory device. Information is stored in a core by coincident currents flowing through two write wires. Information is read by observing whether there is sense current when a core is written with a known value. This read procedure is destructive, and the original contents of a core must be restored. On the other hand, auxiliary storage units provide additional on-line storage. Most of these hold information via magnetic fields induced into ferromagnetic coatings. Magnetic tape drives must access information in series and are said to be sequential devices, whereas magnetic disks and drums can access information in any order and are referred to as random- or direct-access devices.

SELECTED REFERENCES

1. DAVIS, GORDON B., *Introduction to Electronic Computers*, 2nd ed., McGraw-Hill Book Company, New York, 1971.

2. "Herman Hollerith," *Systems and Procedures Journal*, November-December, 1963, pp. 18–24.

3. *Introduction to IBM Data Processing Systems*, Student Text, IBM Corp., Form C20–1684, 1967.

4. KNUTH, DONALD E., "Von Neumann's First Computer Program," *Computing Surveys*, Vol. 2, No. 4, December 1970, pp. 247–60.

5. LEHRENBAUM, BURTON, *By the Numbers*, Veeder-Root, Inc., Hartford, Conn., 1966.

6. MORRISON, PHILIP, and EMILY MORRISON, eds., *Charles Babbage and his Calculating Engines*, Dover Publications, Inc., New York, 1961.

7. PARKHILL, D. F., *The Challenge of the Computer Utility*, Addison-Wesley Publishing Co., Inc., Reading, Mass., 1966.

8. ROSEN, SAUL, "Electronic Computers: A Historical Survey," *Computing Surveys*, Vol. 1, No. 1, March 1969, pp. 7–36.

9. SAMMET, JEAN E., *Programming Languages: History and Fundamentals*, Prentice-Hall, Inc., Englewood Cliffs, N. J., 1969.

10. STIBITZ, GEORGE, as told by Mrs. Evelyn Loveday, "The Relay Computers at Bell Labs," *Datamation*, April 1967, pp. 35–44, and May 1967, pp. 45–49.

3 Problems of Using a Computer

A computer by its very nature presents problems to a computer user. These hurdles must be overcome each time a computer is used to solve a problem. Before we turn our attention to problem solving, we should study the drawbacks of using a computer. Only in this way can problem-solving procedures be developed that will help a user in his effort to overcome the limitations of a computer and to reach a successful solution to his problems.

A _model_ is an abstract representation of a physical object or situation. Its purpose is to simulate that object or situation and to produce the same results as if the actual object or situation were used or were present. An architect studies building models to forsee construction problems just as a stockbroker studies market models to predict stockmarket performance; thus, a computer user can study a computer model to discover and understand the capabilities and limitations of a digital computer.

3.1 A Computer Model

Many different models have been proposed for simulating the operation of a digital computer. Some are so exact that they actually describe the detailed internal operations of specific computers. The purpose here is to discover and understand how computers themselves cause problems; therefore, the model described in this chapter includes only sufficient detail to illustrate those problems.

3.1.1 Components of the model

A block diagram of our model of a stored program digital computer is shown in Figure 3.1. As we discussed before, the diagram depicts components as blocks and represents their interconnections by directed arrows. Solid arrows indicate paths of information flow and dashed arrows indicate control flow. The diagram shows that the model consists of four components: a *central processing unit*, *memory*, an *input unit*, and an *output unit*. A comparison of this diagram with the one in Figure 2.8 reveals several differences. First, the CPU of the model has been split into five subcomponents: a *control unit*, an *instruction address register*, an *instruction unit*, an *arithmetic unit*, and an *accumulator*. This subdivision facilitates a more detailed discussion of a CPU's operation. Second, the model has only one input unit and one output unit, thereby satisfying the requirement that a computer have one of each. Third, auxiliary storage units have been omitted. This omission does not restrict the usefulness and validity of the model as long as its memory capacity is not exceeded.

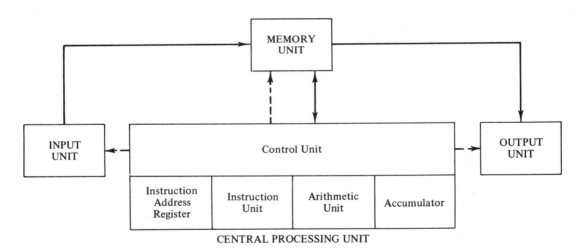

Figure 3.1 *Block diagram of a computer model.*

The *control unit* (CU) in the CPU acts as supervisor or manager of the other components. It organizes and schedules the work of each component and controls all communications. For example, if the arithmetic unit requires a data value that is stored in memory, the CU retrieves that value from memory and transmits it to the arithmetic unit. In the model, you, the reader, perform the control unit function; therefore, it is important that you understand the operation of the remaining components.

The *memory unit* is used by the CU to store information necessary for the operation of the model. Memory can be visualized as a set of boxes arranged

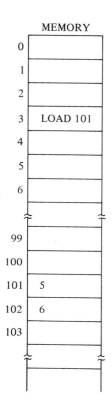

MEMORY	
0	
1	
2	
3	LOAD 101
4	
5	
6	
99	
100	
101	5
102	6
103	

in sequence and numbered consecutively starting at zero, as shown in Figure 3.2. Each box is referred to as a *memory location* or *word*, and the number given each location is known as its *address*. Thus, memory is analogous to a set of post office boxes, and memory addresses are equivalent to post office box numbers.

Each memory word always contains one and only one piece of information. This information can be pictured as being written on a slip of paper with each location always containing one slip. Since the model represents a stored program digital computer, information recorded on each slip can be either a piece of *data* used or produced during computations or an individual *instruction* used to control these computations. Later, we shall see that it is the CU that decides whether a word contains an instruction or data.

Figure 3.2 *Model of a memory unit.*

Because the purpose of this chapter is to explore the hurdles of using a computer as a problem-solving tool, we make several assumptions concerning the operation of memory. First, in an actual computer the binary number system is used to represent both data and instructions. In the model, information to be used as data is shown as decimal numbers. For example, the data values stored in locations 101 and 102 of Figure 3.2 represent the decimal numbers 5 and 6. Information meant as an instruction is shown in an assembly language format rather than machine language. For example, the information in word three of Figure 3.2 represents an instruction that directs the CU to ask memory for the contents of location 101. The second assumption concerns the numerical size of data values that can be stored in a single cell. Because of physical and economical constraints, actual computer memories can store numbers with magnitudes between some minimum and maximum value, depending upon the particular computer. We assume here that a word can store any numerical value regardless of magnitude. Finally, we presume that memory can have an unlimited number of words, which is impossible in a real computer because memory would be either too bulky or too expensive.

The *input unit* is the communication channel into the model. Actual input devices, such as card readers, paper tape readers, and keyboards, have one important characteristic in common—they all transmit information one piece at a time in sequence. This property is incorporated into the model by simulating an input unit by an in-basket, as shown in Figure 3.3a. Here, slips are spread out and tilted so that their numbers can be seen. Whenever the model requires a piece of information, the CU asks the input unit to give it the slip that is *currently* on *top* of the basket. Thus, the first input value must be on the top slip, the second value must be on the slip just under the top, and, finally, the last must be at the bottom. In Figure 3.3a, the number 3 will be the first value transmitted by the input unit to the CU, followed by 7, 2, 11, and 7. Figure 3.3b shows a more convenient representation of the same input.

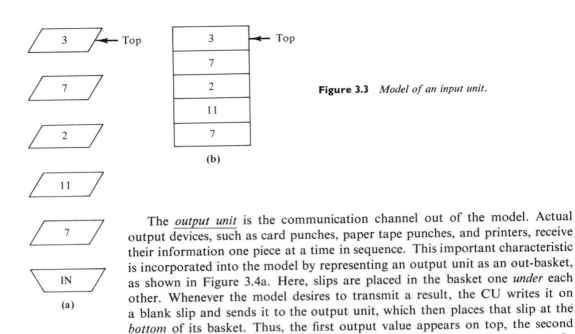

Figure 3.3 *Model of an input unit.*

The *output unit* is the communication channel out of the model. Actual output devices, such as card punches, paper tape punches, and printers, receive their information one piece at a time in sequence. This important characteristic is incorporated into the model by representing an output unit as an out-basket, as shown in Figure 3.4a. Here, slips are placed in the basket one *under* each other. Whenever the model desires to transmit a result, the CU writes it on a blank slip and sends it to the output unit, which then places that slip at the *bottom* of its basket. Thus, the first output value appears on top, the second appears just under the top, and, finally, the last appears at the bottom. In Figure 3.4a, 6 is the first value transmitted by the CU to the output unit, followed by 1, 5, 8, and 0. Figure 3.4b shows the same output.

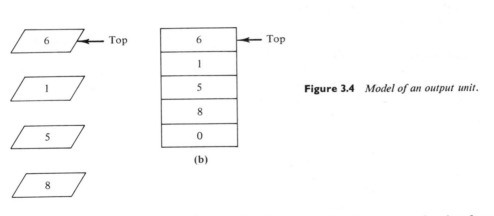

Figure 3.4 *Model of an output unit.*

Output values are placed *under* rather than over each other for two reasons. First, they can be moved back to the input unit for reprocessing in a first-out-first-in sequence without rearrangement. Such is the case with the output produced by card and paper tape punches. Second, printers start at the top of a page and, consequently, their output is read from top to bottom.

The *arithmetic unit* (AU) performs all calculations. Whenever the model needs a computation performed, the CU transmits the necessary directions and data to the AU for processing. When completed, the AU returns its results to the CU. It is assumed that the AU can add, subtract, multiply, and divide two numbers and that it can test a number and report to the CU whether that number is positive (greater than zero), equal to zero, or negative (less than zero).

The *accumulator* (AC) is a special word or *register* that accumulates results in a manner similar to the dials or summary tape of a desk calculator. The CU employs the AC as an intermediate storage location for transmitting data from one memory word to another. For certain instructions, the AU assumes that at least one of its operands is located in the AC and that it is to return its arithmetic results to the AC. Since the AC is a special register and known by name, it does not need a number as an identifying address. The model representation of an AC is shown in Figure 3.5.

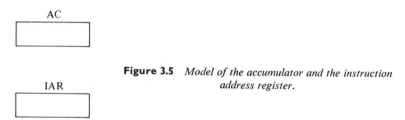

Figure 3.5 *Model of the accumulator and the instruction address register.*

The *instruction address register* (IAR) is used by the model to store the memory address of its next instruction. Whenever the CU is ready to perform its next instruction, it finds the address of that instruction by looking at the contents of the IAR. Like the AC, the IAR can be visualized as a separate, special word, as shown in Figure 3.5; since it is known by name, an identifying address is not required.

The *instruction unit* (IU) tells the CU how to perform each instruction. For our purposes, the IU can be considered as a procedures manual, as shown in Figure 3.6. Each entry in the manual is identified by the name of a particular instruction followed by its operation code, format, and description. In general, each instruction consists of a mnemonic operation code and an operand that specifies a single memory address. The symbol A is used to represent a *numerical* memory address, whereas the notation C(A) refers to the *current contents* of that address. Likewise, the symbols C(AC) and C(IAR) refer to the current contents of the AC and IAR. Finally, a left arrow ($\leftarrow$) is used to indicate *replacement* or *assignment*. For example, the description of the load accumulator instruction states that

$$C(AC) \leftarrow C(A)$$

which is read as follows: the contents of the AC are replaced by the contents of A. It is important to remember that the symbol A represents a numerical address. When an instruction is actually written, a specific number must be prescribed in place of A, such as LOAD 100.

Figure 3.6 *Instruction unit procedures manual.*

LOAD ACCUMULATOR

Operation Code	Format	Description
LOAD	LOAD A	C(AC)←C(A)

Example: | LOAD 101 |

The contents of the AC are replaced by a copy of the contents of word 101. The contents of word 101 are not disturbed while the original contents of the AC are destroyed.

STORE ACCUMULATOR

Operation Code	Format	Description
STORE	STORE A	C(A)←C(AC)

Example: | STORE 17 |

The contents of word 17 are replaced by a copy of the contents of the AC. The contents of the AC remain unchanged while the original contents of word 17 are destroyed.

ADD

Operation Code	Format	Description
ADD	ADD A	C(AC)←C(AC) + C(A)

Example: | ADD 207 |

The contents of the word 207 are added to the contents of the AC, and the result is then placed into the AC. The original contents of the AC are destroyed while the contents of word 207 remain unchanged.

SUBTRACT

Operation Code	Format	Description
SUB	SUB A	C(AC)←C(AC) − C(A)

Example: | SUB 134 |

The contents of word 134 are subtracted from the contents of the AC, and the result is then placed into the AC. The original contents of the AC are destroyed while the contents of word 134 remain unchanged.

MULTIPLY

Operation Code	Format	Description
MPY	MPY A	C(AC)←C(AC) × C(A)

Example: | MPY 365 |

The contents of the AC are multiplied by the contents of word 365, and the result is then placed into the AC. The original contents of the AC are destroyed while the contents of word 365 remain unchanged.

Figure 3.6 (*cont.*)

DIVIDE

Operation Code	Format	Description
DIV	DIV A	$C(AC) \leftarrow C(AC) / C(A)$

Example: ‖ DIV 263 ‖

The contents of the AC are divided by the contents of word 263, and the result is then placed into the AC. The original contents of the AC are destroyed while the contents of word 263 remain unchanged.

BRANCH ABSOLUTELY

Operation Code	Format	Description
BRA	BRA A	$C(IAR) \leftarrow A$

Example: ‖ BRA 9 ‖

The number 9 is placed into the IAR, destroying its original contents. This causes the model to execute the contents of word 9 as its next instruction.

BRANCH IF PLUS

Operation Code	Format	Description
BPL	BPL A	If $C(AC) > 0$, then $C(IAR) \leftarrow A$
		otherwise
		If $C(AC) \leq 0$, then continue

Example: ‖ BPL 102 ‖

If the contents of the AC are currently greater than zero, the number 102 is placed into the IAR, destroying its original contents. This causes the model to execute the contents of word 102 as its next instruction. If the AC is less than or equal to zero, the IAR is not modified and the model's next instruction follows the BPL.

BRANCH IF MINUS

Operation Code	Format	Description
BMI	BMI A	If $C(AC) < 0$, then $C(IAR) \leftarrow A$
		otherwise
		If $C(AC) \geq 0$, then continue

Example: ‖ BMI 58 ‖

If the contents of the AC are currently less than zero, the number 58 is placed into the IAR, destroying its original contents. This causes the model to execute the contents of word 58 as its next instruction. If the AC is greater than or equal to zero, the IAR is not modified and the model's next instruction follows the BMI.

Figure 3.6 (*cont.*)

BRANCH IF ZERO

Operation Code	Format	Description
BZE	BZE A	If $C(AC) = 0$, then $C(IAR) \leftarrow A$
		otherwise
		If $C(AC) \neq 0$, then continue

Example: | BZE   175 |

If the contents of the AC are currently zero, the number 175 is placed into the IAR, destroying its original contents. This causes the model to execute the contents of word 175 as its next instruction. If the AC is not equal to zero, the IAR is not modified and the model's next instruction follows the BZE.

READ

Operation Code	Format	Description
READ	READ A	$C(A) \leftarrow C(\text{Input Slip})$

Example: | READ 100 |

The top slip is read from the input unit, and its contents are placed into word 100. The original contents of word 100 are destroyed.

WRITE

Operation Code	Format	Description
WRITE	WRITE A	$C(\text{Output Slip}) \leftarrow C(A)$

Example: | WRITE 22 |

The contents of word 22 are copied onto a slip and placed at the bottom of the output unit. The original contents of word 22 remain unchanged.

STOP

Operation Code	Format	Description
STOP	STOP	CU stops execution
		of instructions

Example: | STOP |

Since the operand of each model instruction contains no more than one memory address, it is said to be a *single-address* machine. In general, basic operations need more than one data value. The model handles this problem by using its accumulator as an implied address. For example, an addition instruction must tell a machine where to find two data values and where to store their sum. The ADD instruction of the model uses its single address to specify the memory location of one value and the CU assumes that the AC contains the other. Furthermore, the ADD instruction directs the AU to return its results to the AC. Thus, an ADD A instruction is described as

$$C(AC) \leftarrow C(AC) + C(A)$$

Machines have also been built with instructions that contain more than one memory address. For example, in a *double-address* machine, an addition instruction would be written as ADD A,B and might be executed as

$$C(B) \leftarrow C(A) + C(B)$$

Likewise, in a *triple-address* machine, the same addition could be specified as ADD A,B,C and might indicate

$$C(C) \leftarrow C(A) + C(B)$$

Such multi-address machines would not need an accumulator as an implied data address.

3.1.2 The instruction cycle

Although the CU is the manager and supervisor of the model, even it must follow a rigid set of directions as it controls the execution of instructions. These directions are known as an *instruction cycle* and are repeated by the CU for each instruction. An instruction cycle consists of five steps, summarized in Figure 3.7. The first three steps are referred to as the *fetch* phase; the last two are known as the *execute* phase.

INSTRUCTION
CYCLE

Fetch

1. The CU asks the IAR for the location of the current instruction and then increments the IAR by 1.

2. The CU asks memory for a copy of the current instruction.

3. The CU asks the IU for directions on how to perform the instruction.

Execute

4. The CU executes the instruction as specified by the IU.

5. The CU returns to step 1.

Figure 3.7 *Steps of an instruction cycle.*

During the first step of each instruction cycle, the CU determines the address of its next instruction. Since the purpose of the IAR is to save this address, the CU need only ask the IAR for a copy of its contents. Before the CU moves to the next step, it must adjust the IAR for the start of the next cycle. Since the next instruction is assumed to *follow* the current instruction, the CU increments or adds 1 to the contents of the IAR. Now the IAR again contains the address of the next instruction—a requirement that it must always satisfy.

In the second step, the CU retrieves its instruction from memory. Since the CU now knows the address of that instruction, it asks memory for a copy of the contents of that location. Note that the instruction is still retained in memory at its original location and can be executed again during a later cycle.

In the third step, the CU determines what operations must be performed for the current instruction. Since the IU contains this information, the CU identifies the name of its current instruction and then asks the IU how to execute that instruction. At this point, the CU assumes it has received information from memory that represents a valid instruction. If it has not, the CU is unable to identify the instruction and thus cannot find an IU entry. Whenever this happens, the CU can progress no further and must stop.

During the fourth step, the CU performs the operations as directed by the IU. It is in this step that the CU executes the actual instruction. Once all IU operations have been performed, the CU completes the cycle by automatically returning to the first step to begin the execution of the next instruction.

(It is important to realize that the instruction cycle tells the CU how to *interpret* the contents of a memory location.) During the fetch phase, the CU anticipates that memory will send it a copy of a valid instruction. In contrast, during the execute phase, the CU expects data. In an actual computer, both instructions and data are stored in memory as binary numbers. Therefore, if by mistake the IAR is set to an address that contains data, the CU will obediently attempt to execute that value as an instruction. When this happens, the machine literally is out of control and stops as soon as it reaches a data value that is not equivalent to a valid machine instruction.

3.1.3 Examples of an instruction cycle

As the first example of an instruction cycle, let us follow the CU as it executes the load accumulator (LOAD) instruction shown in Figure 3.8. Figure 3.8a specifies the initial condition of the model before it begins its next cycle. Figure 3.8b shows the model after the CU has completed one cycle; it can be derived from Figure 3.8a by the application of the five cycle steps, as follows. In the first step, the CU asks the IAR for the address of the next instruction and receives a value of 2. The CU then advances the IAR by 1 so that it again indicates the address of the next instruction. In the second step, the CU asks memory for a copy of location 2 and is given the instruction, LOAD 101. In the third step, the CU identifies the instruction as a load accumulator and then asks the IU how to execute such an instruction. In the fourth step, the CU follows the directions of the IU and loads a copy of location 101 into the AC. Since the CU receives a copy of word 101, that location still contains its original value. However, the original contents of the AC are destroyed. At the end of the cycle, the AC contains a new value of 7 and the IAR indicates that location 3 contains the next instruction.

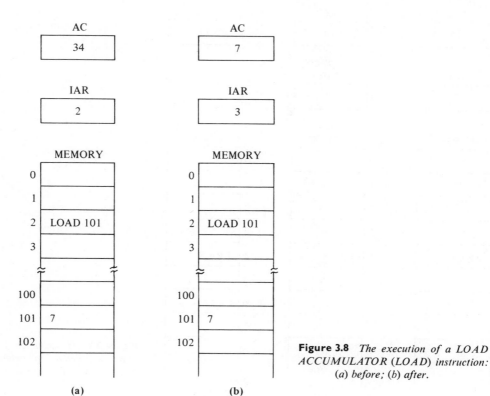

Figure 3.8 *The execution of a LOAD ACCUMULATOR (LOAD) instruction: (a) before; (b) after.*

As a second example of an instruction cycle, Figure 3.9 shows the effect of a branch absolutely (BRA) instruction. In the first step, the IAR tells the CU that its instruction is located in location 4; then, as always, the CU advances the IAR by 1. Now, the IAR, as shown in Figure 3.9b, specifies that memory location 5 contains the next instruction. In the second and third steps, the CU receives a copy of word 4 and asks the IU how to perform a BRA 8 instruction. The IU tells the CU to place the value 8 into the IAR, destroying its present contents. Now, the IAR indicates that the next instruction is actually contained in location 8. It is important to realize that the number contained in the BRA instruction itself is transmitted directly to the IAR. This modification of the IAR by an instruction *overrides* the assumption that the next instruction *follows* the current one. Thus, a BRA instruction can be used to alter the execution sequence of the model. In this case, the CU jumps from location 4 to location 8, ignoring the words in between.

As a final example of an instruction cycle, consider the execution of the branch if plus (BPL) instruction shown in Figure 3.10. As always, in the first cycle step the CU asks the IAR for the location of its next instruction and then increments the IAR by 1, as shown in Figure 3.10b. In the second and third steps of the cycle, the CU asks memory for a copy of location 4 and then

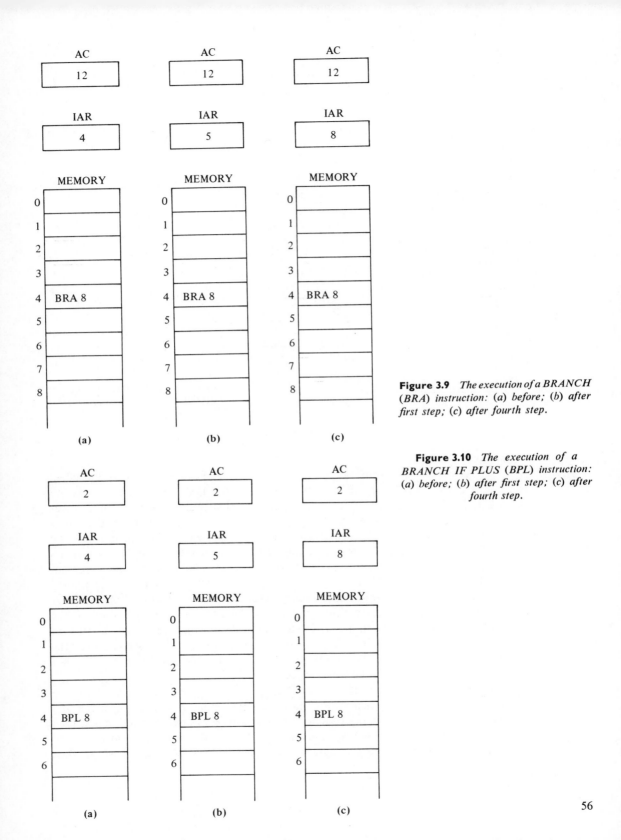

Figure 3.9 *The execution of a BRANCH (BRA) instruction: (a) before; (b) after first step; (c) after fourth step.*

Figure 3.10 *The execution of a BRANCH IF PLUS (BPL) instruction: (a) before; (b) after first step; (c) after fourth step.*

asks the IU for directions on how to execute a BPL 8 instruction. In the fourth step, the CU asks the AU to determine whether the contents of the AC are positive, i.e., greater than zero. Since the AC contains a value of 2, which is greater than zero, the CU places the value 8 into the IAR. Now, when the CU begins the next cycle, it will find that its next instruction is located in word 8. Thus, a BPL instruction is equivalent to a BRA instruction when the AC is positive. Otherwise, if the AC is zero or negative, its only effect is to advance the IAR by 1.

3.2 Using the Model

In the previous section, we described the steps of an instruction cycle and discussed execution of individual instructions. Now we can ask the model to execute a sequence of instructions and thus perform a series of calculations. In this section, we briefly consider two such sequences.

In the first example, the model computes the difference between any two numbers; in the second, it calculates the sum of a set of numbers. Since the purpose of this chapter is to analyze the operation of a stored program digital computer, the model is shown ready to perform its calculations; i.e., the memory already contains the proper instructions, the IAR contains the location of the first instruction, and the input unit contains sample data.

3.2.1 Finding the difference between two numbers

The first example of the use of the model to perform a sequence of instructions is the calculation of the difference between any two numbers. Figure 3.11a shows the model before the start of the first instruction cycle. The instruction sequence occupies 10 memory locations. The first seven words contain instructions, whereas the last three are reserved for data. The IAR contains a value of zero, indicating that the first instruction is in location zero. The input unit contains two numbers, 10 and 15, and the output unit is empty.

During the first instruction cycle, the CU advances the IAR to 1 and then learns that it must execute the instruction, READ 7. Following directions from the IU, the CU asks the input unit for its next data value. Since the number 10 is at the top of the input, the CU receives that value and then sends it to memory for storage in location 7. When all five steps of the instruction cycle have been completed, the CU automatically begins the next cycle. Figure 3.11b shows the model after completion of the first instruction cycle.

In the second cycle, the CU executes the instruction contained in location 1. Since that instruction is also a read, its execution is similar to the previous one. This time, when the CU asks for the next input value, it receives the number 15, thus emptying the input. After the CU transmits its latest input value to memory for storage in location 8, it reverts to the first step of the next cycle. Figure 3.11c shows the model after completion of the second cycle.

During the third, fourth, and fifth cycles, the CU calculates the difference between the input values by subtracting the second from the first. The LOAD

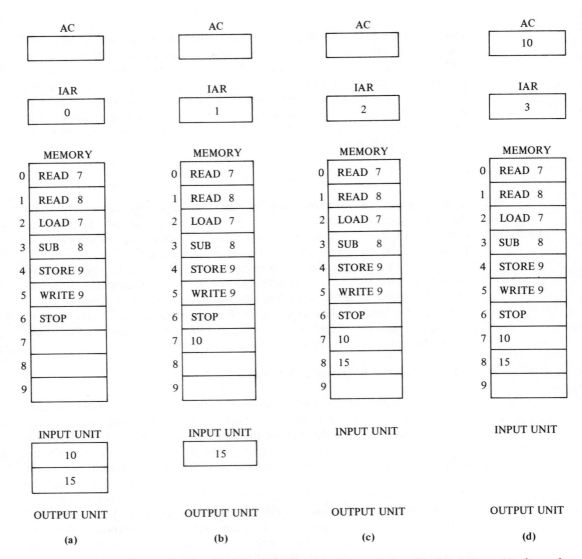

Figure 3.11 *Finding the difference of two numbers: (a) before; (b) after cycle one; (c) after cycle two; (d) after cycle three; (e) after cycle four; (f) after cycle five; (g) after cycle six; (h) after cycle seven.*

instruction directs the CU to retrieve the first input number from memory and to place that value in the AC. The SUB instruction tells the CU to retrieve the second number and to send it along with the first to the AU with a request that the second number be subtracted from the first. After the difference is returned to the AC, the STORE instruction directs the CU to save the AC in location 9.

In the sixth cycle, the CU reaches the instruction at location 5. The IU entry for a WRITE instruction directs the CU to request memory for the

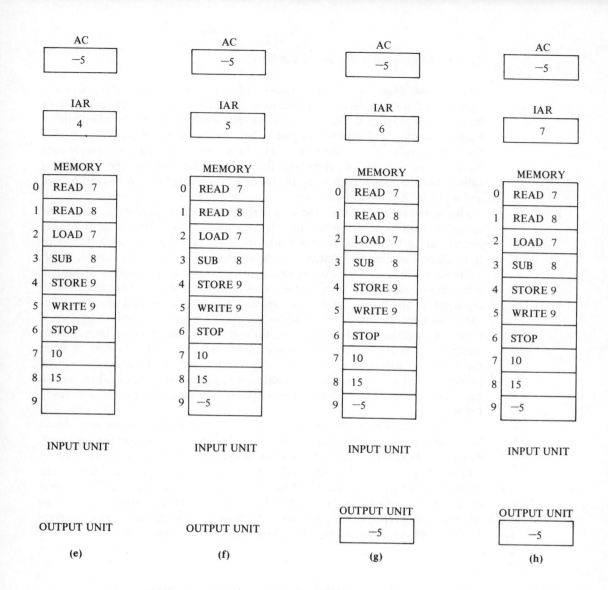

AC
−5

AC
−5

AC
−5

AC
−5

IAR
4

IAR
5

IAR
6

IAR
7

MEMORY

0	READ 7
1	READ 8
2	LOAD 7
3	SUB 8
4	STORE 9
5	WRITE 9
6	STOP
7	10
8	15
9	

MEMORY

0	READ 7
1	READ 8
2	LOAD 7
3	SUB 8
4	STORE 9
5	WRITE 9
6	STOP
7	10
8	15
9	−5

MEMORY

0	READ 7
1	READ 8
2	LOAD 7
3	SUB 8
4	STORE 9
5	WRITE 9
6	STOP
7	10
8	15
9	−5

MEMORY

0	READ 7
1	READ 8
2	LOAD 7
3	SUB 8
4	STORE 9
5	WRITE 9
6	STOP
7	10
8	15
9	−5

INPUT UNIT

INPUT UNIT

INPUT UNIT

INPUT UNIT

OUTPUT UNIT

OUTPUT UNIT

OUTPUT UNIT
−5

OUTPUT UNIT
−5

(e)

(f)

(g)

(h)

contents of location 9 and to send them to the output unit for placement at the bottom of the output. Figure 3.11g shows that the output unit now contains the value minus 5.

Finally, in the seventh cycle, the CU reaches the STOP instruction stored in location 6, and the IU directs the CU to terminate its operation. Notice in Figure 3.11h that the IAR contains a final value of 7, which is the address of the location following the STOP instruction, (because the CU increments the IAR as part of the fetch phase of the instruction cycle before it performs the STOP instruction in the execute phase.) Therefore, after the CU executes a STOP instruction, the IAR always contains the address of the location following that STOP.

3.2.2 Finding the sum of a set of numbers

As a second example of the execution of a complete instruction sequence, Figure 3.12 shows a set of instructions that calculates the sum of a set of input values. Figure 3.12a shows the model before it begins its calculations. Memory contains 12 instruction and 5 data locations. The IAR indicates that the first instruction is at location 0. The input unit contains four sample data values: 3, 6, -3, and 4. Here, the first input value specifies the number of values that the model is to sum. In this case, it is to sum three values: 6, -3, and 4. Finally, the output is empty.

Basically, the model finds the sum as follows. First, it determines how many values it must process by reading the top input value. This is done by the instruction in location 0. It then reads one value at a time and adds that value to a subtotal in a manner similar to a desk calculator. The instructions in words 1 through 4 read and sum input values, whereas those in locations 5 through 9 determine whether all input values have been read. Word 12 is used to store input values and word 13 saves the subtotal. Location 14 is used to count input values as they are processed. It initially contains 0 and is increased by 1 each time a value is read. Word 15 contains the constant 1, which is used to increment location 14. Word 16 saves the number of input values and is subtracted from the count in location 14 to determine whether all input values have been processed. If the result of this subtraction is negative, more input values remain to be processed. If the result is non-negative, the sum is complete and ready for output.

Figure 3.13 traces the execution of this instruction sequence and shows how and when the contents of the AC, IAR, and memory locations are changed. For example, location 12 is set to 6 during cycle 2 and remains 6 until cycle 11 which changes it to -3. You should now pause and trace the execution of the instruction sequence of Figure 3.12 to insure that you understand the effect of each instruction cycle, as shown in Figure 3.13. Note that this solution sums any number of input values. All that is necessary is to make appropriate changes to the input. In other words, no instructions need be modified.

3.3
An Analysis
of the Model
The previous sections of this chapter described a simplified model of a stored program digital computer. The individual components of the model were discussed, and then their operation under the direction of a control unit was illustrated. A model was used to introduce the study of problem solving via a computer for two reasons. First, the model illustrates how an actual computer performs its calculations; second, it can be used to *predict* how the computer itself causes problems for a computer user as he attempts to solve his own problems. Now that the model has been discussed, let us analyze its operation.

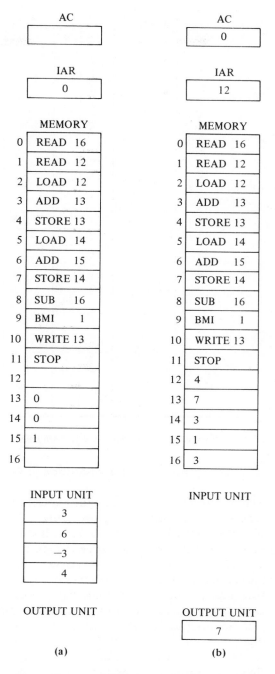

Figure 3.12 *Finding the sum of a set of numbers: (a) before; (b) after.*

Instruction Cycle	Instruction Address	IAR	AC	12	13	14	15	16	Test	Result
Start		0			0	0	1			
1	0	1						3		
2	1	2		6						
3	2	3	6							
4	3	4	6							
5	4	5			6					
6	5	6	0							
7	6	7	1							
8	7	8				1				
9	8	9	−2							
10	9	1							−2 < 0	Yes
11	1	2		−3						
12	2	3	−3							
13	3	4	3							
14	4	5			3					
15	5	6	1							
16	6	7	2							
17	7	8				2				
18	8	9	−1							
19	9	1							−1 < 0	Yes
20	1	2		4						
21	2	3	4							
22	3	4	7							
23	4	5			7					
24	5	6	2							
25	6	7	3							
26	7	8				3				
27	8	9	0							
28	9	10							0 < 0	No
29	10	11								
30	11	12								

Figure 3.13 *The instruction cycles for finding the sum of a set of numbers.*

3.3.1 The data-instruction coordination problem

DATA INSTRUCTION COORDINATION

The first problem that a computer creates for a user is that he must ensure that he has *data-instruction coordination*. A user must coordinate his data with his instructions in three ways. *First,* his input data must be arranged in the input unit in the proper sequence and must have the expected number of values. *Second,* data must be correctly passed from instruction to instruction, which means that read instructions must store input data in memory words known to processing instructions and that processing instructions must store their results in locations known to write instructions. *Third,* write instructions must place results into the output unit in a known sequence so that a user can correctly interpret each output value.

The three parts of the data-instruction coordination problem can best be illustrated through an example. The model shown in Figure 3.14 is set to calculate the sum and difference of any two numbers. Figure 3.14a and 3.14b show the model before and after its calculations. The first 11 memory words contain instructions; the last 4 are reserved for data. Locations 11 and 12 store the two input values, whereas words 13 and 14 save the resulting sum and difference.

The arrangement of the input data becomes significant when the operation of the subtraction sequence in words 5, 6, and 7 is studied. The LOAD instruction brings the contents of location 11 into the AC, and then the SUB instruction subtracts the contents of location 12 from the AC. Consideration of the READ instructions indicate that word 11 contains the first input value and word 12 contains the second. If the two numbers, 10 and 15, are reversed as input, the result of the SUB instruction changes from -5 to $+5$ because subtraction is *not* commutative, i.e., $a-b \neq b-a$. Finally, it is important to notice that the model expects two input values. If there are less than two, it is unable to complete its read operations and stops. If there are more than two, the excess are simply ignored and left unnoticed in the input unit.

The passing of data from instruction to instruction becomes important when one studies the interaction between instructions. Notice that the READ instructions store their input values in words 11 and 12 and that the LOAD, ADD, and SUB instructions assume that these locations contain data. Figure 3.15 shows a modification of the sum and difference example and illustrates improper data-instruction coordination through incorrect passage of data. Study of this figure shows that the READ instructions store their input values in words 11 and 12, whereas the LOAD, ADD, and SUB instructions expect data values to have been previously stored in words 13 and 14. Since locations 13 and 14 already contain values, the model produces the output shown in Figure 3.15b. Certainly, 10 plus 15 does not equal 11, and 10 from 15 is not 3. The model has produced incorrect results because the input data are incorrectly passed from the read instructions to the processing instructions. Thus, a computer user must carefully consider how he stores his data in memory.

The importance of output arrangement becomes evident when the output values in Figure 3.14b are considered. From previous discussions, one assumes that the first output value is always the sum of the two input numbers, whereas the second is their difference. Consider for a moment what happens if the two WRITE instructions in words 8 and 9 are interchanged. This switch rearranges the output such that the difference appears first followed by the sum. If one does not know about the interchange of instructions, one would continue to interpret the two output values with their previous meaning. Thus, a computer user must ensure that his output values are sent to the output unit in a known sequence so that he can correctly interpret each value.

3.3.2 The instruction sequence problem

The second problem that a computer creates for a user is that he must ensure that he has a correct instruction sequence. First, each instruction must perform the appropriate individual calculation, such as ADD, SUB, etc. Second, these individual instructions must be arranged into a sequence that produces an accurate and complete set of results.

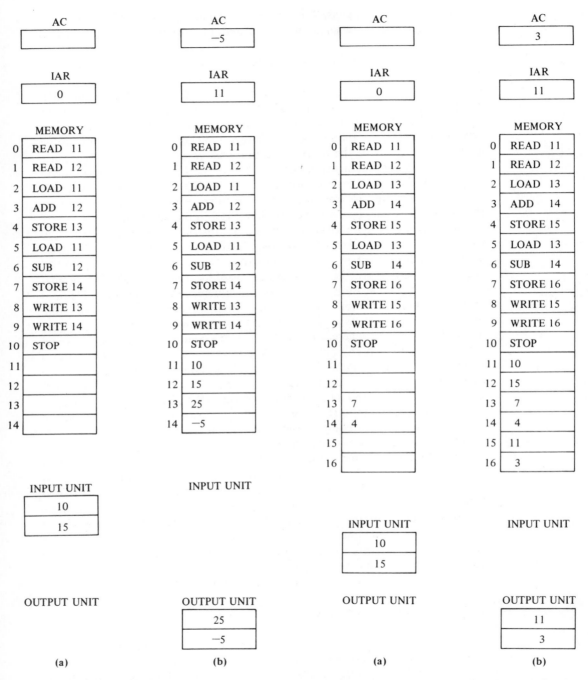

Figure 3.14 *Finding the sum and difference of two numbers: (a) before; (b) after.*

Figure 3.15 *An example of improper coordination between data and instructions: (a) before; (b) after.*

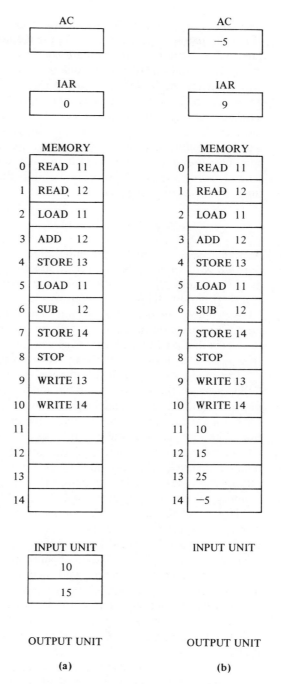

Figure 3.16 *An example of an incorrect instruction sequence: (a) before; (b) after.*

Figure 3.16 shows the model set up to calculate again the sum and difference of two numbers. Figure 3.16a shows the model before it begins its calculations. The first 8 memory words contain the same instructions as before; however, the WRITE and STOP instructions have been interchanged so that the STOP now precedes the WRITE. Figure 3.16b shows the model after it terminates its calculations. In this case, the output unit is empty, yet the words reserved for data storage contain correct values. This occurs because the model executes the STOP before it can perform its output operations. The model produces incorrect results because its instructions are not in proper sequence. Thus, a computer user must ensure that he gives a computer an instruction sequence that not only performs the appropriate individual calculations but also performs them in the correct sequence.

3.4
Summary

A model is an abstract representation of a physical object or situation. Its purpose is to simulate the object or situation and to produce the same results as if the actual object or situation were used or were present. A model of a stored program digital computer was introduced for two reasons. First, it allows you, the reader, to study and understand how a computer operates and how it performs its calculations. Second, the model can be used to predict the problems that a computer will cause you, the computer user, when you attempt to employ it as a problem-solving tool to solve your own problems.

The model presented in this chapter is composed of four components. The CPU oversees the operation of the model and is divided into five subcomponents. The CU acts as supervisor or manager of the other components. The IAR is a special register that contains the memory address of the next instruction. The AU performs the calculations for the model. The AC is used by the CU and the AU as an intermediate storage register. The IU is a procedures manual that tells the CU how to perform each instruction. The input and output units are channels of communication into and out of the model. Finally memory serves as storage for the CU.

The model performs its calculations by executing a sequence of instructions. The CU oversees this execution by rigorously following the steps of the instruction cycle, which is divided into two parts: fetch and execute. During the fetch portion, the CU performs three operations. First, it asks the IAR for the location of its next instruction, and then it increments the IAR by 1. Second, it asks memory for a copy of the current instruction. Third, it identifies the name of its instruction and asks the IU for directions on how to perform that instruction. During the execute portion, the CU performs operations as directed by the IU. The CU then automatically begins the next instruction cycle.

The analysis of the operation of this model exposes two problems that a computer user must solve whenever he uses a computer. *First*, he must ensure that he provides a computer with a coordinated set of data and instructions. His input data must be arranged in proper sequence and must contain the proper number of values. Data values must be passed from instruction to instruction such that each instruction receives the proper values. Results must be placed into the output unit in a known sequence so that the user knows the meaning of each value. *Second*, a user must provide a computer with a sequence of instructions that performs the correct calculations and produces the desired results. Not only must the individual instructions be correct, but they must also be arranged in proper sequence.

PROBLEMS

In each of the problems on pages 68–72, a figure shows the model before it begins its calculations. Perform the function of the CU and execute the instruction cycles as directed by the model. Show how the model appears after completion of its calculations. In general, what does the model calculate?

3.1

Before	After
AC	AC
[ ]	[ ]
IAR	IAR
0	[ ]

MEMORY (Before)

0	READ 11
1	READ 12
2	READ 13
3	READ 14
4	LOAD 11
5	ADD 12
6	ADD 13
7	ADD 14
8	STORE 15
9	WRITE 15
10	STOP
11	
12	
13	
14	
15	

MEMORY (After)

0	
1	
2	
3	
4	
5	
6	
7	
8	
9	
10	
11	
12	
13	
14	
15	

INPUT UNIT

6
0
−3
1

OUTPUT UNIT

INPUT UNIT

OUTPUT UNIT

3.2

Before	After
AC	AC
[ ]	[ ]
IAR	IAR
0	[ ]

MEMORY (Before)

0	READ 8
1	LOAD 8
2	BPL 6
3	LOAD 9
4	SUB 8
5	STORE 8
6	WRITE 8
7	STOP
8	
9	0

MEMORY (After)

0	
1	
2	
3	
4	
5	
6	
7	
8	
9	

INPUT UNIT

−5

OUTPUT UNIT

INPUT UNIT

OUTPUT UNIT

3.3

Before	After
AC	AC
[ ]	[ ]

IAR	IAR
0	[ ]

MEMORY (Before)

0	READ 11
1	READ 12
2	LOAD 11
3	SUB 12
4	BPL 8
5	WRITE 12
6	WRITE 11
7	STOP
8	WRITE 11
9	WRITE 12
10	STOP
11	
12	

MEMORY (After)

0	
1	
2	
3	
4	
5	
6	
7	
8	
9	
10	
11	
12	

INPUT UNIT (Before)

12
15

INPUT UNIT (After)

OUTPUT UNIT   OUTPUT UNIT

3.4

Before	After
AC	AC
[ ]	[ ]

IAR	IAR
0	[ ]

MEMORY (Before)

0	READ 12
1	LOAD 12
2	MPY 12
3	ADD 13
4	STORE 13
5	LOAD 14
6	ADD 15
7	STORE 14
8	SUB 16
9	BMI 0
10	WRITE 13
11	STOP
12	
13	0
14	0
15	1
16	3

MEMORY (After)

0	
1	
2	
3	
4	
5	
6	
7	
8	
9	
10	
11	
12	
13	
14	
15	
16	

INPUT UNIT (Before)

2
−3
1

INPUT UNIT (After)

OUTPUT UNIT   OUTPUT UNIT

3.5

Before

AC

IAR
0

	MEMORY
0	READ 16
1	READ 17
2	LOAD 16
3	SUB 17
4	BMI 7
5	LOAD 18
6	STORE 19
7	LOAD 17
8	STORE 16
9	LOAD 20
10	ADD 18
11	STORE 20
12	SUB 21
13	BMI 1
14	WRITE 19
15	STOP
16	
17	
18	1
19	0
20	0
21	3

INPUT UNIT

13
17
−11
167

OUTPUT UNIT

After

AC

IAR

	MEMORY
0	
1	
2	
3	
4	
5	
6	
7	
8	
9	
10	
11	
12	
13	
14	
15	
16	
17	
18	
19	
20	
21	

INPUT UNIT

OUTPUT UNIT

3.6

Before

AC

IAR
0

	MEMORY
0	READ 14
1	LOAD 14
2	ADD 15
3	STORE 15
4	LOAD 16
5	ADD 17
6	STORE 16
7	SUB 18
8	BMI 0
9	LOAD 15
10	DIV 18
11	STORE 15
12	WRITE 15
13	STOP
14	
15	0
16	0
17	1
18	5

INPUT UNIT

7
3
15
2
8

OUTPUT UNIT

After

AC

IAR

	MEMORY
0	
1	
2	
3	
4	
5	
6	
7	
8	
9	
10	
11	
12	
13	
14	
15	
16	
17	
18	

INPUT UNIT

OUTPUT UNIT

3.7

Before

AC

IAR
0

MEMORY

0	READ 18
1	READ 14
2	LOAD 14
3	BMI 7
4	LOAD 15
5	ADD 16
6	STORE 15
7	LOAD 17
8	ADD 16
9	STORE 17
10	SUB 18
11	BMI 1
12	WRITE 15
13	STOP
14	
15	0
16	1
17	0
18	

INPUT UNIT

5
2
−1
7
10
−135

OUTPUT UNIT

After

AC

IAR

MEMORY

0	
1	
2	
3	
4	
5	
6	
7	
8	
9	
10	
11	
12	
13	
14	
15	
16	
17	
18	

INPUT UNIT

OUTPUT UNIT

3.8

Before

AC

IAR
0

MEMORY

0	READ 19
1	READ 15
2	READ 16
3	LOAD 15
4	SUB 16
5	BPL 8
6	LOAD 16
7	STORE 15
8	LOAD 17
9	ADD 18
10	STORE 17
11	SUB 19
12	BMI 2
13	WRITE 15
14	STOP
15	
16	
17	1
18	1
19	

INPUT UNIT

5
100
1
2
101
17

OUTPUT UNIT

After

AC

IAR

MEMORY

0	
1	
2	
3	
4	
5	
6	
7	
8	
9	
10	
11	
12	
13	
14	
15	
16	
17	
18	
19	

INPUT UNIT

OUTPUT UNIT

3.9

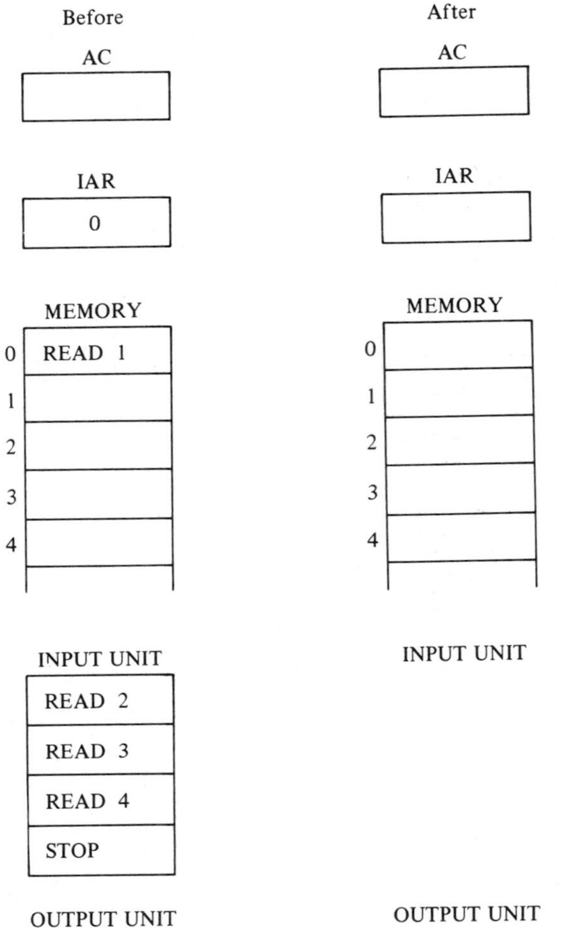

Before
AC

IAR

0

MEMORY

0	READ 1
1	
2	
3	
4	

INPUT UNIT

READ 2
READ 3
READ 4
STOP

OUTPUT UNIT

After
AC

IAR

MEMORY

0	
1	
2	
3	
4	

INPUT UNIT

OUTPUT UNIT

3.10

AC

IAR

0

MEMORY

0	READ	16
1	READ	12
2	LOAD	12
3	ADD	13
4	STORE	13
5	LOAD	14
6	ADD	15
7	STORE	14
8	SUB	16
9	BMI	1
10	WRITE	13
11	STOP	
12		
13	0	
14	0	
15	1	
16		

INPUT UNIT

OUTPUT UNIT

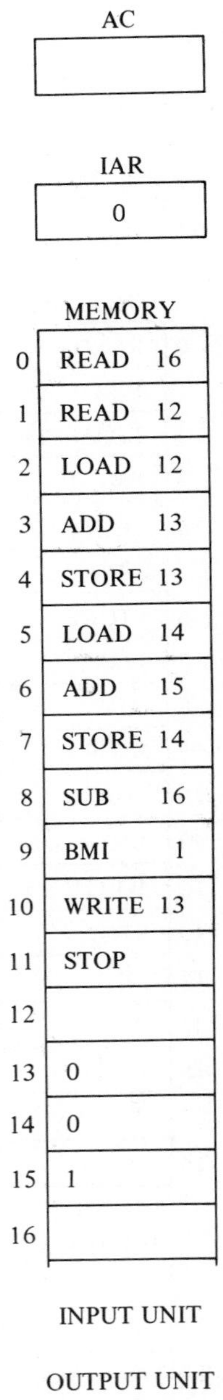

3.10 In Section 3.2.2, the model was used to calculate the sum of a set of numbers where the first input value specified the number of values to be summed. Unfortunately, that solution, shown above at right, does not handle all input possibilities. Find and describe these situations. *Hint:* Consider a range of first input values.

4 A Problem-Solving Procedure

Problem solving is an acquired skill. Like any skill, it must be developed from scratch by imitation and practice. Swimming is a good example of an acquired skill. In the beginning, when you learned to swim, you imitated the arm and feet movements of those you saw swimming. At first you were barely able to keep your head above water, but with practice and coaching from more experienced swimmers you were able to improve your performance. Learning to solve problems is similar to learning to swim. In the beginning you observe and imitate what other people do when they solve problems. You start by solving small problems and then gradually advance to larger ones. If you want to refine your swimming ability, you practice swimming; likewise, if you want to develop your problem-solving ability, you practice problem solving.

This chapter introduces a procedure that should help you learn to use a computer as a problem-solving tool. This procedure incorporates a *systems approach* and covers the total process of using a computer to solve problems. It is not limited to just one part of the solution process, such as learning the grammar rules of a particular programming language. Rather, it starts by encouraging you to define and understand your problem so that you realize what is required from your solution. It then continues through a series of steps designed to guide you to a successful solution. The procedure utilizes four graphical techniques, which are intended to help you produce satisfactory results while overcoming the inherent problems of using a computer. The first three graphical techniques—the *input list*, *output list*, and *data chart*—should help you overcome the data-instruction coordination problem, whereas the fourth technique—the *flow chart*—should help with the instruction sequence problem.

4.1
A Procedure
for Using a
Computer as
a Problem-
Solving Tool

To the beginner, problem solving is difficult because he does not understand what to do. He does not know where to begin, and, once started, he does not know how to continue. People who can already solve problems seem to have one thing in common—they all have some plan of attack. Their problem-solving procedures vary from individual to individual, but each person has some way of knowing where to start and how to continue. If you are a beginner, you probably do not have a solution procedure for using a computer as a problem-solving tool. This section introduces you to such a procedure. Adopt it as your own, and it should help you learn to solve problems. As you develop your own problem-solving skill, you can adapt this procedure to fit your own style and situation. Whenever you find yourself having trouble with a particular problem, stop and make sure that you are still following your plan of attack.

4.1.1 The steps of the procedure

Figure 4.1 summarizes a six-step procedure designed to help you learn to use a computer as a problem-solving tool. The *first* step tells you to define your problem and to break it into subproblems. It is foolish to try to solve any problem without first understanding it. Furthermore, it is easier to solve small problems. Consequently, whenever possible, you should subdivide your problem into smaller ones. The *second* step tells you to specify your desired output.

1. Define your problem and break it into subproblems.

2. Specify your desired output.

3. Specify the required input.

4. Determine what data are to be retained in memory.

5. Devise a calculation procedure.

6. Write a computer program and then test it.

Figure 4.1 *Steps of a problem-solving procedure.*

You must know what answers your solution must produce and their output sequence. By doing so, you have a concrete goal at which to aim. The *third* step tells you to specify the required input. Here, you must determine what information a computer needs to produce your desired results. In addition, you must specify the sequence of your input values. The *fourth* step tells you to determine what data are to be retained in memory. In the *fifth* step, you develop a calculation procedure that transforms the required input into your desired output. Finally, in the *sixth* and last step, you convert your procedure into an actual computer program using some programming language. Once your program is complete, you must test it by having a computer use it to process sample sets of input data to ensure that your solution produces the correct results.

You should notice that the six solution steps ensure that you face and attempt to overcome the inherent problems of using a computer, as discussed in Chapter 3. The second, third, and fourth steps handle the three parts of the data-instruction coordination problem, whereas the fifth step is aimed at the instruction sequence problem. You should also notice that an actual computer program is not written and tested until the *last* step. Certainly, a program is essential and important because it tells a computer how to solve your problem. However, you cannot produce a successful computer program without at least subconsciously considering the first five steps. Thus, this procedure is designed to help you ensure that you have covered all the important aspects of problem solving.

As you start through the steps of the procedure, you will undoubtedly change your point of view about your problem. For example, you may discover that you have made unnecessary or even incorrect assumptions. Thus, at some point in the solution process, you may have to stop and fall back to repeat one or more solution steps. When this happens, you should not feel discouraged. There is a lot of cut-and-try in problem solving, and some rework is almost always necessary and should be considered normal.

4.1.2 An example of using the procedure

Since imitation is a most successful problem-solving technique for a beginner, let us illustrate the problem-solving procedure by applying it to a problem that has already been considered. Let us assume that we wish to use the model to find the sum and difference of any two numbers. The solution to this problem was discussed in Section 3.3.1. Repeating a previous example has several advantages. By now, you should understand the operation of the model; in addition, you are already familiar with how the model calculated the sum and difference. Thus, you should be free to concentrate on how each procedure step is applied to produce a solution to the problem at hand.

The first step of the problem-solving procedure tells you to define the problem and to break it into subproblems. In this case, the problem has been given to you. However, you should always be sure that you fully understand a problem. You should acquire the habit of reading the problem statement several times before you begin to work. This should help you keep the complete problem in mind as you work toward a solution. Here, the statement says "to use the model to find the sum and difference of any two numbers." After studying this statement, you should notice the following. First, you are to produce a solution for the model. Second, your solution must work for any two numbers, not just those that are positive or nonzero. Third, this problem can be subdivided into two smaller ones: finding the sum of two numbers, and finding their difference.

The second step of the solution procedure tells you to specify the desired output. This must include both the number of values and their output sequence. From the statement of the problem, two values are required. One value must be the sum of the two input numbers and the other must be their difference. Since the problem statement does not specify an output arrangement, let us arbitrarily agree that the sum shall appear first followed by the difference. You should realize that this choice is ours to make, but once made, the procedure that outputs these results must arrange them in this order. Figure 4.2a illustrates how the output unit should look after the model finishes its calculations.

The third step tells you to specify your input data. As with the output, the input specification must include both the number of data values and their sequence. The problem statement says to find the sum and difference of two numbers. Thus, there must always be two input values. Once again, the statement of the problem does not specify input arrangement. Furthermore, it does not mention which number should be subtracted from the other. Let us arbitrarily agree to subtract the second input value from the first. This is an example of learning about a problem while solving it. We have had to make an assumption about input order to solve our problem. Figure 4.2b shows how the input unit should look before the model begins its calculations.

The fourth step directs you to determine what data are to be retained in memory. So far, four different values have been mentioned: two input values, their sum, and their difference. Once in memory, these four data values can each be stored in separate words, as shown in Figure 4.2c. It does not matter which four are used, but once a word is selected for one of these numbers, only that number should be stored in that word. Otherwise, data values can be destroyed and data-instruction coordination can be lost.

The fifth step directs you to devise a calculation procedure that converts the required input into your desired output. From our discussion of the problem, we should realize that basically we must direct the model to perform three separate operations. First, it must read two input numbers and save them in memory. Second, the model must access two input values, calculate their sum and difference, and store the results back in memory. Finally, the model must retrieve the results from memory and send them to the output unit in expected order. Figure 4.2d lists this calculation procedure.

The last step tells you to write and test a program. Figure 4.2e shows how the results of the previous steps are combined together to produce a complete solution for the model. Since four values must be retained in memory, let us arbitrarily reserve locations 100 and 101 for the first and second input values and words 102 and 103 for their sum and difference. Now, we are ready to convert our calculation procedure into a sequence of instructions. The input

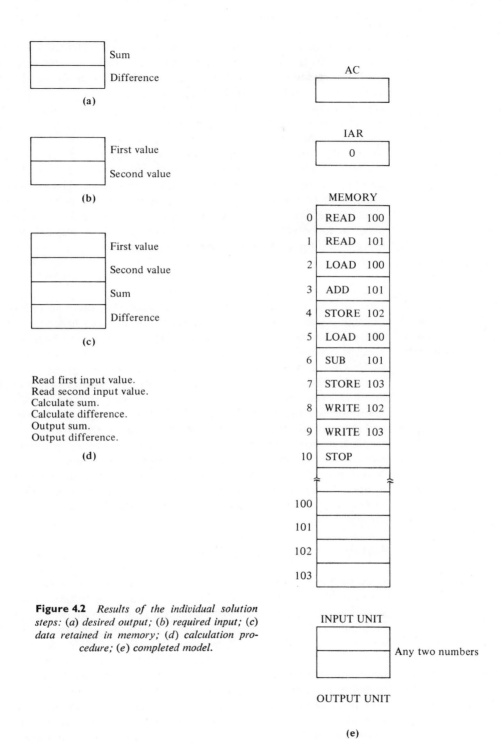

Read first input value.
Read second input value.
Calculate sum.
Calculate difference.
Output sum.
Output difference.

(d)

Figure 4.2 *Results of the individual solution steps: (a) desired output; (b) required input; (c) data retained in memory; (d) calculation procedure; (e) completed model.*

values can be read into memory by separate read instructions. The statement, READ 100, reads the first input value into word 100, whereas READ 101 reads the second into word 101. The addition is then performed by the sequence LOAD 100, ADD 101, STORE 102, and the subtraction is performed by LOAD 100, SUB 101, STORE 103. Finally, the results are sent to the output unit in expected order by the instructions WRITE 102 and WRITE 103. You should realize that the two READ instructions must be in the order shown. Otherwise, the result of the subtraction sequence is altered, and the sign of the difference is reversed. The addition and subtraction sequences can be interchanged without affecting the results. In other words, the difference can be calculated before the sum; however, the addresses used in the subtraction sequence must be as shown. Finally, the WRITE instructions must appear as shown if expected output order is to be achieved. You should now devise several different input data sets and use them to test this instruction sequence.

4.2 Problem-Solving Techniques

Even though problem solving is an acquired skill that can only be developed through practice, there are known techniques that can help you solve problems. These techniques have been devised by successful problem solvers, just as successful swimming coaches have developed improved swimming techniques. If, by chance, you wanted to improve your swimming skill quickly, it would be most efficient for you to study and adopt these known swimming techniques. Similarly, you can improve your problem-solving abilities quickly by studying known problem-solving techniques. This section introduces these techniques and incorporates them into the problem-solving procedure.

George Polya, the great mathematician, worked on problem solving and reported his findings in a series of volumes. His book, *How to Solve It: A New Aspect of Mathematical Method*, is an introduction to his methodology and is now published by Doubleday Anchor Books in paperback. It would be worthwhile for you to purchase a copy of this book or borrow one from a library.

4.2.1 Hints on defining a problem

Reading the problem is perhaps the most important aspect of defining and understanding it. As we said earlier, it is pointless to answer a problem that you do not yet understand. There is no reason to waste time solving the wrong problem. You should acquire the habit of rereading the statement of a problem until you can repeat it from memory. You should understand the meaning of all its words. How can you solve a problem if you do not understand its description? If you are puzzled by a description, stop and review some reference or textbook that will help you understand the concept of the problem. For example, assume that you are asked to calculate a home mortgage repayment schedule. If you do not already understand such schedules, you should first consult a reference. Is there a figure or table associated with the problem?

If yes, do you understand it? If no, can you draw a diagram that will help you visualize the problem? Finally, you should test your comprehension of the problem by asking yourself the following questions: What is required? What are the data? What are the conditions? What are the restrictions?

Once you fully understand a problem, you should ask yourself if you have solved this problem before. If you have, you need only ensure that your previous solution did truly solve the problem correctly and completely. Perhaps your earlier solution was produced when you were less experienced. If such is the case, you probably can improve upon your previous solution. If you have not seen the problem before, you should ask whether you have seen one that is similar. If so, how does that problem differ from the problem you have now? How do the data differ? How do the conditions differ? How do the restrictions differ?

Usually, it is easier to understand and solve smaller problems than larger ones. Because of this, you should attempt to divide your problem into sub-problems. By chance, some subproblems may not require solution by computer, or perhaps you may have already solved some or have at least seen similar ones. Once the smaller problems have been solved, individual solutions can be combined together to form a total solution. The problem-solving procedure introduced in the previous section is an example of this technique. The procedure is divided into six steps, each to be solved separately. Since each step is similar and less complicated than the total process, it should be easier to solve these individual steps.

4.2.2 Input and output lists

Only you can decide what data values produce a satisfactory solution to your own particular problem. Nevertheless, it is important that you specify your desired output as soon as you understand your problem. By doing so, you know where you are going and where you must be once you have finished your solution.

In the previous chapter, an output unit was simulated by a list. As each individual output was produced, it was placed at the bottom of that list. This representation was selected because it incorporates the sequential nature of physical output devices. Consequently, computer output can also be visualized as a list. This is the case whether the actual output values are printed across a page of paper or punched into cards or tape. Values still come out of a computer one at a time in sequence. Since computer output forms a list, a list is a convenient way for you to specify your desired output. This special list can show both the number of output values and their sequential arrangement and is referred to as an *output list*.

As examples of the use of an output list, assume you have the following situations. Suppose that your output should consist of three values arranged in numerical order as follows: the largest value, the middle value, and the smallest value. A suitable output list, shown in Figure 4.3a, indicates that three separate values are required. The labels at the side of that figure specify

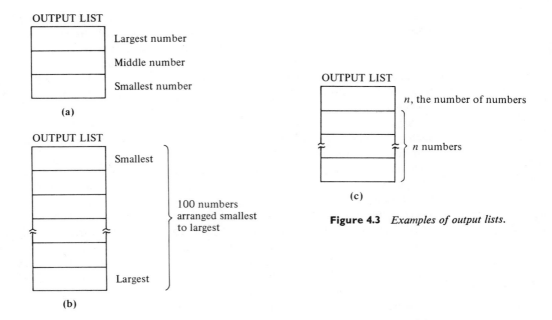

Figure 4.3 *Examples of output lists.*

their desired sequence. As a second example, assume that your output must consist of 100 data values arranged from smallest to largest. Figure 4.3b shows a suitable output list. Finally, suppose that your output is to be $n+1$ numbers, where the first value specifies the number of values, n, that follow on the list. Figure 4.3c shows such an output list.

The output list is a graphical device that can be used to specify your desired output during the second solution step. Once you have drawn your output list, you can use it for reference in later solution steps. Because the output list is drawn on paper with appropriate labels, it can help you remember exactly what output values must be produced and how they are to be sequenced. Likewise, you can use a similar list to specify your required input during the third solution step. This list is referred to as an *input list*. The use of output and input lists as graphical problem-solving aids are illustrated in more detail in later chapters.

4.2.3 Data structures and data charts

Once you have specified your desired output and required input, you are ready to determine what data are to be retained in memory. During the discussion of the model, each piece of information was considered as a separate, independent data value. As such, these values were stored in separate words, which were reserved for just that purpose. However, individual members of a data set can possess interrelationships, and these relationships can be quite important in determining how data should be stored in memory. Furthermore, the method of data storage can greatly affect the complexity of the procedure that is required to transform input data into output.

The *data structure* of a data set is the interrelationships that exist between individual members of that set. These relationships can exist naturally, or they can be established arbitrarily to suit your convenience. Notice that relationships between data values, not the values themselves, determine the structure of a set. Thus, it is possible for dissimilar data sets composed of different values to have identical structures. A *data chart* is a graphical or pictorial device that exhibits the structure of a data set. Now, let us consider different data sets and illustrate their structure via data charts.

A data set composed of a single value has the simplest possible data structure. Because it contains one value, it cannot possess any data interrelationships.

21

(a)

Figure 4.4 *A single-cell data structure: (a) data set; (b) its data chart.*

(b)

Such a set is said to have a *single-cell* data structure. Figure 4.4a shows an example of a data set possessing a single-cell structure, and Figure 4.4b illustrates its data chart. This chart is composed of a single box, referred to as a *cell*, which indicates that its set contains just one value. Note that any data set containing one value has this same data chart. The single cell was the only type of structure used during the discussion of the model. Although the single cell is the simplest of all structures, it is the most often used. The single-cell structure is discussed in more detail in Chapter 6.

As a second example of data structure, consider a data set that results from a series of rolls of a single die. Figure 4.5a shows an example of such a set. Here, each value ranges from 1 to 6 and is related to other values by its position in the roll sequence. Figure 4.5b shows that the data chart of such a structure consists of a set of cells laid out in sequence in a *line* or *single dimension*. Each cell represents one data value, and their arrangement indicates their sequential relationship. This structure resembles what might naturally be termed a list.

5
4
6
1
2
3
4
6

(a)

Figure 4.5 *A linear list data structure: (a) data set; (b) its data chart.*

Unfortunately, that name is used for a more complicated data structure; therefore, this structure is referred to as a *single-dimension* data structure or *linear list*. In mathematics, vectors are an example of a linear list. Chapter 7 discusses linear lists in more detail.

As a third example of data structure, consider a data set that describes the position of players on a checkerboard, as shown in Figure 4.6a. Here, each data value represents one square and indicates whether that square is occupied, and, if so, by which team. The board forms a set of x, y coordinates; consequently, each data value is related to other values by two relationships: row and column. Figure 4.6b shows that the data chart of this structure consists of cells laid out in rows and columns. Each cell represents one data value, and

(b)

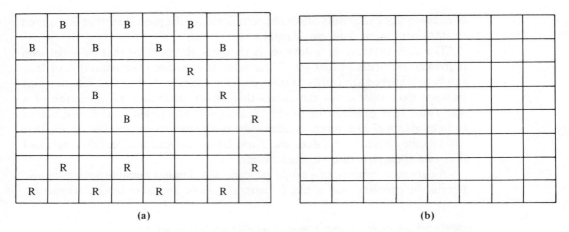

Figure 4.6 *A two-dimension data structure: (a) data set; (b) its data chart.*

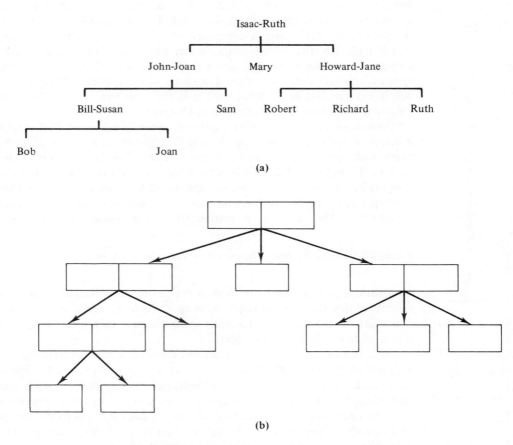

(a)

(b)

Figure 4.7 *A tree structure: (a) data set; (b) its data chart.*

the arrangement of cells indicates their relationship. This structure is referred to as a *two-dimension* data structure or *array*. In mathematics, matrices and determinants are examples of data sets having a two-dimension data structure. In contrast, a data set that describes three-dimensional tic-tac-toe has a three-dimension structure. Multidimensional data structures are discussed in detail in Chapter 8.

As a final example of data structure, consider a data set that describes a genealogical diagram. Figure 4.7a shows an example of such a set, where each data value represents one family member. Figure 4.7b shows the data chart of such a structure. Here, separate cells represent each member, and directed arrows specify family relationship. For example, vertical arrangement shows a father-son relationship, whereas horizontal placement indicates husband-wife, brother-sister, and cousin relationship. Certainly, these relationships differ from those of single cells, linear lists, and arrays. This latest structure is referred to as a *tree*. Actually, its chart looks more like an inverted tree, because its roots point upward and its branches grow downward. Notice that a tree structure includes not only cells but also arrows that *link* data values. Structures that incorporate *links* are discussed in Chapter 11.

4.2.4 Algorithms and flow charts

Once a data chart is drawn showing the structure of all data sets, we must devise a procedure that transforms input data into output. In the discussion of the model, the number of operations in any one example was purposefully kept to a minimum so that instruction sequences were relatively simple. However, it is possible to develop intricate processes that perform extremely complicated calculations. As your problems become more involved, it will be necessary for you to generate longer and more sophisticated procedures. Therefore, it is worthwhile to study techniques that can help you specify these procedures.

An *algorithm* is a set of step-by-step instructions for carrying out some process. A recipe from a cookbook is a straightforward, everyday example of an algorithm. The recipe breaks down the preparation of what might be a complicated dish into a series of simple steps so that even an inexperienced cook can follow them. In general, the most popular cookbooks contain the most detailed cooking algorithms.

Good algorithms have at least three characteristics in common. First, each step of an algorithm must be so precisely stated that there can be no possible ambiguity or uncertainty about the operations to be performed. Second, the set of steps must specify the performance of a limited or finite number of operations; in other words, it must be possible to finish the execution of an algorithm. Finally, an algorithm must be complete and allow for all possible conditions and situations.

As a second example of an algorithm, let us consider the everyday process of using a telephone. Figure 4.8a shows one possible telephone dialing algorithm that consists of four operations. After reading the algorithm, anyone who has

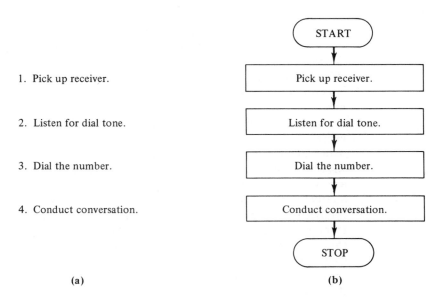

1. Pick up receiver.

2. Listen for dial tone.

3. Dial the number.

4. Conduct conversation.

(a)

(b)

Figure 4.8 *Placing a telephone call: (a) algorithm; (b) flow chart.*

ever used a telephone will realize that the algorithm is not precise. In fact, it would be of little use to someone who has never made a telephone call. The statement of the algorithm fails to mention such important details as waiting for a dial tone or dialing the digits one at a time. In addition, the algorithm does not handle all possible situations. For example, what should be done if there is no dial tone or if the telephone does not ring?

A *flow chart* is a graphical display or diagram of an algorithm. Figure 4.8b shows a flow chart of the telephone dialing algorithm. By convention, each flow-chart statement is enclosed in a specially shaped box that indicates the general nature or function of the statement it encloses. For example, a flow chart always indicates the beginning of its algorithm by the word *START* enclosed in a rectangular box with rounded ends, referred to as a *terminal box*. An algorithm can have only one beginning, and thus a flow chart can have only one START. Each algorithmic step that performs an operation is written inside a separate, rectangular box, referred to as a *process box*. Directed arrows, known as *flow lines*, are used to indicate the order of performance of individual operations. Each process box can have only one outgoing arrow and must have at least one incoming arrow. An algorithm is performed by beginning with START and executing each statement one at a time in sequence as indicated by the flow lines. Execution is terminated when a *STOP* statement, enclosed in a terminal box, is reached.

Earlier, it was noted that the telephone dialing algorithm shown in Figure 4.8 suffers from a lack of detail and omits possible situations. For example, no instructions were given for waiting for a dial tone or an answer; in addition, no thought was given to the possibility of an unknown number or an inoperative

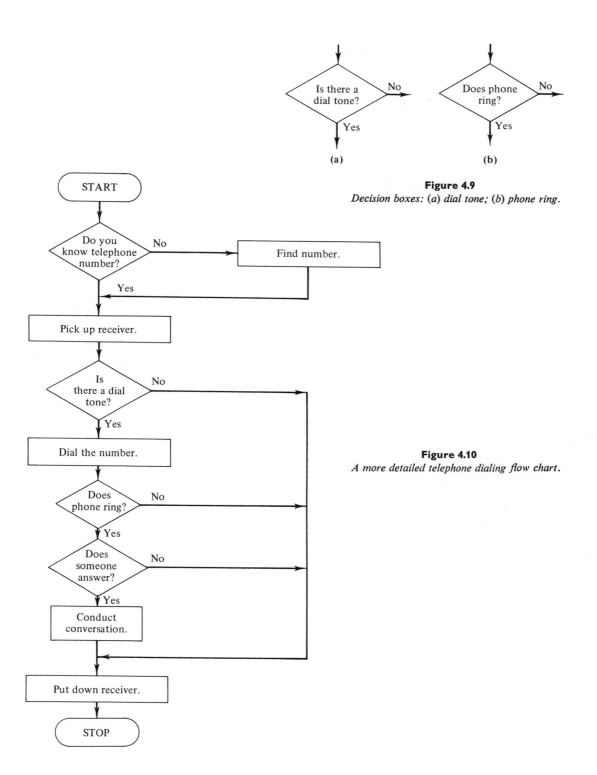

Figure 4.9
Decision boxes: (a) dial tone; (b) phone ring.

Figure 4.10
A more detailed telephone dialing flow chart.

telephone. These situations can be handled by asking and answering questions, which is done in a flow chart by enclosing a question inside a diamond-shaped box, as shown in Figure 4.9. Such a box is referred to as a *decision box*. Each outward arrow is labeled with a possible answer to the enclosed question. If the answer to the question matches the label on an arrow, that arrow indicates the path to the next flow-chart statement. For example, in Figure 4.9a if there is no dial tone, the path to the right is followed. Otherwise, if a dial tone is heard, the downward path is taken. Thus, a decision box provides a means for changing the sequence of steps once the execution of an algorithm is under way. Notice that a decision box must have outward arrows for all possible answers to its question. Otherwise, the algorithm displayed by the flow chart is incomplete, because it does not handle all possible situations. Figure 4.10 shows a revised flow chart for a telephone dialing algorithm that includes more detail and handles these additional situations.

It is possible to make the flow chart in Figure 4.10 even more detailed. For example, the process of dialing a number requires one operation per digit. Therefore, the flow chart statement "Dial the number" can be subdivided and rewritten as shown in Figure 4.11a. However, such a flow chart represents an algorithm that assumes that there will always be seven digits. The flow chart in Figure 4.11b does not make this restrictive assumption. As soon as one digit is dialed, the outward arrow leads back to repeat the same statement.

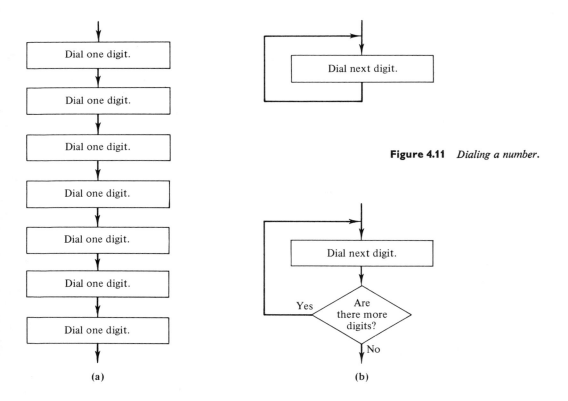

Figure 4.11 *Dialing a number.*

(a)   (b)

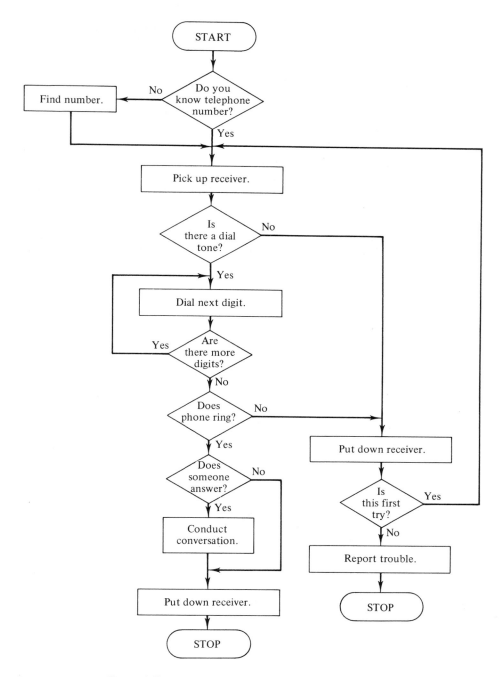

Figure 4.12 *An even more detailed telephone dialing flow chart.*

The repetition of a set of statements is known as a *loop*. However, in this case the loop is endless, because there is no way to terminate its execution. This is remedied in Figure 4.11c by adding a decision box to ask whether all digits have been dialed. If at least one digit remains, the flow chart loops back to dial the next digit. When all digits have been dialed, the flow chart breaks out of the loop and goes on to the next statement. Figure 4.12 shows an even more detailed flow chart. This process of adding statements to the flow chart could be continued until even the most inexperienced person could use it to dial a telephone.

It is not necessary to follow each and every path through a flow chart during the execution of an algorithm. For example, Figure 4.13 shows the portion of the flow chart in Figure 4.12 that is executed if you know the number you wish to dial but your telephone is out of order with no dial tone. A flow chart shows all possible conditions and operations to be performed under those conditions. Thus, a flow chart is a *static* representation of a *dynamic* process. Finally, you should notice that each statement of a flow chart is related to every other flow-chart statement. Thus, flow charts have structure just as data have structure. In Chapter 5, a flow-chart language is introduced and flow charts in that language are used to study program structures.

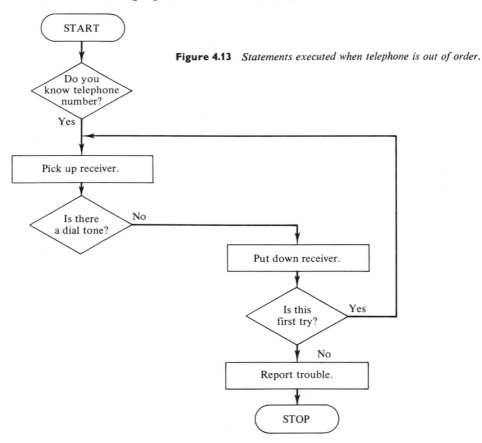

Figure 4.13 *Statements executed when telephone is out of order.*

4.3
Summary

Learning to solve problems is an acquired skill. Like any such skill, it can be developed only through practice. In the beginning, you learn to solve problems by imitating more experienced problem solvers. Later, you improve your problem-solving ability by solving additional problems. Successful problem solvers all have one thing in common—they all have some step-by-step plan of attack for solving problems. This chapter described a problem-solving procedure designed to help you solve your own problems using a computer as a problem-solving tool. As a beginning problem solver, adopt it and follow it as your own. As you become more experienced, you can adapt it to fit your own needs and situation. Whenever you find yourself having trouble with a problem, you should stop and make sure that you are following your plan of attack.

The problem-solving procedure described in this chapter is purposefully designed to help you solve your own problems while overcoming the intrinsic hazards of using a computer. The procedure begins by telling you to define your problem and break it into subproblems, so that you understand its requirements, conditions, and restrictions. The second step directs you to define your desired output. The output list was introduced as a graphical device that can be used to specify the quantity and sequence of output data. The third step asks you to specify the required input. The input list was suggested as a graphical device for specifying input data. The fourth step tells you to determine what data are to be retained in memory. The data structure of a data set was defined as the relationships existing between individual members of that set. The data chart was introduced as a graphical device for displaying the data structure of a data set. In the fifth step, you devise a procedure that converts the required input into your desired output. An algorithm was defined as a set of step-by-step instructions for performing a process. A flow chart was introduced as a graphical technique for specifying an algorithm. The sixth step tells you to write and test a computer program. Here, you use your output and input lists and data and flow charts to produce an actual computer program, using some programming language. The particular language you use depends on your personal preference, or your instructor's, and on the languages available at your computer center.

SELECTED REFERENCES

1. BERZTISS, ALFS T., *Data Structures: Theory and Practice*, Academic Press, Inc., New York, 1971.

2. GRUENBERGER, FRED, *Computing: An Introduction*, Harcourt, Brace & World, Inc., New York, 1969.

3. KNUTH, DONALD E., *The Art of Computer Programming*, Vol. 1, "Fundamental Algorithms," Addison-Wesley Publishing Co., Inc., Reading, Mass., 1968.

4. POLYA, GEORGE, *How To Solve It*, Doubleday & Co., Inc., Garden City, N. Y., 1957.

PROBLEMS

4.1 Describe the data structure of the following data sets:

(a) Numbers on an adding machine tape;
(b) The steps in constructing a building;
(c) The stops on a bus route;
(d) The playing squares on a monopoly board;
(e) Results of a horse race;
(f) An organization chart;
(g) Seats in an auditorium;
(h) The results of a coin flipping experiment;
(i) A sequence of rolls of a pair of dice;
(j) A table showing average height as a function of height and age;
(k) A table showing average weight as a function of height, age, and sex;
(l) Numbers on a roulette wheel.

4.2 Give examples of data sets having the following structures:

(a) Single cell;
(b) Linear list;
(c) Two dimension;
(d) Three dimension;
(e) Tree.

4.3 The flow chart on the facing page describes an algorithm for changing a flat tire. Unfortunately, it contains errors. Redraw the flow chart using the *same* steps in such a way that it specifies a valid algorithm.

4.4 Draw a flow chart for each of the following everyday operations:

(a) Waking up and getting ready for your class;
(b) Getting a haircut or having hair set;
(c) Cooking an egg.

4.5 Draw a flow chart that describes the algorithm that you followed while revising the flow chart in Problem 4.3.

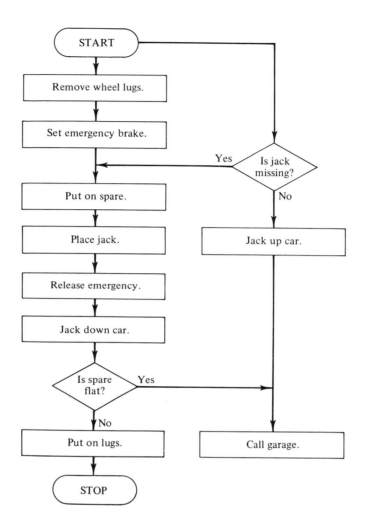

5 A Flow-Chart Language

Languages are systematic means of communicating ideas or feelings. They convey their messages through the use of conventionalized signs, gestures, marks, or vocal sounds. As long as their conventions are followed, communications are precise and messages are understood. Since flow charts are a language for expressing algorithms, it is necessary to have flow-chart conventions. In the previous chapter, flow charts were written in English with little or no concern for form or format. Such charts, while sufficient for describing mechanical procedures, are often wordy and are not precise enough for specifying computer algorithms.

The purpose of this chapter is to introduce a flow-chart language that can be used to specify such algorithms. This language is a tool that can help you develop algorithms; it does not produce them—you must do that yourself. It does, however, allow you to concentrate upon your algorithm without concerning yourself with the details of a particular programming language. Once produced, you can use your flow chart to verify that your algorithm is valid and handles all possible situations and conditions. Furthermore, your flow chart can be used to show others how your algorithm works.

During the discussion of the model, it was assumed that words could store decimal numbers regardless of magnitude. Actual memory is constructed of magnetic cores or electronic circuits that can each store one bit. A *memory word* consists of a sequence of cores or circuits that can store a numerical value coded as a binary number, and the number of bits in a memory word is known as its *word length*. Some computers have small word lengths and must use more than one word to store a large number. Such computers are referred to as *character* machines, because they store one digit or character per word. In contrast, machines with longer word lengths can store larger numbers in a single word and are known as *word* machines. In any case, the word length of a computer must be finite; thus, there is always some maximum value that can be stored in a single word. Let us now consider three forms of data representation that have been devised to overcome this limitation.

5.1.1 Forms of data

The *integer* form of data representation is used to store integers or whole numbers. Such numbers are represented inside a machine as a sequence of binary bits. For example, assume for simplicity that a computer has a word length of four, as shown in Figure 5.1a. The first bit of each word might

Figure 5.1 *Data representation:*
(a) integer; (b) floating point; (c) alphanumeric.

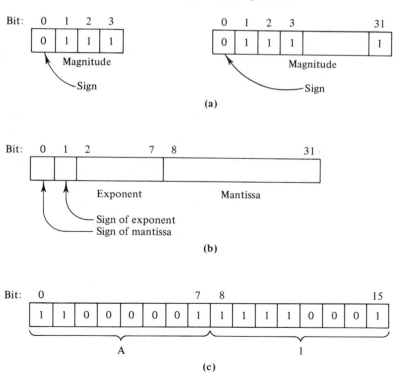

indicate the sign of the number, 0 for plus and 1 for minus, whereas the last three might store its magnitude. Such a machine has a maximum storage magnitude of 111 in binary, which is 7 in decimal. On the other hand, a computer with a word length of 32 can store a binary number whose magnitude consists of a sequence of 31 one's or 2,147,483,647 in decimal. Thus, the maximum value that can be stored as an integer depends upon the particular computer and its word length.

When arithmetic calculations are performed upon integer data, care must be taken to ensure that numerical values stay within the storage capacity of a single word. Again, for the sake of simplicity, consider a machine whose word length is four. Suppose that a memory word contains the largest value that can be stored as an integer, in this case 0111 in binary. If the contents of that word are incremented by 1, the result must be 8, or 1000 in binary. Since this new value requires four bits, it cannot be stored in a single four-bit word without destroying the sign. Such a situation is referred to as *integer overflow*, because the magnitude of a number has exceeded the integer storage capacity of a single word.

The *floating point* form of data representation is used to store decimal numbers and to extend the range of values that a computer can process. To understand floating point notation, recall that a number, such as

$$-429.571$$

can also be written with an exponential power of 10 as

$$-4.29571 \times 10^2 \quad \text{or} \quad -429571.0 \times 10^{-3}$$

Numbers that contain a decimal point or an exponential power of 10 are said to be in floating point notation. When the decimal point is at the left and precedes a nonzero digit, such as

$$-.429571 \times 10^3$$

the floating point number is said to be *normalized*. Floating point numbers are usually stored in a single word in normalized form, as shown in Figure 5.1b. Here, some bits are used for the exponent and the remainder for the fraction or mantissa, with both represented as binary integers. Sometimes floating point representation is also referred to as *scientific notation*, because it can represent easily very large and very small numbers, often required in science.

Even though floating point representation with its exponent permits the processing of larger numerical values, a finite word length still causes problems, just as it does with integer notation. For example, during a sequence of calculations, the magnitude of a floating point exponent can exceed the storage capacity of the exponential portion of a single word. When this happens, the number cannot be stored in memory. If the exponent sign is positive, a *floating point overflow* is said to occur; if the sign is negative, it is a *floating point underflow*. Also, during a sequence of calculations, the fractional portion can lose accuracy. For ease of discussion, assume that a computer can store only three fractional digits and that it performs the following multiplication:

$$.799 \times 10^2$$
$$.682 \times 10^3$$

$$1598$$
$$6392$$
$$4794$$

$$.544918 \times 10^5$$

When the machine attempts to save the product, it can store only three digits. Either it can *truncate* the results to $.544 \times 10^5$ by dropping off the last three digits, or it can *round off* the result to $.545 \times 10^5$. In either case, the stored result does not equal the true product. The loss of accuracy in the first case is called *truncation error*, whereas the second is referred to as *round-off error*.

The *alphanumeric* form of data representation is used to store characters, including alphabetic characters, numeric digits, and special symbols, such as +, \$, *, and space. Each character is represented in memory by its own unique combination of binary bits. Figure 5.2 shows the representation of selected characters in commonly used coding schemes. For example, the letter A is represented in 7-bit BCD (Binary Coded Decimal) by the binary sequence 0110001. This same character is 000001 in 6-bit ASCII (U.S.A. Standard Code for Information Interchange), 11000001 in 8-bit ASCII, and 11000001 in 8-bit EBCDIC (Extended Binary Coded Decimal Interchange Code).

Character	7-Bit BCD	6-Bit ASCII	8-Bit ASCII	EBCDIC
Space	1000000	100000	10100000	01000000
+	1110000	101011	10101011	01001110
\$	1101011	100100	10100100	01011011
*	0101100	101010	10101010	01011100
.	.	.	.	.
.	.	.	.	.
.	.	.	.	.
A	0110001	000001	11000001	11000001
B	0110010	000010	11000011	11000010
.	.	.	.	.
.	.	.	.	.
.	.	.	.	.
Z	0011001	011010	11011010	11101001
.	.	.	.	.
.	.	.	.	.
.	.	.	.	.
1	0000001	110001	10110001	11110001
2	0000010	110010	10110010	11110010
3	1000011	110011	10110011	11110011
.	.	.	.	.
.	.	.	.	.
.	.	.	.	.
9	1001001	111001	10111001	11111001

Figure 5.2 *Representation of selected characters in different codes.*

The number of characters that can be stored in a single computer word depends upon the number of bits used to code each character and the word length of a particular machine. For example, Figure 5.1c shows how the characters A1 are stored in a single 16-bit word using EBCDIC. Notice that the alphanumeric representation of a decimal digit is quite different from its integer representation. For example, the integer form of the number 3 is 11 in binary; on the other hand, Figure 5.2 shows its alphanumeric representation in EBCDIC as 11110011. Certainly, the two are not equivalent. In fact, the EBCDIC number 3 equals 243 in decimal, if interpreted by mistake as an integer.

5.1.2 Variables and constants

As we work examples, we shall need to refer in our flow charts to various data values. This is done by giving each data structure a unique name. Because the contents of the cells of a structure can change during the execution of an algorithm, data structures are also referred to as *variables*, and their names are known as *variable names*. A variable name consists of a string of alphabetic and numeric characters where the first character is always alphabetic. The characters of a variable name are limited to the 26 uppercase Roman letters A through Z and the 10 digits 0 through 9. Lowercase Roman and special symbols, such as $+$, $-$, $=$, and space. are not permitted. Thus, a variable name can be a single letter, such as A, B, C, or X; a combination of letters, such as SPEED, TAX, or RATE; or a combination of letters and numbers, such as R1, X12, or A1B2. Variable names are purely *arbitrary* and can be chosen to indicate the purpose of their data structures. For example, if a structure contains distance data, it can be given the variable name DISTANCE, or DIST for short. If there are two such structures, the names DIST1 and DIST2 might be used. On the other hand, the names ZEBRA and HIPPO would be just as permissible.

A variable name is used to reference or access the contents of its data structure. If we wish to know the value that is currently contained in a single cell with the variable name of RATE, we need only mention that name. When a program is converted into machine language, the compiler keeps track of where it has stored each different variable. Thus, it is *no longer necessary* to specify numeric memory locations as was done previously with the model. In future examples, a data chart is used to display all data structures and to indicate their variable names. Sometimes it is necessary to indicate the current contents of a variable. This is done by placing that value inside the particular cell. Figure 5.3 shows a data chart that includes three single cells containing sample data values.

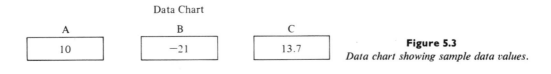

Data Chart

A	B	C
10	−21	13.7

Figure 5.3
Data chart showing sample data values.

Sometimes, we need to refer in our flow charts to a data value that is already known and does not change during the execution of an algorithm. Such a value is known as a *constant*. Since there are three forms of data representation, there are three forms of constants. Examples of all three are shown in Figure 5.4. *Integer constants* are written as whole numbers without a decimal point

Integer: 9, $+3$, -17, 1973, 0, -127, -1

Floating point: 9.0, 75.6, $-19.3E4$, $1.75E-3$, $-.03$, $-.0725E+7$

Alphanumeric: 'ALPHA', '123', 'N1', 'X=', 'BAD DATA', 'CAN''T', '⊔ ⊔'

Figure 5.4 *Constants*

using the 10 decimal digits, 0 through 9. *Floating point constants* contain either a decimal point or an exponential power of 10 or both. However, an off-the-line exponent or power of 10 is not permitted. Here, the letter E replaces the "$\times 10$" and is read as "times 10-to-the." Both integer and floating point constants may or may not include plus or minus signs.

Alphanumeric constants consist of strings of arbitrary characters enclosed by single quotation marks. These single quote marks are necessary to distinguish alphanumeric constants from variable names. For example, DISTANCE is a variable name whereas 'DISTANCE' is an alphanumeric constant. If a quote mark is required within an alphanumeric constant, it is represented by two successive single quotes. For example, the contraction, don't, is written as 'DON''T'. Sometimes, an alphanumeric constant includes a space. Here, the symbol ⊔ is used to represent a space when there might be confusion. For example, an alphanumeric constant that consists of a single blank, ' ', is written as '⊔' for clarity. Finally, alphanumeric constants are sometimes referred to as *literals*.

Previously, it was shown that data storage is machine dependent. The word length of a particular machine determines the maximum allowable magnitude of integer and floating point values and the number of alphanumeric characters that can be stored in a single computer word. However, most programming languages permit a user to combine memory locations under one variable name when data values exceed the storage capacity of single words. For this reason, we shall assume here that there is no limit to the numerical magnitude or the number of alphanumeric characters that can be stored in any one cell of a data structure. Thus, there is no one-to-one correspondence between data structure cells and actual memory words. Several memory words may be required to store the contents of one cell of a data structure. On the other hand, the contents of several data structure cells might be stored in one physical memory location. The actual situation depends upon the particular computer, the programming language, and the nature of the data values. Therefore, further discussion of data storage is left to your instructor, who can give you the details that are appropriate to your own particular programming language and computer.

5.2
Flow-Chart
Operations

Now that we are able to name data structures, we are ready to perform calculations upon the contents of their cells. During the discussion of the model, calculations were specified by a sequence of instructions where each instruction denoted a single operation, such as addition or subtraction. The flow-chart language permits you to combine a series of operations by using algebralike statements. Let us now study a set of operations that serve as basic building blocks for flow-chart statements that are discussed next.

5.2.1 Arithmetic operators

Figure 5.5 lists seven arithmetic operations along with their algebraic and flow-chart symbols. Since these symbols indicate that an arithmetic operation

Operation		Algebraic Symbol	Flow-Chart Symbol
Plus	Unary	$+$	$+$
Negation		$-$	$-$
Addition	Binary	$+$	$+$
Subtraction		$-$	$-$
Multiplication		$\cdot$ or $\times$	$\times$
Division		$\div$ or $/$	$/$
Exponentiation		$-^2$ (e.g., A^2)	$\uparrow$ (e.g., $A \uparrow 2$)

Figure 5.5 *Arithmetic operators.*

is to be performed, they are known as *arithmetic operators*. These operators are used in flow charts just as their counterparts in algebra. For example, suppose that you wish to have calculations performed upon the contents of two cells, A and B. Figure 5.6 displays a data chart indicating that these cells contain sample values of 2 and 4. The figure illustrates how each operator is combined with these variable names to specify a calculation, and then it indicates the result of that operation.

Data Chart

A	B
2	4

Operation		Flow-Chart Representation	Result
Plus	Unary	$+A$	2
Negation		$-A$	-2
Addition	Binary	$A+B$	6
Subtraction		$A-B$	-2
Multiplication		$A \times B$	8
Division		A/B	.5
Exponentiation		$A \uparrow B$	16

Figure 5.6 *Arithmetic operations.*

Before proceeding, perhaps multiple occurrences of plus and minus signs in Figures 5.5 and 5.6 should be explained. When used to specify addition and subtraction, they are said to be *binary* operators because they manipulate two quantities or operands. In the examples, $A + B$ or $A - B$, A and B are the two operands. On the other hand, when used to specify plus or negation, these signs are said to be *unary* operators because they manipulate a single operand. In the example, $+A$ or $-A$, A is the single operand.

Even though the use of arithmetic operators is straightforward, there are two points that should be noted. First, there is no *implied* multiplication as there is in algebra. For example, suppose that AB is written rather than $A \times B$. Since AB is a valid variable name, a reference to the single cell AB is assumed, not A times B. Likewise, A times the sum of B and C must be written as $A \times (B + C)$, not $A(B + C)$. Consequently, a multiplication operator must always be used whenever multiplication is intended. Second, as was said earlier, off-the-line notation, such as A^B, is unacceptable. Therefore, an exponentiation operator, $\uparrow$, is introduced, so that exponentiation can be written on a single line. Thus, A^B is written as $A \uparrow B$.

5.2.2 Arithmetic expressions

An *arithmetic expression* is a sequence of variables and constants connected by arithmetic operators. Because algorithms must be precise and unambiguous, it is necessary to have rules for constructing and evaluating expressions. This requirement is best illustrated by an example. Suppose that one wants to evaluate the expression $A + B \times C$. Figure 5.7 shows that if the addition is performed first, this expression has a value of 20; otherwise, its value is 14.

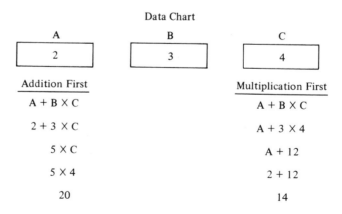

Figure 5.7 *An ambiguous expression.*

Such ambiguity cannot be tolerated in an algorithm or flow chart. Since arithmetic expressions play a key role in flow charts, let us consider them in more detail.

Previously, an arithmetic expression was said to be a sequence of constants and variables connected by operators. This definition is made more precise by the rules listed in Figure 5.8. These rules are *recursive* in that they can be

The following are arithmetic expressions:

1. A constant

2. A variable

3. An arithmetic expression preceeded by a unary operator or two arithmetic expressions connected by a binary operator

4. An arithmetic expression contained within parentheses

Figure 5.8 *Recursive rules for constructing arithmetic expressions.*

applied repetitively to existing expressions to form new ones. Their recursive nature is best illustrated by example. Figure 5.9 shows how these rules are used to form the expression $(X + 4)\uparrow-2$. Since 4 is a constant, it alone forms an expression according to rule 1. Likewise, since X is a variable, it is an expression via rule 2. Since rule 3 says that two expressions connected by a binary operator are also an expression, $X + 4$ is an expression. Enclosing $X + 4$ within parentheses forms yet another expression according to rule 4.

Expression	Rule Used
4	1
X	2
X + 4	3
(X + 4)	4
2	1
−2	3
$(X+4)\uparrow-2$	3

Figure 5.9 *Forming the arithmetic expression $(X+4)\uparrow-2$.*

Since 2 is a constant and therefore an expression, -2 is an expression under rule 3. Finally, $(X + 4)\uparrow-2$ is an expression via rule 3. In this way, complicated expressions can be constructed by using simpler ones as building blocks.

Earlier in this section, an example of an ambiguous expression was discussed. This ambiguity is removed when there is an assumed order of performance for arithmetic operators. The table in Figure 5.10 shows the precedence of arithmetic operators in parenthesisfree expressions. Such expressions are evaluated by scanning them from left to right, looking for first-level operators, unary plus and minus. When one is found, it is performed and the left-to-right scan is resumed. When all first-level operations have been evaluated, the left-to-right scan is repeated for the second-level operator, exponentiation. Like-

Level	Operation		Operator
1.	Plus	} Unary	+
	Negation		−
2.	Exponentiation		↑
3.	Multiplication		×
	Division		/
4.	Addition	} Binary	-|-
	Subtraction		−

Figure 5.10 *Precedence levels for evaluating parenthesisfree expressions.**

Note: Where operations have the same precedence level (like binary addition and subtraction), they are performed from left to right.

wise, when the second level scan is completed, the expression is scanned for third-level operators, multiplication and division, and then, in turn, for fourth-level operators, addition and subtraction.

Before using the precedence rules, perhaps we should discuss plus and minus signs in more detail. Since the minus is potentially the most perplexing, let us consider it first. Actually, there are three ways that a minus can appear in an expression. First, it can be a binary operator and indicate subtraction, as in X − 4. Second, a minus can be unary and specify negation, as in −X. Finally, a minus can be part of a negative number, as in −4. Here, the minus is actually part of a constant and is not really an operator. The use of the same symbol in three different roles should not cause confusion because its meaning can be determined from its position in an expression. For example, the expression

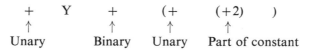

shows a minus in each of its three roles. A minus is binary unless it occurs at the beginning of an expression or immediately after a left parenthesis. If the minus occurs in one of these two positions, then it is part of a constant if the character following the minus is a digit or a decimal point. Otherwise, the minus is unary. The same discussion can be applied to the plus sign in the following expression.

$$+ \quad Y \quad + \quad (+ \quad (+2) \quad)$$
$$\uparrow \qquad \uparrow \qquad \uparrow \qquad \uparrow$$
Unary   Binary   Unary   Part of constant

When these precedence rules are applied to the expression A + B × C, the multiplication is performed first because the plus sign indicates binary addition. Thus, the expression has only one value, and the precedence rules have removed any possible ambiguity. Figure 5.11 demonstrates a step-by-step evaluation of a more complicated parenthesisfree expression. This figure

Data Chart

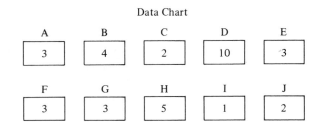

A	B	C	D	E
3	4	2	10	3

F	G	H	I	J
3	3	5	1	2

Step Number	Action	Appearance of Expression After Each Step
	Original expression	−A×B/C−D×E↑F/G+H/I×J
1.	Calculate −A	−3×B/C−D×E↑F/G+H/I×J
2.	Calculate E↑F	−3×B/C−D×27/G+H/I×J
3.	Calculate −3×B	−12/C−D×27/G+H/I×J
4.	Calculate −12/C	−6−D×27/G+H/I×J
5.	Calculate D×27	−6−270/G+H/I×J
6.	Calculate 270/G	−6−90+H/I×J
7.	Calculate H/I	−6−90+5×J
8.	Calculate 5×J	−6−90+10
9.	Calculate −6−90	−96+10
10.	Calculate −96+10	−86

Figure 5.11 *Step-by-step evaluation of a parenthesisfree expression.*

1. Scan the expression from left to right for the first right parenthesis, i.e., '')''.

2. At the first right parenthesis, scan right to left for the first left parenthesis, i.e., ''(''.

3. Evaluate the parenthesisfree expression contained between the parenthesis pair according to the precedence relationships in Figure 5.10 and remove the parenthesis pair.

4. If the expression still contains parentheses, return to step 1.

5. Otherwise, evaluate the remaining parenthesisfree expression.

Figure 5.12 *Rules for evaluating expressions with parentheses.*

indicates an assumed value for each variable, and shows how the expression changes as each operation is performed. Solid triangles (▲) designate the operator that is next, according to the precedence rules. You should stop and study each step to ensure that you understand the evaluation process.

Parentheses can be used to override precedence relationships. In other words, if the assumed rules do not express the correct arithmetic relationship, parentheses can be added, as in algebra. Essentially, the rules as shown in Figure 5.12 specify that when an expression contains parentheses, the expression within those parentheses is evaluated first. As an example, consider the expression $A + B \times C$. As it stands, the multiplication is performed first, followed by addition. However, if the reverse order is desired, the expression must be written with parentheses, as $(A + B) \times C$. Notice that a sequence of equal precedence operators is performed left to right. Thus, $\frac{A}{2} \cdot B$ can be written as $A/2 \times B$, whereas $\frac{A}{2 \cdot B}$ must be written as $A/(2 \times B)$. If you are ever in doubt about the necessity of parentheses, put them in. Extra parentheses are not harmful.

Figure 5.13 shows the evaluation of an expression that contains parentheses. Once again, the figure indicates an assumed value for each variable and then illustrates how the original expression changes as each set of parentheses is identified. Initially, the first right parenthesis is found by a left-to-right scan, and its matching parenthesis is identified by a reverse scan to the left. This

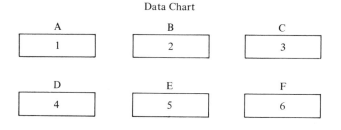

Data Chart

A	B	C
1	2	3

D	E	F
4	5	6

Figure 5.13 *The step-by-step evaluation of an expression with parentheses.*

Step Number	Action	Appearance of Expression After Each Step
	Original expression	A+B×(C×(D+E)+F)
1.	Find first)	A+B×(C×(D+E)+F) 　　　　　　　▲
2.	Find matching (	A+B×(C×(D+E)+F) 　　　　　▲
3.	Evaluate D+E	A+B×(C×9+F)
4.	Find first)	A+B×(C×9+F) 　　　　　　▲
5.	Find matching (	A+B×(C×9+F) 　　　　▲
6.	Evaluate C×9+F	A+B×33
7.	Evaluate A+B×33	67

process separates out D + E, which can be evaluated as a parenthesisfree expression. Since the remaining expression still contains parentheses, the preceding process must be repeated. The second scan identifies the expression C × 9 + F. Finally, A + B × 33 can be evaluated as a parenthesisfree expression.

Expressions containing parentheses are evaluated from inside out. This means that the first left-to-right scan identifies a parenthesisfree expression contained within parentheses which might well be contained within other parentheses. Furthermore, expressions must contain an equal number of right and left parentheses. Figure 5.14 specifies an algorithm that checks an expression for matching parentheses and illustrates its use. This algorithm is limited in that it can only verify a match or mismatch and cannot determine whether parentheses are correctly located.

1. Start with a parenthesis counter whose value is zero.

2. Scan the expression from left to right.

3. When a left parenthesis is found, add 1 to the counter.

4. When a right parenthesis is found, subtract 1 from the counter.

5. If the count is zero at the end of the scan and was never negative, the expression has matching parentheses.

6. Otherwise, the expression has a parentheses mismatch.

Parentheses match	A + B × (C × (D + E) + F)
	1 2 1 0
Parentheses mismatch	A + B × (C × D + E) + F)
	1 0 −1
Parentheses mismatch	A + B × (C × (D + E + F)
	1 2 1
Parentheses mismatch	A + B ×)C × (D + E) + F(
	−1 0 −1 0

Figure 5.14 *A parentheses-checking algorithm.*

So far, only variables and constants in integer form have been used to evaluate expressions. Some programming languages, such as early versions of FORTRAN, did not permit intermixing of data forms in the same expression. Names of integer variables had to start with letters I, J, K, L, M, or N; and if an expression referenced one integer value, all variables and constants in that expression had to be integer. Since then, many programming languages, including later versions of FORTRAN, have allowed intermixing of integer and floating point data. For this reason, we shall no longer distinguish between integer and floating point, but instead shall refer to them as *decimal*. Your instructor will give you further details if such is not the case for your programming language.

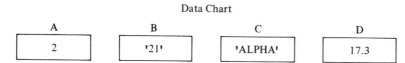

Data Chart

A	B	C	D
2	'21'	'ALPHA'	17.3

Proper Expressions	Improper Expressions
2 × A	A + B
B	'41' + B
C	C + D
'BETA'	B / C
A/2 × D	2 × 'ALPHA'

Figure 5.15
Expressions using alphanumeric values.

Sometimes, expressions are used to process alphanumeric data. Since it rarely makes sense to perform arithmetic operations upon such data, mixing of decimal and alphanumeric data is best avoided. Consequently, expressions that reference alphanumeric data are generally restricted in form to

alphanumeric constant

or

variable

Figure 5.15 illustrates both proper and improper expressions. For example, the expression A + B should not be used because A contains a decimal value whereas B is alphanumeric. You must know which data structures contain decimal data and which contain alphanumeric data, and that it is your responsibility to keep them separate.

5.2.3 Logical operators

In the previous section, arithmetic operators were used to specify arithmetic calculations. Let us now consider a set of operators than can be used to compare the results of such calculations. As a group, these operators are commonly known as *logical operators*. Sometimes, they are separated into two functional groups and referred to as *relational operators* and *Boolean operators*.

Relational operators are used to compare the values of two arithmetic expressions. Figure 5.16 lists six relational operations and indicates their flow-chart symbols. Note that the last three are actually combinations of the first three. For example, greater than or equal ($\geq$) includes both greater than ($>$) and equal ($=$). Relational operators are binary and thus require two operands, both of which must be arithmetic expressions. The result of a relational operation is either *true* or *false*. If the two arithmetic expressions have the same relation as specified by the relational operator, the operation is said

Data Chart

A
4

B
2

Operation	Flow-Chart Symbol	Flow-Chart Representation	Result
Greater than	>	A > B	True
Less than	<	A < B	False
Equal	=	A = B	False
Greater than or equal	≥	A ≥ B	True
Less than or equal	≤	A ≤ B	False
Not equal	≠	A ≠ B	True

Figure 5.16 *Relational operators.*

to be true; if not, it is false. Figure 5.16 illustrates how each operator is used to compare arithmetic expressions, displaying sample results. For example, since the value of A is greater than that of B, the result of A > B is true.

Boolean operators are used in conjunction with relational operators to compare more than two arithmetic expressions. Figure 5.17 lists two Boolean

			Truth Table		
Operation	*Flow-Chart Symbol*	*Flow-Chart Representation*	*Value of Operand 1*	*Value of Operand 2*	*Result*
Or	∨	Operand 1 ∨ operand 2	False	False	False
			False	True	True
			True	False	True
			True	True	True
And	∧	Operand 1 ∧ operand 2	False	False	False
			False	True	False
			True	False	False
			True	True	True

Figure 5.17 *Boolean operators.*

operators, *or* and *and*, and shows their flow-chart symbol. These operators are binary and require two operands, the values of which are either true or false. The *or* operation is said to be true if either or both of its operands are true; otherwise, it is false. The *and* operation is true if both operands are true; otherwise, it is false. Figure 5.17 also displays the flow-chart representation and a *truth table*, specifying the result of each operation as a function of the values of its two operands. There are other Boolean operators, such as *not* ($\neg$), *inclusion* ($\supset$), *identity* ($\equiv$), and *exclusive-or* ($\oplus$), but since they are not necessary for the specification of algorithms discussed in this book, they are purposefully omitted. If your particular programming language includes these additional Boolean operators, your language manual should explain their use.

5.2.4 Logical expressions

A sequence of arithmetic expressions connected by logical operators is known as a *logical expression*. Figure 5.18 lists a set of rules that can be used to construct such sequences. As was the case with arithmetic expressions, the rules

The following are logical expressions:

1. Two arithmetic expressions connected by a relational operator;

2. Two logical expressions connected by a Boolean operator;

3. A logical expression contained within parentheses.

Figure 5.18 *Rules for constructing logical expressions.*

are recursive and can be applied repetitively to existing expressions to form new ones. Figure 5.19 shows how these rules are used to construct a logical

Expression	Rule Used
$X < 5$	1
$X \geq 3$	1
$X < 5 \wedge X \geq 3$	2

Figure 5.19 *Forming the logical expression* $X < 5 \wedge X \geq 3$.

expression that determines whether the current contents of X are less than 5 and also greater than or equal to 3. First, the relational operator ($<$) is used to compare the contents of X with the constant 5. According to rule 1, $X < 5$ is a logical expression and has a value of true or false depending upon the current contents of X. Second, the relational operator ($\geq$) is used to compare X with 3. According to rule 1, $X \geq 3$ is also a logical expression, and likewise its value depends upon X. Finally, since X must satisfy both conditions, an *and* operator is used to combine these two logical expressions to form $X < 5 \wedge X \geq 3$, according to rule 2. Notice that the required conditions would also be satisfied if the logical expression were written as

$$5 > X \wedge X \geq 3$$

or

$$5 > X \wedge 3 \leq X$$

Level	Operation		Operator
1	Plus	} Unary	+
	Negation		−
2	Exponentiation		↑
3	Multiplication		×
	Division		/
4	Addition	} Binary	+
	Subtraction		−
5	Greater than		>
	Less than		<
	Equal		=
	Greater than or equal		≥
	Less than or equal		≤
	Not equal		≠
6	And		∧
7	Or		∨

Figure 5.20 *Precedence levels for evaluating parenthesisfree logical expressions.*

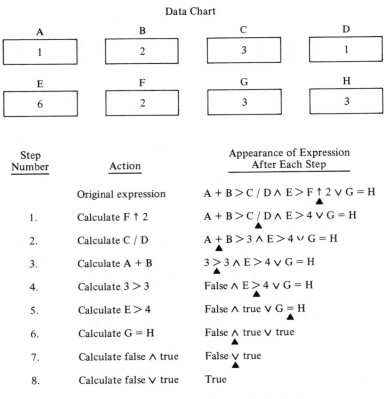

Data Chart

A	B	C	D
1	2	3	1

E	F	G	H
6	2	3	3

Step Number	Action	Appearance of Expression After Each Step
	Original expression	$A + B > C / D \wedge E > F \uparrow 2 \vee G = H$
1.	Calculate $F \uparrow 2$	$A + B > C / D \wedge E > 4 \vee G = H$
2.	Calculate C / D	$A + B > 3 \wedge E > 4 \vee G = H$
3.	Calculate $A + B$	$3 > 3 \wedge E > 4 \vee G = H$
4.	Calculate $3 > 3$	False $\wedge$ $E > 4$ $\vee$ $G = H$
5.	Calculate $E > 4$	False $\wedge$ true $\vee$ $G = H$
6.	Calculate $G = H$	False $\wedge$ true $\vee$ true
7.	Calculate false $\wedge$ true	False $\vee$ true
8.	Calculate false $\vee$ true	True

Figure 5.21 *The step-by-step evaluation of a logical expression.*

Figure 5.20 shows a precedence table that includes both arithmetic and logical operators. Logical expressions are evaluated by a series of left-to-right scans, as was done with arithmetic expressions. Notice that arithmetic operators are performed first followed by relational operators and finally by Boolean operators. Figure 5.21 shows the step-by-step evaluation of a logical expression.

You should appreciate that each programming language has its own set of operators with its own particular precedence relationships. Before you switch from one language to another, you should first ensure that you understand the precedence relationships for the new language. In addition, operator precedence rules of some languages have been changed from time to time.

Actually, the rules for evaluating logical expressions are quite similar to those for arithmetic expressions. If the precedence relationships of Figure 5.20 cannot express the desired logical relationship, parentheses can be inserted to override the standard performance order. As was the case with arithmetic expressions, logical expressions with parentheses are evaluated from the inside out using the same left-to-right parentheses scan as was discussed in Figure 5.12.

<h2>5.3 Flow-Chart Statements</h2>

The flow-chart language consists of six basic statements. Since a flow chart must be precise and unambiguous, each of these statements has its own grammar and construction rules. Fortunately, the rules are straightforward and can be memorized in a matter of minutes. In fact, two of the six statements were discussed in the previous chapter. A single *start* statement indicates the beginning of a flow chart, whereas one or more *stop* statements signals the end.

Each flow-chart statement is enclosed within its own particular outline or symbol so that its purpose or intent can be seen at a glance. For example, a rectangular box with rounded ends always contains a start or stop statement. The number of these special symbols is kept to a minimum, but when used, they conform to American National Standards Institute (ANSI) flow-chart standards.

5.3.1 The read statement

A *read* statement is used to bring data into memory from the input unit. The basic form of a read statement is

READ variable name

The execution of this statement causes a computer to take the next data value from the top of the input list and to store that value in the cell specified by the variable name. The original contents of that cell are lost.

Figure 5.22 demonstrates the effect of the execution of the statement, READ A. Figure 5.22a indicates that a read statement is enclosed by a parallelogram-shaped outline known as an *input-output* symbol. This outline can be used irrespective of input or output media, format, or equipment. The ANSI flow-chart standard permits specification of the data-carrying media via

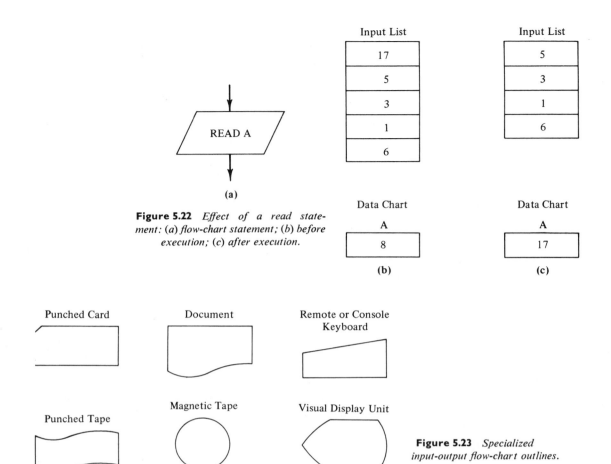

Figure 5.22 *Effect of a read statement: (a) flow-chart statement; (b) before execution; (c) after execution.*

Figure 5.23 *Specialized input-output flow-chart outlines.*

specialized outlines, as shown in Figure 5.23. In general, algorithms discussed in this text are not a function of data media; thus, specialized outlines are avoided. Figure 5.22b displays an input list and single cell A before execution of the READ A statement. Notice that the top value on the input list is 17 and that A contains an arbitrary value of 8. Figure 5.22c shows the same items after execution. Now the top value on the input list is 5 and A contains 17. The original contents of A have been destroyed.

Sometimes it is necessary to read more than one data value. Rather than use a sequence of statements, it is more convenient to use a single read statement of the form

READ variable name, variable name, . . . , variable name

The computer executes this statement by filling the variables from left to right as it reads values from the top of the input list. Notice that individual variable names are separated by commas and that no comma follows the last name.

Figure 5.24 shows the effect of the execution of the statement, READ A, B, C. Here, the first input value is placed in A, the second in B, and the third in C. Note that in this example, the input is comprised of alphanumeric data values. As was said earlier, you must remember which variables are decimal and which are alphanumeric so that you do not mix them by mistake in the same expression.

Whenever a read statement is executed, the input unit should contain enough values to fill all variables listed in that statement. If it does not, the read cannot be completed. When this happens, the input unit is said to have reached an *end of file* (EOF). Most input units transmit a message to their CPU when an EOF is encountered. This message can be detected and used to

Figure 5.24 *Combining read statements: (a) the flow-chart statements; (b) before execution; (c) after execution.*

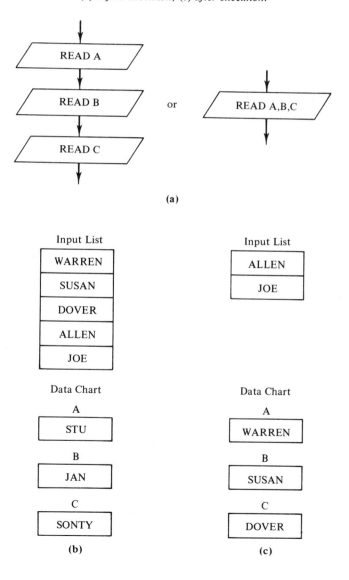

instruct a computer on how it is to proceed. The following read statement incorporates this feature:

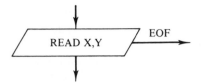

Here, if input is exhausted during a read, the arrow labeled EOF indicates the path to the next statement. Otherwise, the unlabeled arrow is followed.

5.3.2 The write statement

A *write* statement is used to send data from memory to the output list. The basic form of a write statement is

WRITE variable name

The execution of a write statement causes a computer to take the data value contained in the cell referenced by the variable name and to place that value at the bottom of the output list. The original contents of the cell are not disturbed. Figure 5.25 demonstrates the effect of the statement, WRITE A. Figure 5.25a indicates that a write statement is enclosed by an input-output

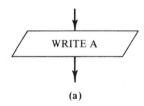

(a)

Output List

7
3
12
4

Output List

7
3
12
4
15

Figure 5.25 *Effect of a write statement: (a) flow-chart statement; (b) before execution; (c) after execution.*

Data Chart

A

15

(b)

Data Chart

A

15

(c)

112

symbol. Figure 5.25b shows an output list and single cell A before execution. Notice that the last number on the output list is 4 and that A contains 15. Figure 5.25c displays the same items after execution. Now the bottom number on the output list is 15 and A still contains 15. Figure 5.26 shows how a number of data values can be placed on the output list by a single write statement. In this case, the output values are alphanumeric.

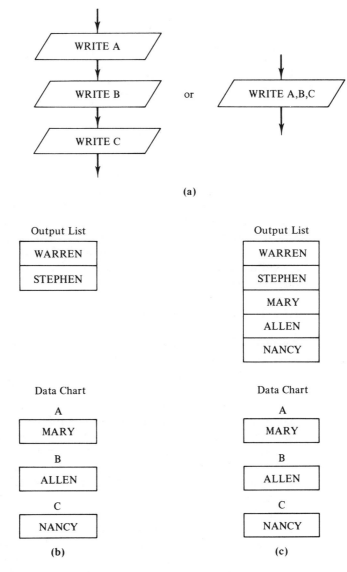

Figure 5.26 *Combining write statements: (a) flow-chart statements; (b) before execution; (c) after execution.*

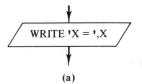

(a)

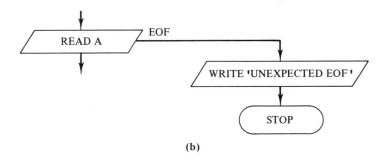

Figure 5.27 *Output messages: (a) output label; (b) error message.*

(b)

Sometimes it is desirable to label output values or to terminate execution with an error message. This is done by inserting appropriate literals or alphanumeric constants into write statements. For example, Figure 5.27a shows how to output the current contents of X along with a label that identifies that value as X. On the other hand, Figure 5.27b illustrates how a write statement is used to explain that an error condition has been encountered and that execution has been terminated for that reason.

5.3.3 The assignment statement

An *assignment* statement is used to specify calculations that a computer is to perform. The general form of an assignment statement is

Variable name←arithmetic expression

where the left arrow is known as an *assignment operator*. An assignment statement directs a computer to calculate the value of the arithmetic expression and then to place that value into the cell referenced by the variable name to the left of the assignment operator. The arithmetic expression is evaluated using the current contents of the variables in that expression. The original contents of the cell referenced by the variable name to the left of the assignment operator are destroyed. Figure 5.28 indicates that an assignment statement is enclosed within a rectangular outline, known as a *process box*; it shows examples of using assignment statements to perform arithmetic calculations. The figure first displays current values for several single-cell variables and then indicates the effect of the execution of assignment statements using those values.

Notice that assignment statements do not specify algebraic equalities. For example, X←X + 1 is not true in the algebraic sense, but it is a valid assignment statement. On the other hand, $X + 1 \leftarrow X$ is not proper because it is impossible to assign a value to an expression. Likewise, $2 \leftarrow A$ is not permitted because the value of a constant cannot be changed. Some programming languages use other symbols for the assignment operator because most keypunches do not have a left arrow symbol. FORTRAN, MAD, PL/I, and BASIC use the equal sign $(=)$, whereas ALGOL uses a colon, equal sign combination $(:=)$.

Figure 5.28 *Effect of an assignment statement using numeric data.*

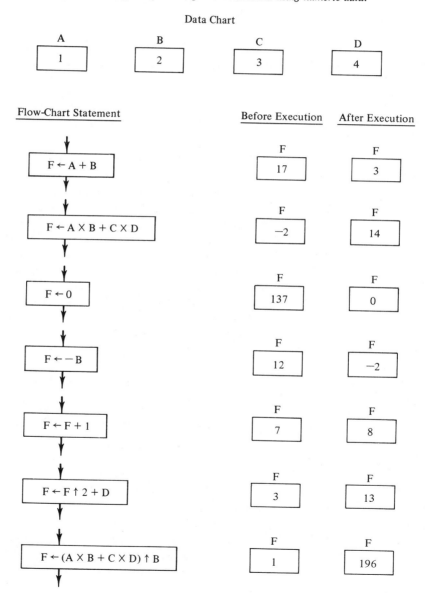

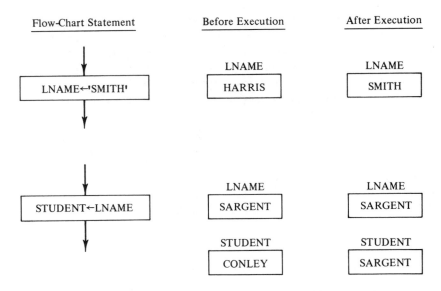

Figure 5.29 *Effect of an assignment statement using alphanumeric data.*

The left arrow ($\leftarrow$) is used here to distinguish the assignment operator from the relational equal sign ($=$) employed in logical expressions.

Assignment statements can also be used to manipulate alphanumeric data. Figure 5.29 shows two such statements. In the first example, the alphanumeric constant, 'SMITH', is assigned to the single cell, LNAME. As was the case with numeric data, the original contents of LNAME are lost. In the second example, the current contents of LNAME are moved to the single cell, STUDENT, so that after execution both variables have the same value. As was said earlier, it generally does not make sense to perform arithmetic calculations upon alphanumeric data. For example, statements of the form

$$\text{NAME} \leftarrow 2 \times \text{'SMITH'}$$

or

$$\text{NAME} \leftarrow \text{'LARRY'} + \text{'SMITH'}$$

have no meaning in a conventional arithmetic sense. Therefore, assignment statements referencing arithmetic data should be limited to the form

$$\text{Variable} \leftarrow \text{alphanumeric constant}$$

and

$$\text{Variable} \leftarrow \text{variable}$$

5.3.4 The test statement

A *test* statement tells a computer how to determine its next instruction. Figure 5.30 shows two general forms of test statements and indicates that test statements are enclosed in a diamond-shaped outline known as a *decision box*.

Note that test statements differ from others in that they must always have more than one outgoing arrow. Execution of a test statement determines which outgoing arrow is followed and which instruction is executed next. Thus, test statements interrupt and alter an instruction execution sequence.

An *arithmetic test* statement directs a computer to calculate the value of both expressions, determine their arithmetic relationship, and then use that relationship to decide which statement is executed next. A *colon* (:) is used to separate the two arithmetic expressions and is referred to as the *comparison* operator. Figure 5.31 shows examples of arithmetic test statements. The figure first displays a data chart that indicates current values for four single cells. Next, it displays sample test statements, the values of the two arithmetic expressions, and the path that is followed for the assumed values. In the first example, the current contents of single cells A and B are compared. If A is less than (<) B, the path to the left is followed to find the next statement. If A is greater than (>) B, the downward path is followed. If A is equal to (=) B, the path to the right is followed. Since A has a current value of 1 and B has a current value of 2, A is less than B and the path to the left points to the next instruction. Because an algorithm must be unambiguous and complete, an arithmetic test statement must allow for all possible arithmetic relations. Since the result of a comparison can be either greater than (>), equal (=), or less than (<), all three possibilities must be included in an arithmetic test statement. It is possible to combine two of these three conditions into one, as shown in the last three examples in Figure 5.31. Consequently, an arithmetic test statement must have either two or three outgoing arrows.

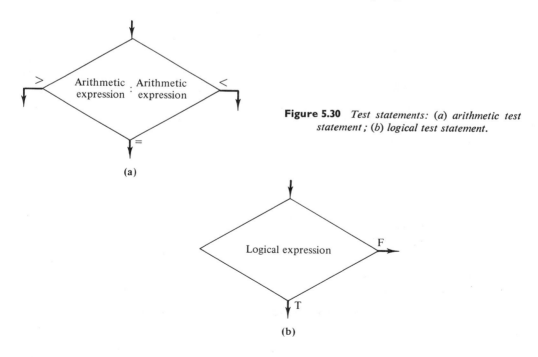

Figure 5.30 *Test statements: (a) arithmetic test statement; (b) logical test statement.*

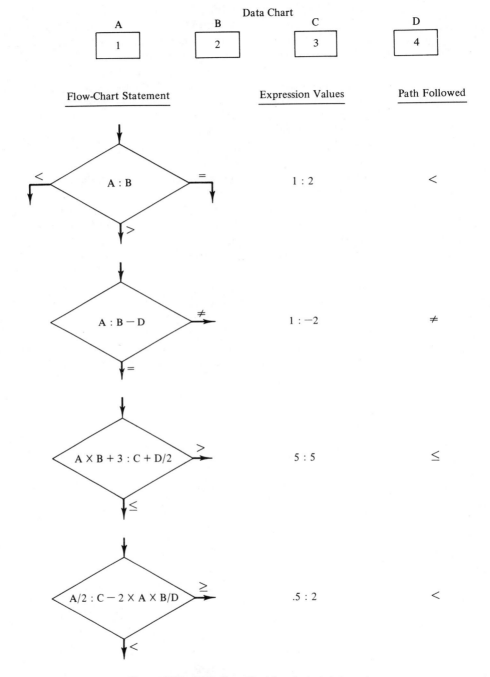

Figure 5.31 *The effect of arithmetic test statements.*

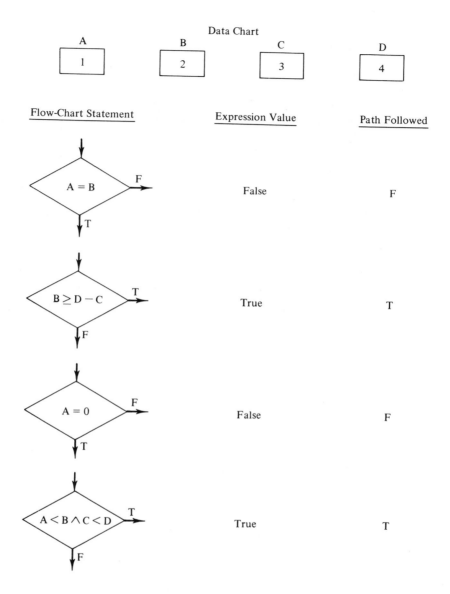

Figure 5.32 *The effect of logical test statements.*

The *logical test* statement shown in Figure 5.30b directs a computer to determine the value of the logical expression and then to use that value to decide which statement is executed next. Figure 5.32 shows examples of logical test statements. In the first example, the logical expression compares the current contents of A and B for equality. If they are equal, the logical expression is true and the arrow labeled T points to the next instruction. If they are unequal, the expression is false and the arrow labeled F is followed. Since in this situation A does not equal B, the expression is false, and the false arrow points to the next instruction. Since a logical expression can have two values, true or false, a logical test statement must always have two outgoing arrows.

Two forms of test statements have been included for convenience. Sometimes it will seem easier to use an arithmetic test while at other times a logical test will seem more appropriate. The actual choice is up to you. Figure 5.33 shows a comparison of the two forms under the same conditions. In the first example, a three-way split is performed by one arithmetic test, whereas the two logical tests are required for the same decision. On the other hand, the second example shows that one logical test can do the work of two arithmetic statements. Some programming languages, such as 1620 FORTRAN, FORTRAN II, and 1130 BASIC FORTRAN IV, do not permit logical expressions. Arithmetic test statements are more appropriate for these languages.

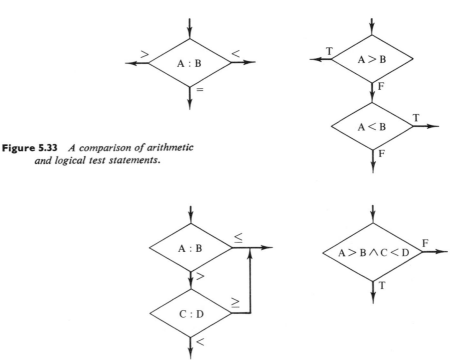

Figure 5.33 *A comparison of arithmetic and logical test statements.*

5.4
Basic
Flow-Charts
Now that we have a set of flow-chart statements, let us use them to illustrate basic flow-chart techniques. In doing so, we begin to solve problems by following the problem-solving procedure discussed in Chapter 4. Previously, it was said that flow charts display the structure of algorithms just as data charts display the structure of data sets. The problems that follow are chosen so as to illustrate five forms of program structure: straight line, branch, loop, function, and subroutine.

5.4.1 The straight-line structure

As a first example of program structure, let us repeat the solution of the sum and difference problem discussed earlier in Chapter 4. Basically, that problem required us to produce a solution that finds the sum and difference of any two numbers. By now, this particular problem should be well understood; thus, the first problem-solving step is satisfied. Remember that our solution must work for any two numbers, and that this problem can be divided into two smaller subproblems, finding the sum of two numbers and then their difference.

The second and third problem-solving steps tell us to specify our desired output and required input. From the problem statement, we know that our solution must produce two values. Since output order is not stated, we can arbitrarily agree that the first output value will be the sum, whereas the second will be the difference. Likewise, since the problem statement says nothing about input order, let us further agree to subtract the second input value from the first. Figure 5.34 shows output and input based upon these assumptions. Note that both contain two values, each of which is labeled for easy reference.

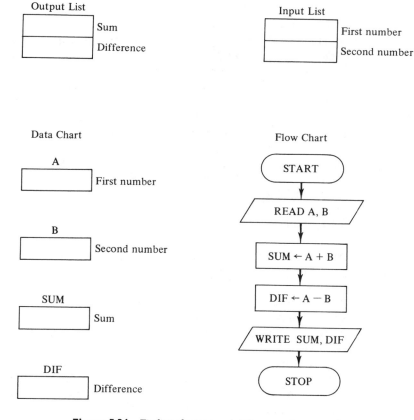

Figure 5.34 *Finding the sum and difference of two numbers.*

The fourth solution step directs us to determine what data are to be retained in memory. From previous discussions of this problem, we know that we must process four data values, two input values and their sum and difference. Since these four numbers are single, unrelated values, they have single-cell data structures. Consequently, each value can be stored in a separate cell with its own variable name, as illustrated in the data chart in Figure 5.34.

Finally, we are ready to develop an algorithm that converts two input values, A and B, into two output values, SUM and DIF. Every algorithm must have a beginning; thus, the flow chart in Figure 5.34 begins with a single start statement. Before the sum and difference can be calculated, the input values must be read and stored in their respective data structures. This can be done with a single read statement. Since the first input number must go into A, the variable name, A, appears first in the read statement. Once two values are read, calculations can be performed. Since there are two separate calculations, two assignment statements are required, one for SUM and one for DIF. Remember that the value of an arithmetic expression to the right of an assignment operator is determined from current contents of the variables in that expression. With calculations complete, we can transmit results to the output list, making sure that SUM is placed at the top followed by DIF. As always, an algorithm ends with a stop statement.

The flow chart in Figure 5.34 displays an algorithm that has the simplest of structures, a *straight line*. Here, each flow-chart statement is preceded and followed by one and only one statement. When this algorithm is performed, each statement is executed one at a time in sequence beginning with start and ending with stop. Although necessary for this problem, a straight-line algorithm does not take full advantage of the capabilities of a modern computer. Since there is just one path through such an algorithm, a computer need not make decisions on how to process its data. Furthermore, because each statement is executed once, a computer does not reuse any of its instructions. Consequently, this algorithm can be executed by a computer in less time than it takes us to write it.

5.4.2 The branch structure

As a second example of a program structure, let us develop a *computerized procedure* that finds the absolute value of a single number. By a computerized procedure, we always mean an output and input list and a data and flow chart. There should be no trouble defining this problem if the concept of absolute value is understood. If it is not, a review of an introductory algebra text would reveal that the *absolute value* of a number is formed by making that number positive.

From the problem definition, it should be clear that both output and input consist of single values, as shown in Figure 5.35. Since the input number and its absolute value are separate entities, they can be stored in single cells. Arbitrarily, the input value is stored in A, whereas its absolute value is in ANS. From the problem discussion, an algorithm for forming an absolute value is

Output List
| | Absolute value

Input List
| | The number

Data Chart

A
| | Input number

ANS
| | Absolute value

Flow Chart

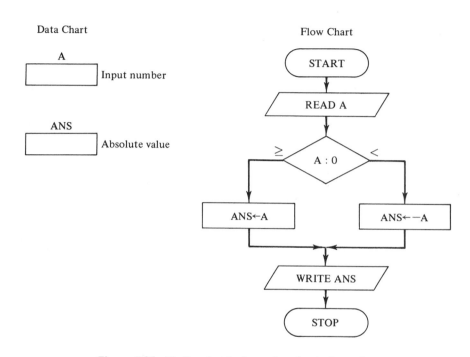

Figure 5.35 *Finding the absolute value of a single number.*

quite straightforward. If the input value is positive, it is its own absolute value. Otherwise, if it is negative, the absolute value is the negation of that value.

The flow chart in Figure 5.35 contains what is known as a *branch*. The arithmetic test, A : 0, permits a computer to choose its own execution path depending upon the current contents of A. If the input value is positive or zero, the left-hand path is followed. Otherwise, the right-hand one is taken. Note that during each execution of this algorithm, just one of two possible paths is traversed and the other is unused. Thus, the structure of this flow chart differs from that of the previous example.

Finally, the flow chart indicates that the contents of A are not referenced after the test statement is executed. Thus, A can be used to store its own absolute value, as shown in Figure 5.36. This solution requires a single storage cell, whereas the previous one needs two. At first glance, one might be tempted to say that this second solution is "better" because it requires fewer cells.

Output List

| | Absolute value
|---|

Input List

| | The number
|---|

Data Chart

A

| | Input number and its absolute value
|---|

Flow Chart

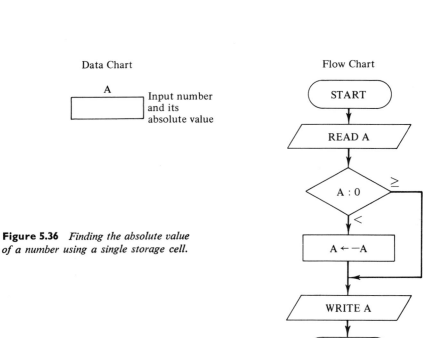

Figure 5.36 *Finding the absolute value of a number using a single storage cell.*

However, using the same data structure for more than one purpose is bad practice, because it sometimes makes it harder to find errors in one's algorithms. Of course, there is no choice if memory capacity is limited.

5.4.3 The loop structure

As a third example of program structure, let us suppose that we are to develop a computerized procedure that finds the sum of a set of positive numbers. From the problem statement, the output is a single value, the sum of all input numbers. In the previous two problems, the number of input quantities was rigidly specified in the problem definition. For example, the sum and difference problem always has two input values, whereas the absolute value problem has just one. However, in this situation, we are told that we have a set of positive numbers. This means that we must be prepared to handle any number of input values ranging from zero to infinity. In reality, we cannot process an infinite set because we would never receive an answer. Figure 5.37 shows a suitable representation of an input list of unspecified length.

With the specification of the output and input, we are ready to analyze the data sets and determine their structures. Certainly, the sum of the input numbers is a separate value and can be stored in a single cell, SUM. As has been done in previous examples, each input value can be stored in a separate cell with a unique name. But if the number of input values is unknown, how do we know how many cells to specify in our data chart? Figure 5.37 shows a data chart that is unsatisfactory because it does not specify each structure by name. Furthermore, the flow chart contains invalid statements since the read and assignment statements do not conform to flow-chart rules.

Now that an impasse has been reached, let us stop and consider how one might add a set of numbers by hand. Figure 5.38 shows two manual methods. First, one might write all numbers in a single column and then produce their

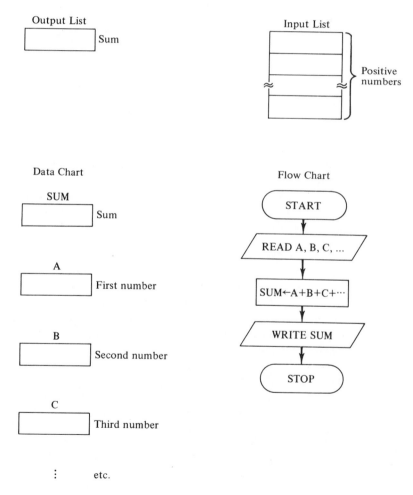

Figure 5.37 *Finding the sum of a set of positive numbers—a first attempt.*

sum in one operation, as shown in Figure 5.38a. This procedure was tried unsuccessfully in Figure 5.37. In contrast, one might produce a *running total* by summing one value at a time, as in Figure 5.38b. Since the first method did not work, let us now try the second.

$$
\begin{array}{r}
17 \\
102 \\
56 \\
3 \\
+\ 25 \\
\hline
203 \\
\end{array}
\qquad
\begin{array}{r}
17 \\
+\ 102 \\
\hline
119 \\
+\ 56 \\
\hline
175 \\
+\ 3 \\
\hline
178 \\
+\ 25 \\
\hline
203 \\
\end{array}
$$

(a)

(b)

Figure 5.38 *Two methods of addition.*

The running sum procedure involves reading one input number and then adding it to a total before the next value is read. As before, a cell is required for the sum, but in this case it contains the current value of the running total. A second cell is needed to store the latest input number. Once that value is added to the running total, its cell can be used to hold the next input value. Consequently, this procedure can process a complete input list with just two cells.

Figure 5.39 shows a flow chart that incorporates a running summation algorithm. It first reads the next input value into A and then uses that value to update the running total, SUM. The flow chart then inputs the next value by going back and reusing the same read statement. Such a repetition of statements is known as a *loop*. A quick glance at the flow chart reveals that this loop is endless. Some method must be devised that enables a computer to determine when it has read its last data value.

For the time being, let us assume that our computer system does not recognize end of files. Such systems terminate execution when input data are exhausted during a read. This can be avoided by adding a special number at the end of the input to act as an *end-of-data signal*. Since the problem statement specifies that all input values must be greater than zero, let us arbitrarily use a value of zero. Notice that this end-of-data signal must not appear anywhere else in the input except at the end. Now as each value is read, a test statement can check for this end-of-data signal. When it is detected, the test statement

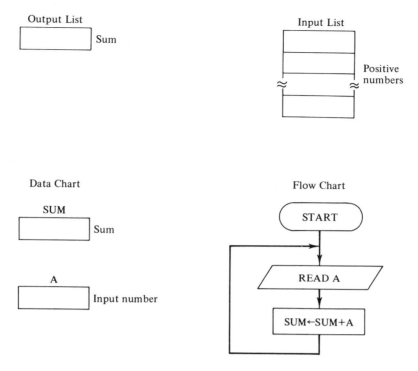

Figure 5.39 *Finding the sum of a set of positive numbers—a second attempt.*

terminates the loop, causing a branch to a write that outputs the sum. The flow chart in Figure 5.40 incorporates this method.

This flow chart still contains one flaw. Remember that the value of an arithmetic or logical expression is determined from the current contents of its variables. Therefore, it is necessary to ensure that each cell contains a value before it is used to evaluate an expression. For example, in the test statement, A receives its value from the previous read. However, when the assignment statement SUM←SUM + A is executed for the first time, SUM does not contain a value. This is rectified by setting SUM to zero via an assignment statement, SUM←0, at the beginning of the flow chart in Figure 5.41. This operation is referred to as *initialization*.

A loop is a most powerful program structure. Since it permits a computer to reuse statements, a loop allows you to specify more computer processing with fewer program statements. Furthermore, a loop makes it possible for you to design one algorithm that handles a variety of input conditions. For example, the summation solution just discussed processes 100,000 numbers just as well as 10. The only difference is that execution time is longer for the larger set.

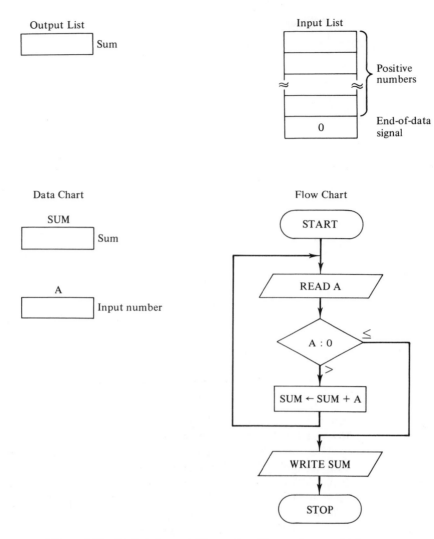

Figure 5.40 *Finding the sum of a set of positive numbers—a third attempt.*

5.4.4 Functions and subroutines

During the discussion of problem solving in Chapter 4, it was stated that it is usually easier to understand and solve smaller problems rather than larger ones. It was therefore suggested that you always ask yourself whether or not a problem can be broken into subproblems. By doing so, you may discover that you have already solved or know of someone else's solution to one or more of your subproblems. Once these smaller problems have been solved, individual solutions can be combined to form a total solution. Since problem subdivision

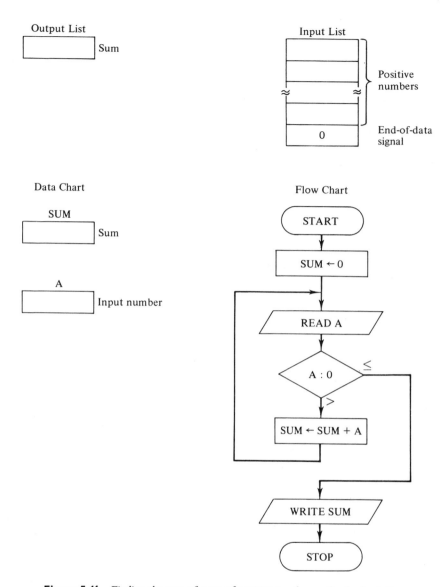

Figure 5.41 *Finding the sum of a set of positive numbers—the final solution.*

is such a successful problem-solving technique, Chapter 9, entitled Functions and Subroutines, is devoted to problem subdivision. However, it is appropriate to introduce the concepts of *functions* and *subroutines* so as to complete our discussion of program structures.

Basically, a *function* is a correspondence between two sets of numbers called the *domain* and *range* of a function, such that for every number x of the domain there is associated exactly one number y in the range. This y is called the value of the function for the given x. A function is said to be *defined* for all numbers in its domain. Mathematically, we denote that y is a function of x by

$$y = f(x)$$

For example, the algebraic equation

$$y = x^2$$

represents y as a function of x, i.e., for each value of x there is one and only one value of y. Likewise, it is possible to have a function of more than one variable, such as

$$z = f(x, y)$$

as in

$$z = \sqrt{x^2 + y^2}$$

For the time being, we shall limit ourselves to the functions listed in Figure 5.42. In general, a function is represented in flow-chart language by the notation

function name (arguments)

where the *function name* identifies the desired function. The arguments, separated by commas, specify the operands. For example, the function, ABS(X), has a value that equals the absolute value of the current contents of X. On the other hand, SQRT (X↑2 + Y↑2) equals the square root of the current value of the expression $x^2 + y^2$.

Function	Description	Value
ABS(arg)	Absolute value	$\lvert arg \rvert$
SQRT(arg)	Square root	$\sqrt{arg}$
EXP(arg)	Exponential	e^{arg}
SIN(arg)	Sine	Sin(arg)
COS(arg)	Cosine	Cos(arg)
TAN(arg)	Tangent	Tan(arg)
MAX(arg$_1$,arg$_2$)	Maximum value	Larger of two arguments
MIN(arg$_1$,arg$_2$)	Minimum value	Smaller of two arguments
CEIL(arg)	Ceiling	Smallest integer greater or equal to arg
FLOOR(arg)	Floor	Largest integer less than or equal to arg

Figure 5.42 *Built-in functions.*

In the recursive definition of an expression, a function is itself an expression. Thus, functions can appear in expressions in a manner similar to constants and variables. Functions have the *highest* precedence level and are performed first when an expression is evaluated. Of course, if the arguments of a function are themselves expressions, those expressions must be evaluated before the function

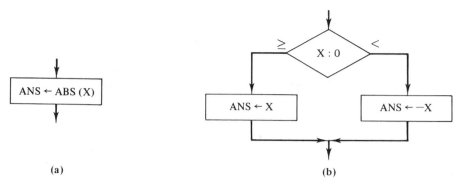

(a)   (b)

Figure 5.43 *Using a function in a flow-chart statement*

is performed. For example, the flow-chart statement in Figure 5.43a deposits the absolute value of X into a single cell, ANS, and thus is equivalent to the three statements in Figure 5.43b. Now, the absolute value problem discussed in Section 5.4.2 can be solved by using the absolute value function, as shown in Figure 5.44.

A function can be considered as a set of predefined operations. As such, you can use them as building blocks as you construct your solution. Each programming language has its own set of functions that can be employed simply by mentioning the desired function name along with the proper arguments. Such functions are usually referred to as *built-in* functions. Sometimes it is convenient to be able to define your own functions; this topic is discussed in Chapter 9.

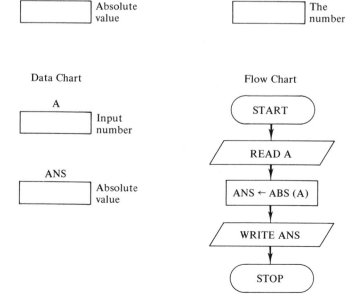

Figure 5.44 *Finding the absolute value of a number using a function.*

The usefulness of functions for problem subdivision is limited by their inability to produce more than one value. This drawback is overcome by *subroutines*, which can be considered functions that produce multiple values. Since subroutines are designed to generate more than one value, they are better suited for use with more advanced data structures. Therefore, further consideration of subroutines is left for Chapter 9.

5.5 Flow-Chart Debugging

An error or mistake in an algorithm or program is commonly referred to as a *bug*, and the process of detecting and correcting such errors is known as *debugging*. Now that we have solved several examples, let us see how a flow chart can be used as a debugging aid. Certainly, it is more convenient to debug an algorithm while it is still a flow chart than to wait until it has been converted into a program and punched into cards. Because flow-chart debugging can be performed at a table or desk without the need of an actual computer, the process is known as *table-top debugging* or *desk checking*.

1. Ensure that your flow chart has one and only one start statement and at least one stop statement.

2. Verify that each statement conforms to the construction rules of the flow-chart language.

3. Make certain that every outgoing arrow leads to one and only one flow-chart statement.

4. Confirm that each statement has the proper number of incoming and outgoing arrows, as shown:

Statement Type		Incoming	Outgoing
START		0	1
READ		At least 1	1 or 2
ASSIGNMENT		At least 1	1
TEST	LOGICAL	At least 1	2
	ARITHMETIC	At least 1	2 or 3
WRITE		At least 1	1
STOP		At least 1	0

5. Check that all outgoing arrows from test statements are labeled, showing their exit conditions, and that all possible conditions are covered.

6. Substantiate that all variables are properly initialized before they take part in any calculation.

7. Use your flow-chart with sample input lists to verify that your algorithm produces correct output lists.

Figure 5.45 *Guidelines for table-top debugging.*

Figure 5.45 shows a set of guidelines designed to help you table-top debug a flow chart. Begin by examining your flow chart to see that it has just one start statement and at least one stop statement. Then check each statement one at a time ensuring that it conforms to flow-chart rules and that it has the proper number of incoming and outgoing arrows. If it is a test statement, confirm that all test conditions are covered and that all outgoing arrows are properly labeled. Pay particular attention to ensure that all variables have been properly initialized. Before any variable can be used in a write statement or in an expression of an assignment or test statement, that variable must have *previously* appeared in a read statement or on the left-hand side of an assignment statement. In other words, every variable must have a value before it can take part in any calculation. Figure 5.46 uses the summation flow chart from Figure 5.41 to illustrate how variable initialization can be verified by tracing a flow chart *in reverse*. For example, the dashed arrow from the arithmetic test statement, A : 0, indicates that A is initialized in the previous read. Likewise, in the assignment statement SUM←SUM + A, SUM is initialized in the first statement of the flow chart. Finally, notice that SUM has an initial value even if the write statement is reached without a single execution of the addition loop.

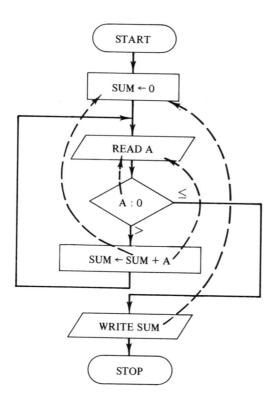

Figure 5.46 *Initialization of variables.*

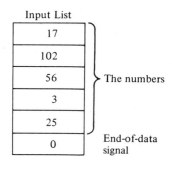

Input List

17	
102	
56	} The numbers
3	
25	
0	} End-of-data signal

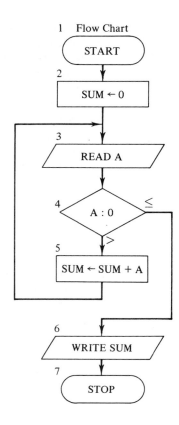

1 Flow Chart

START

2 SUM ← 0

3 READ A

4 A : 0

5 SUM ← SUM + A

6 WRITE SUM

7 STOP

Figure 5.47 *Flow-chart tracing.*

Flow-Chart Trace					
		Value of Variables			
Step Number	Flow-Chart Statement Number	A	SUM	Test	Result
1	1	?	?		
2	2		0		
3	3	17			
4	4			17 : 0	>
5	5		17		
6	3	102			
7	4			102:0	>
8	5		119		
9	3	56			
10	4			56 : 0	>
11	5		175		
12	3	3			
13	4			3 : 0	>
14	5		178		
15	3	25			
16	4			25 : 0	>
17	5		203		
18	3	0			
19	4			0 : 0	≤
20	6				
21	7				

Once all statements have been individually checked and variable initialization has been confirmed, the flow chart along with sample input can be used to verify that your algorithm does, in fact, produce your desired output. Selection of sample input is critical. The values themselves can be simple, but they must be chosen so that *all* possible input conditions are checked. Consequently, your test data must be selected so that they force execution of all possible paths through your chart. Sometimes, you may have to use more than one input set if you are to test it exhaustively. Figure 5.47 shows how sample input is used to *trace* the execution of the summation algorithm. It indicates the sequence in which flow-chart statements are performed and how and when the contents of variables are changed. For example, A is set to 17 during step 3 by the third flow-chart statement and remains 17 until step 6 where the third statement changes it to 102. At the beginning of the trace, variable contents are shown as question marks because their values have not yet been initialized.

Table-top debugging is useful because it allows you to detect algorithmic errors before you convert your flow chart into an actual program. Nevertheless, it is still necessary for you to test your final program, which is done by having a computer execute your program using sample input. Since you have already used sample data to debug your flow chart and since you know the output that data should produce, you can use these same data to test your program.

Sometimes it is useful to have a computer help you discover where your program is going wrong. This can be done by having it output the contents of selected variables as it performs its calculations. For example, it produces a trace of the contents of A and SUM if the statement

WRITE A, SUM

is inserted into the summation loop in Figure 5.47. When you have tested your program under all input conditions, you can remove these extra write statements.

Correct problem solutions produced in minimum time are a mark of a good problem solver. If you use a computer as a problem-solving tool in your profession, your employer wants you to be a good problem solver so that his production costs are minimized and so that he can assign you to another problem as quickly as possible. If, on the other hand, you are a student using a computer in your classwork, you want to solve your problems quickly so that you can use your time for other courses. Therefore, it pays to use good problem-solving techniques, such as flow charts and table-top debugging. Do not believe those who say they do not need to table-top debug because they can produce the correct and best algorithm at a keypunch. They are the ones who spend too much time in the hubbub of a computer center looking for obvious errors.

5.6
Summary

From the beginning, you are encouraged to use flow charts to specify algorithms. In so doing, you separate the production of an algorithm from the generation of a program. Once produced, the flow chart with its graphical display permits you to study your algorithm to ensure that it does, in fact, perform the correct calculations. As you study your flow chart, you will sometimes discover ways of improving its performance. Only when you are convinced that you have a correct algorithm should you convert a flow chart into a computer program using an actual programming language.

The examples in this chapter illustrate five forms of program structure. In a straight-line algorithm, each flow-chart statement is preceded and followed by one and only one statement. Every time such an algorithm is performed, each statement is executed one at a time in sequence, beginning with start and ending at stop. An algorithm that contains a branch permits a computer to choose its own execution path depending upon the outcome of its calculations. Thus, a branch structure differs from a straight-line structure in that it contains more than one path. A loop structure permits a computer to reuse the same algorithmic statements, therefore allowing you to specify more processing with fewer statements. Finally, functions and subroutines were introduced as program structures that are useful in subdividing problems for easier solution. These last two structures are discussed in detail in Chapter 9.

SELECTED REFERENCES

1. BOHL, MARILYN, *Flowcharting Techniques*, Science Research Associates, Inc., Chicago, Ill., 1971.

2. CHAPIN, NED, "Flowcharting With the ANSI Standard: A Tutorial," *Computing Surveys*, Vol. 2, No. 2, June 1970, pp. 119–46.

3. ———, *Flowcharts*, Auerbach Publishers, Inc., Princeton, N. J., 1971.

4. FARINA, MARIO V., *Flowcharting*, Prentice-Hall, Inc., Englewood Cliffs, N. J., 1970.

5. *Flowcharting Symbols in Information Processing*, (X3.5–1966), American Standards Institute, New York, 1966.

6. SCHRIBER, THOMAS J., *Fundamentals of Flowcharting*, John Wiley & Sons, Inc., New York, 1969.

PROBLEMS

5.1 Which of the following are not constants? Why are they incorrect?

(a) 12	(d) *5	(g) 5/2
(b) 1.34	(e) 0.0	(h) 3.14
(c) −6	(f) 1.72E7	(i) A7

(j) 6×10^5	(m) 0	(p) $4 + 2$
(k) STU''S	(n) 'BAKER'	(q) $-7.13 \times E - 6$
(l) ALPHA	(o) 6.1.2	(r) 'STU'DENT'

5.2 Which of the following are incorrect variable names? Why are they incorrect?

(a) 'ALPHA'	(f) 1.12	(k) GOTO
(b) A1	(g) (X)	(l) GO TO
(c) $-J$	(h) M123456	(m) 1ZETA
(d) B4J	(i) A*B	(n) END
(e) $X = Y + Z$	(j) 9B	(o) -1.0

5.3 Which of the following are not arithmetic expressions? Why are they incorrect?

(a) $A \times A + B$	(g) $(C + D) \times (/E)$	(m) $(A + B)/6$
(b) $AX + B$	(h) $2.0 - A, B$	(n) $(A + B) \uparrow 2$
(c) $C*D/+E$	(i) B7	(o) $A \uparrow .5$
(d) $N + 1.0$	(j) $6 \uparrow \uparrow 2$	(p) $3 + X$
(e) $X \leftarrow Y + Z$	(k) $3 - 1 - 2$	(q) 'LITERAL'
(f) $2/Z$	(l) $(A + B)(C + D)$	(r) $(A + B)/C + D$

5.4 Write expressions for each of the following algebraic forms:

(a) $a - b$	(f) $\sqrt{a^2 + b^2}$	(k) $1 + r^n$
(b) $a + b^2$	(g) $\dfrac{1}{m + n}$	(l) $a(b/c - d)^3$
(c) $\dfrac{a + b}{c + d}$	(h) $\dfrac{a}{b + c} + \dfrac{d}{e + f}$	(m) $d(d(d - 1) - 1) - 1$
(d) $\dfrac{a + b}{c}$	(i) $\dfrac{a/b}{c}$	(n) $\dfrac{w^2 + x^2}{y^2 + z^2}$
(e) $x^2 + y^2$	(j) $\dfrac{a}{b/c}$	(o) $\sqrt{\dfrac{b^2 - 4ac}{2a}}$

5.5 Given the following variables, determine a value for each arithmetic expression:

A	B	C	D
4	3	2	1

(a) $A \times (A + 1)$	(g) $(A \uparrow 2 + B \uparrow 2) \uparrow .5$
(b) $A \uparrow 2 + A$	(h) $A/B/C$
(c) $(A + B)/(C + D)$	(i) $A/B \times C$
(d) $C + D/A$	(j) $A \times B/C$
(e) $A/B + C/D$	(k) $-A \uparrow B$
(f) $A/B + C$	(l) $A \times (B \times (C \times (D - 1) - 1) - 1) - 1$

5.6 Given the following variables, determine a value for each logical expression:

A	B	C	D
1	2	3	4

(a) $A > B$

(b) $A + D = B + C$

(c) $(B - C)/A \le D$

(d) $C \uparrow (B - A) \ge (D + 1)/2$

(e) $B < C \wedge C < D$

(f) $A \uparrow B - (D - C) \uparrow A = 0$

(g) $D - 1 > B + 1 \vee A \ne 1$

(h) $A = 1 \wedge B = 2 \wedge C = 3 \wedge D = 4$

5.7 Which of the following are incorrect assignment statements? Why are they incorrect?

(a) $A \leftarrow B + C$

(b) $A + 2 \leftarrow XY$

(c) $XY \leftarrow A + 2$

(d) $'DATE' \leftarrow '12/02/74'$

(e) $L + M)(N + 0$

(f) $A + (-B)$

(g) $W = X/Y$

(h) $W + \uparrow 2$

(i) THE SUM $\leftarrow X + Y$

(j) $((A + B) + C)$

(k) NAME $\leftarrow 'FIRST' + 'LAST'$

(l) $-X$

5.8 Which of the following expressions exhibit a proper use of parentheses?

(a) $A + B \times (C + D)$

(b) $(A + B)/C + D)$

(c) $X + Y$

(d) $(X + Y) > D)$

(e) $A + B) \times (C + D$

(f) $X \uparrow (-Y)$

(g) $(M + N/(X \uparrow 2 - 1))$

(h) $A = B \vee (C \ne D \wedge E)$

(i) $1/(1/(1/(1 - X) - X) - X)$

(j) $((A - 1) \times B - 1) \times C - 1) - 1) - 1$

5.9 For the following variables, determine which path is taken for each test statement:

A	B	C	D
4	2	3	1

(a)

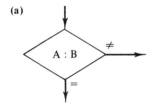

(b)

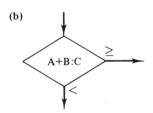

(c)

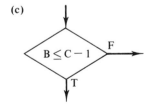

(d)

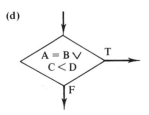

5.10 Combine each of the following examples into a single test statement:

(a)

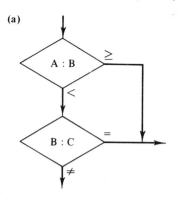

(b)

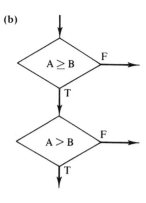

5.11 Which of the following are incorrect flow-chart statements? Why are they incorrect?

(a)

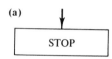

(f) $C \leftarrow (A \uparrow 2 + B \uparrow 2) \uparrow .5$

(b)

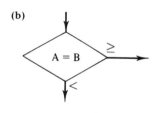

(g)

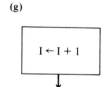

(c)

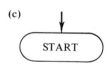

(h)

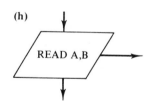

(d)

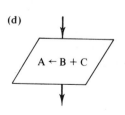

(i)

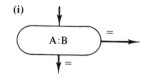

(e)

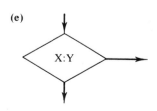

(j)

6 Single-Cell Data Structures

The previous chapter presented a flow-chart language for specifying computer algorithms. The discussion began by introducing such basic concepts as data representation, variables and constants, and operators and expressions. Next, these concepts were used as building blocks to construct six different flow-chart statements. Start and stop statements are used to designate the beginning and end of algorithms, whereas input and output operations are indicated by read and write statements. Assignment statements specify the performance of calculations, and test statements are used to compare the results of calculations. Finally, these individual statements were combined to specify complete algorithms.

This chapter shows how single-cell data structures are used to solve problems. It begins by formalizing the characteristics of data that have a single-cell data structure and then describes how these structures are stored in memory. Next, a number of problems are solved that involve data best stored in single-cell data structures. At all times, complete examples are solved so as to illustrate the problem-solving procedure discussed in Chapter 4.

So far, the single cell has been used as an example of a data structure without formal consideration. Now let us briefly discuss its structure in more detail to see how it is used and how it is stored in memory.

6.1.1 Characteristics and uses of single cells

Previously, a data set consisting of a single value was said to have a *single-cell* data structure. Its representation in a data chart shows a single rectangle, indicating that it is a separate, individual value with no interrelationships with other values. In the examples that follow, single-cell structures perform a variety of functions. They store individual input values for later processing. They act as temporary storage for results of intermediate computations and save final results for later output. Finally, they tell a computer how to perform and when to stop its calculations.

Sometimes, you use single cells because they naturally fit the data you wish to process. If you have a small number of data values, you can assign each to a single cell that has its own variable name. On the other hand, you may wish to force a data set to fit the single cell because you know that you can produce a simpler and more convenient algorithm if you use that structure. For example, you might be able to process a large data set one value at a time, thus requiring only a single cell for the whole set. The examples that follow are designed to illustrate both approaches.

6.1.2 Storing single cells in memory

Figure 6.1 shows our representation of a computer memory. It is a sequence of words similar to that of the model in Figure 3.2, except that numerical addresses have been omitted. In the case of the model, these numbers were used as addresses to reference the contents of individual memory locations. Now, variable names perform that function.

A computer automatically assigns memory locations to your data structures by using the variable names in your computer program. The assignment process depends upon the particular programming language, but it can usually be described as follows. A computer scans your program one statement at a time looking for variable names. When it finds a name that it has not seen before, it assigns that variable to the next free location in memory. For the remainder of the program, that variable name is associated with that particular word. This allocation process continues through the complete program until each variable name is assigned a memory location.

The assignment of memory space to single cells is quite straightforward. Each structure is always allocated a fixed number of memory locations. If the word length of a particular computer is sufficient, each variable is assigned one memory word; otherwise, more than one is required. In any case, a com-

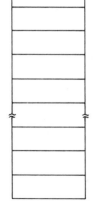

Figure 6.1 *Representation of a computer memory.*

puter knows in advance how many locations are required for each structure and can continue the assignment process as long as it does not exhaust memory. If this happens, you must adjust your program so that fewer memory locations are required.

6.2
Using
Single-Cell
Data
Structures

Now that we have seen how single cells are stored in memory, let us continue to solve problems. After all, the best way to improve your problem-solving skill is actually to solve problems. Each of the following examples can be solved with just single cells. Study each example carefully, for many of the problems at the end of this chapter are variations of examples discussed here.

6.2.1 Calculating simple interest

As our first example of the use of single-cell data structures, let us suppose that we are required to develop a computerized procedure for calculating the effect of simple interest upon a savings account deposit. We are told to use the standard interest equation, $b = p(1 + ni)$ where p is the value of the principal on deposit in the account, n is the number of years that this principal remains on deposit, i is the simple yearly interest rate, and b is the savings account balance after starting with a principal, p, that remains on deposit for years, n, at yearly interest rate, i.

This problem definition specifies that the output must consist of a single value, a savings account balance, as labeled in Figure 6.2. From the simple interest equation, we see that three input numbers are required: p, n, and i. These input values each perform a unique function and have no interrelationships. Consequently, their relative input order is arbitrary, and Figure 6.2 shows one possible arrangement. It is important to realize that even though this sequence is arbitrary, any arrangement once chosen must be followed throughout the remainder of the solution.

From the discussion of the output and input, we know that we must store values for p, n, i, and b. Since these numbers are unrelated, they each have a single-cell data structure and can be stored in four separate cells, as shown in Figure 6.2. Here, each cell has been given a variable name corresponding to its interest equation symbol.

Finally, we are ready to develop an algorithm that converts three input values, p, n, and i, into a single output value, b. First, it is necessary to input three values into their respective cells, which can be done in a single read, as shown in Figure 6.2. Note that the order of variable names corresponds to data value arrangement on the input. If this input sequence is changed, so must that of the variable names in the read statement. Once input values have been read, a single assignment statement calculates a value for B, and then a write statement outputs that value. Notice that this flow chart exhibits a straight-line structure and that all statements are executed each time it is performed.

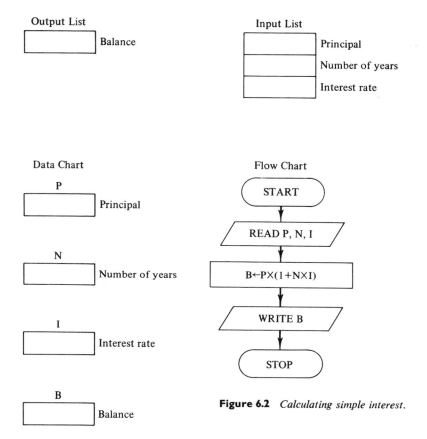

Figure 6.2 *Calculating simple interest.*

6.2.2 Making change from a dollar

As our second example of the use of single cells, let us develop a computerized procedure that tells a sales clerk how to make change in a minimum number of coins. For simplicity, let us assume that all purchases cost at least a penny and never more than one dollar, and that a customer always pays for his purchase with a single one-dollar bill. A clerk can make change if we tell him how many coins of each denomination he should give his customer. Since there are five different coins, we must output five different values: the number of half-dollars, quarters, dimes, nickels, and pennies, as shown in Figure 6.3. In contrast, input consists of a single value, a purchase price.

So far, we know that we must store at least six data values, a purchase price and the number of each of five coins. Since these values are unrelated, they can each be stored in a single cell. In addition, a cell is required for calculating the value of change that must be given to a customer. Figure 6.3 shows a data chart that displays these seven single cells and indicates their variable names.

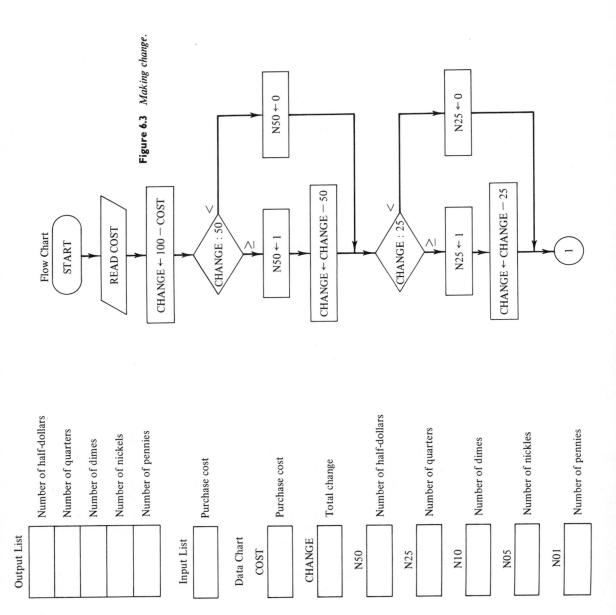

Figure 6.3 *Making change.*

144

Figure 6.3 (*cont.*)

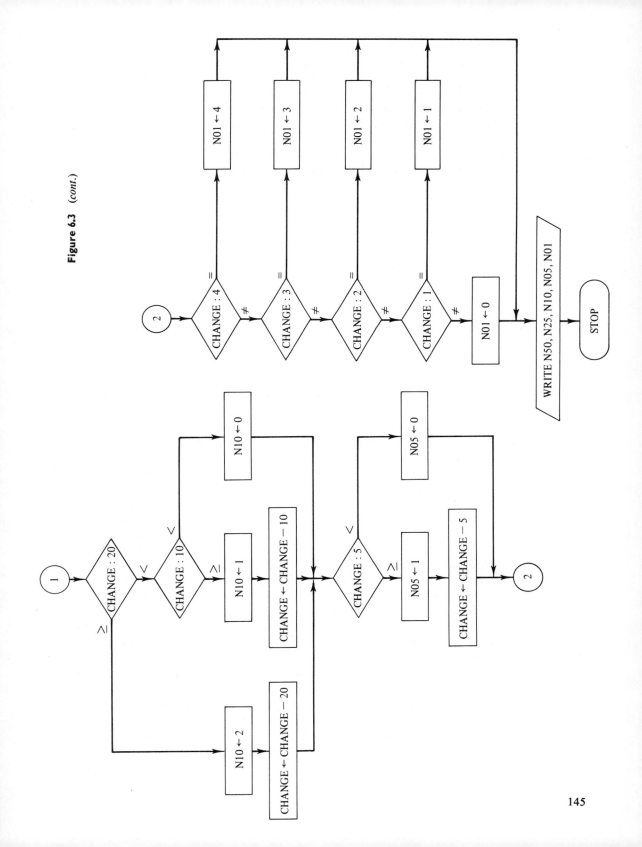

145

Now we are ready to develop an algorithm and draw its flow chart. From the problem definition, we know that our result must make change in a minimum of coins. To see how this might be done, consider the following example. Assume that a purchase costs seven cents. Figure 6.4 illustrates some possible change combinations. The top line indicates that change can be given in 93 coins as pennies; in contrast, the bottom shows how it can be done in just 7. Here, the number of coins is minimized by using as many of the larger ones as possible. Further examples should convince you that this is always the case.

Total Number of Coins	Number of Each Coin				
	50¢	25¢	10¢	5¢	1¢
93					93
21				18	3
12			9		3
8		3	1	1	3
7	1	1	1	1	3

Figure 6.4 *Table of coin combinations for 7¢ purchase.*

Our algorithm begins by reading a purchase price and calculating the total value of a customer's change. At this point, let us agree that costs are stated in cents rather than dollars. In other words, an item priced at 37 cents has a cost of 37 rather than .37. Customer change is calculated by subtracting the cost of an item from 100. This remainder is stored in CHANGE, as shown in the flow chart in Figure 6.3. Now, the number of each denomination is determined starting with the largest coin.

The number of half-dollars is calculated by comparing CHANGE with 50. If CHANGE is greater than or equal to 50, the customer's change includes one half-dollar. Because N50 is reserved for half-dollars, N50 is set to one. Since the customer is receiving a half-dollar, the remaining change is reduced by 50 cents by subtracting 50 from CHANGE. If, on the other hand, CHANGE is less than 50, the customer receives no half-dollars and N50 is set to zero. After the number of half-dollars is calculated, we go to the next largest coin and determine the number of quarters. Here, the procedure is the same as for the half-dollars, except that N25 and 25 are substituted for N50 and 50.

For the two largest denominations, change consists of either zero or one of each coin. However, in the case of dimes, there can be either zero, one, or two coins. Therefore, we must allow for three possibilities. If CHANGE is greater than 20, there are two dimes; otherwise, CHANGE must be compared with 10 to see if there is at least one. Consequently, N10 is set to two, one, or zero, depending upon the outcome of these comparisons. Once the number of dimes is calculated, we can proceed to nickels. Since there can be at most one nickel, we can use the same process employed for half-dollars and quarters. Finally, the number of pennies remains to be determined. Here, there can be zero to four coins. Each of these five situations must be included in the flow chart.

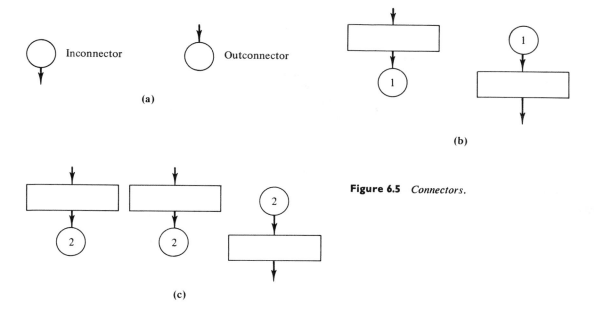

Figure 6.5 *Connectors.*

Figure 6.3 shows a finalized flow chart. Unfortunately, it is too large to fit onto a single page; thus, it must be broken into parts. In such cases, a circle, known as a *connector* outline, is used to indicate how various parts fit together. In general, there are two types of connectors: the inconnector or entry connector, and the outconnector or exit connector, as shown in Figure 6.5a. An *inconnector* has an arrow or flowline leaving it but none entering: an *outconnector* has an entering arrow but none leaving. Connectors must be used at least in pairs, and their contents are used to match an outconnector with its associated inconnector. For example, the connector pair in Figure 6.5b indicates that the flow chart broken by an outconnector encircling a 1 continues at the inconnector, which also contains a 1. In other words, an outconnector can be thought of as being tied to its matching inconnector by an imaginary arrow. Each inconnector may have one or more outconnectors associated with it, but each outconnector must have only one associated inconnector. For example, in Figure 6.5c, there are two outconnectors encircling a 2 but just one inconnector.

Tracing the flow chart in Figure 6.3 should convince you that its algorithm actually does calculate the minimum number of coins for any purchase price from 1 to 100 cents. However, one purpose of a flow chart is to help you improve your algorithm. For example, consider the portion of the chart that calculates the number of dimes, as shown in Figure 6.6a. Notice how its algorithm handles the three cases as individual situations with separate flow-chart paths. Figure 6.6b shows a more compact chart that first assumes that there are no dimes. If CHANGE is less than 10, that assumption is correct. Otherwise, there is at least one dime, and N10 is increased by 1 while CHANGE is reduced by 10. The chart checks for a second dime by looping back to repeat this process.

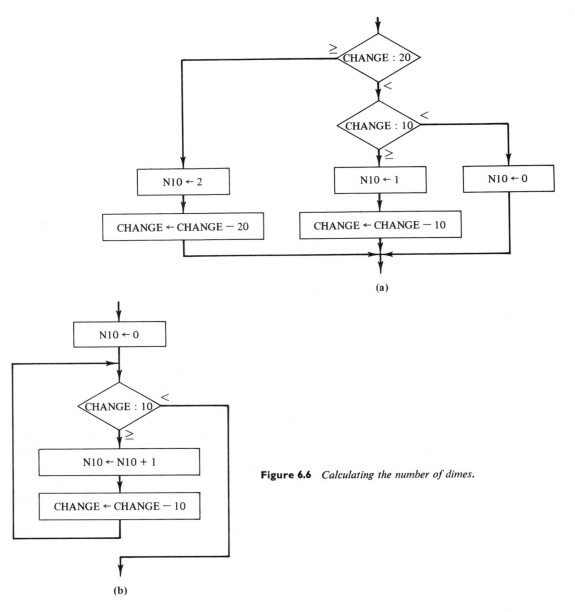

(a)

(b)

Figure 6.6 *Calculating the number of dimes.*

Figure 6.7 compares two methods for calculating the number of pennies. Figure 6.7a shows the original method, whereas Figure 6.7b displays a one-statement equivalent. Notice that in Figure 6.7a, N01 is set to a value that equals CHANGE. If such is the case, this can be done in a single statement, as shown in Figure 6.7b. In other words, once the value of half-dollars, quarters, dimes, and nickels has been removed from CHANGE, the remaining value in CHANGE must equal the number of pennies.

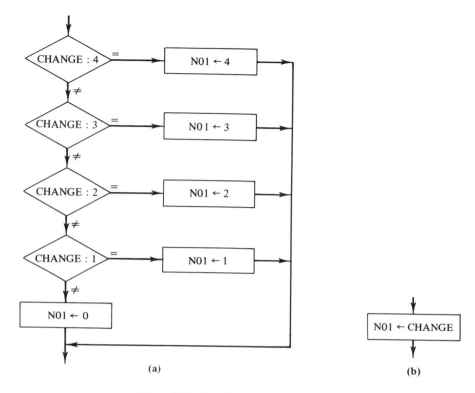

Figure 6.7 *Calculating the number of pennies.*

Figure 6.8 shows a final flow chart. Actually, it is no more correct than the earlier one. It does, however, use fewer statements, and for that reason might be considered "better."

6.2.3 Counting a set of positive numbers

As a third example of the use of single cells, let us develop a computerized procedure that determines how many numbers are in a set. We are told that a set can contain any number of values, but may not contain any zeros or negative values. From the problem definition, we are required to produce one output value, a number count, as shown in Figure 6.9. The problem statement tells us that our input is a set of numbers. Since we need only count them, their input arrangement is not important. In other words, our result is independent of input sequence. This problem has an unknown and potentially unlimited number of input values. Consequently, we must tell a computer how to recognize that it has read all of its input. As in the summation problem in Section 5.4.3, let us agree that the last input number shall be special. Since all input values are positive, let us use a zero or a negative number as an end-of-data signal. When a computer finally detects this signal, it knows it has exhausted its input.

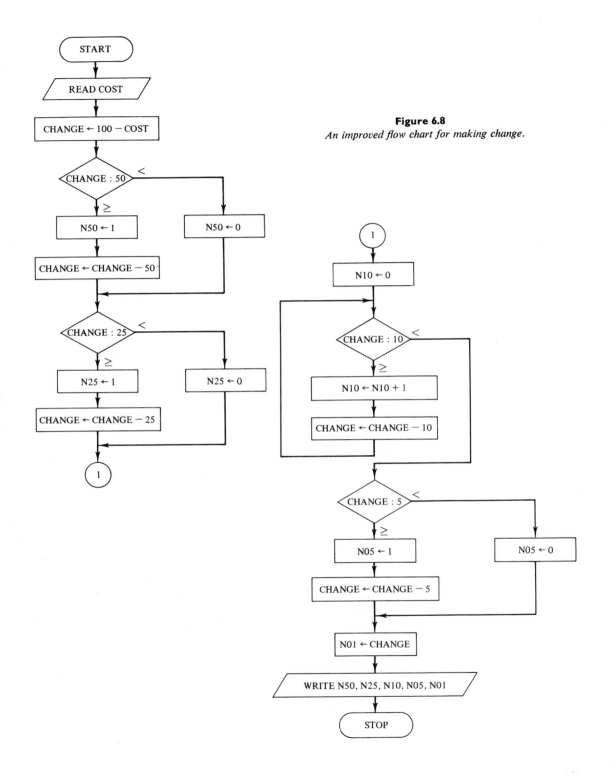

Figure 6.8
An improved flow chart for making change.

150

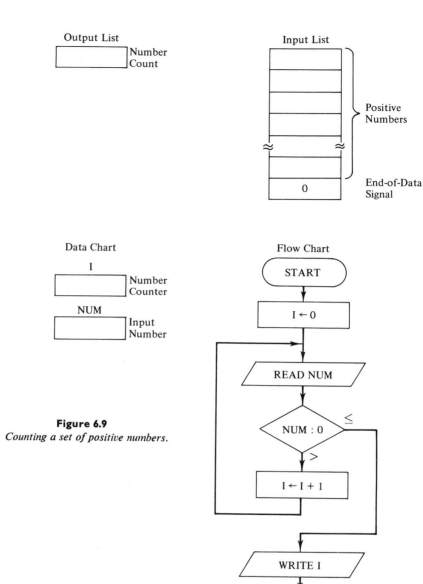

Figure 6.9
Counting a set of positive numbers.

Now that we have specified the output and input, let us determine the data structures and produce a data chart. From the output requirements, we know that we must count a set of numbers. For this, let us use a single-cell data structure, I. Each time a number is read, I is incremented by one. In addition, we need a single cell to hold input values as they are read one at a time. Let us refer to this second cell by the name NUM.

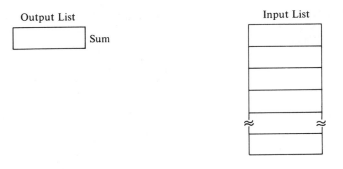

Figure 6.10 *Summing a set of numbers—
a first attempt.*

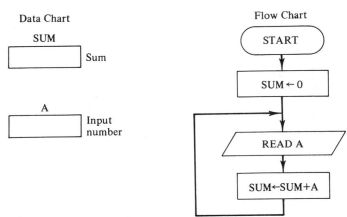

Finally, we can develop an algorithm and draw its flow chart. Each number can be read one at a time into NUM. After a number is read, it must be checked to ensure that it is not the end-of-data signal, which can be done by testing NUM to determine if it is zero or negative. If it is, the end has been reached and a test statement should cause a branch to a write that ouputs I. Otherwise, I is incremented by one, followed by a loop back to read the next value. Figure 6.9 shows a flow chart that incorporates this algorithm. This counting process is straightforward, but what are the initial contents of I? Certainly, after the first number has been counted, I should contain a value of one, which implies that I should be initialized to zero before counting begins. Note that if an input set is empty and the end-of-data signal is the only input, this flow chart outputs a zero.

6.2.4 Finding the sum of a set of numbers

As our fourth example of the use of single cells, let us develop a computerized procedure that finds the sum of a set whose numbers can take on any value. In addition, we are told that the set can contain any number of values, but that we shall know in advance exactly how many numbers are in each set.

As you gain an understanding of this problem by rereading it, you should ask yourself whether you have seen this problem before. If your answer is no, you should then ask if you have seen a similar one. In this case, you should remember that a summation problem was discussed in Section 5.4.3, when the concept of a loop was introduced. At this point, you should reread that problem to see how it differs from this one. Your review should reveal that in the earlier one, all input numbers were positive; in this problem they can have any value. Further study should remind you that the earlier input restriction permitted the use of an end-of-data signal.

Now that we have our problem defined, let us continue the solution process. From the problem statement, we know that our solution must produce a single output value from a variable length input, as shown in Figure 6.10. In the earlier summation problem, we employed a running total. If we are to use that procedure here, we need single cells to store a running sum and one input value. Finally, we might use the flow chart shown in Figure 6.10. Unfortunately, it contains an endless loop.

In the earlier summation problem, an endless loop was overcome by adding a zero to the end of the input as a termination signal. Since input numbers in this problem can take on any value including zero, a different approach is required. Review of the statement of this problem reveals that we shall be told how many numbers are in each input set before we begin. Therefore, why not count each number as it is read, as was done in the previous section? When the count exceeds the number of input values, a test statement can cause a branch out of a loop to a write statement, which outputs the sum.

This *read-and-count* approach requires that an input count appear at the head of the input, as shown in Figure 6.11. Furthermore, two new single cells must be added to the data chart. Here, N stores the number of input values while I counts those values as they are read; I is initialized at one and then incremented by one as each value is read. However, before the next read, I must be compared with N to ensure that there is at least one remaining input value. When I exceeds N, a test should cause a branch to a write. Flow chart 1 in Figure 6.11 incorporates this algorithm.

A table-top trace of flow chart 1 reveals that its loop is *always* executed at least once. In other words, if N is less than 1, the flow chart still attempts to read one value, because its test statement appears after those that process the input. Since a good algorithm must handle all possible conditions, the test should be placed in front of the read, as shown in flow chart 2. In this case, if N is less than 1, this test causes an immediate branch to the write without executing the loop.

The flow charts in Figure 6.11 illustrate two methods for controlling the processing of data, and Figure 6.12 compares them in more detail. Both charts consist of the same four steps. In the *initialize* step, a single cell acting as a counter is given its first value. The *test* step compares a counter with a final count to see if more data values remain to be processed. In the *process* step, input values are read and necessary calculations performed. Finally, the *increment* step advances a counter in preparation for the next performance of

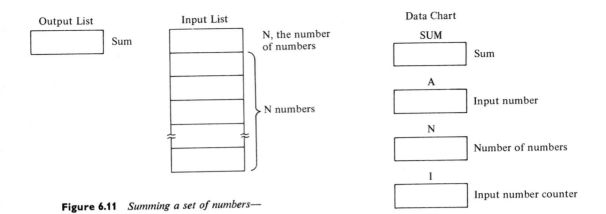

Output List

Sum

Input List

N, the number of numbers

N numbers

Data Chart

SUM
Sum

A
Input number

N
Number of numbers

I
Input number counter

Figure 6.11 *Summing a set of numbers—
a final attempt.*

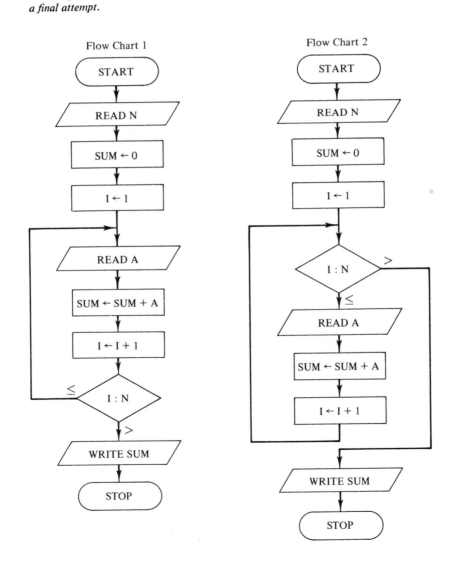

Flow Chart 1

START

READ N

SUM ← 0

I ← 1

READ A

SUM ← SUM + A

I ← I + 1

I : N

≤

> WRITE SUM

STOP

Flow Chart 2

START

READ N

SUM ← 0

I ← 1

I : N

>

≤

READ A

SUM ← SUM + A

I ← I + 1

WRITE SUM

STOP

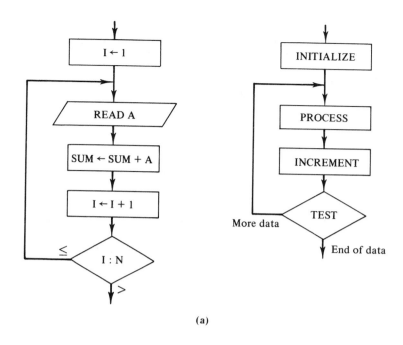

(a)

Figure 6.12 *Two methods of counting;*
(a) test after process; (b) test before process.

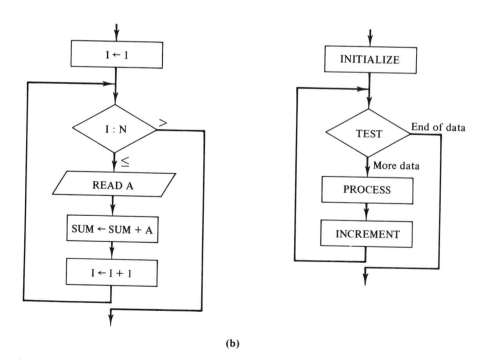

(b)

the loop. Each step consists of a single statement, except the process step, which can contain more than one. In this example, it has two: a read and an assignment. Since process appears before test in Figure 6.12a, it is referred to as *test after process*. In contrast, Figure 6.12b illustrates *test before process*. Generally, it is best to adopt test before process because it helps avoid difficulties such as those encountered here.

6.2.5 Checking a set of numbers for numerical sequence

As our fifth example of the use of single cells, let us develop a computerized procedure that checks a set for numerical sequence. Each number in the set must be less than or equal to the one that follows it. The set can contain any number of values, but we shall know in advance how many are in each one. We are told to output a value of 1 if the set is in sequence; otherwise, we output a 0. Consequently, the output contains one number, a yes or no code, shown in Figure 6.13. Let us agree to tell a computer how many numbers it must read by placing a count at the top of its input. Thus, a computer can input this count and know immediately how many numbers it must read. It is important to appreciate that this first input value is not part of the sequence that follows.

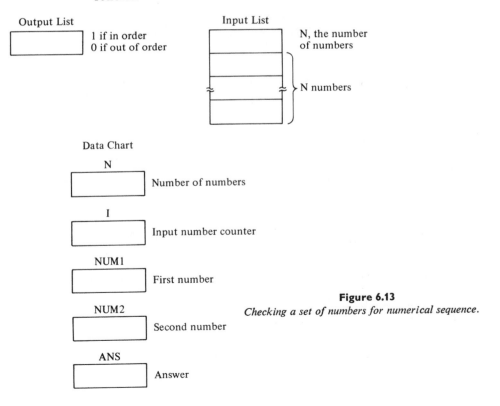

Figure 6.13
Checking a set of numbers for numerical sequence.

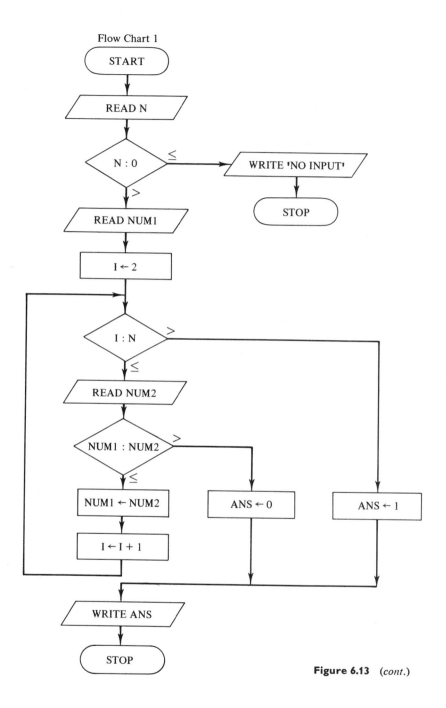

Flow Chart 1

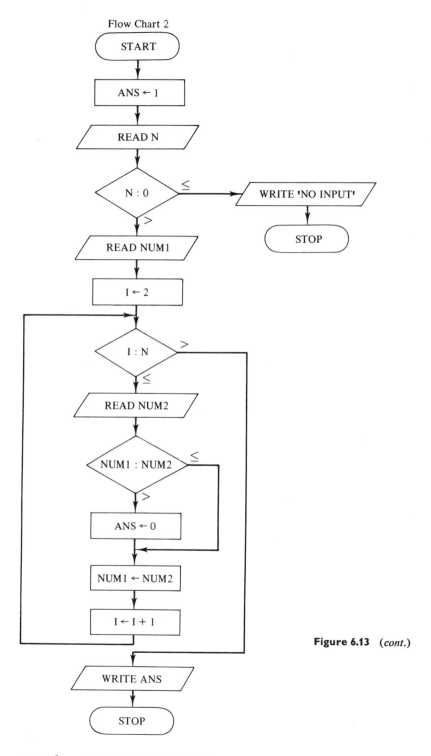

Flow Chart 2

Figure 6.13 (*cont.*)

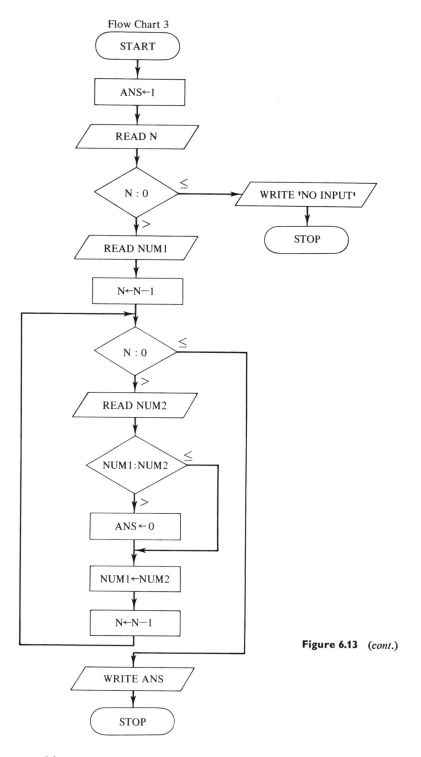

Flow Chart 3

Figure 6.13 (*cont.*)

Now that we have specified our output and input, let us determine the data structures. The output requirement tells us to produce an answer of 0 or 1. For this, let us use a single cell, ANS. If the set is in sequence, ANS is 1; otherwise, 0. The first input value specifies the size of the data set that follows. Let us save this value in a single cell, N. If we are to know when all input values have been processed, we must count them as they are read. Let us use a single cell, I, as an input counter. We can then compare I with N to determine if all values have been read. Finally, there must be storage for input numbers. Since we must compare successive number pairs, two single cells are required, one for each number. Let us refer to them as NUM1 and NUM2.

Finally, we can devise an algorithm and draw its flow chart. From the problem definition, we realize we must read successive number pairs, i.e., adjacent numbers, and determine whether the first number is less than or equal to the second. The first number is read into NUM1 and the second into NUM2; then, a test compares them. If NUM1 > NUM2, the input is out of order, and ANS is zero. If NUM1 ≤ NUM2, the current number pair is in order and the next pair must be checked. Since the first number of the next pair is already in memory at NUM2, it must be moved to NUM1 before the second number is read into NUM2. If input is exhausted before an inverted pair is found, ANS is 1.

Flow chart 1 in Figure 6.13 displays this algorithm. Basically, it consists of a loop that reads the second number, NUM2, of each number pair and compares it with the first number, NUM1, which is already in memory. If NUM1 ≤ NUM2, then the input is still in order, and NUM2 must be moved to NUM1 in preparation for the next comparison. Otherwise, if NUM1 > NUM2, the set is not in sequence, and ANS is 0.

As in the previous summation example, the loop consists of four steps: initialize, test, process, and increment, as follows:

Initialize:	I←2
Test:	I : N
Process:	READ NUM2
	NUM1 : NUM2
	NUM1←NUM2
Increment:	I←I + 1

Here, the input counter I is initialized at 2, because two values must be read before the first number pair can be compared.

As always, you should stop and table-top debug this flow chart with sample input. Your trace should convince you that this chart does, in fact, produce a 1 if input sequence is correct. Notice that N must be checked for zero before the first data value is read to ensure that there is at least one input value. Finally, you should realize that this chart outputs a 0 immediately upon detection of an inverted pair, leaving any remaining values on the input list.

Flow chart 2 reads the complete input and still produces the correct result. As before, number-pair comparisons are made in a loop which consists of the four steps: initialize, test, process, and increment. At the beginning of this chart, input is assumed to be in order and ANS is set to 1. As long as number pairs are in sequence, a test causes a branch around the assignment statement, ANS←0. If an inversion is found, the original assumption is revised by setting ANS to 0.

So far, a separate cell has been used as an input counter. In flow charts 1 and 2, I is incremented by 1 as each input value is read. On the other hand, it is possible to count down on N, as shown in flow chart 3. Here, the input count is read into N, which is then reduced to 1 as each value is read. The test statement terminates processing when N reaches 0. In general, this procedure should be avoided because it destroys original input values, which can complicate computer tracing and debugging.

6.2.6 Finding the largest value in a set of numbers

As a sixth example of using single cells, let us develop a computerized procedure that determines the largest value in a set of numbers. A set may contain any number of values, and the values themselves can by any size, i.e., positive, negative, or zero. Our solution must input such a set and determine the largest

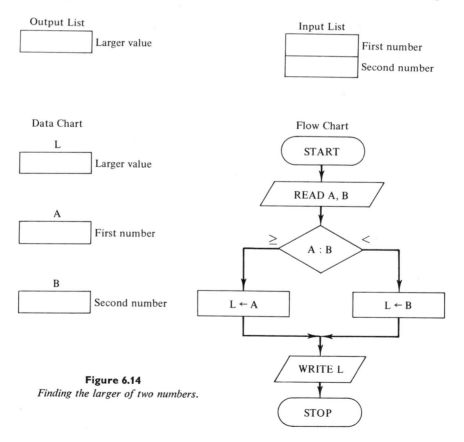

Figure 6.14
Finding the larger of two numbers.

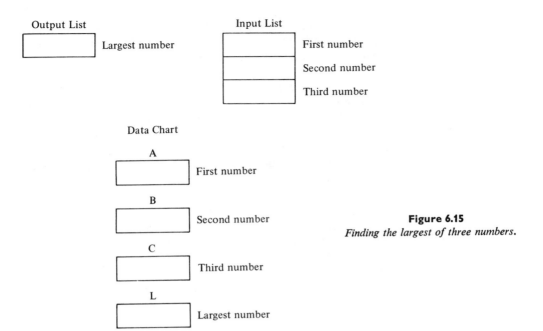

Output List
[   ] Largest number

Input List
[   ] First number
[   ] Second number
[   ] Third number

Data Chart

A
[   ] First number

B
[   ] Second number

C
[   ] Third number

L
[   ] Largest number

Figure 6.15
Finding the largest of three numbers.

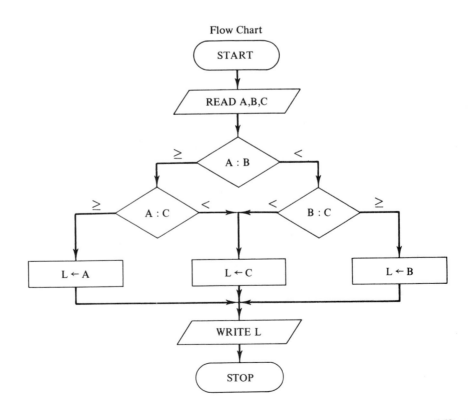

Flow Chart

START

READ A,B,C

A : B

≥   <

A : C   B : C

≥ <   < ≥

L ← A   L ← C   L ← B

WRITE L

STOP

value without indicating which one has that value. If, by chance, two or more are equal and have the largest value, we are only required to produce the largest value and need not note how many numbers have that value.

Sometimes it is easier to solve a problem by beginning with a smaller one. Once solved, it can be expanded in steps until it fits the original. For the time being, let us assume that we are to find the larger of two values. The solution to this problem is straightforward and is shown in Figure 6.14. Here, output is the larger of two input quantities. The data chart consists of three single cells, L for output and A and B for input. The flow chart incorporates an algorithm that reads both input values and uses a single test to determine which input is the larger.

Now that we have solved this problem for two input values, let us expand it to three, as shown in Figure 6.15. Here, output is still a single value, only now it is the largest of three input numbers. An additional cell, C, is needed in the data chart for the third input value. The flow chart handles this additional value by using the previous algorithm twice. First, A is compared with B to

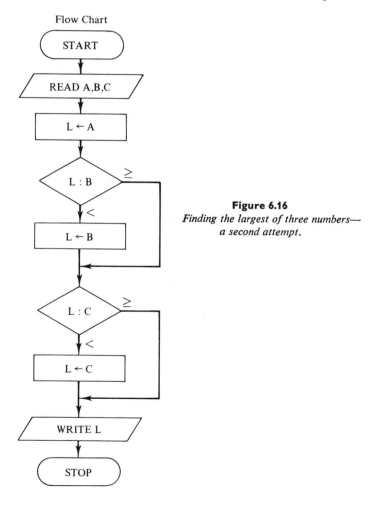

Figure 6.16
*Finding the largest of three numbers—
a second attempt.*

find the larger of these values. If A is larger, then it is compared with C to find the largest; if B is larger than A, B is compared with C. The placement of equal signs in the three test statements is arbitrary because we need not determine whether the largest value occurs more than once.

This expansion process can be continued as new values are added. Unfortunately, each additional value means that another row of test statements must be added to the flow chart. For example, a fourth value requires three more tests, whereas a fifth necessitates yet another four. In general, adding an nth value to the input requires a row of $n-1$ more tests for a total of $n(n-1)/2$ for n input values. Since the number of statements grows as n squared, a different approach is required for this problem.

The flow chart in Figure 6.16 incorporates a different algorithm for finding the largest of three values. Here, the first input is assumed to be the largest and is immediately assigned to L. Next, B is compared with L to determine if this assumption is correct; if not, it is revised by assigning B to L. Finally, C is compared with L. If C is larger than L, C is assigned to L. Now, L contains the largest of the three. Although an improvement over the previous approach, this method still grows as n, since an additional test statement is required for each new input.

Study of the flow chart in Figure 6.16 indicates that it contains a repeating structure. Specifically, test statements are followed by assignments, as illustrated in Figure 6.17a. This repetition can be eliminated by incorporating these statements into a loop, as shown in Figure 6.17b. Here, one value at a time is read and then compared with L to determine if it is larger than the largest value found so far. If it is, it is used to revise L; otherwise, the test branches back to read the next input.

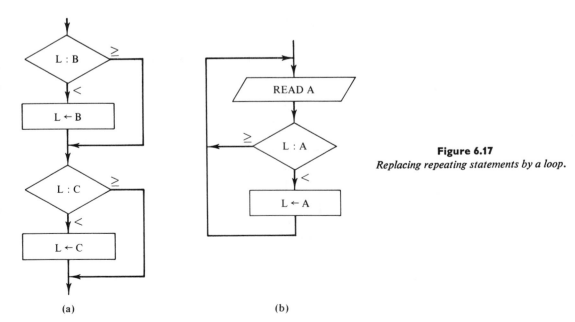

Figure 6.17
Replacing repeating statements by a loop.

(a)   (b)

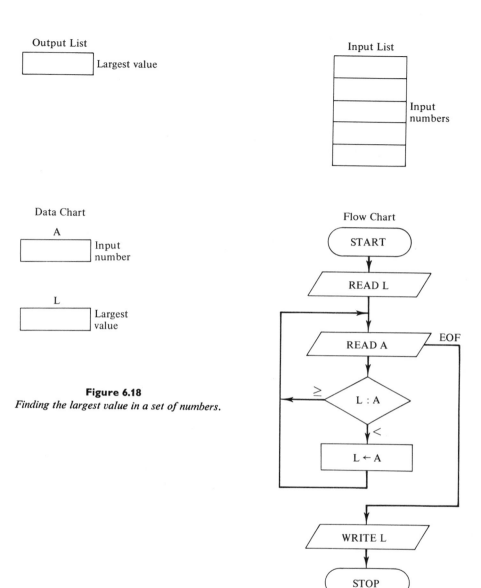

Output List

| | Largest value

Input List

| | Input
| | numbers

Data Chart

A
| | Input
| | number

L
| | Largest
| | value

Figure 6.18
Finding the largest value in a set of numbers.

Flow Chart

START

READ L

READ A   EOF

L : A   ≥

<

L ← A

WRITE L

STOP

Figure 6.18 specifies a final solution that finds the largest value in a set of numbers. Since this value must occur somewhere in the input, the first value is assumed to be the largest and is read directly into L. Values are then read one at a time and compared with L to see if this assumption is correct. Here, an end-of-file exit on a read statement is used to signal end of data. If our computer does not permit such exits, we must either know or count by hand how many numbers are in each set. In this problem, we cannot use a special value as an end-of-data signal because there are no input restrictions.

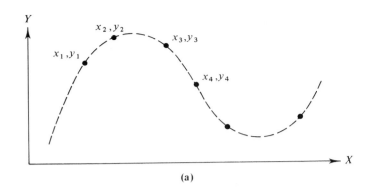

(a)

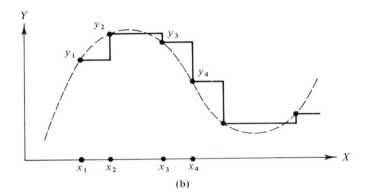

(b)

Figure 6.19 *Representing a curve by horizontal line segments.*

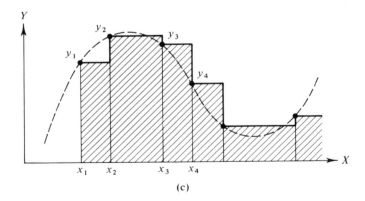

(c)

6.2.7 Approximate integration

As a seventh example of the use of single cells, let us assume that we have the following problem. We are given a set of data values, (x_i, y_i), said to represent some unknown curve, as shown in Figure 6.19a; we are asked to find the area under that curve from x_1 to x_n. Our directions tell us to assume that the actual curve is represented by a series of horizontal straight lines, as shown in Figure 6.19b. Consequently, the area under this curve can be approximated by the sum of the individual rectangles formed by the line segments in Figure 6.19c.

The problem definition tells us that our solution must calculate an approximate area. Consequently, our output is a single value, as shown in Figure 6.20. In contrast, the input is a set of data points, two values per point. Here, x_i is paired with and precedes y_i. The sequence of these values must be maintained. Otherwise, the shape and area of the curve are changed.

Figure 6.20 *Approximate integration using the rectangular rule.*

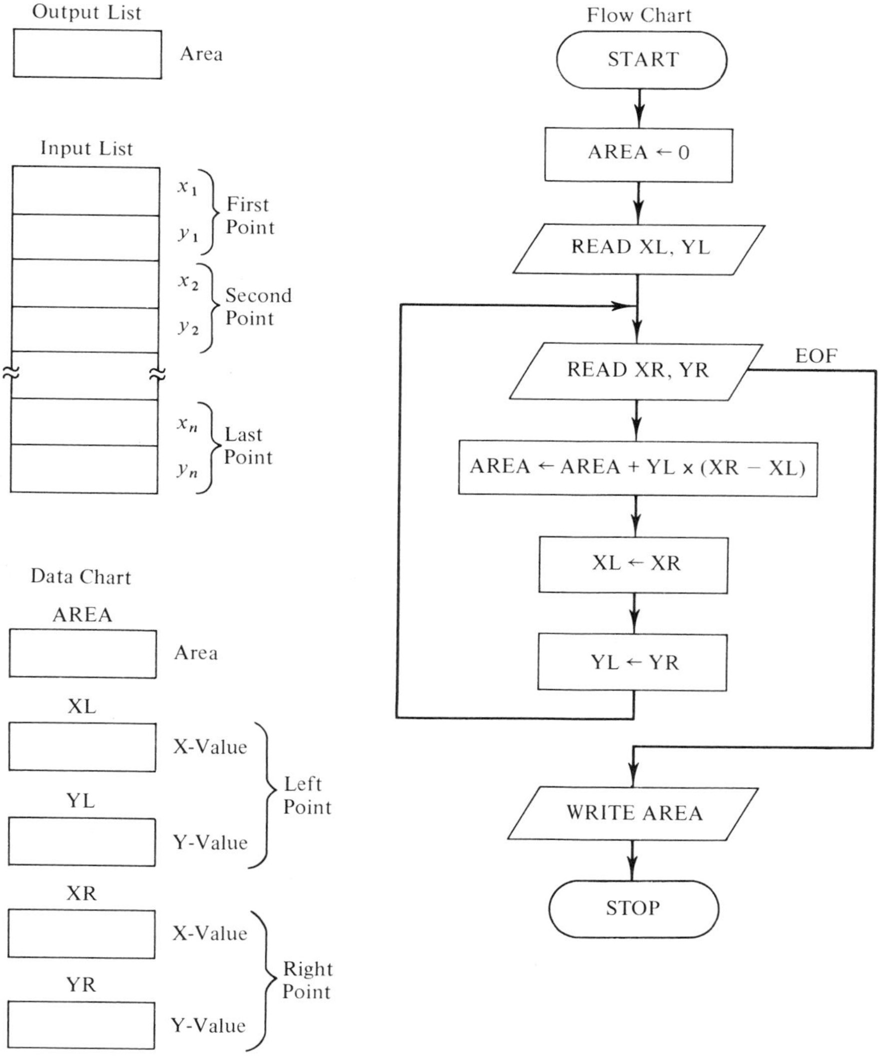

h

w

Area $= h \cdot w$

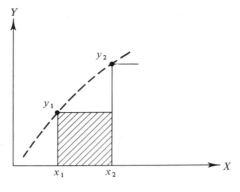

$h = y_1$

$w = x_2 - x_1$

Area $= y_1 (x_2 - x_1)$

Figure 6.21
Area of a rectangle.

Now, we are ready to select our data structures. Since the output is a single value, let is store it in a single cell, AREA. In contrast, the input contains an unspecified number of values. Consequently, it is impossible to assign each value to its own single cell; therefore, we have no choice but to develop a procedure that processes this input a few values at a time.

Figure 6.21 shows an enlarged view of the first rectangle. Its height is y_1 and its base is the difference between x_2 and x_1. Since the area of a rectangle equals its height times its base, the area of this rectangle is

$$y_1(x_2 - x_1)$$

In other words, this area can be determined from the first two data points. Similarly, the area of the second rectangle is

$$y_2(x_3 - x_2)$$

and requires the second two data points. Consequently, if the areas are calculated from left to right, only two data points are required in memory at any one time. Let us use XL and YL for the left point and XR and YR for the right.

Finally, we can develop our algorithm and draw its flow chart. By now we know that we are going to sum the individual areas working left to right. Since we are going to use AREA as a running sum, it must be initialized to 0. Next, the first two data points can be read into XL and YL and XR and YR. The area of this rectangle can be added into the running sum by the statement

$$\text{AREA} \leftarrow \text{AREA} + \text{YL} \times (\text{XR} - \text{XL})$$

Once this is done, XR and YR can be moved to XL and YL in preparation for a loop back to read the next XR and YR. This process can be terminated by an EOF during a read. The flow chart in Figure 6.20 incorporates this algorithm. Since this procedure calculates area via rectangles, it is known as the *rectangular rule* for approximate integration.

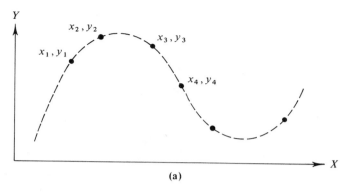

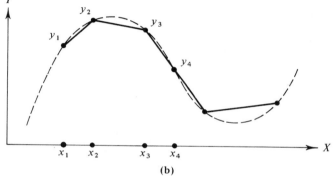

Figure 6.22 *Representing a curve by line segments.*

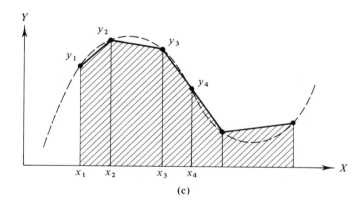

In this example, we were given a set of data points that fell on some unknown curve and were asked to find the area under that curve. We represented the curve by a series of horizontal straight lines and then found an approximate area by summing a set of rectangles formed by those lines. On the other hand, if we suspected that the actual curve was smooth, i.e., does not have any sharp turns, we might better represent the curve by a series of straight lines drawn directly between points, as shown in Figure 6.22b. Now the area under this

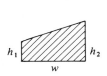

$$\text{Area} = \frac{h_2 + h_1}{2} \cdot w$$

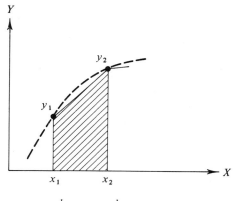

Figure 6.23
Area of a trapezoid.

$$h_1 = y_1 \qquad h_2 = y_2$$

$$w = x_2 - x_1$$

$$\text{Area} = \frac{(y_2 + y_1)}{2} \cdot (x_2 - x_1)$$

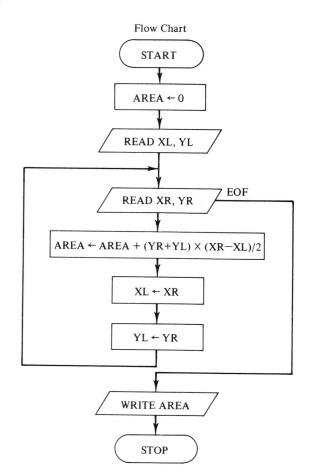

Figure 6.24
Approximate integration using trapezoidal rule.

curve can be approximated by the sum of the areas formed by the trapezoids in Figure 6.22c. Figure 6.23 shows an enlarged view of the first trapezoid and indicates that its area is

$$\frac{y_2 + y_1}{2} \cdot (x_2 - x_1)$$

Thus, the flow-chart statement

$$\text{AREA} \leftarrow \text{AREA} + (YR + YL) \times (XR - XL)/2$$

can be used to find the area, as shown in Figure 6.24. Since this procedure uses trapezoids, it is referred to as the *trapezoidal rule* for approximate integration.

6.2.8 Calculating a grade-point average

As our last example of the use of single cells, let us develop a computerized procedure that analyzes a student's scholastic record. We are told that we shall be given a student's transcript showing letter grades and number of credits for all courses. As output, we are directed to produce four values: total credits taken, total credits passed, total quality points, and grade-point average. An instruction sheet indicates that the school uses a four-point grading system, where $A = 4.0$, $B = 3.0$, $C = 2.0$, $D = 1.0$, and $F = 0.0$, It defines the following:

Total Credits Taken—total number of credits for all courses taken;

Total Credits Passed—total number of credits for all courses passed;

Course Quality Points—number of credits in a course multiplied by the equivalent numerical grade received in that course, e.g., an A in a 3-credit course earns 4×3, or 12 quality points;

Total Quality Points—sum of all course quality points;

Grade-Point Average—total quality points divided by total credits taken.

From the problem definition, we know that we must produce four values. Since output order is not specified, let us arbitrarily use the arrangement shown in Figure 6.25. For input, we know that we shall be given two values per course, a letter grade and number of credits. Let us agree to arrange these data by course, as shown in Figure 6.25, where course grade appears first followed by number of credits. Placement by course is not important, but order within course is critical. In other words, it makes no difference which course is placed first, but within that course, its grade must come before number of credits. Since the number of courses can vary from student to student, let us use an end-of-file exit from a read statement to signal end of input. By doing so, we are saved the trouble of counting courses in advance of each computer run. After all, a computer can count faster and more accurately than we can.

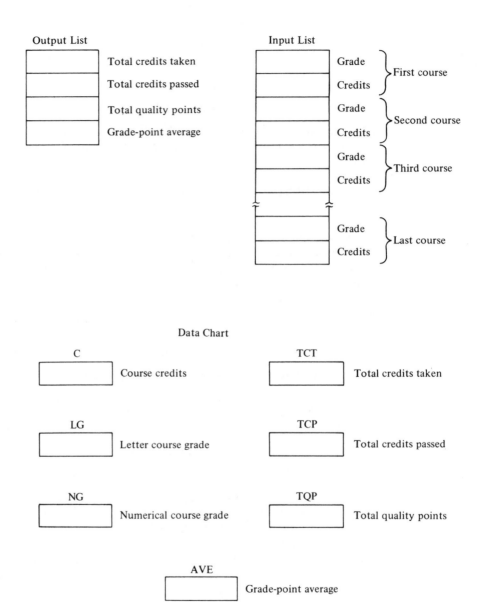

Figure 6.25
Calculating a grade-point average.

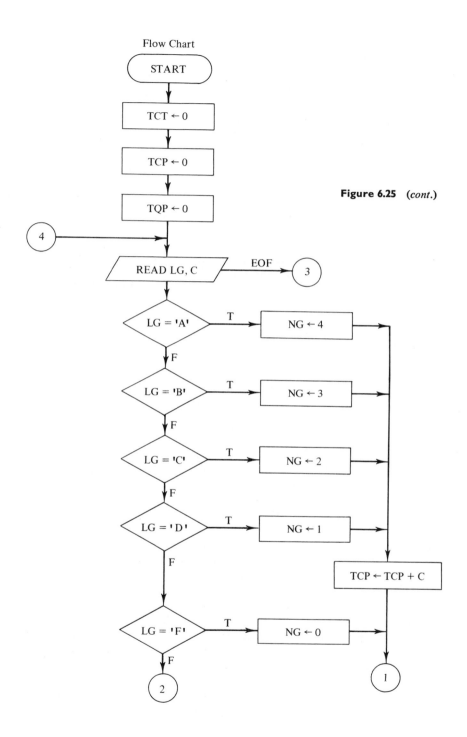

Flow Chart

Figure 6.25 (cont.)

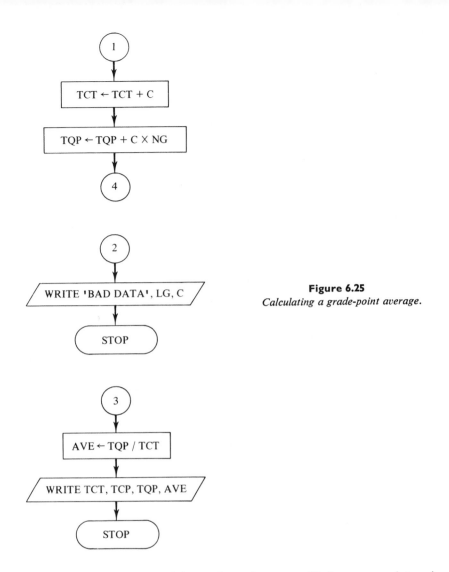

Figure 6.25
Calculating a grade-point average.

Now that output and input have been specified, we can determine the necessary data structures. From the output, we see that four values must be calculated. Since each is a single value, these can be assigned to single cells. Let us use the variable name TCT for total credits taken, TCP for total credits passed, TQP for total quality points, and AVE for grade-point average. The instruction sheet defines total credits taken as the sum of the credits for all courses taken; total credits passed as the sum of the credits for all courses passed; and total quality points as the sum of the individual course quality points. These three sums can be calculated by using a running sum technique. Consequently, each course can be processed one at a time; therefore, two cells are required for input data. Let us use LG for course letter grade and C for course credits.

To calculate these three sums via a running sum technique, we need to incorporate the statements

$$TCT \leftarrow TCT + C$$
$$TCP \leftarrow TCP + C$$
$$TQP \leftarrow TQP + C \times LG$$

inside a loop. As it stands, this last statement mixes a decimal variable, C, with an alphanumeric variable, LG. To avoid this, each letter grade must be converted into its numerical equivalent before it can be used in a calculation. This can be done by comparing LG with alphanumeric constants, 'A' through 'F'. In general, it is not good practice to use the same variable to store both numerical and alphanumeric data. Therefore, let us add a new single cell, NG, to the data chart in Figure 6.25. Now the last assignment statement becomes

$$TQP \leftarrow TQP + C \times NG$$

Finally, note that if LG equals 'F', total credits passed, TCP, is not incremented.

Application of table-top debugging guidelines to the flow chart indicates that TCT, TCP, and TQP must be initialized. Since we are calculating sums, they should all be set to zero before the summation loop is entered. The loop is repeated until an end-of-file is encountered by the read statement. Finally, notice how this algorithm terminates with a message 'BAD DATA' if a numerical equivalent cannot be found for any letter grade. Besides this error message, the erroneous data are also written out so that they can be identified quickly. Note that the flow chart contains two stop statements. Additional stops are sometimes used to avoid crossing arrows, which can confuse the appearance of a chart and camouflage its structure.

6.3
Summary

Sometimes you may use single cells because your data sets naturally fit that structure. If you must process a small number of values, you can assign each value to a separate cell with its own variable name. For example, this was done in the interest problem because it had just three input values and one output value. In contrast, you may wish to force your data to fit a single cell because it allows you to produce a simpler and more convenient algorithm. This was done when we found the sum of a set of numbers. By reading values one at a time and by keeping a running total, we processed a variable length input list with a limited number of cells. Thus, data structure selection depends upon the characteristics of data and also upon how they are to be processed.

Finally, this chapter has used the problem-solving procedure to solve problems. Several of these examples illustrated how false starts are made and how dead ends are reached. Sometimes it is necessary to fall back and rework some or all of the problem-solving steps. In the beginning, do not be discouraged when this happens to you. There is no other way to learn how to solve problems except by actually solving them. Each problem you solve should help you with your next one. Never expect to produce the best algorithm or to draw a perfect flow chart on the first try. After all, a flow chart is for studying and table-top debugging an algorithm so that you can improve and verify its performance.

SELECTED REFERENCES

1. ARDEN, BRUCE W., *An Introduction to Digital Computing*, Addison-Wesley Publishing Co., Inc., Reading, Mass., 1963.

2. GROVE, WENDELL E., *Brief Numerical Methods*, Prentice-Hall, Inc., Englewood Cliffs, N. J., 1966.

3. HULL, THOMAS E., *Introduction to Computing*, Prentice-Hall, Inc., Englewood Cliffs, N. J., 1966.

4. McCRACKEN, DAVID D., and WILLIAM S. DORN, *Numerical Methods and Fortran Programming*, John Wiley & Sons, Inc., New York, 1964.

5. SHERMAN, PHILIP M., *Techniques in Computer Programming*, Prentice-Hall, Inc., Englewood Cliffs, N. J., 1970.

6. WILKINSON, J. H., *Rounding Errors in Algebraic Processes*, Prentice-Hall, Inc., Englewood Cliffs, N. J., 1963.

PROBLEMS

For each of the following problems, develop a computerized solution that includes an output list, input list, data chart, and flow chart.

6.1 Rework the problem in Section 6.2.1, but calculate the effect of both simple interest and compound interest upon a savings account.

Simple interest: $b = p(1 + ni)$

Compound interest: $b = p(1 + i)^n$

6.2 (a) Repeat the problem of finding the largest of three values discussed in Section 6.2.6, but do not use a cell to save the largest value; i.e., eliminate the need for the structure, L.

(b) Repeat the same problem but produce a flow chart that uses only two test statements.

(c) Repeat the same problem but produce a data chart containing a minimum of data structures.

6.3 The economic order quantity, q, for inventory control of an item may be found by the equation

$$q = \sqrt{\frac{2dc}{us}}$$

where d is the demand for the item, c is the cost of placing the order, u is the cost of the item, and s is the cost of carrying the item in inventory. Develop a computerized procedure that inputs values for d, c, u, and s and outputs a value of q.

6.4 Read two numbers, n and m, and determine whether m satisfies the condition $-m \leq n \leq m$. If it does, output n, m, and the message: inside interval. Otherwise, output n, m, and the message: outside interval.

6.5 Before the English converted their coinage to a decimal system, there were 12 pence in a shilling and 20 shillings in a pound. Assume that the pound has an exchange rate of $2.40. Develop a computerized procedure that converts English money in pounds, shillings, and pence into U.S. dollars and cents.

6.6 Repeat Problem 6.5, but convert U.S. dollars and cents into English pounds, shillings, and pence.

6.7 Read three unequal numbers and output the value that is neither the largest nor the smallest.

6.8 Modify the solution shown in Section 6.2.5 so that it counts the times a value is greater than the one that follows it.

6.9 Read three numbers and set a variable, TYPE, to one of the following numbers:

TYPE	CONDITIONS
1	If the three numbers are arranged in increasing order,
2	If the numbers are arranged in decreasing order,
3	If neither of the above

Output the three numbers and TYPE.

6.10 Input any three numbers and determine whether they represent the lengths of the sides of a triangle. Output one or more values according to the following table:

Triangle Type	Output Value
Not triangle	0
Equilateral	1
Isosceles	2
Right	3
None of the above	4

6.11 Read three numbers and determine how many are less than zero, equal to zero, and greater than zero. *Hint:* Do not read the three numbers into three separate cells. Use only one cell by reading and processing one number at a time.

6.12 Read three numbers and then output them in the following order: first, the largest of the three numbers; second, the next largest; and third, the smallest.

6.13 Determine how many values in a set are greater than 10 but less than 25. The total number of values in a set is always known in advance and is placed at the top of the input list.

6.14 Count the number of heads and tails in a coin-tossing experiment. The input is a sequence of zeros and ones, where zero represents a tail and one represents a head. End of input is signalled by a number unequal to either zero or one. The procedure must also calculate the percentage of tails and the percentage of heads.

6.15 The equation
$$y = ax^3 + bx^2 + cx + d$$
is to be evaluated for 50 values of x. For each value of x, calculate and output both x and y. Constants a, b, c, and d are supplied along with the x values.

6.16 Find the sum of 10 numbers and the sum of the squares of the same 10 numbers. *Hint:* Read one number and process it completely before reading the next number.

6.17 Develop a computerized procedure that calculates an individual's withholding tax and net pay. Assume that the number of individuals, n, is known and that they pay taxes at the rate, r_1, if their gross salary is above s dollars. Otherwise, they pay at the rate, r_2. Output gross salary, tax, and net salary of each individual plus total taxes withheld for all individuals.

6.18 Read two positive integers, n and m, and determine the quotient q and the remainder r such that $qm + r = n$, where $0 \leq r < m$.

6.19 Read a non-negative integer n, and determine whether it is even or odd. An integer is even if it can be divided by 2 with a remainder of 0. Output should include the input value, and indicate whether it is even or odd.

6.20 Read a number n, and determine if that number can be divided evenly, i.e., with a remainder of 0, by 3, 4, or 5. Output n and either 3, 4, 5, or the message: none, depending upon the results of the division. *Hint:* Some numbers can be divided evenly by more than one number.

6.21 Read two positive integers, n and m, and calculate the largest integer, r, such that $r^m \leq n$. In addition, if $r^m = n$, then write r, m, n, and the message; exact root. Otherwise, write r, m, n, and the message: not exact root.

6.22 Read a positive integer number n, and find all integer numbers that divide n evenly. Output n and all numbers found.

6.23 A positive integer, n, which is greater than 1, is a prime number if the only integers that divide it evenly are 1 and n. Read a number n, and determine whether it is a prime number. Output an appropriate message.

6.24 Read a single value of n and calculate the sum of the first n integers, i.e.,

$$\text{Sum} = 1 + 2 + 3 + \cdots + n = \sum_{i=1}^{n} i$$

Output n and the sum; n is a positive integer.

6.25 Develop a computerized procedure that calculates a value of s from the geometric series

$$s = a + ar + ar^2 + ar^3 + \cdots + ar^n = \sum_{i=0}^{n} ar^i$$

given values for a, r, and n.

6.26 Read two numbers, a and n, and compute a value for the following expression:

$$s = 1 + (1 + a) + (1 + 2a) + (1 + 3a) + \cdots + (1 + na) = \sum_{i=0}^{n} (1 + ia)$$

6.27 The factorial of a number n is represented by $n!$, mathematically defined as

$$n! = 1 \cdot 2 \cdot 3 \cdot \cdots \cdot (n - 1) \cdot n$$

which is the product of all integers from 1 to n where zero factorial is defined as 1. Read an integer that is greater than or equal to zero and output both the integer and its factorial.

6.28 One limitation of an actual computer is that it has a finite word size. Because factorials grow quite rapidly, word size can become extremely critical. As a result, it has been suggested that an additional number be read into a computer which will specify the absolute maximum value that a machine can hold. With this discussion in mind, modify Problem 6.27 so that it reads this additional number and checks to insure that n factorial does not exceed the capacity of a machine. If capacity is exceeded, print an appropriate message. Do you see any difficulty in using this checking procedure?

6.29 Develop a computerized procedure that reads an expression one character at a time and determines whether that expression exhibits proper use of parentheses.

6.30 Assume that in 1960 the populations of the United States and of Brazil were 180,000,000 and 85,000,000, respectively. If the United States has a 2% growth rate and Brazil has a 4% growth rate, in what year will Brazil's population equal or exceed that of the United States?

6.31 Given a set of positive numbers, determine its largest, smallest, and range (range is the difference between its largest and smallest number). Output this information along with the number of values in the set. The last input number will be negative. The largest number is known not to be greater than 99,999.

6.32 Social security taxes (F.I.C.A) are withheld from an individual's earnings at a rate of 4.8% of the amount earned during a period. Once total earnings for a year exceed $7800, the withholding rate drops to 0. Given earnings to date this year and earnings this pay period, calculate the F.I.C.A. tax withheld this period and the new total earnings to date this year.

6.33 Assume that two lists, A and B, contain a sequence of numbers $A_1, A_2, A_3, \ldots, A_n$ and $B_1, B_2, B_3, \ldots, B_m$. Develop a computerized procedure which collates these two lists into a single list in the sequence $A_1, B_1, A_2, B_2, A_3, B_3$, etc. Your computer will have two input devices, one for each list. The statement READ1 reads from the first; the statement READ2 reads from the second. The first number on each input list tells how many numbers are on the list, i.e., n and m. If one list is exhausted before the other, copy the remaining numbers onto the collated list.

6.34 Assume that two lists, A and B, contain numbers $A_1, A_2, A_3, \ldots, A_n$, and $B_1, B_2, B_3, \ldots, B_m$, which are in ascending numerical sequence. A list of numbers is in ascending sequence if each number is greater than or equal to the number it follows. Develop a computerized procedure that inputs the two ascending lists and outputs a single ascending list. Your computer will have two input devices, one for each list. The statement READ1 reads from the first list; the statement READ2 reads from the second list. The first number on each input list tells how many numbers are on the list, i.e., n and m.

6.35 Calculate the mean, m, and the standard deviation, d, of a set of numbers using the equations

$$m = \left(\sum_{i=1}^{n} x_i \right) / n$$

$$d = \left[\frac{\sum_{i=1}^{n} x_i^2 - \left(\sum_{i=1}^{n} x_i \right)^2 / n}{n-1} \right]^{0.5}$$

where

$$\sum_{i=1}^{n} x_i = x_1 + x_2 + x_3 + \cdots + x_n$$

$$\sum_{i=1}^{n} x_i^2 = x_1^2 + x_2^2 + x_3^2 + \cdots + x_n^2$$

6.36 (a) Develop a computerized procedure that calculates a depreciation schedule showing yearly depreciation, d, and undepreciated value, u, for each year throughout an item's expected life, y. Use straight-line depreciation equations shown, where c represents original cost and s represents salvage value after y years.

$$d = \frac{c - s}{y}$$

$$u = \text{(last year's } u) - d$$

(b) Repeat the preceding process, but use the following declining balance depreciation equations:

$$d = 2 \cdot \frac{\text{last year's } u}{y}$$

$$u = (\text{last year's } u) - d$$

(c) Combine steps (a) and (b) to find the year in which straight-line undepreciated value becomes less than that of declining balance.

6.37 A home mortgage repayment schedule can be calculated from the annual interest rate, r, mortgage amount, a, and constant monthly payment, m. Develop a computerized procedure that calculates values for the monthly interest payment, i, monthly principal payment, p, and new principal balance, b, for each month until b goes to zero. Assume that the monthly interest rate is $r/12$ and that $m > ar/12$. Care must be taken to ensure that the final payment reduces b exactly to 0.

6.38 Suppose you are given eight balls, all of which look alike. You are told that one ball is heavier than all others, which have identical weights. Develop a computerized procedure to identify the heavy ball by *executing* no more than three test statements in your flow chart. Assume that the balls are numbered from 1 to 8 and that the weights of the balls are supplied in numerical order, i.e., the weight of ball 1 comes first, etc.

6.39 A small company has three departments, X, Y, and Z. Each department has direct expenses and is also charged with a portion of the total expenses of the other two departments. The following table shows the direct expenses for each department and the percentage of its expenses charged to the other departments.

Department	Direct Costs	Percentage Charged		
		X	Y	Z
X	$25,000	—	2	8
Y	15,000	3	—	5
Z	40,000	7	4	—

Develop a computerized procedure that calculates the final costs, X, Y, and Z, for each department. *Hint:* This problem can be solved by using an iterative procedure where the costs of each department are calculated using the following equations:

$$X = \$25,000 + 0.02Y + 0.08Z$$
$$Y = \$15,000 + 0.03X + 0.05Z$$
$$Z = \$40,000 + 0.07X + 0.04Y$$

This process involves using each department equation in turn to calculate a new or closer approximation to the actual department cost. For example, the first iteration would calculate the following:

First, a new value of X is calculated, using the first equation and the direct costs of Y and Z.

$$X = \$25,000 + 0.02(15,000) + 0.08(40,000)$$
$$= 25,000 + 300 + 3200$$
$$= 28,500$$

Second, a new value of Y is calculated, using the second equation, the new value of X, and the direct cost of Z.

$$Y = \$15,000 + 0.03(28,500) + 0.05(40,000)$$
$$= 15,000 + 755 + 2000$$
$$= 17,755$$

Third, a new value of Z is calculated, using the third equation and the new values of X and Y.

$$Z = \$40,000 + 0.07(28,500) + 0.04(17,755)$$
$$= 40,000 + 1995 + 30.20$$
$$= 42,025.20$$

The preceding process is repeated until the sum of the changes of X, Y, and Z vary less than some small value, e.g., 1.0.

7 Single-Dimension Data Structures

Chapter 6 illustrated the use of single cells as a data structure for solving problems. The discussion showed that, in general, single cells are appropriate for problems involving relatively few data values or those having solutions that do not require all values in memory simultaneously. In the first case, individual values are assigned to separate cells, and all values are read into memory before computations begin; in the second, a few values are read and processed completely before additional ones are required in memory. In both situations, it is possible to process input data with a limited number of cells; however, not all problems fall into these two categories. Consequently, it is necessary to study other data structures.

This chapter introduces the *single-dimension* data structure as a structure that can be used for solving problems not suitable for single cells. It begins by illustrating limitations of single cells and by showing how single-dimension data structures overcome these drawbacks. Once the data- and flow-chart representations of a single-dimension data structure are presented, hazards and techniques of using this new structure are considered. Finally, a number of problems are solved that involve data that are best stored in single-dimension data structures.

7.1
Need for
Single-
Dimension
Data
Structures

So far, only single cells have been used to solve problems. As additional data structures are introduced, you will have to determine which structures are appropriate for your data. Let us begin our discussion of single-dimension data structures by solving a problem that is inappropriate for single cells. In so doing, we shall discover the limitations of single cells and, at the same time, illustrate how one realizes that he has selected the wrong data structure.

For purposes of discussion, let us suppose that we are required to calculate the average of a set of numbers and then determine how many of those numbers are above average. In other words, we must solve two smaller problems. First, we must calculate the average of a set of numbers, which involves summing individual values and then dividing the result by the number of values in that set. Second, we must compare each value with that average and count those that exceed it. Here, it is important to realize that the solution of the second subproblem is dependent upon that of the first.

This problem statement tells us that we must produce two values, an average and an above-average count, as shown in Figure 7.1. For the time being, let us assume that there are always three input quantities. Since the number of values is fixed, it is a simple matter to assign each to a separate single cell. Here, A, B, and C save three input quantities, whereas AVE and COUNT are used to calculate their average and above-average count. The flow chart begins by reading three values and then calculates their average. Finally, the above-average count is determined by three separate test statements, one for each input value.

Study of this flow chart reveals that input values are used twice. First, they are added to form an average; second, they are compared, in turn, with this average, which implies that input values must be retained in memory and that each value must have its own single cell. In other words, this problem cannot be solved by reading one input value and processing it completely before the next one is read.

Now that we have solved this problem for three values, let us increase its input and see how this affects our present solution. Since each input must have its own cell with a unique variable name, additional values require extra cells. For example, if the input is increased to 100 values, the data chart must include 100 separate cells with 100 different variable names. Furthermore, flow-chart statements that read these values and calculate their average must be expanded. Likewise, additional test statements are required for extra above-average comparisons. It is important to realize that any change in input necessitates revision of our original solution. This is the case if even a single input value is added or removed. Here, the flow-chart statements are long enough with just three input values, Those with 100 would be unbearably long, whereas 1000 would be out of the question.

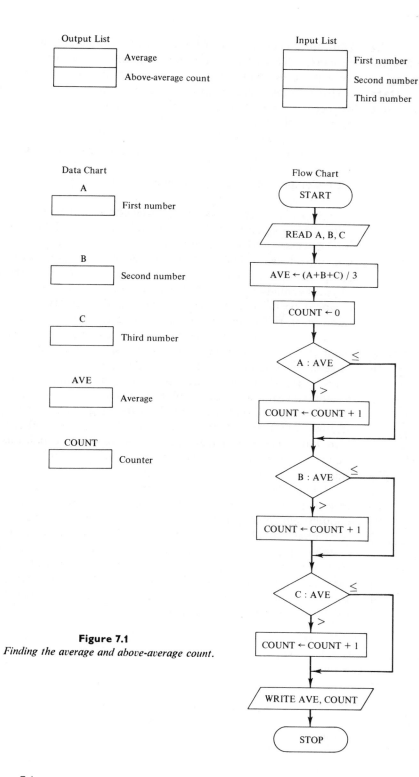

Figure 7.1
Finding the average and above-average count.

Difficulties encountered in the previous example are caused by choice of data structures. This problem no longer fits into one of the two categories suitable for single cells. Not only does it incorporate a variable number of data values, it also requires a large number of values in memory simultaneously. Therefore, we need a structure that handles such problems. To be successful, it must be able to store a large number of data values such that the number of values can be varied without revising problem solutions. Furthermore, it must permit us to reference any or all of its values without writing excessively long statements.

7.2.1 Components of a single-dimension data structure

A variety of structures have been designed to overcome the limitations of single cells. The most basic of these, the *single-dimension* data structure or *linear list*, was discussed briefly in Section 4.2.3 when the concept of data structure was introduced. Figure 7.2 shows that a single-dimension data structure is composed of a sequence of cells. Thus, this structure derives its name from its physical configuration, a set of cells laid out in a line in one dimension. Actually, it would be more convenient to refer to this structure as a *list*; but, as was said earlier, this term is reserved for a more complicated structure.

As always, each structure must have a name, and in Figure 7.2 the variable name A refers to all cells in the linear list. Cells of this structure are laid out in sequence one after another, and the number of cells in any one structure is arbitrary. However, once chosen, this number cannot, in general, be changed without revising a problem solution. Each cell is given a number, known as its *cell number*. Usually, cell numbers are integers and are assigned sequentially, starting with 1. In Figure 7.2, the linear list contains 100 cells, numbered from 1 to 100. Once in a while, other cell numbering schemes are employed. For example, sometimes it is easier to solve a particular problem if cell numbers start at 0, or even some negative value.

A linear list stores data values, one value per cell. Since the number of cells in a linear list is arbitrary, its size or length can be set such that it contains enough cells to store the largest anticipated data set. Usually, values are stored sequentially in a linear list starting with the first cell. When a data set does not contain enough values to fill a structure completely, excess cells are simply left vacant, as shown in Figure 7.2. Thus, it is necessary to know where in a structure data values end and where unused cells begin. This is done by storing the cell number of the last data value in a separate single cell, which will be referred to as the *last cell number*.

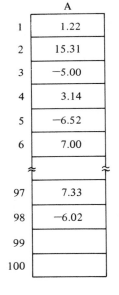

Last cell number

Cell pointer

Figure 7.2 *Data chart representation of a single-dimension data structure.*

Even though the last cell number is used in conjunction with a linear list, it alone is a data structure and, therefore, has its own variable name. In Figure 7.2, N is the last cell number and contains 98, the cell number of the last data value in A. Since a last cell number has a name, its contents can be changed via assignment or read statements just like any other single cell. Thus, a linear list handles different size data sets with only a change in the contents of its last cell number. Sometimes a linear list is used to store different data sets that always contain the same number of values. In such cases, the number of data values is a known constant; therefore, a last cell number is superfluous and need not be used.

Cell numbers, along with a structure name, are used to access contents of cells of a linear list. This is done by the notation

Variable name (cell number)

where the variable name identifies a linear list and the cell number specifies the particular cell within that structure. The absence of an arithmetic or logical operator between the variable name and left parenthesis indicates a reference to a specific cell in a linear list rather than an arithmetic or logical operation. In other words, A(3) specifies a reference to the third cell of A, whereas A × (3) denotes multiplication of a single cell, A, and a constant, 3. As a more complete example, let us assume that we wish to place the contents of the third cell of A into a single cell, X. Flow chart 1 in Figure 7.3 indicates how this is specified by an assignment statement, X←A(3). Before this statement is executed, X contains an arbitrary value, 12.2; afterward, it contains 8.7 and equals the contents of the third cell of A.

Sometimes it is necessary to reference different cells in a linear list from the same statement. This is done by the notation

Variable name (cell pointer)

As before, a variable name identifies a particular linear list, but now the *cell pointer* is a variable name of a single cell that contains the cell number of the desired cell. Flow chart 2 in Figure 7.3 shows how a cell pointer is used to reference a specific cell. Here, the assignment statement X←A(I) directs a computer first to find the current contents of cell pointer I, and then to use that value as a cell number to reference A. Since in this case I contains 3 the statement X←A(I) is equivalent to X←A(3); thus, both flow charts in Figure 7.3 produce the same results.

A cell pointer should literally be thought of as a *cell* that *points* to a specific cell in a linear list. When you see or use the notation A(I), you should visualize the single cell, I, as an arrow pointing to a specific cell in A. For example, in data chart 1 in Figure 7.4, I contains a value of one, and thus points to the first cell of A. In data chart 2, I has been incremented by one and now points to the second cell of A. Thus, changing the contents of a cell pointer implies shifting the termination point of its imaginary arrow.

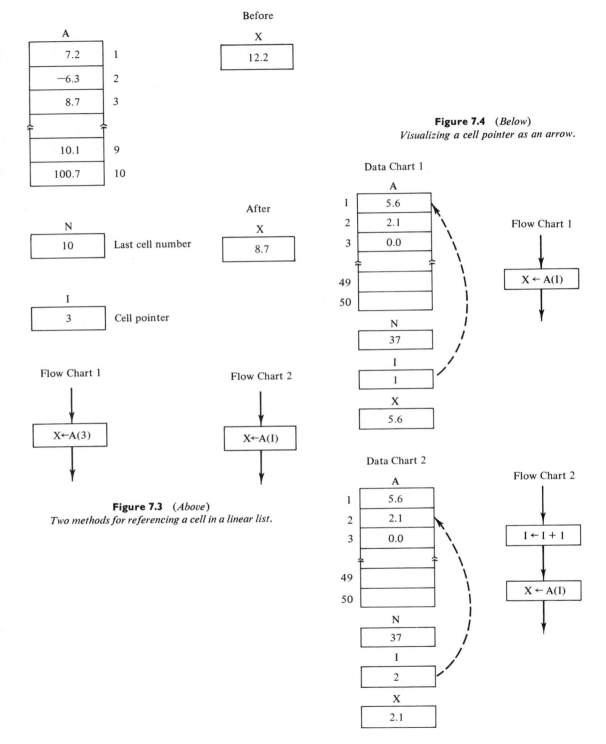

A

7.2	1
−6.3	2
8.7	3
10.1	9
100.7	10

Before

X

| 12.2 |

Figure 7.4 (*Below*)
Visualizing a cell pointer as an arrow.

N

| 10 | Last cell number

After

X

| 8.7 |

I

| 3 | Cell pointer

Data Chart 1

A

1	5.6
2	2.1
3	0.0
49	
50	

N

| 37 |

I

| 1 |

X

| 5.6 |

Flow Chart 1

X ← A(I)

Flow Chart 1

X←A(3)

Flow Chart 2

X←A(I)

Figure 7.3 (*Above*)
Two methods for referencing a cell in a linear list.

Data Chart 2

A

1	5.6
2	2.1
3	0.0
49	
50	

N

| 37 |

I

| 2 |

X

| 2.1 |

Flow Chart 2

I ← I + 1

X ← A(I)

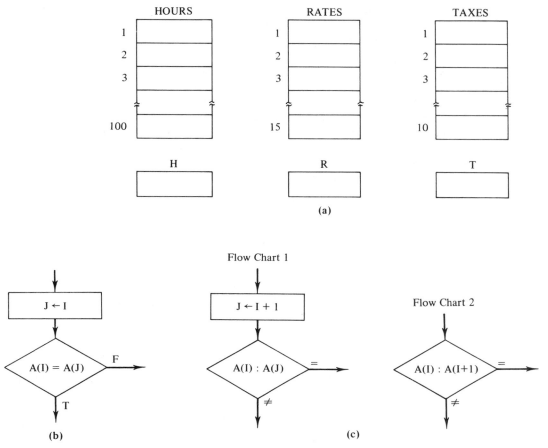

Figure 7.5 *Examples of cell pointers: (a) a separate cell pointer for each structure; (b) using two different cell pointers; (c) an expression as a cell pointer.*

As you produce your data and flow charts, you will find it a good practice to use a different cell pointer for each linear list. In that way, each cell pointer has its own unique function, and you should be less likely to confuse or intermix them. For example, Figure 7.5a shows a data chart that contains three linear lists, each with its own cell pointer. On the other hand, a separate cell pointer for each structure is not an absolute requirement. Sometimes, problem solutions require that the same cell pointer be used for two or more linear lists or that more than one cell pointer access the same structure. For example, the flow chart in Figure 7.5b illustrates the use of two different cell pointers to access the same structure. Since the assignment statement, J←I, ensures that both cell pointers contain the same value, the result of the logical test is always true. Although trivial, this chart illustrates that there is nothing magical about the variable name of a cell pointer. A computer cares about the current contents

−2.3, 7.3, 0, −1.7, 2.6

	X
1	−2.3
2	7.3
3	0
4	−1.7
5	2.6
6	
7	
8	
9	
10	

N
5

of a cell pointer, not its variable name. Finally, we will find it desirable to be able to access cells of a linear list by combining a cell pointer into an expression and using the current value of that expression as a cell number. For example, suppose that we wish to compare adjacent cells of a linear list, A. We could use the sequence of statements shown in flow chart 1 of Figure 7.5c, but the single statement in flow chart 2 is certainly more convenient. In general, a cell pointer can be any expression whose value is an integer.

Since a linear list is itself a sequence of cells, it can store a set of numbers such that the sequence of those numbers is retained in memory. For example, in a linear list X, the first cell of X appears before the second cell, and the second appears before the third, etc. Thus, data values stored in X can be thought of as forming an ordered set

$$X(1), X(2), X(3), \ldots, X(N)$$

where N is the last cell number of X. Figure 7.6 shows an example of how an ordered set is stored in a linear list such that its original sequence is maintained.

Figure 7.6 *Storing an ordered data set in a linear list.*

In the field of mathematics, an ordered data set is referred to as a *vector*, and the vector, X, is written using the notation

$$x_1, x_2, x_3, \ldots, x_n$$

where a *subscript* indicates the arrangement or sequence of individual data values. Therefore, when a linear list is used to store an ordered data set, it is the equivalent of a mathematical vector and its cell pointer is the counterpart of a subscript.

Linear lists are sometimes classified by the manner in which data are added to or removed from them. A *stack* is a linear list in which all additions and removals are made at one end. Stacks are often referred to as LIFO (Last In, First Out) or *push-down* lists. A *queue* is a linear list in which all additions are made at one end and all removals are made at the other. Queues are sometimes known as FIFO (First In, First Out). Finally, a *deque* (pronounced "deck") is a linear list in which additions and removals are made at either end.

7.2.2 Storing a single-dimension data structure in memory

Section 6.1.2 described how memory space is assigned to single cells. Basically, when a computer compiles a program into machine language, it scans that program looking for variable names. When it finds one that it has not seen before, it assigns that variable to the next available memory location. For the remainder of the program, that name is associated with that location. This allocation process continues until memory space has been assigned to all variables.

When a program incorporates both single cells and linear lists, a computer must be able to distinguish them and must assign the proper number of words to each. It is easy for a computer to differentiate the two because a variable name of a linear list is always followed by a left parenthesis. When a computer finds a single cell, it can immediately reserve one location, but such is not the case for linear lists. Since they consist of an arbitrary number of cells, we must tell a computer the size or length of each linear list. This is done when you convert your data and flow charts into an actual program by using a special instruction, whose form depends upon your particular programming language. In FORTRAN, a dimension statement is used to specify the length of a linear list, whereas a declare statement is used in PL/I.

Once a computer is told the length of each linear list, memory space allocation is straightforward. Since a linear list has the same construction as memory —i.e., a sequence of locations—a computer assigns words to a linear list by simply allocating the required number starting with the next free location in memory. Figure 7.7 illustrates how a portion of memory might look for a program that includes both single cells and linear lists. This figure shows that a computer first allocated three locations to single-cell variables, X, Y, and Z, and then reserved 10 words for a linear list A, followed by single cells N and I. Once space is allocated to a linear list, there is a high probability that it will be trapped between or bounded on both sides by other data structures, as in Figure 7.7. Consequently, it is usually not possible to change the size or length of a linear list without first moving or rearranging other structures. Some programming languages, such as PL/I, do provide a facility for readjusting data structure size after original allocation of memory space. Such a procedure is referred to as *dynamic storage allocation*. Finally, you should be aware that cell numbers of a linear list do not appear in memory but are implicit in the sequential arrangement of its individual cells. In other words, a computer need remember only the address of the first cell of a linear list, and then it can use that address plus a cell number or the contents of a cell pointer to locate any desired cell. Thus, cell numbers should be thought of as being *relative* to the first cell of a structure.

7.2.3 Overcoming cell pointer hazards

When a cell pointer is used to access the contents of a linear list, care must be taken to ensure that it always contains the correct cell number relative to the first cell of its structure. Figure 7.8 illustrates a memory layout that includes a linear list preceded by three single cells, X, Y, and Z. This linear list has a variable name A and consists of 10 cells containing 8 data values. It has a last cell number, N, and I is its cell pointer. Suppose, for example, that one wishes to use the cell pointer I to move the contents of the third cell of A into X. Flow chart 1 shows two assignment statements that correctly perform this operation. Here, the first statement ensures that I contains the correct cell number before the second uses it to access A(I).

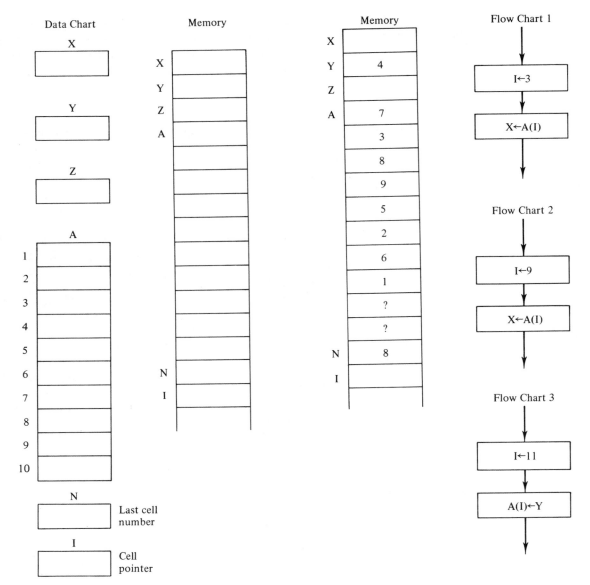

Figure 7.7
Storing a linear list in memory.

Figure 7.8
The hazards of using a cell pointer.

As a second example, suppose that the situation is as shown in flow chart 2. Here, the cell pointer is set to 9 and then is used to move A(I) into X. The last cell number, N, indicates that only the first 8 cells of A currently contain data values. Not knowing the difference, a computer would obediently use I to access the ninth cell of A. Consequently, the computer would reference a cell whose contents have not previously been defined; now the contents of X are likewise unknown.

Flow chart 3 shows a similar example. Here, a cell pointer is set to 11 and then used to move the contents of Y into A(I). As previously described, a computer finds the eleventh cell by counting from the first cell. For the memory layout shown in Figure 7.8, A(11) is at the same memory location as N. Therefore, when I is 11 the statement A(I)←Y destroys the original contents of N and replaces them by a value of 4. Now, when N is used as a last cell number it will indicate that the last data value is stored in A(4). Thus, data values in cells 5 through 8 will be ignored and, in effect, are lost.

The preceding examples indicate that faulty cell pointers can produce incorrect results and even destroy data values. In the last two, the value of a cell pointer became too large and exceeded the last cell number of its linear list. On the other hand, a pointer also causes trouble if its contents are less than one. In either case, a computer accesses cells that contain data values which are not members of the data set currently stored in the structure. When this happens, a cell pointer is said to be *out-of-bounds*.

If we are to use cell pointers successfully, we must always ensure that they stay *in-bounds*, which implies that we should examine the contents of each cell pointer before it is used to access a linear list. In the examples that follow, we shall see that we can control the contents of a cell pointer by following the same four-step sequence of initialize, test, process, and increment, that we used in Chapter 6. In this case, a cell pointer acts as a data counter in the generalized flow chart shown in Figure 7.9. In the initialize step, a cell pointer is given an initial value. In many cases, we shall want to start by accessing the first cell of a structure; thus, we shall give its cell pointer an initial value of 1. By so doing, we ensure that the cell pointer is in-bounds at the lower end of the structure. Next, in the test step, we check to see that it is also in-bounds at the upper end.

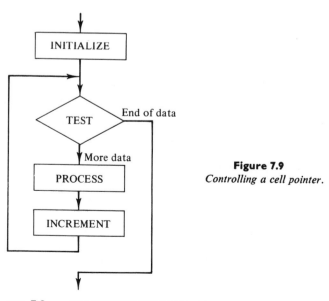

Figure 7.9
Controlling a cell pointer.

Usually, this means comparing the cell pointer with the last cell number of a structure. In the process step, the cell pointer can be used in any number of flow-chart statements without fear of accessing an out-of-bounds or undefined location. Finally, the cell pointer is advanced in the increment step so that it points to the next data value; then the flow chart loops back to the test step to check that the cell pointer is still in-bounds.

7.3 Using Single-Dimension Data Structures

Now that we know how the structure of a linear list differs from that of a single cell, let us use it to solve problems. After all, the purpose of studying linear lists is to have a structure that makes it possible to solve problems the data of which are inappropriate for single cells. With the availability of this second structure, it becomes necessary to be able to determine when and where to use each structure.

7.3.1 Finding the sum of a set of numbers

As our first example of the use of single-dimension data structures, let us develop a computerized procedure that finds the sum of a set of numbers. In the next section, we rework the above-average problem previously discussed in Section 7.1. Since that problem requires us to find the sum of a set of numbers already in memory, let us solve that smaller problem here. In other words, our solution must input all values before it begins to calculate their sum. By so doing, we shall see how linear lists overcome the limitations of single cells.

Let us begin by solving this problem for three input values. Once this is done, we can expand our solution to handle more. For this restriction, our output and input are shown in Figure 7.10. Previously, we had only one form of data structure, the single cell, and had no choice but to use it to store all data values. Now that we have a second form, we must be able to decide when it is best to use each type of structure. Since the sum of the input is still a single value, let us assign it to a single cell, SUM. In contrast, input consists in three numbers that must all be in memory at the same time. In this case, let us store them in a linear list, A, which contains three cells numbered from 1 to 3, as shown in the data chart in Figure 7.10. Since A always contains three values, its last cell number is constant, and there is no need for a separate single cell to act as a last cell number. Finally, let us use a single cell, I, as a cell pointer for A.

From the previous discussions, an algorithm for this problem is obvious. First, we read three input values; then we find their sum. Only now, data values must be stored into and accessed from a linear list via a cell pointer. Of course, we can explicitly reference each value by variable name and cell number using statements,

$$\text{READ } A(1), A(2), A(3)$$

and

$$\text{SUM} \leftarrow A(1) + A(2) + A(3)$$

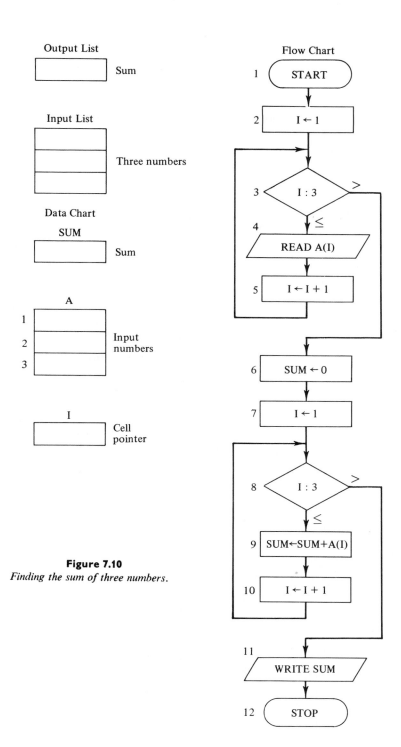

Output List

	Sum

Input List

Three numbers

Data Chart

SUM

Sum

A

1	
2	
3	

Input numbers

I

Cell pointer

Figure 7.10
Finding the sum of three numbers.

Flow Chart

1 START

2 I ← 1

3 I : 3   >

4 READ A(I)   ≤

5 I ← I + 1

6 SUM ← 0

7 I ← 1

8 I : 3   >

9 SUM←SUM+A(I)   ≤

10 I ← I + 1

11 WRITE SUM

12 STOP

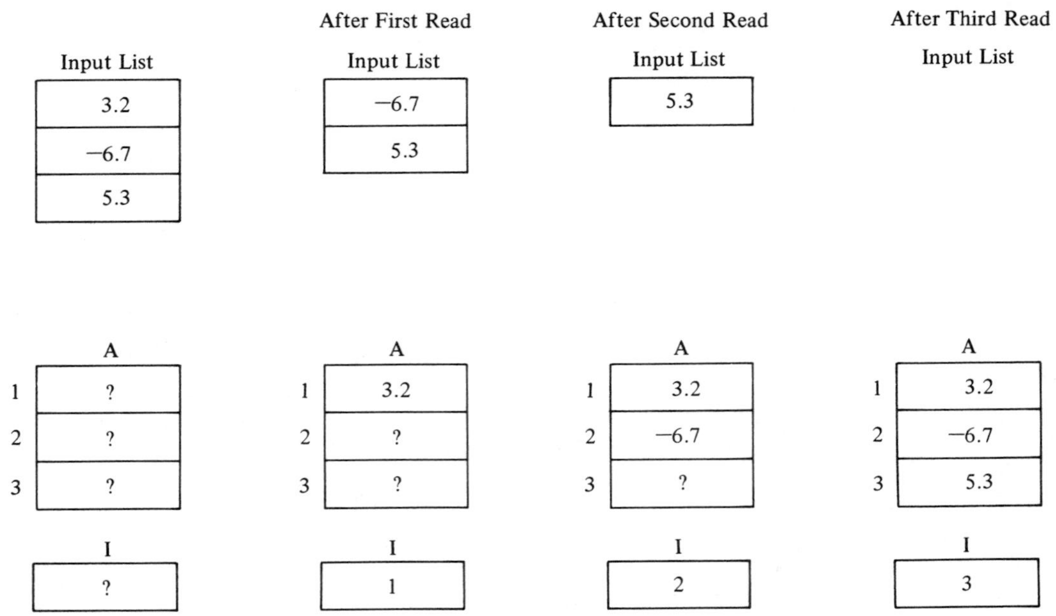

	After First Read	After Second Read	After Third Read
Input List	Input List	Input List	Input List
3.2	−6.7	5.3	
−6.7	5.3		
5.3			

	A		A		A		A
1	?	1	3.2	1	3.2	1	3.2
2	?	2	?	2	−6.7	2	−6.7
3	?	3	?	3	?	3	5.3

I	I	I	I
?	1	2	3

Figure 7.11 (*Above*) *The effect of the execution of the READ A(I) instruction.*

Figure 7.12 (*Below*) *Trace of flow chart in Figure 7.10.*

Step No.	Flow Chart No.	Value of Variables					Test	Result
		I	SUM	A(1)	A(2)	A(3)		
1	1	?	?	?	?	?		
2	2	1						
3	3						1 : 3	≤
4	4			3.2				
5	5	2						
6	3						2 : 3	≤
7	4				−6.7			
8	5	3						
9	3						3 : 3	≤
10	4					5.3		
11	5	4						
12	3						4 : 3	>
13	6		0					
14	7	1						
15	8						1 : 3	≤
16	9		3.2					
17	10	2						
18	8						2 : 3	≤
19	9		−3.5					
20	10	3						
21	8						3 : 3	≤
22	9		1.8					
23	10	4						
24	8						4 : 3	>
25	11							
26	12							

Although valid, these statements have the same limitations as those with single cells in the previous section. Because each cell is referenced explicitly by name, these statements must be revised whenever the number of input values is changed. Furthermore, these statements become unmanageable as input increases. Let us now use a cell pointer to overcome these obstacles.

We see that we wish to input three numbers into cells: A(1), A(2), A(3). Examination of this sequence shows that cell numbers begin at 1 and increase by 1 until a value of 3 is reached. Thus, the statement READ A(I) can be used to input all data values if it is executed with the proper values of I. This can be done by using the four-step procedure of initialize, test, process, and increment, which was discussed in the previous section as a means of controlling cell pointers. The first part of the flow chart in Figure 7.10 incorporates these four steps as follows:

Initialize:	$I \leftarrow 1$
Test:	$I : 3$
Process:	READ A(I)
Increment:	$I \leftarrow I + 1$

In the initialize step, the cell pointer I is set to 1 and is, therefore, in-bounds at the lower end of A. The test step then checks the upper boundary by comparing I with 3. Only when I is known to be in-bounds is it used in the processing step to access a cell in A. Since I has a value of 1, the read statement appears as READ A(1), and the first input value is transmitted to the first cell of A. The increment step adds 1 to I, and then the flow chart loops back to see if the cell pointer has reached its upper bound. Since I is less than or equal to 3, the process step is repeated and now appears as READ A(2). The loop is executed for each value of I until it becomes larger than 3. When I equals 4, the test terminates the read loop. Figure 7.11 shows how each execution of the read statement changes the appearance of both sample input and the linear list, A.

Now that input values have been read into memory, we are ready to develop a procedure that finds their sum. In the previous chapter, we performed addition by processing each value as it was read into a single cell, A, using the statement,

$$SUM \leftarrow SUM + A$$

In this case, since input values are stored in a linear list, A, we can find their sum by executing the statement,

$$SUM \leftarrow SUM + A(I)$$

for values of I from 1 to 3, after the single cell, SUM, has been given an initial value of 0. The same four-step sequence can again be used to control the cell pointer, as shown in the lower portion of the flow chart in Figure 7.10, where the steps are as follows:

Initialize:	$I \leftarrow 1$
Test:	$I : 3$

Process: SUM←SUM + A(I)
Increment: I←I + 1

When a computer reaches the statement SUM←SUM + A(I), SUM is 0 and I equals 1. Therefore, the statement is executed as SUM←A(1). After I is incremented by 1, the flow chart loops back to see if the upper bound of A has been exceeded. Since I is less than 3, the summation statement is reached for a second time, with SUM containing a value equal to A(1) and with I at 2. Thus, the statement is executed as SUM←A(1) + A(2). Each time the loop is repeated, the next value from A is added to SUM. After three times through the loop, the test stops the process, and SUM contains a value, A(1) + A(2) + A(3). Figure 7.12 shows the results of a step-by-step table-top debug trace of the complete flow chart, using the input list of Figure 7.11.

Now that we have solved this problem for three input values, let us expand our solution so that it sums any number of values. However, we are told that the size of the input set never exceeds some known maximum, which, for this discussion, is assumed to be 100. Since the result is still a single number, the output contains one value, as shown in Figure 7.13. However, because input size varies, we must tell a computer how to recognize when it has read all its input. In this case, let us assume that a data value count is placed at the top of the input, as was done in the previous chapter.

A variable input list affects our selection of data structures. Of course, a single cell is required to store the sum; but now we need a structure that can save up to 100 data values. This is done by specifying a linear list, A, with 100 cells numbered from 1 to 100. Since A contains a variable number of data values, it is necessary to remember where the last one is stored. For this, let us use a single cell, N, as a last cell number for A. Finally, let I be a cell pointer for A.

Now, we must modify our flow chart so that it handles a variable number of values. Since the number of input data values also equals the last cell number of A, we should read the input data count into N. Therefore, it is necessary to insert the statement READ N between the start statement and the initialize step of the read loop. Previously, we compared the cell pointer, I, with a constant, 3, to see if all input values had been read. Now, we wish to know when I exceeds the last cell number of A. Consequently, N replaces 3 in the test step of the read loop—likewise in the addition loop, so that it, too, is executed N times.

Figure 7.13 shows a final solution for finding the sum of a set of numbers that must all be in memory simultaneously. Individual flow-chart statements are quite compact and need not be revised when the number of input values is altered. Furthermore, the solution handles any number of values from 0 to 100. Thus, for this problem, a linear list overcomes the limitations of single cells. Actually, this flow chart can handle more than 100 values, but that upper bound is placed upon our solution by the size of the linear list A. Great care must be exercised to ensure that the number of input values never exceeds 100. If it does, the flow chart as presently drawn will not detect this error, and the read loop will store excess data values beyond the upper boundary of A.

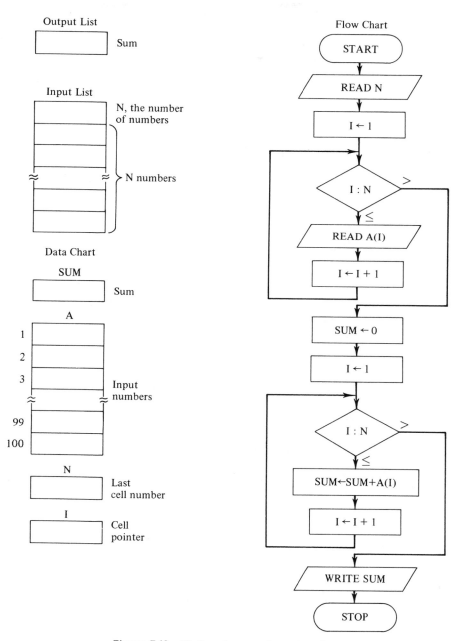

Figure 7.13 *Finding the sum of a set numbers*

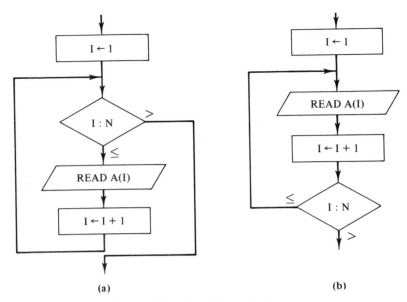

Figure 7.14 *Controlling cell pointers:*
(a) test-before-process; (b) test-after-process.

At this point, one might wonder why it is necessary to test a cell pointer immediately after it has just been assigned a value in the initialize step. In other words, why not test after the process step has been completed for the first time? The flow charts in Figure 7.14 illustrate two possible arrangements of the four cell pointer control steps. As in the previous chapter, when the test is located before the process step, it is referred to as *test before process*; if the order is reversed, it is known as *test after process*. A table-top trace of these two charts reveals that the read loop in the first is executed only if I is less than or equal to N; in the second, the loop is always executed at least once. This difference can be significant if N happens to be less than 1. In the first case, the chart branches around the read loop; in the second, the chart directs a computer to read one value into A(1), even though the input may be empty. Since we must always produce flow charts that handle all possibilities, it is a good policy to use test before process.

7.3.2 Calculating an average and above-average count

As our second example of single-dimension data structures, let us now extend our summation solution so that it calculates the average of a set of numbers and then determines how many are above average. We are told that a set can contain any number of values up to some known maximum, which, for this discussion, is assumed to be 500. We are also told that individual numbers can have any value—i.e., positive, negative, or zero—and that we shall know in advance how many values are in each set.

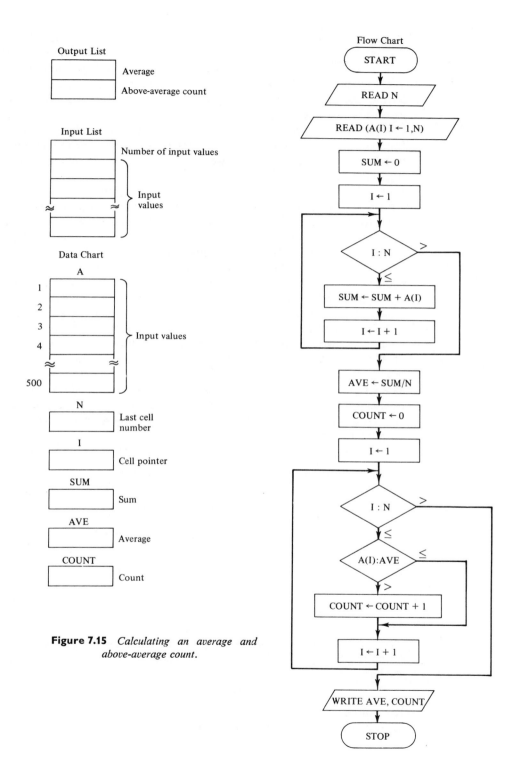

Figure 7.15 *Calculating an average and above-average count.*

Since this problem is similar to the one solved with single cells in Section 7.1, we know that our solution must produce two output values, as shown in Figure 7.15. Only now, our input consists of a variable number of values. Since we must always tell a computer how to recognize the end of its input, let the first input quantity specify the number of values that follow. Inasmuch as we are just interested in finding an average and above-average count, input order is not important, which means that individual values can be arranged in any sequence. In contrast, if we wished to determine the location of those numbers that exceed average, we would be forced to retain values in their original sequence.

Now that we have specified the output and input, let us select our data structures. From the output, we see that two values must be saved. Let us use AVE for the average and COUNT for the above-average count. Furthermore, calculation of an average requires summing the input. For this, let us use a single cell, SUM. Input requirements dictate that we store a set of numbers. Since the size of this set varies and since all values must be in memory simultaneously, let us store them in a linear list. Arbitrarily, let us name this structure A; the problem definition tells us that A must contain 500 cells, as shown in Figure 7.15. Finally, we must specify two single cells as a last cell number and cell pointer for A. For this, let us use N and I, respectively.

Finally, we can devise an algorithm and draw its flow chart. From the problem definition, we know that we must first read all input data. At this point, we should notice that input for this problem has the same construction as that of the previous one. Consequently, we can employ the same read procedure as was used in that problem. Since we shall use such read loops in solving various problems, let us agree to compress them into a single flow-chart statement

$$READ(A(I) \ I \leftarrow 1,N,1)$$

which is shorthand for a read loop, as follows:

Here, a pair of parentheses specifies the scope or boundaries of the loop. If the increment value is 1, it can be omitted; the read statement is further shortened to

$$READ \ (A(I) \ I \leftarrow 1,N)$$

Remember that these shorthand statements specify the same four operations as the read loop in Figure 7.16, and also imply test before process.

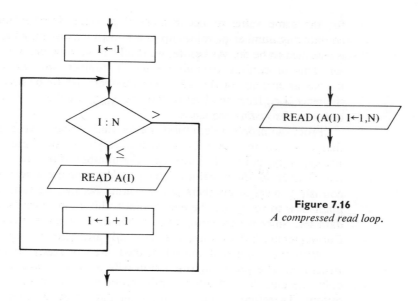

Figure 7.16
A compressed read loop.

Once input is in memory, we are ready to calculate its average. This involves finding a sum and then dividing it by the number of values in the set. Here, we need only append an assignment statement, AVE←SUM/N, after the summation loop that was used in Figure 7.13. Now we are ready to compare each input value one at a time in sequence with AVE. As before, we use the same four-step sequence to control our cell pointer:

Initialize:	I←1
Test:	I : N
Process:	A(I) : AVE
	COUNT←COUNT + 1
Increment:	I←I + 1

Note that in this case, the process step includes two statements. Here, if A(I) is greater than AVE, COUNT is incremented by 1. In general, there is no limit to the number of statements in this step, but the other three always consist of just one. You should now stop and trace the flow chart in Figure 7.15 with sample input to ensure that you understand how these four steps provide cell pointer control.

7.3.3 Sorting a set of numbers

As our third example of single-dimension data structures, let us suppose that we have the following problem. We are given a set of numbers and are asked to develop a computerized procedure that arranges it into numerical sequence such that the smallest input number is the first output value, the next smallest input is the second output, etc., until, finally, the largest input is the last output. We are told that input numbers can take on any value and that it is possible for the same value to occur more than once. Furthermore, the input can contain any number of values up to a known maximum, which for this problem is assumed to be 50. As before, we shall be told how many numbers are in each set. This process of arranging a set of numbers into numerical sequence is known as *sorting*. In this case, the numbers are to be arranged in *ascending* sequence, i.e., from smallest to largest. They could also be arranged in reverse order or *descending* sequence.

From the problem definition, we see that our solution must produce output that is sorted in ascending sequence, as shown in Figure 7.17. The output size can vary, but we do know that the number of output values always equals the number of input values. The problem statement tells us that the input consists of a set of numbers plus a count. Because we must always tell a computer how to recognize the end of input, this count must be at the front of the data set. Since we are going to sort this set, its input sequence is unimportant. Consequently, it does not matter how it is arranged as long as its count is first.

With the input and output defined, we are ready to determine the data structures. The preceding discussion tells us that we are actually dealing with only one data set. In other words, every input number must also appear as output. Therefore, we can use the same data structure to store both input and output. To do so, this structure must be able to store a large number of data values, and, at the same time, must retain their numerical order. A linear list with its sequential cell arrangement satisfies these requirements. Thus, let us use a linear list A, which contains 50 cells with a last cell number, N, and a cell pointer, I, as shown in Figure 7.17.

Finally, we can determine an algorithm and produce its flow chart. From the preceding, we realize that we must first read the complete input into A. From the problem definition, we know that every number in A must be less than or equal to the one that follows it, i.e., $A(I) \leq A(I+1)$ must be true. When this relationship is true for all adjacent numbers in A, its values are sorted. Thus, we must compare $A(I)$ with $A(I+1)$ for all values of I. If $A(I)$ is greater than $A(I+1)$, these two values are out of sequence and must be interchanged. When we compare all number pairs in A without making a single interchange, the set is in sequence and ready for output. Let us use a single cell, SWITCH, to remember whether an interchange has been made. Initially, SWITCH is set to 0; when an interchange is performed, SWITCH is set to 1. If SWITCH is still 0 after all number pairs have been compared, the set is in sequence. In contrast, if SWITCH is 1, it must be reset to 0, and the comparison process repeated. Since SWITCH was not anticipated earlier, it must be added to the data chart.

Figure 7.17 shows a flow chart that incorporates this algorithm. Because it works by interchanging number pairs, it is commonly known as an *interchange sort*. Notice that in the test step, I is compared with $N-1$ rather than N. The reason is that there are just $N-1$ adjacent number pairs in N numbers. If the comparisons are stopped when I exceeds N rather than $N-1$, a computer would compare $A(N)$ with $A(N+1)$, which is beyond the upper boundary of the input data set.

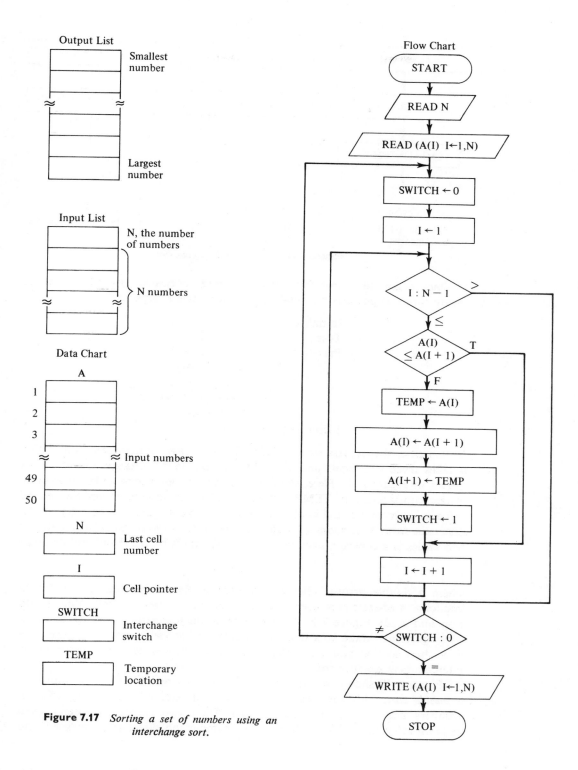

Output List

Smallest number

Largest number

Input List

N, the number of numbers

} N numbers

Data Chart

A

1
2
3

≈ Input numbers

49
50

N   Last cell number

I   Cell pointer

SWITCH   Interchange switch

TEMP   Temporary location

Figure 7.17 *Sorting a set of numbers using an interchange sort.*

Flow Chart

START

READ N

READ (A(I) I←1,N)

SWITCH ← 0

I ← 1

I : N − 1   >

≤

A(I) ≤ A(I + 1)   T

F

TEMP ← A(I)

A(I) ← A(I + 1)

A(I+1) ← TEMP

SWITCH ← 1

I ← I + 1

SWITCH : 0   ≠

=

WRITE (A(I) I←1,N)

STOP

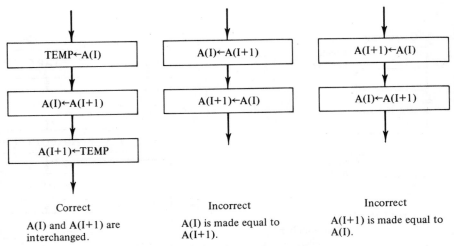

Figure 7.18 *Interchanging two numbers.*

Once again, the same four steps are used to control processing and to ensure that cell pointers stay in-bounds. Here, these steps are

$$
\begin{array}{ll}
\text{Initialize:} & \text{I}\leftarrow 1 \\
\text{Test:} & \text{I : N}-1 \\
\text{Process:} & \text{A(I) : A(I}+1) \\
& \text{TEMP}\leftarrow\text{A(I)} \\
& \text{A(I)}\leftarrow\text{A(I}+1) \\
& \text{A(I}+1)\leftarrow\text{TEMP} \\
& \text{SWITCH}\leftarrow 1 \\
\text{Increment:} & \text{I}\leftarrow\text{I}+1
\end{array}
$$

In this case, the process step includes five flow-chart statements. Notice that it takes three statements and an additional cell to interchange two values, as shown in Figure 7.18. Here, the first statement saves a copy of the first value in temporary location, TEMP, whereas the next statement moves the second value in over the first. Finally, the third statement transfers the copy of the first value from its temporary location to that of the second. Since interchanging two values is a common occurrence, let us specify it by the shorthand notation

$$\text{A(I)}\leftrightarrow\text{A(I}+1)$$

where a double arrow indicates interchange. Remember that this notation implies a three-statement operation that includes a temporary cell. You should stop and study Figure 7.17 to ensure that you understand this interchange-sort algorithm. Make up a small input data set and use it to table-top trace the flow chart so that you can actually see how it moves data into sequence by interchanging number pairs.

Figure 7.19 shows two variations of a second sorting algorithm known as a *bubble sort*. This sort scans down an input data set comparing adjacent numbers until it finds an inverted pair. These two values are interchanged as in an interchange sort, only now, the comparison direction is reversed, and

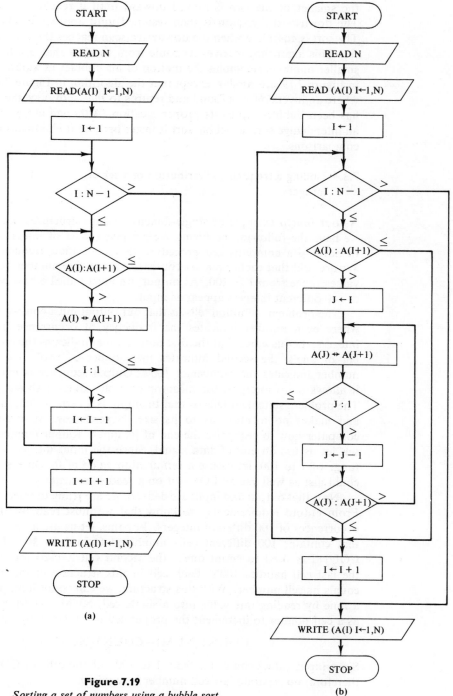

Figure 7.19
Sorting a set of numbers using a bubble sort.

the smaller of the two is moved upward until it reaches its proper position. The downward direction is then resumed until another inversion is detected. The sort is complete when the downward scan reaches the end of the input data set. This algorithm receives its name from the fact that upward movement of smaller numbers resembles the motion of air bubbles in water. The flow charts in Figure 7.19 are similar, except that the algorithm in Figure 7.19b remembers where an inversion was found and returns to that spot once the smaller number has been bubbled up to its proper location. Although more complicated than an interchange sort, a bubble sort is faster because it eliminates many unneeded comparisons.

7.3.4 Finding a frequency distribution of a set of integers

As our fourth example of single-dimension data structures, let us assume that we have the following problem. We are given a set of integers and are asked to develop a computerized procedure that finds their frequency distribution. We are told that each input set consists of a variable number of integers whose values range from 1 to 100. As output, we must indicate how many times each of 100 different integers appear as input.

The problem definition tells us that our output must consist of 100 numbers, where each number indicates the frequency of occurrence of 1 of the 100 integers. Let us agree that the first output value indicates the count of the number of one's, the second indicates the number of two's, etc., until the last number indicates the number of 100's. Output sequence is important because it allows us to interpret the meaning of each value, as shown in Figure 7.20. The problem statement tells us that the input is a variable length set of numbers and makes no mention as to its size. Nevertheless, we must always tell a computer how to recognize the end of its input. Rather than count each input set, let us use an end-of-data signal, Since the input integers are limited to a range of 1 to 100, let us use a termination value of 0. On the other hand, we could just as well use an EOF exit on a read statement.

Now that output and input are defined, we are ready to select data structures. From output requirements, we know that we must read the input and count occurrences of 100 different integers. For this, let us use a linear list, COUNT, that contains 100 different cells numbered from 1 to 100. The first cell of COUNT is used to count one's, the second cell is used for two's, etc., until the last cell handles 100's. Each cell in this structure counts the integer that equals its cell number. With this structure, we can count input numbers one at a time by reading one value into a single cell, NUM. NUM can then be used as a cell pointer to increment the proper cell in COUNT by the statement

$$COUNT(NUM) \leftarrow COUNT(NUM) + 1$$

Since input values can range from 1 to 100, all 100 cells of COUNT are used; therefore, no separate last cell number is required.

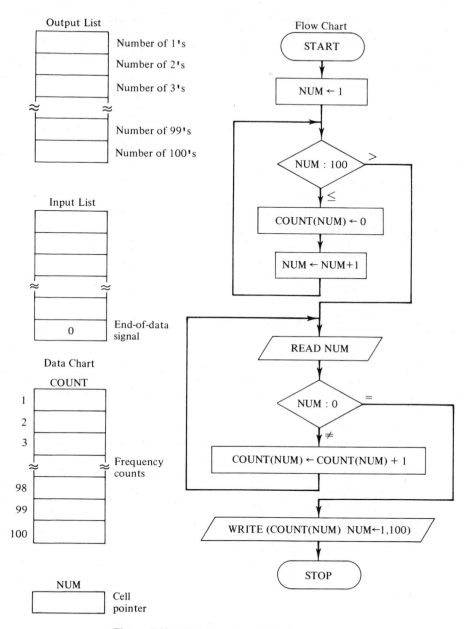

Figure 7.20 *Finding an integer frequency count.*

With these data structures, we are ready to develop an algorithm and to draw its flow chart. Since we are going to use COUNT as a set of 100 separate counters, it is necessary that all 100 cells be initialized to 0. In this way, if a given integer does not occur as input, its cell contains 0 at the end. COUNT can be zeroed by using a loop, as shown in Figure 7.20, where the four cell pointer steps are

Initialize:	NUM$\leftarrow$1
Test:	NUM : 100
Process:	COUNT(NUM)$\leftarrow$0
Increment:	NUM$\leftarrow$NUM $+$ 1

Once COUNT has been initialized properly, the counting operation begins by reading one value at a time and processing it completely before the next value is read. As each input value is read, it is necessary to check to see if it is the end-of-data-signal. If it is not, the input value is used as its own cell number to increment the proper cell of COUNT. The flow chart then loops back to read the next input number. Once the termination signal is detected, 100 COUNT values are transmitted as output. In previous examples, cells of linear lists were accessed in sequence starting at the top. Here, they are referenced at random depending upon input values.

7.3.5 Using a table lookup

As our fifth example of single-dimension data structures, let us assume that we are asked by a company to develop a computerized procedure that analyzes and summarizes a set of sales transactions. As background, we are told that this company has assigned a unique number to each of its different items. Furthermore, the sale of an item is considered a transaction and is reported separately by item number and quantity sold. Thus, we receive a set of transactions and are to produce a sales summary that lists total items sold as a function of item number.

In the previous section, we found a frequency count of a set of integers. There, output order indicated the meaning of each count. For example, the first result specified the number of one's present as input. Here, each sales total should be labeled with its associated item number, as shown in Figure 7.21, for easier identification. This is particularly important for a report that may be read by indivuduals who have no reason to understand how it was generated. If we are to label each count explicitly with an item number, we must know these item numbers in advance. Consequently, they are placed at the top of the input. If these numbers are preceded by a count, it is possible to add and delete item numbers without modifying our solution. Finally, there are two input values per transaction, where the first value indicates item number and the second specifies quantity sold. For the time being, let us assume transactions occur randomly, as they would if processed directly from salesmen.

With output and input specified, we are ready to consider data characteristics in order to select data structures. Output requirements tell us to produce labeled

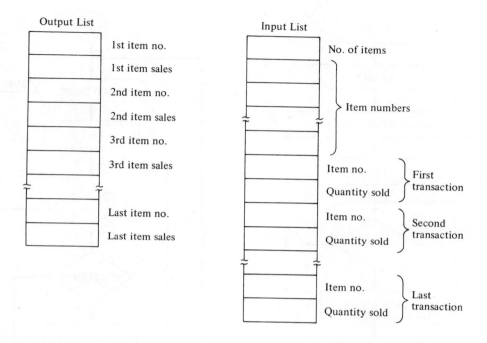

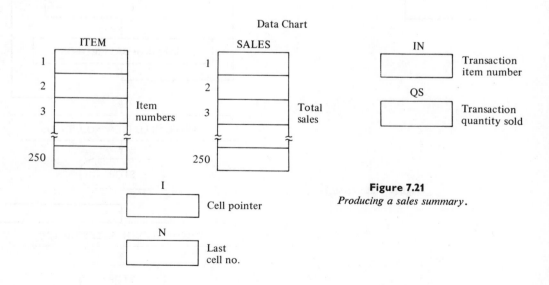

Figure 7.21
Producing a sales summary.

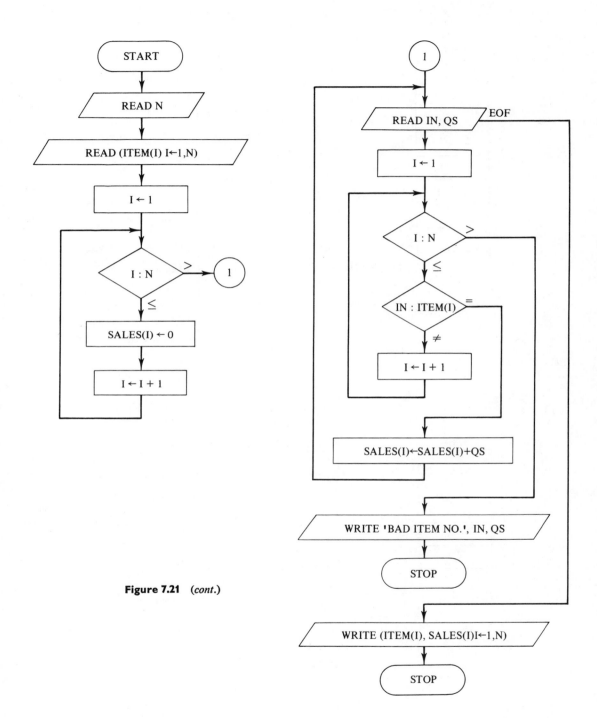

Figure 7.21 *(cont.)*

sales totals. Thus, it is necessary to associate item numbers with sales counts. Since the number of different items can vary, item numbers can be stored in a linear list, ITEM. Let us assume that never more than 250 different products are for sale at any one time. Therefore, ITEM contains 250 cells numbered from 1 to 250, as shown in Figure 7.21. With a possibility of 250 different items, we must be prepared to calculate 250 separate sales totals. This necessitates a linear list, SALES, consisting of 250 cells also numbered from 1 to 250, where SALES(1) counts the number of items sold for the item whose item number is stored in ITEM(1); SALES(2) counts the sales of ITEM(2); etc. Since these structures are used in conjunction with each other and since they both have the same number of data values, they can use the same last cell number, N, and cell pointer, I. As in the previous example, let us process one input at a time. Since each transaction consists of two values, this requires two single cells: IN for item number and QS for quantity sold.

Basically, we must develop an algorithm and flow chart similar to those of an integer frequency count. In that problem, each integer was its own cell number. Here, we must determine a cell number before we can increment the proper sales count. We can do so by viewing the entries of ITEM and SALES as *columns* in a table where their cell numbers act as *line numbers*, as shown in Figure 7.22. Initially, item numbers are read into the left-hand column, whereas the right-hand column is zeroed in preparation for counting. As each transaction is read, we can look up its item number in the table as we might do manually by scanning down the left-hand column. When a match is found, we move across the line and increment the desired total. For example, assume that a transaction covers a sale of 17 items for item number 21. We then take the number 21 and begin comparing it sequentially with the item numbers in Figure 7.22a. A match is found on the third line, and 17 is added to its sales column, as shown in Figure 7.22b. Using one data structure as a table to find an entry in another is referred to as a *table lookup*.

The flow chart in Figure 7.21 uses this technique to summarize sales data.

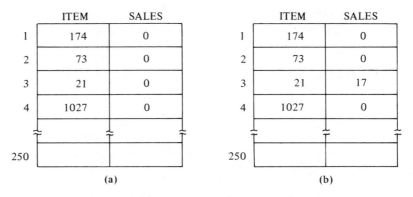

Figure 7.22 *Combining linear lists into a table.*

Initially, item numbers are read into ITEM, and then the cells of SALES are set to 0. Note that SALES is initialized by a loop that terminates when I exceeds N rather than 250, since only the first N cells are used. Next, a single transaction is read into IN and QS. Another loop performs the table lookup and determines the cell number of the cell in ITEM that matches the transaction item number, IN. When IN equals ITEM(I), I is used as a cell pointer to increment SALES(I) by QS, and then the flow chart loops back to read the next transaction. This chart displays a loop within a loop, where the inner one performs a table lookup and the outer one reads the input, starts the inner loop, and increments the proper sales total using a cell pointer value from the inner one. If during a table lookup the end of ITEM is reached before a match is found, then one of two errors has occurred. Either an item number has been omitted from the original list, or the transaction item number is incorrect. In both cases, an error message should be written so that this situation can be investigated and corrected.

As an extension to this problem, let us assume that we are not given a list of valid item numbers. In this case, an item number table must be built as transactions are processed. In Figure 7.23, the flow chart begins by setting N to 0, indicating that both tables are empty. Transactions are read one at a time, and the same table-lookup procedure is used to locate an item number. If no match occurs, it is assumed that a new transaction item number has been found, meaning that another entry must be made at the end of ITEM, provided there is room. Here, the quantity sold, QS, is used as an initial value for the appropriate cell in SALES. By doing so, we avoid the necessity of initially setting SALES to 0. Of course, this procedure suffers from the disadvantage that it cannot detect incorrect transaction item numbers. However, it does eliminate the need for a list of item numbers as input.

As a final consideration of this example, let us remove the restriction that transactions occur in random order. In particular, let us assume that they have previously been sorted by item number using techniques that will be introduced in Chapter 10. With transactions in ascending sequence, a running total can be used where transactions are read and processed one at a time. If the current transaction has the same item number as the previous one, its quantity sold is added to a running sum. Otherwise, the sum for the previous item is written out and the quantity sold for the new item is used to reinitialize the sum. Figure 7.24 displays data and flow charts that incorporate this procedure. Note that preordering the input eliminates the need for linear lists.

7.3.6 Text editing

As our last example of single-dimension data structures, let us assume that we are to develop a computerized procedure for text editing. In particular, we are given a string of characters that represents a paragraph and are asked to break it into lines such that each line ends on a complete word. Before each computer run, we shall be told a maximum line length, and all output lines are to be less than or equal to that length.

Flow Chart

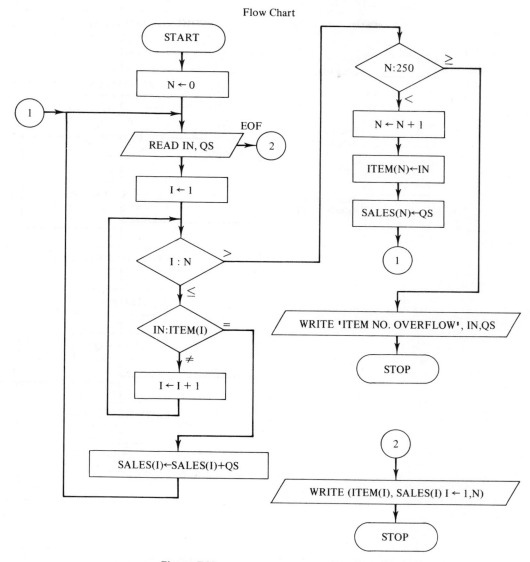

Figure 7.23 *Building a table as transactions are processed.*

Data Chart

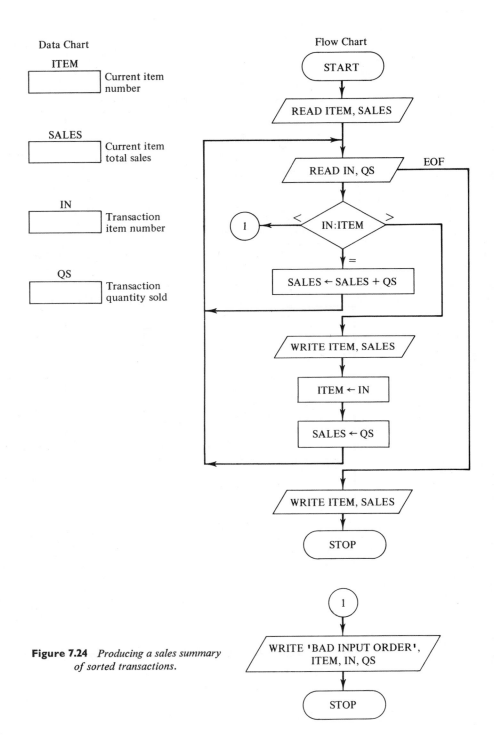

Flow Chart

ITEM
[   ] Current item number

SALES
[   ] Current item total sales

IN
[   ] Transaction item number

QS
[   ] Transaction quantity sold

START

READ ITEM, SALES

READ IN, QS   EOF

IN:ITEM   < → 1   >

=

SALES ← SALES + QS

WRITE ITEM, SALES

ITEM ← IN

SALES ← QS

WRITE ITEM, SALES

STOP

1

WRITE 'BAD INPUT ORDER', ITEM, IN, QS

STOP

Figure 7.24 *Producing a sales summary of sorted transactions.*

As further explanation, we are given a sample, shown in Figure 7.25. Here, input is a single sentence that is to be considered as a continuous character string. Each word is separated by one blank, and these blanks are characters,

The purpose of studying linear lists is to have a data structure that makes it possible to solve problems whose data is inappropriate for single cells.

(a)

The purpose of studying
linear lists is to have a
data structure that makes
it possible to solve
problems whose data is
inappropriate for single
cells.

(b)

Figure 7.25 *Sample text editing: (a) input character string; (b) output lines.*

just as is any other letter or digit. The output is a set of lines with a maximum length of 25. For example, the first line consists of 23 characters, including 3 blanks. The word "linear" starts the second line because it contains 6 characters, which, with a preceding blank, would produce a first line of length 30. Consequently, our output must be a set of lines, as shown in Figure 7.26, where the number of lines depends upon paragraph size and line length. In contrast, our input is a variable length character string. But since this string is to be broken into lines, let the line length precede it as input.

We are now ready to select data structures. From the output, we know that we must generate a set of lines that do not exceed a certain length. If we construct each line separately, we need store just one line at a time. Since a line is a string of characters, it can be saved in a linear list, LINE, where each cell holds one character. Let us assume that maximum line length never exceeds 100 characters; therefore, LINE contains 100 cells. Let LL be its last cell number and L its cell pointer.

In contrast, the input is a maximum line length followed by a continuous character string. Here, maximum line length is a single value and can be stored in a single cell, MLL. But since each output line must end on a complete word, let us process the character string one word at a time. Each word is a string of characters and can be saved in a linear list, WORD, where each cell holds one character. Since a word should not exceed the maximum line length, WORD need contain just 100 cells. Let WL be its last cell number and W its cell pointer.

Finally, we are ready to develop an algorithm and draw its flow chart. Basically, we must read one word at a time into WORD and determine if it can be added to the end of LINE without exceeding the maximum line length,

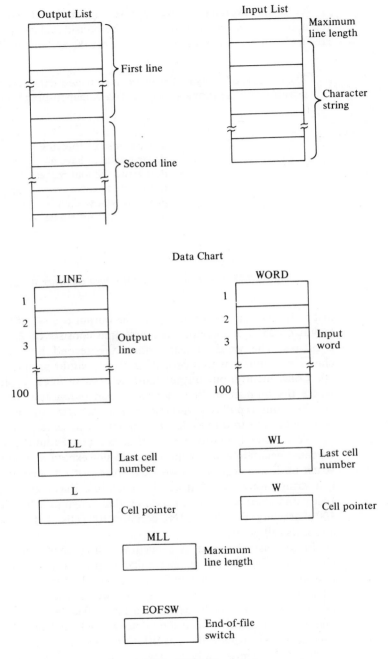

Figure 7.26 *Text editing.*

Partial Flow Chart

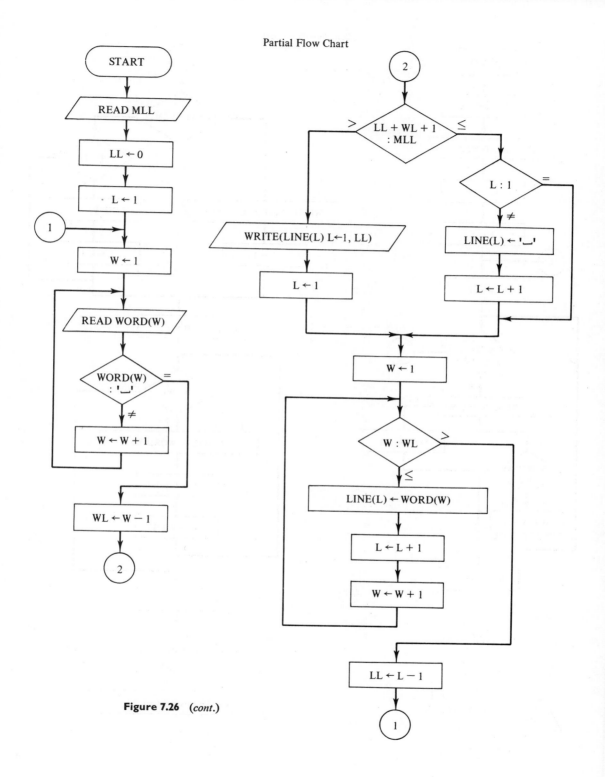

Figure 7.26 *(cont.)*

Complete Flow Chart

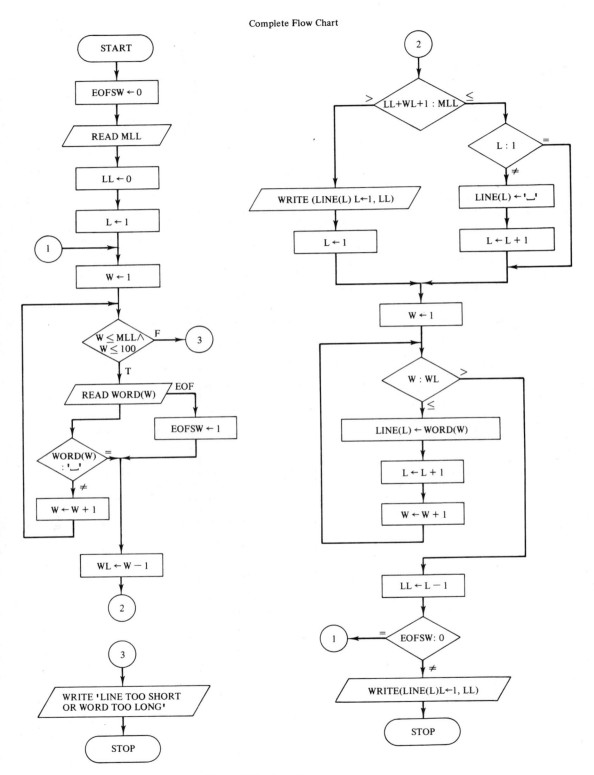

Figure 7.26 (*cont.*)

MLL. If it can, it is moved from WORD to LINE one character at a time. If the latest input word causes a line overflow, the current contents of LINE must be written out before this word is moved into LINE.

The partial flow chart in Figure 7.26 incorporates this algorithm. It begins by reading the first input value into MLL. It then initializes LL at 0, showing that the current line is empty, and L at 1, indicating that the next output character goes into LINE(1). Next, it reads a word one character at a time into WORD. When a space signals end of word, the read loop terminates, and the length of the current word is saved in WL. Here, WL is one less than W so as to eliminate the blank at the end of the current word.

We are now ready to determine if there is room at the end of the current line for the latest word. We do so by comparing the maximum line length with the length of the current line, assuming the new word has been added. Remembering that a space must be inserted before the latest word, the length of the new line is LL + WL + 1. If LL + WL + 1 is greater than MLL, the new word is too long for the current line, and the present line is ready for output. Once this line is written, L can be reset to 1.

On the other hand, if LL + WL + 1 is less than or equal to MLL, there is room for the new word at the end of the current line. But if L is 1, the latest word is the first word on the new line and there is no need for an intervening blank. If L does not equal 1, this blank must be added. Now, the current word can be moved into LINE, and then LL is set to point to the last character in LINE.

A trace of this chart reveals two defects. First, it is possible to input a word that exceeds the length of WORD, which we can rectify by inserting a test in the loop that reads each word as shown in the complete chart in Figure 7.26. Second, the partial flow chart contains an endless loop and does not terminate after the last word, which we can correct by using a single cell, EOFSW, as a switch that remembers whether an end of file has been detected. Initially, EOFSW is set to 0. When an EOF is sensed, this switch is set to 1 and processing continues. Now, after each word is moved into LINE, EOFSW is tested for 0. If it contains a 1, the last word has been read and this test causes a branch to a write, which outputs the last line.

Finally, the solution shown in Figure 7.27 incorporates a second algorithm. Here, the complete paragraph is first read into a linear list, PAR. The start of the next line is assumed to be at PAR(1) and a start-of-line pointer, LS, is set to 1. Since all lines contain MLL characters or less, the end of line must occur at or before PAR(LS+MLL). Thus, an end-of-line pointer, LE, can be set to LS+MLL. Now, LE is reduced by 1 until PAR(LE) equals a blank, which signals an end of word. At this point, the next line lies between LINE(LS) and LINE(LE−1) and is ready for output. The start of the next line is then found at LE+1. This process finally terminates when LE exceeds the end of paragraph, PE. In this solution, words are not moved from one structure to another once in memory. On the other hand, it requires more storage, because its input area must be able to hold a complete paragraph.

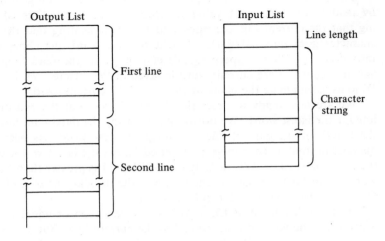

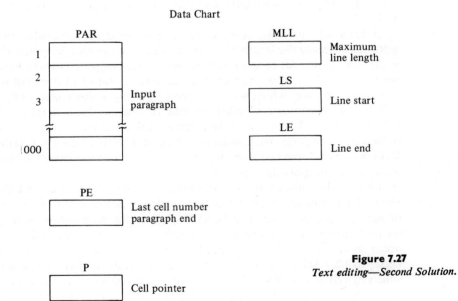

Figure 7.27
Text editing—Second Solution.

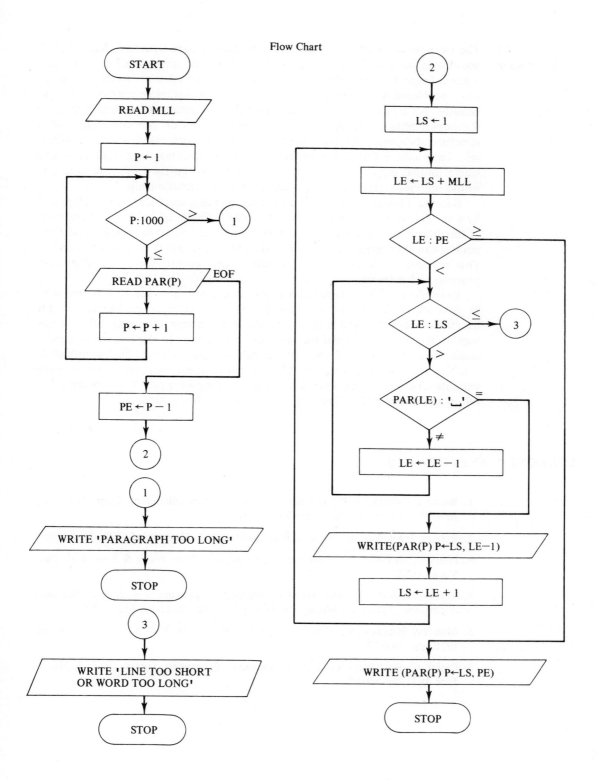

Flow Chart

**7.4
Summary**
The purpose of studying linear lists is to have a data structure that makes it possible to solve problems the data of which are inappropriate for single cells. Since a linear list can contain an arbitrary number of cells, it can be used to solve problems requiring a large number of data values in memory simultaneously. All that is necessary is to ensure that it contains enough cells to store the largest anticipated data set. When smaller sets do not completely fill a structure, its excess cells are simply left vacant. In such cases, a separate single cell, known as a last cell number, is used to indicate where data ends and where unused cells begin. Finally, linear lists can be used to store data sets whose individual data values possess a single interrelationship.

Because a linear list contains more than one cell, specific cells are referenced by a variable name and cell number. Usually, a single cell holds the cell number of the desired cell and acts as a pointer to that cell. Since the contents of a cell pointer can vary, great care must be taken to ensure that it is always in-bounds. This requirement leads to the four cell pointer control steps: initialize, test, process, and increment.

Example problems were solved that illustrated how linear lists are used as data structures. In the summation and above-average problems, a linear list stored variable length data sets. In the sort problem, sequential cell arrangement of a linear list retained the order of sorted data. In the integer frequency count, linear list cell numbers identified cell contents; a linear list functioned as a table in the sales analysis problem. Finally, linear lists were used to store variable length character strings in the text editing example. The problems that follow are designated to illustrate further uses of linear lists.

SELECTED REFERENCES

1. BROOKS, FREDERICK P., and KENNETH E. IVERSON, *Automatic Data Processing*, John Wiley & Sons, Inc., New York, 1963.

2. FLORES, IVAN, *Sorting Methods*, Prentice-Hall, Inc., Englewood Cliffs, N. J., 1969.

3. IVERSON, KENNETH E., *A Programming Language*, John Wiley & Sons, Inc., New York, 1962.

4. KNUTH, DONALD E., *The Art of Computer Programming*, Vol. 1, "Fundamental Algorithms," Addison-Wesley Publishing Co., Inc., Reading, Mass., 1968.

5. MARTIN, WILLIAM A., "Sorting," *Computing Surveys*, Vol. 3, No. 4, December 1971, pp. 147–174.

6. PRICE, C. E., "Table Lookup Techniques," *Computing Surveys*, Vol. 3, No. 2, June 1971, pp. 49–65.

PROBLEMS

For each of the following problems, develop a computerized solution that includes an output list, input list, data chart, and flow chart.

7.1 Rework the problem in Section 7.3.1, but calculate the sum of the squares of the input numbers rather than just the sum, i.e.,

$$\text{Sumsq} = \sum_{i=1}^{n} a_i^2 = a_1^2 + a_2^2 + \cdots + a_n^2$$

7.2 Read N and N numbers into a linear list and then find and output the largest value and its cell number; N is always less than 500.

7.3 Rework Problem 7.2, but also output the number of times the largest value occurs as input.

7.4 Rework Problem 7.2, but find the two largest values in a set of numbers. Output the largest number first, followed by the second largest number. If the largest number appears more than once, output that value twice.

7.5 Rework the problem in Section 7.3.4 so that the solution calculates a weighted average, WAVE, after it has produced a frequency count.

$$\text{WAVE} = \frac{\displaystyle\sum_{\text{NUM}=1}^{100} \text{NUM}^2 \times \text{COUNT(NUM)}}{\displaystyle\sum_{\text{NUM}=1}^{100} \text{COUNT(NUM)}}$$

7.6 Assume that $X(1), \ldots, X(50)$ and $Y(1), \ldots, Y(50)$ are available. Develop a computerized procedure that first inputs the X's and Y's, then produces $Z(I) = X(I) + Y(I)$, and finally outputs the Z's.

7.7 Suppose that N, $X(1), X(2), X(3), \ldots, X(N)$ are available. Calculate the sum, S, the average, A, and the difference, $A - X(I)$, for all N numbers; N is always less than 1000.

7.8 Develop a computerized procedure that first inputs $A(1), \ldots, A(100)$, second inverts the numbers such that $A(1)$ becomes $A(100)$, $A(2)$ becomes $A(99)$, etc., and third outputs the rearranged list.

7.9 Read N numbers into a linear list, where N is never greater than 50. If N is odd, output the midelement of the linear list; if N is even, output its two midelements.

7.10 Read N data values into a linear list. Switch the positions of the first N/2 values so that $A(1)$ moves to $A(N/2)$, $A(2)$ moves to $A(N/2 - 1)$, etc. Switch the second set of N/2 numbers in a similar fashion so that $A(N/2 + 1)$ moves to $A(N)$, $A(N/2 + 2)$ moves to $A(N - 1)$, etc. Output the rearranged data set; N is always even and never more than 1000.

7.11 Assume that the numbers N, A(1), B(1), A(2), B(2), ..., A(N), B(N), X are available, where N is always less than 200; X is known to equal one of the A's. Develop a computerized procedure that will output the value of B(I) for which X equals A(I).

7.12 Assume that the numbers N, A(1), A(2), ..., A(N) are available, where N is never more than 100. Furthermore, the A's have been arranged in ascending order and no two numbers are alike. Read an additional number, NUM, and output two or three values as follows:

(a) If NUM is less than A(1), output NUM and A(1).
(b) If NUM equals some value in A, output NUM and that value.
(c) If NUM falls between two values of A, output NUM and those two values.
(d) If NUM is greater than A(N), output NUM and A(N).

7.13 Read N and N elements into a linear list. Output three separate lists as follows:

(a) All positive numbers;
(b) All negative numbers;
(c) All zero numbers.
N never exceeds 50.

7.14 Assume that you have a set of N numbers, where N is never more than 100. You are required to input these numbers, sort them into ascending order, and eliminate any duplicates. Output the revised set of numbers and the new value of N.

7.15 The mode of a set of numbers is that number which occurs most frequently. There may be more than one mode if several different numbers appear in the set an equal number of times. Assume that input values are integers which are greater than 0 and less than or equal to 50. Develop a procedure to determine the mode or modes.

7.16 The problem in Section 7.3.3 sorts a set of numbers by first reading all input values into a linear list. Develop a procedure that accomplishes the same thing by keeping the contents of the linear list in ascending order as each individual number is read.

7.17 Develop a computerized procedure that calculates the coefficient of correlation, R, for two sets of numbers, X and Y, both containing N numbers. The input data are arranged as follows: first, the single value of N; second, the N numbers of X; third, the N numbers of Y. N will always be less than 100.

$$R = \frac{N*SUMXY - SUMX*SUMY}{\sqrt{(N*SUMXX - SUMX^2)\,(N*SUMYY - SUMY^2)}}$$

where

$$SUMX = \sum_{i=1}^{N} X_i \qquad SUMY = \sum_{i=1}^{N} Y_i \qquad SUMXX = \sum_{i=1}^{N} X_i^2$$

$$SUMYY = \sum_{i=1}^{N} Y_i^2 \qquad SUMXY = \sum_{i=1}^{N} X_i Y_i$$

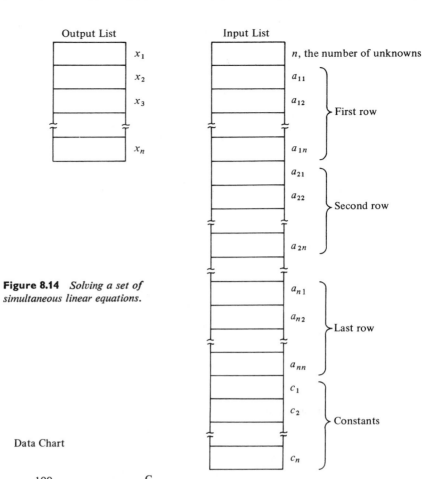

Output List — x_1, x_2, x_3, x_n

Input List — n, the number of unknowns

a_{11}, a_{12}, a_{1n} — First row

a_{21}, a_{22}, a_{2n} — Second row

a_{n1}, a_{n2}, a_{nn} — Last row

c_1, c_2, c_n — Constants

Figure 8.14 *Solving a set of simultaneous linear equations.*

Data Chart

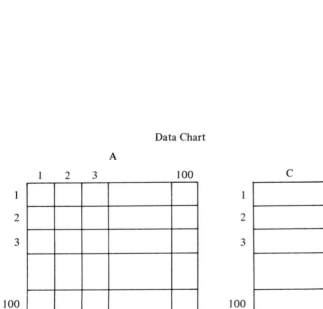

A

1 2 3 100

1
2
3
100

C

1
2
3
100

First Dimension   Second Dimension

N

Last cell number

I   J

Cell pointer

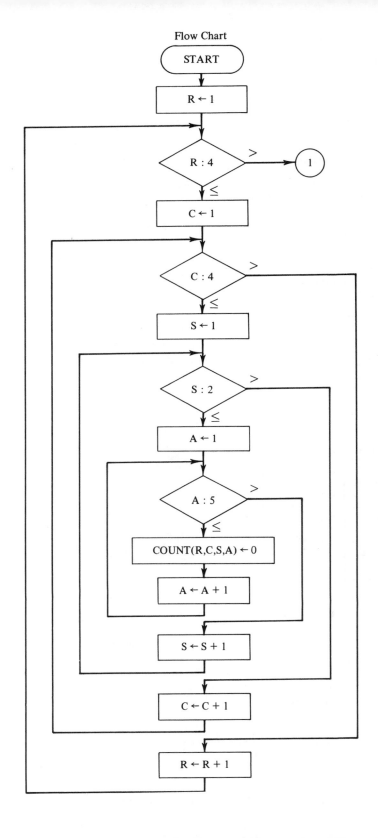

Flow Chart

Figure 8.23 (cont.)

272

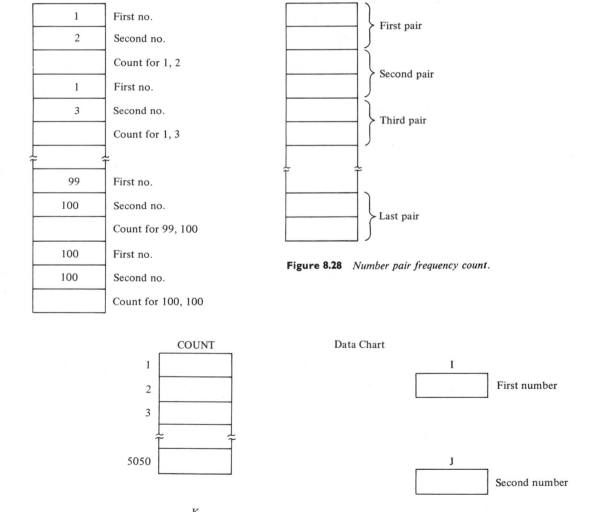

and by defining

$$a'_{32} = a_{32} - m_3 a_{12}$$

$$a'_{33} = a_{33} - m_3 a_{13}$$

$$c'_3 = c_3 - m_3 c_1$$

equation (7) becomes

$$a'_{32} x_2 + a'_{33} x_3 = c'_3 \tag{8}$$

At this point, x_1 has been removed from the last two equations and the three equations now appear as

$$a_{11} x_1 + a_{12} x_2 + a_{13} x_3 = c_1 \tag{9}$$

$$a'_{22} x_2 + a'_{23} x_3 = c'_2 \tag{10}$$

$$a'_{32} x_2 + a'_{33} x_3 = c'_3 \tag{11}$$

This procedure can be repeated for x_2 in equation (11). Here, a new multiplier is defined as

$$m'_3 = \frac{a'_{32}}{a'_{22}}$$

Now, equation (10) is multiplied by m'_3, and the resulting equation is subtracted from equation (11), which becomes

$$(a'_{32} - m'_3 a'_{22}) x_2 + (a'_{33} - m'_3 a'_{23}) x_3 = c'_3 - m'_3 c'_2 \tag{12}$$

However,

$$a'_{32} - m'_3 a'_{22} = 0$$

and by defining

$$a''_{33} = a'_{33} - m'_3 a'_{23}$$

$$c''_3 = c'_3 - m'_3 c'_2$$

equation (12) becomes

$$a''_{33} x_3 = c''_3 \tag{13}$$

Finally, the original equations have been transformed to

$$a_{11} x_1 + a_{12} x_2 + a_{13} x_3 = c_1 \tag{14}$$

$$a'_{22} x_2 + a'_{23} x_3 = c'_2 \tag{15}$$

$$a''_{33} x_3 = c''_3 \tag{16}$$

From their appearance, these equations are referred to as *triangular*.

Now that these equations have been triangularized, it is a straightforward process to solve them for their unknowns. Since the third equation (16) contains only one unknown, it can be used to determine x_3. Once x_3 is known, its value can be substituted into equation (15) to find x_2. Finally, with x_2 and x_3 known, equation (14) can be used to find x_1. This process is specified by

$$x_3 = \frac{c_3''}{a_{33}''}$$

$$x_2 = \frac{(c_2' - a_{23}'x_3)}{a_{22}'}$$

$$x_1 = \frac{(c_1 - a_{12}x_2 - a_{13}x_3)}{a_{11}}$$

and is known as the *back substitution* of a Gauss elimination.

As an example of a Gauss elimination, let us solve the following equations:

$$x_1 + x_2 + x_3 = 6$$
$$2x_1 - x_2 + 3x_3 = 7$$
$$-x_1 + 2x_2 - 3x_3 = -2$$

The multiplier, m_2, for the second equation is 2, and m_3 for the third is -1. After elimination of x_1 from the second and third equations, the equations have the form

$$x_1 + x_2 + x_3 = 6$$
$$-3x_2 + x_3 = -5$$
$$3x_2 - 2x_3 = 4$$

Now, $m_3' = -1$, and when x_2 is removed from the last equation, the triangular result is

$$x_1 + x_2 + x_3 = 6$$
$$-3x_2 + x_3 = -5$$
$$-x_3 = -1$$

Finally, the back solution produces a value of $x_3 = 1$; $x_2 = 2$; and $x_1 = 3$.

As a second example of a Gauss elimination, let us solve the following set of equations.

$$x_1 + x_2 + x_3 = 6$$
$$2x_1 - x_2 + 3x_3 = 7$$
$$-x_1 + 2x_2 - 2x_3 = -1$$

As before, the multipliers m_2 and m_3 are 2 and -1, respectively; thus, the equations have the form

$$x_1 + x_2 + x_3 = 6$$
$$-3x_2 + x_3 = -5$$
$$3x_2 - x_3 = 5$$

after the elimination of the first unknown. In this case, m_3' is -1, and the triangular result is

$$x_1 + x_2 + x_3 = 6$$
$$-3x_2 + x_3 = -5$$
$$0 = 0$$

Now, there are actually only two equations in three unknowns. Therefore, these equations have no unique solution.

Finally, consider the equations

$$x_1 + x_2 + x_3 = 6$$
$$2x_1 - x_2 + 3x_3 = 7$$
$$-x_1 + 2x_2 - 2x_3 = 0$$

which reduces to

$$x_1 + x_2 + x_3 = 6$$
$$-3x_2 + x_3 = -5$$
$$3x_2 - x_3 = 6$$

and then to

$$x_1 + x_2 + x_3 = 6$$
$$-3x_2 + x_3 = -5$$
$$0 = 1$$

Now, the last equation states an impossibility: zero cannot equal one. In this case, these equations have no solution.

From the discussion of the problem, we know that our solution must produce a value for each unknown. Let us agree to output these unknowns in sequence: $x_1, x_2, x_3, \ldots, x_n$. Furthermore, since the input order is not specified, let us use the arrangement shown in Figure 8.14. The first input value specifies the number of unknowns and is followed by equation coefficients arranged by row or equation. Each row contains n coefficients and there are n rows. Consequently, n^2 coefficients must appear as input. Finally, the last n input values represent equation constants arranged in equation order.

Now that the output and input have been specified, let us determine suitable data structures. For the equation coefficients, let us use a two-dimension array, A. Since the number of equations must equal the number of unknowns, A is a *square* array. For this discussion, let us assume that there are never more than 100 unknowns. Therefore, A must be a 100 by 100 array. Initially, let us use I and J as cell pointers for the first and second dimensions, respectively. For any particular coefficient, A(I,J), the first cell pointer indicates its equation and the second identifies its position within that equation. Since there are as many rows as columns, a single last cell number, N, can be used for both dimensions. Finally, equation constants can be saved in a 100-cell linear list, C.

Output List

Input List

x_1

x_2

x_3

x_n

n, the number of unknowns

a_{11}

a_{12} } First row

a_{1n}

a_{21}

a_{22} } Second row

a_{2n}

a_{n1}

a_{n2} } Last row

a_{nn}

c_1

c_2 } Constants

c_n

Figure 8.14 *Solving a set of simultaneous linear equations.*

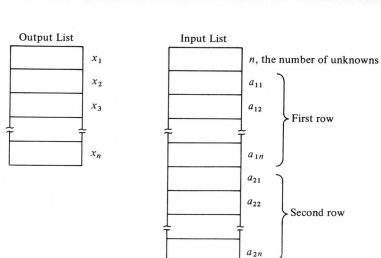

Data Chart

A

C

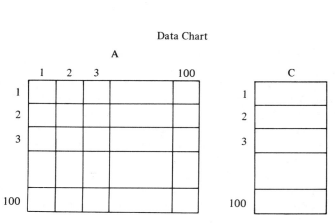

First Dimension

Second Dimension

N

Last cell number

I

J

Cell pointer

$$
\begin{array}{ccccc}
a_{11} & a_{12} & a_{13} & a_{14} & c_1 \\
0 & a_{22} & a_{23} & a_{24} & c_2 \\
0 & a_{32} & a_{33} & a_{34} & c_3 \\
0 & a_{42} & a_{43} & a_{44} & c_4
\end{array}
$$

(a)

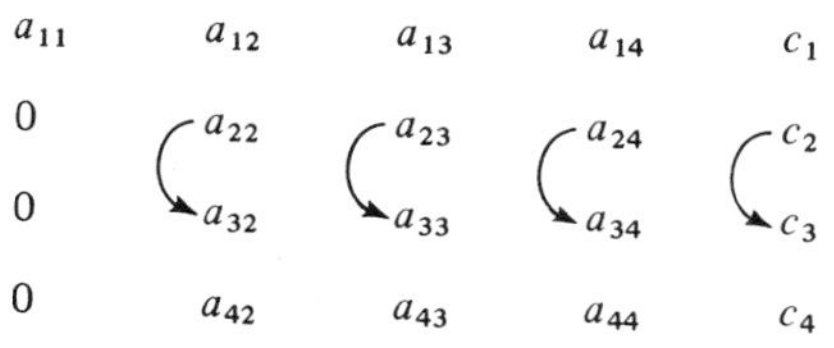

$$
\begin{array}{ccccc}
a_{11} & a_{12} & a_{13} & a_{14} & c_1 \\
0 & a_{22} & a_{23} & a_{24} & c_2 \\
0 & a_{32} & a_{33} & a_{34} & c_3 \\
0 & a_{42} & a_{43} & a_{44} & c_4
\end{array}
$$

(b)

$$
\begin{array}{ccccc}
a_{11} & a_{12} & a_{13} & a_{14} & c_1 \\
0 & a_{22} & a_{23} & a_{24} & c_2 \\
0 & 0 & a_{33} & a_{34} & c_3 \\
0 & a_{42} & a_{43} & a_{44} & c_4
\end{array}
$$

(c)

Figure 8.15 *Coefficients before, during, and after an elimination: (a) before; (b) during; (c) after.*

Let us begin with the development of our algorithm by assuming that we are in the middle of a Gauss elimination and that the procedure has progressed as far as shown in Figure 8.15a. Here, primes are omitted from coefficients to simplify notation. The first column contains zeros except for the first row, implying that the elimination process has been completed for the first unknown and is ready to proceed with the second. The arrows in Figure 8.15b indicate which coefficients are used to eliminate the second unknown from the third equation. When this step is completed, the coefficients must appear as shown in Figure 8.15c.

At this point, let us assume that the cell pointers, I, J, and K, are used in Figure 8.16 as follows:

K specifies the unknown being eliminated and also refers to the equation being subtracted from the equation below it.

I indicates the equation from which an unknown is currently being eliminated.

J refers to the column being processed.

Using these cell pointers, the Kth unknown can be eliminated from the Ith equation by the statements

$$A(I,J) \leftarrow A(I,J) - M \times A(K,J)$$

and

$$C(I) \leftarrow C(I) - M \times C(K)$$

where J is varied from K to N with an appropriate multiplier, M. The partial flow chart in Figure 8.16 incorporates these statements and forms the core of a Gauss elimination algorithm.

The flow chart in Figure 8.16 removes the Kth unknown from the Ith row; but before it can be executed, an appropriate value of M must be calculated.

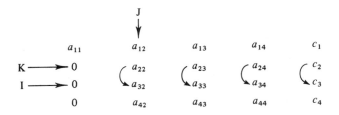

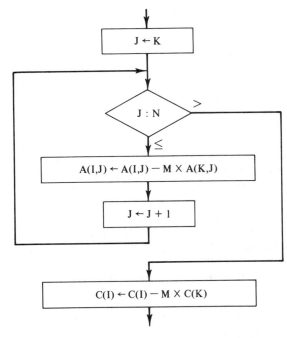

Figure 8.16 *Eliminating the Kth unknown from the Ith row.*

From earlier discussions, we know that M is a ratio of coefficients, such that when $M \times A(K,K)$ is subtracted from $A(I,K)$, the result is zero. In other words, M must satisfy the relationship

$$A(I,K) - M \times A(K,K) = 0$$

Therefore, M is specified by

$$M = \frac{A(I,K)}{A(K,K)}$$

Note that we calculate each value of M using a denominator that resides on the main diagonal of A. This value, $A(K,K)$, is referred to as the *pivot element*. With this value of M, the flow chart in Figure 8.16 produces a zero value of $A(I,K)$. Since this is always the case, $A(I,K)$ can be directly set to zero by an assignment statement. Now, the column pointer, J, can be initialized at $K + 1$ rather than K. These two additions are shown in Figure 8.17.

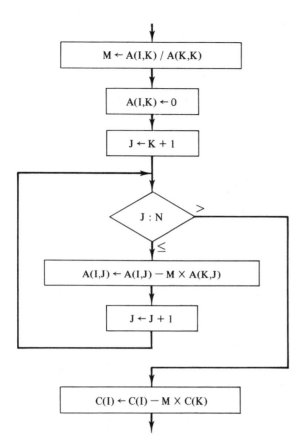

Figure 8.17 *Flow chart for eliminating the Kth unknown from the Ith row.*

So far, our algorithm eliminates the Kth unknown from the Ith equation. However, the Kth unknown must be removed from all equations below the Kth. This can be done by enclosing the flow chart of Figure 8.17 within a loop that varies I from K + 1 to N. Note that we only need one cell for the multiplier, M. Its value is calculated for a particular equation and used for that entire equation before a new value is required. Finally, the complete set of coefficients can be triangularized by varying K from 1 to N − 1. Figure 8.18 shows a flow chart that contains three loops, one within each other. The outer loop varies K and controls the variable that is being eliminated. The middle loop varies I and removes the Kth unknown from the Ith equation. The inner loop varies J and performs the subtractions of individual coefficients.

So far, our discussion has assumed that our set of equations always has a unique solution. However, if such is not the case, our algorithm as it stands can neither detect nor handle the situation. Notice that the flow chart in Figure 8.18 calculates M by the statement

$$M = \frac{A(I,K)}{A(K,K)}$$

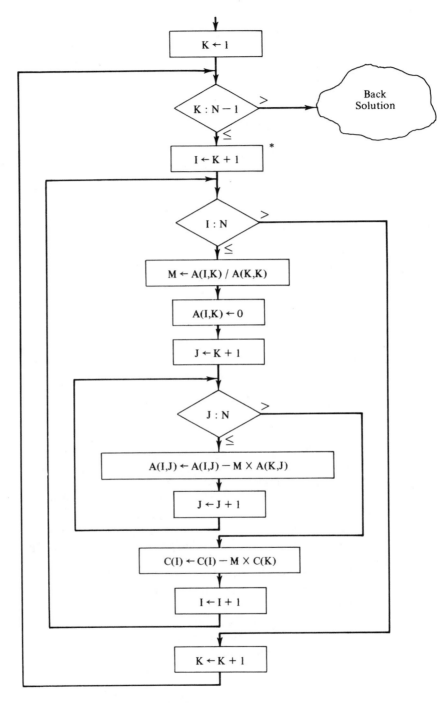

Figure 8.18 *Flow chart for triangularizing a set of linear equations.*

Now, what happens if by chance one of the pivot elements, A(K,K), contains a zero? Since division by zero is undefined, care must be taken to ensure that all pivot elements are nonzero. If A(K,K) happens to be zero, the Kth equation can be interchanged with one of the equations below it. Such an interchange is the same as simply rewriting the original equations in a different order. Certainly, equation order cannot and does not affect their solution, if there is, in fact, a unique solution.

Now, if A(K,K) is a zero, how do we select the equation that is to be interchanged with the Kth equation? In other words, if the Ith equation is to be exchanged with the Kth, how do we select I? It turns out that we should scan down the column under A(K,K) and select I such that the absolute value of A(I,K), written as |A(I,K)|, is a maximum. Furthermore, if we use this selection rule even if A(K,K) is not zero, our results will be more accurate, because this rule attempts to avoid the possibility that we might select an I such that |A(K,K)| is *almost* zero. In such a case, the division by a near-zero value can produce an M that is too large for the word length of our particular computer. The reason a small coefficient can occur is that it may have been formed as the difference between two almost equal numbers. We try to circumvent this problem by suitable row interchanges, but so far no completely satisfactory strategy seems to have been discovered. This process of finding the maximum value for the pivot element is called *partial pivoting*. If a nonzero value of |A(I,K)| cannot be found in the column under A(K,K), then there is no unique solution and the algorithm must halt.

The partial flow chart in Figure 8.19 specifies the partial pivoting operation. Here, L is introduced as an auxiliary cell pointer that is used to remember the row number of the maximum value of |A(I,K)|. In addition, MAX is used to remember that maximum. This process begins by assuming that the maximum value is already in the Kth row. It then verifies its assumption via a single loop that varies I from K + 1 to N. When the loop terminates, L contains the number of the row that is to be interchanged with K. Before this interchange is performed, MAX must be checked for zero. If it is zero, the set of equations has no unique solution and this algorithm halts with an appropriate message. If MAX is not zero, then L is compared with K to see if the Kth row already contains the maximum. If L equals K, no interchange is necessary. Now, this flow chart for partial pivoting can be inserted just before the box labeled with an asterisk (*) in the triangularization flow chart in Figure 8.18.

Now that our algorithm triangularizes the coefficients, we are ready to proceed with the back solution. From earlier discussions, we know that the back solution for three unknowns is

$$x_3 = \frac{c_3}{a_{33}}$$

$$x_2 = \frac{c_2 - a_{23}x_3}{a_{22}}$$

$$x_1 = \frac{c_1 - a_{12}x_2 - a_{13}x_3}{a_{11}}$$

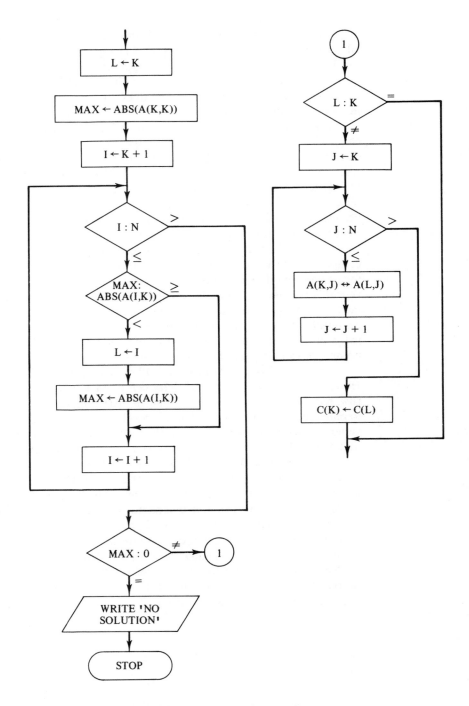

Figure 8.19 *Flow chart for partial pivoting.*

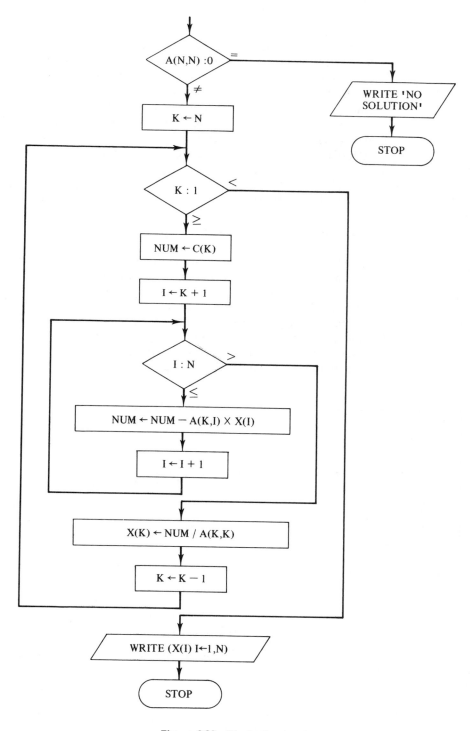

Figure 8.20 *The back solution.*

This can be extended to *n* unknowns, as shown in the flow chart in Figure 8.20. Here, the inner loop uses a single cell, NUM, to calculate the numerator of each unknown, whereas the outer loop controls the number of the unknown. In the latter, note that the *x*'s are, in fact, determined in the reverse order starting at K equal to N. Finally, notice that the flow chart begins by checking A(N,N) for zero. All other A(K,K) are known to be nonzero, since the elimination procedure included the partial pivot operation, which guarantees that A(K,K) is nonzero for K from 1 to N − 1. Since

$$X(N) = C(N) / A(N,N)$$

A(N,N) must not be zero, and thus, must be checked individually for zero.

8.3.4 Cross tabulation

As our last example of the use of multidimension data structures, let us develop a computerized procedure that produces cross tabulations. In particular, let us assume that we are asked to analyze the makeup of a student body by race, class, sex, and age. We are told that the coding scheme in Figure 8.21 is used to record four one-digit numbers for each student. For example, the code 1, 4, 1, 3 represents an Indian senior who is male and 22 years old. We are asked to produce a set of tables showing the age and sex distribution for each race and class. Figure 8.22 shows a sample output table.

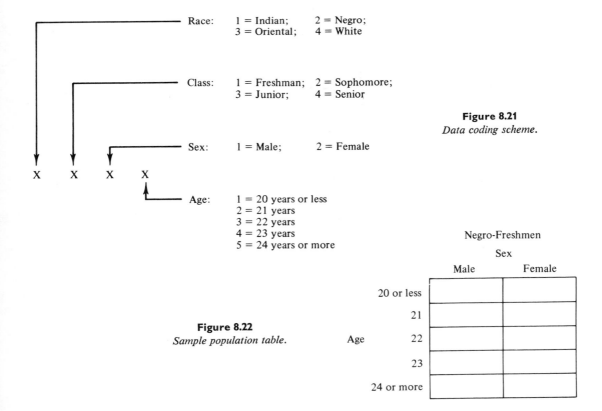

Race: 1 = Indian;   2 = Negro;
        3 = Oriental;   4 = White

Class: 1 = Freshman;   2 = Sophomore;
        3 = Junior;   4 = Senior

Figure 8.21
Data coding scheme.

Sex: 1 = Male;   2 = Female

Age: 1 = 20 years or less
        2 = 21 years
        3 = 22 years
        4 = 23 years
        5 = 24 years or more

Figure 8.22
Sample population table.

Negro-Freshmen

	Sex	
	Male	Female
20 or less		
21		
22		
23		
24 or more		

Age

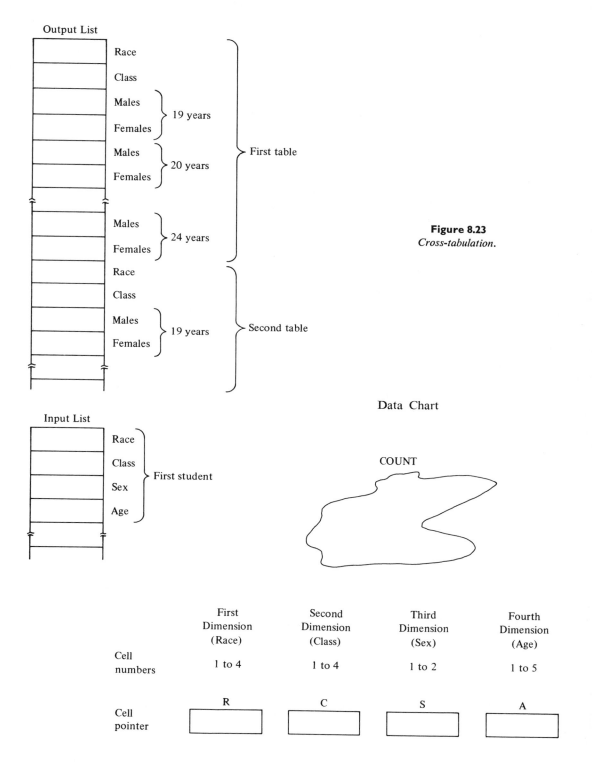

Figure 8.23
Cross-tabulation.

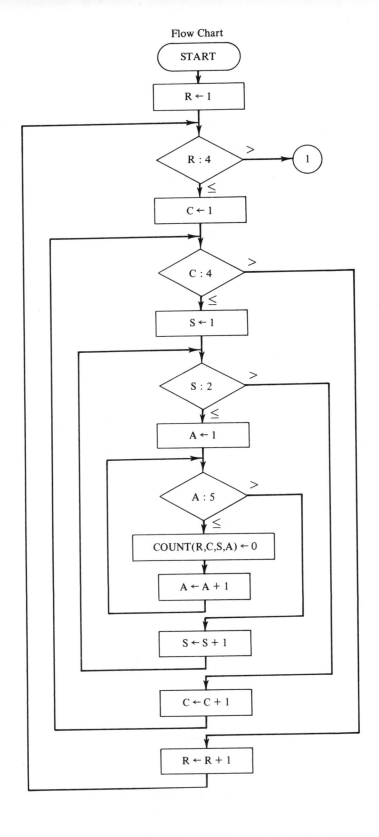

Figure 8.23 (cont.)

272

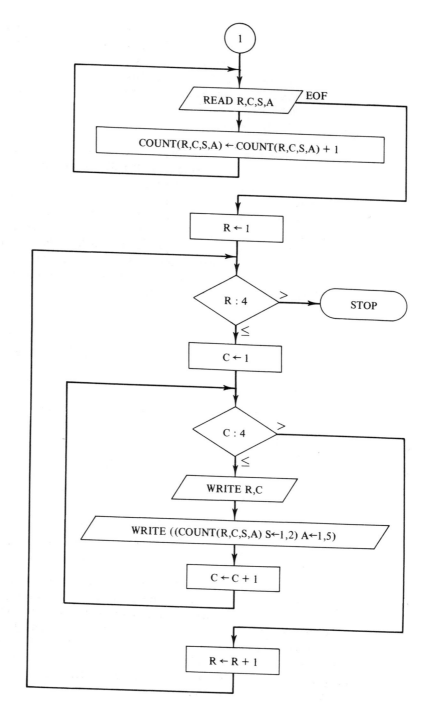

Figure 8.23 (*cont.*)

From the description of this problem, we know that our output must be a set of population tables. Let us agree to output each table by rows, as shown in Figure 8.23. The first two values for each table identify its race and class. The input list consists of four values for each student.

Each input has four identifiers: race, class, sex, and age. If such data are to be tabulated, we must be able to reference them by all their identifiers. Therefore, let us use a four-dimension array, COUNT, as shown in Figure 8.23, whose dimensions represent race, class, sex, and age, in that order. The length of each dimension equals its number of codes. Finally, let us use four cell pointers, R, C, S, and A. Note that all cells are used in each dimension; therefore, no last cell numbers are required.

Finally, we are ready to develop an algorithm and draw its flow chart. If COUNT is to be used to tabulate input values, its cells must initially be zero. Since COUNT has four dimensions, it is zeroed via four nested loops, as shown in Figure 8.23. Next, the coded values for each student are read one student at a time. Since the values are coded as integers starting at 1, they act as their own cell numbers. Finally, when an end of file is encountered, the summary population tables are ready for output.

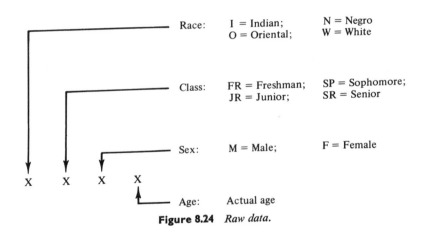

Figure 8.24 *Raw data.*

Before proceeding, we might ask how this problem would be solved had input values not been coded as integers before processing. In other words, suppose that data had been left in raw form, as shown in Figure 8.24. If such data are used directly, a computer must do its own coding. This can be done easily, as shown in the partial flow chart in Figure 8.25. Here, RR, RC, and RS represent raw data in alphanumeric form, whereas R, C, and S are coded integer values. Note that age, A, is already integer and has not been given a raw alphanumeric structure.

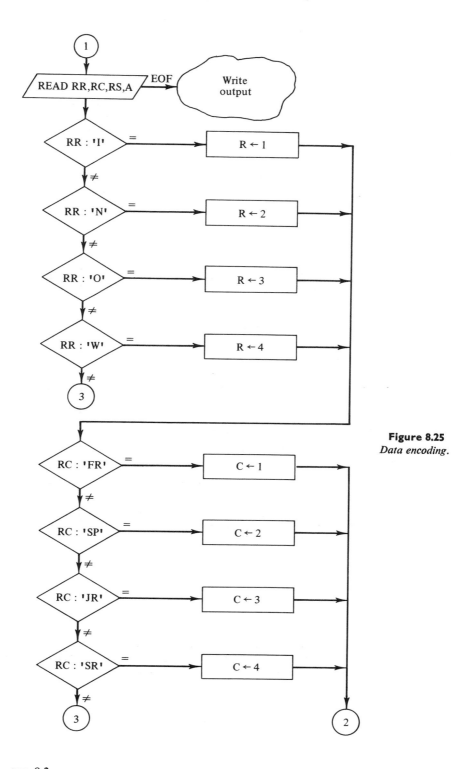

Figure 8.25
Data encoding.

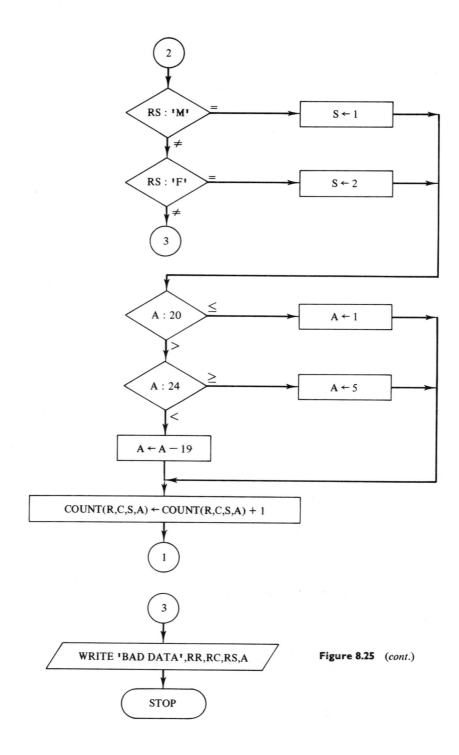

Figure 8.25 (cont.)

8.4
Using Single-
Dimension
Equivalents of
Multi-
Dimension
Data
Structures

At the beginning of this chapter, multidimension arrays were introduced as structures that can be employed to process data possessing more than one property, characteristic, or identifier. Each such identifier is assigned to a separate dimension with its own cell numbers, cell pointer, and last cell number. Individual data values are referenced via a structure name and a combination of cell numbers or pointers. A computer then automatically uses these cell numbers or pointers to calculate its equivalent single pointer. Thus, we can reference data sets by their properties while a computer handles the problem of storing them in memory. We should realize that such convenience actually increases the number of steps or operations that a computer must perform and, at times, can waste memory space. Let us now consider how sometimes we can save processing time and memory space by using single-dimension equivalents of multidimension arrays.

8.4.1 Saving processing time

As an example for discussion, let us repeat part of the cross-tabulation problem discussed previously. In particular, let us assume that we wish to zero all cells in the data structure, COUNT. Since this structure has four dimensions, we would normally initialize it via four nested loops, as was done in Figure 8.23. Thus, each time a computer zeros one cell in COUNT, it must evaluate the single pointer relation

$$s = d_4 d_3 d_2 (p_1 - 1) + d_4 d_3 (p_2 - 1) + d_4 (p_3 - 1) + p_4$$

which, in this case, reduces to

$$s = 40 (R - 1) + 10(C - 1) + 5(S - 1) + A$$

Since COUNT has dimension lengths of 4, 4, 2, and 5, it contains $4 \times 4 \times 2 \times 5$ or 160 cells; therefore, the preceding relationship must be evaluated 160 times.

If COUNT is actually stored as a linear list, why not use one cell pointer to initialize it to zero, as shown in Figure 8.26? Here, a single loop zeros all cells by varying a cell pointer, I, from 1 to 160. In this way, a computer need not calculate values for its single pointer but can use the cell pointer, I, directly. Note however, that a single loop can only access cells in sequence and cannot jump over or skip unused cells.

Now, we can reference multidimension data structures by either multiple cell pointers or just a single pointer. If we wish to reference structures by data properties, we employ multiple cell pointers; if not, we can use a single pointer. Unfortunately, most programming languages do not permit both multiple and single pointers for the same variable name in the same program. However, these languages do permit the use of two different variable names for the same structure. Thus, the first name can be used with multiple pointers whereas the second is used with a single pointer. For example, in FORTRAN, the equivalence statement is used to assign two different variable names to the same data structure.

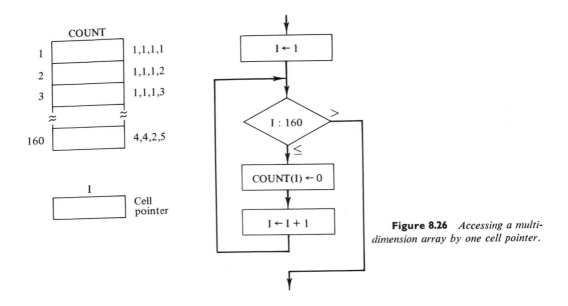

Figure 8.26 *Accessing a multi-dimension array by one cell pointer.*

8.4.2 Saving memory space

In the previous section, we discussed how we can reference multidimension arrays by a single pointer and thereby reduce processing time by eliminating cell pointer conversions. Likewise, it is sometimes possible to save memory cells by using a properly designed linear list in place of a multidimension array. Let us now consider one such example.

Let us assume that we are given a set of number pairs—e.g., 1,7; 3,6; 7,5; 17,17—where each number in all pairs must range from 1 to 100. We wish to know how often any two numbers occur together in the same pair. Here, the order of the two numbers in each pair is not important; e.g., the number pair 7,1 is considered to be the same as 1,7. Our output must show a frequency count for each different number pair. Furthermore, we are asked to label each count with its associated number pair.

Actually, this problem is quite similar to the cross-tabulation example discussed in Section 8.3.4. In fact, we might employ the same solution by changing the cross-tabulation array, COUNT, from four dimensions to two, as shown in Figure 8.27a. However, by doing so, the tabulation for any particular number pair is divided between two cells. For example, the count for the pair 2,3 is split between COUNT(2,3) and COUNT(3,2). Therefore, before we can output the frequency count for any pair, we must combine its partial counts. Of course, the counts for number pairs whose numbers are equal are not split, e.g., the count for 4,4 is found in one cell at COUNT(4,4).

We can avoid splitting tabulation counts by using only one cell for each unique number pair. Let us assume that each pair of numbers is read into single cells, I and J. If $I \leq J$, we increment COUNT(I,J) immediately. Otherwise, if $I > J$, we interchange the contents of I and J before 1 is added to COUNT(I,J). Now the tabulation for any number pair is combined into one cell. For example, whenever the number pairs 2,3 or 3,2 occur, COUNT(2,3) is incremented.

Since I is always less than or equal to J, just the upper half of COUNT contains tabulation data. In other words, all cells below the main diagonal are left unused, as shown in Figure 8.27b. In this case, using the obvious data structure, a two-dimension array, is quite wasteful of memory space. In fact, COUNT is a 100×100 array and contains 10,000 cells, of which 4950 cells are left vacant.

Figure 8.27c shows a single-dimension representation of COUNT in which all unused cells are omitted. The numbers at the left of the figure are single-dimension cell numbers; those to the right are for two dimensions. The two sets of cell numbers are related by the equation

$$K = 100(I - 1) + J - I \times (I - 1) / 2 \quad \text{for} \quad I \leq J$$

where I and J are the two-dimension cell pointers and K is the corresponding single pointer. With this relationship, we can use a linear list of 5050 cells rather than the original two-dimension array of 10,000. In so doing, 4950 unused cells are saved.

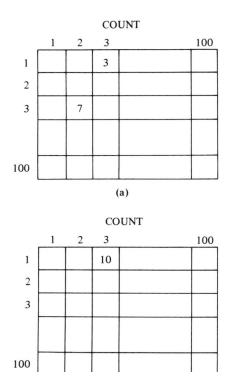

(a)

(b)

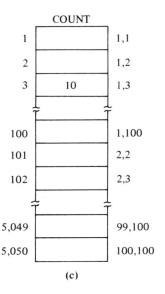

Figure 8.27
Data structures for counting number pairs.

(c)

Finally, Figure 8.28 shows a total solution to this problem. Output is a set of frequency counts where each count is identified by its associated number pair. Input consists of individual number pairs. The data chart contains a linear list, COUNT, with its cell pointer, K, along with I and J, which are used for input pairs. Basically, the flow chart consists of three parts. Initially, the cells of COUNT are set to 0 in a single loop. Next, input values are read and processed one pair at a time. If the first value exceeds the second, the two values are exchanged before a value of K is calculated. When an end of file is sensed during a read, the tabulation loop is terminated and the counts are ready for output. Here, a double loop is used so that the proper values of I and J precede each count as labels.

Output List

1	First no.
2	Second no.
	Count for 1, 2
1	First no.
3	Second no.
	Count for 1, 3
99	First no.
100	Second no.
	Count for 99, 100
100	First no.
100	Second no.
	Count for 100, 100

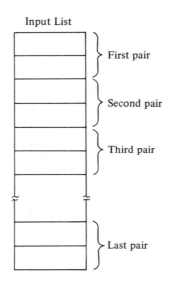

Input List

First pair

Second pair

Third pair

Last pair

Figure 8.28 *Number pair frequency count.*

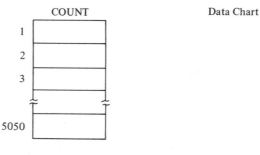

COUNT

1	
2	
3	
5050	

K

Cell pointer

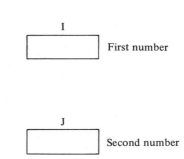

Data Chart

I

First number

J

Second number

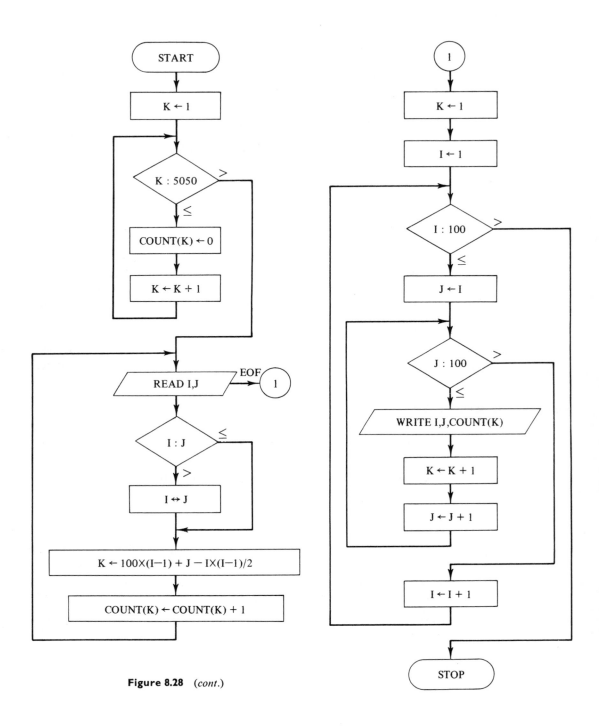

Figure 8.28 *(cont.)*

**8.5
Summary**

So far, three data structures have been introduced. The *single cell* is suitable for problems involving relatively few data values or those having a solution that does not require all data values in memory at the same time. In the first case, data values can be assigned to specific single cells; in the second, a few values can be read and processed completely before the next set of values is required in memory. If a particular problem does not satisfy one of these two conditions, it should not be solved with single cells.

The *linear list* with its cell pointer and last cell number is a data structure that can sometimes be used when single cells fail. Since it can contain an arbitrary number of cells, it can be used to solve problems requiring a large number of data values in memory at the same time. All that is necessary is to ensure that the linear list contains enough cells to store the largest anticipated data set. Smaller sets are then stored by leaving cells vacant, and a separate single cell, the last cell number, indicates where data end and where unused cells begin. Finally, the linear list was found suitable for problems whose data sets possess a single data relationship.

This chapter introduced *multidimension arrays* as a family of structures than can be used for data sets possessing more than one data relationship. Each such property, characteristic, or identifier is assigned to a separate dimention with its own cell numbers, cell pointer, and last cell number. By doing so, individual data values can be accessed and processed by their own data properties. A computer automatically converts multidimension arrays into equivalent linear lists for storage in memory. Finally, we saw how equivalent linear lists can sometimes be used to save processing time and memory space.

SELECTED REFERENCES

1. BARRODALE, IAN, FRANK D. K. ROBERTS, and BYRON L. EHLE, *Elementary Computer Applications*, John Wiley & Sons, Inc., New York, 1971.

2. FROBERG, CARL E., *Introduction to Numerical Analysis*, Addison-Wesley Publishing Co., Inc., Reading, Mass., 1965.

3. HILDEBRAND, F. B., *Methods of Applied Mathematics*, Prentice-Hall, Inc., Englewood Cliffs, N. J., 1960.

4. KNUTH, DONALD E., *The Art of Computer Programming*, Vol. 1, "Fundamental Algorithms," Addison-Wesley Publishing Co., Inc., Reading, Mass., 1968.

5. RALSTON, ANTHONY, and HERBERT S. WILF, *Mathematical Methods for Digital Computers*, John Wiley & Sons, Inc., New York, 1960.

6. STERLING, THEODORE D., and SEYMOUR V. POLLACK, *Introduction to Statistical Data Processing*, Prentice-Hall, Inc., Englewood Cliffs, N. J., 1968.

7. TOMPKINS, CHARLES B., and WALTER L. WILSON, *Elementary Numerical Analysis*, Prentice-Hall, Inc., Englewood Cliffs, N. J., 1969.

PROBLEMS

For each of the following problems, develop a computerized solution that includes an output list, input list, data chart, and flow chart.

8.1 Input a set of numbers into a two-dimension array and then determine the number of zeros. Assume that the input data have entries for 50 rows and 100 columns, and that they are arranged in row order, i.e., 100 entries for the first row come first, then 100 entries for the second row come next, etc.

8.2 Repeat Problem 8.1, but assume that the input is arranged in column order, i.e., 50 entries for the first column come first, then 50 entries for the second column come next, etc.

8.3 Repeat Problem 8.1, but assume that the input data can have up to 25 rows and 50 columns, and that they are arranged in row order. The first input value specifies the number of rows and the second states the number of columns.

8.4 Assume that data having 10 rows and 10 columns are available in column order. Develop a computerized procedure that inputs a set of numbers into a two-dimension array A(I,J), moves the entries A(I,I) into B(I), and then outputs B(I).

8.5 Assume that you have already drawn a partial flow chart that reads data into the four-dimension data structure, A, shown. Finish the chart so that it calculates and outputs the sum of all cells in A.

A
Four-Dimension Data Structure

	1st	2nd	3rd	4th
	M	N	O	P
Last cell number				
	I	J	K	L
Cell pointer				

8.6 Input a set of numbers into a two-dimension array and then calculate and output the sums of individual rows and columns. Assume that input data have entries for 25 rows and 75 columns, and that they are arranged in row order.

8.7 Assume that an input data set can have up to 30 rows and 60 columns and that it is arranged in column order. Input this set and determine and output the largest number in each row. The first input value specifies the number of columns; the second specifies the number of rows.

8.8 Assume that input data having 25 rows and 25 columns are available in row order. Develop a computerized procedure that inputs the data into a two-dimension array, inverts the data such that A(I,J) and A(J,I) are interchanged for all values of I and J, and then outputs the rearranged data in row order.

8.9 Read numbers into an N by N array and determine and output the sum of the elements on the main diagonal and the sum of the elements located above the main diagonal; N is never greater than 100.

8.10 Economic order quantity can be calculated from the following equation:

$$EOQ = \sqrt{\frac{2DC}{US}}$$

Assume that 10 different values of D, C, U, and S are available. Develop a computerized procedure that will input the following:

D(I)	I←1,10
C(J)	J←1,10
U(K)	K←1,10
S(L)	L←1,10

and then calculate

$$EOQ(I,J,K,L) = \sqrt{\frac{2 \times D(I) \times C(J)}{U(K) \times S(L)}}$$

for all combinations of I, J, K, and L.

8.11 Assume that you have just received data collected from a state travel survey on the habits of tourists traveling through the state. Each data piece consists of two road numbers: the first is the number of the road used to enter the state; the second is the number of the road used to leave the state. For convenience, assume that road numbers have been coded from 1 to 200. Develop a computerized procedure that inputs travel data and determines how many cars entered and left the state on each pair of roads.

8.12 In Problem 8.11, you were told to assume that road numbers were already coded into integers from 1 to 200. Rework that problem without that assumption. In other words, input values are actual road numbers as assigned by the Highway Department.

8.13 Determine the total dollar inventory value for each store in a chain of stores, which consists of 25 stores that all sell the same 100 items. The input consists of current inventory quantities on hand for each item in each store and the per unit dollar value of each item.

8.14 Assume that you are in charge of calculating the pay for a group of 50 salesmen who are paid on commission for selling the same 100 items where each item has its own commission rate. Input consists of a sequence of sales information with each data piece giving salesman number, item number, and units sold. Calculate the pay for each of 50 salesmen and output them in salesman number order.

8.15 The tax table shown gives personal income tax rates as a function of salary range code and number of dependents. Input the tax table and calculate after-taxes salary from gross salary. Input is a set of individual payroll values where each individual is represented by employee number, gross salary, salary range code, and number of dependants. Output must show employee number and net salary.

TAX TABLE

No. of Dependents

	0	1	2	3	4	5 or more
1						
2						
3						
4						
5						

(Salary range code)

8.16 Repeat Problem 8.15, where input is actual gross salary rather than a salary range code. Now both a tax table and a salary range table must be read before new salary calculations can be performed. A sample salary range table is shown below.

Salary Range Code	Gross Salary
1	$50.00 or less
2	50.01–100.00
3	100.01–200.00
4	200.01–400.00
5	400.01 or more

8.17 Assume that you receive accident reports for a 100 by 100 block area in a large city. Each report consists of two coded numbers between 1 and 100. These codes represent the two street numbers of the closest intersection to the scene of the accident. The north-south street is designated by the first code, whereas the east-west street is indicated by the second. Determine the compass direction and street number code of the street with the most accidents. In addition, find the street number code of the cross street that forms the intersection having the highest accident rate on the street with the most accidents.

8.18 In problem 7.31 the inventory of a store was compared with the reorder level for each item. You were required to output the order quantities for those items that needed to be ordered. Expand that solution to study the inventory of a chain of stores. Assume that each store has the same reorder point and order quantity for each item. Also the number of items cannot exceed 100 and there are not more than 50 stores. Input is arranged as follows: number of items, number of stores, a list of reorder points for each item, a list of order quantities for each item, and the present inventory for each item for each store. In addition to listing the order quantities by store, total the individual store order quantities into a single item order quantity so that only a single order need be written for any one item.

8.19 A pinochle deck is composed of 48 cards of the usual four suits: diamonds, hearts, clubs, and spades; but there are two cards for each denomination. The cards are nine, ten, jack, queen, king, and ace. An input list, coded by card, is available. The coding scheme is as follows:

Card	Code	Suit	Code
Ace	14	Diamonds	1
King	13	Hearts	2
Queen	12	Clubs	3
Jack	11	Spades	4
Ten	10		
Nine	9		

Read in this input list and "deal" the cards to the players one at a time. Deal to four players. When the deck is dealt, then write out the contents of each hand by suit and denomination.

1. 1st dimension—card code;
2. 2nd dimension—suit;
3. 3rd dimension—player.

Watch out for *two* of the same cards.

8.20 Students at a university can be classified by class and college as follows:

Class	Code	College	Code
Freshman	1	Business administration	1
Sophomore	2	Agriculture	2
Junior	3	Liberal arts & sciences	3
Senior	4	Engineering	4
Graduate	5	Pharmacy	5
		Nursing	6

Each student is assigned a class code and a college code. Read the student information and indicate how many students of each class have enrolled in a particular college.

8.21 Derive an equation that stores the lower half of a symmetric two-dimension array as a linear list.

8.22 Derive an equation that stores a two-dimension array in column order. Expand your equation to n dimensions.

9 Functions and Subroutines

So far, we have concentrated on solution techniques that involve selecting the correct data structure for each data set. Sometimes a particular data structure is chosen because a data set naturally fits its structure. On the other hand, it is sometimes possible to force a data set into a particular structure to produce a simpler or more convenient algorithm.

Previously, the concept of program structure was introduced as the relationship between individual steps of an algorithm. In straight-line structures, each statement is followed by one and only one statement; therefore, all statements are executed each time such an algorithm is performed. Branches allow a computer to select which of several paths it should follow depending upon conditions at the time it makes its decision. In such cases, not all instructions need be executed. Loops permit a computer to reuse statements, and therefore specify more processing in fewer instructions. Finally, functions and subroutines are predefined operations that can be employed as building blocks for constructing algorithms.

This chapter shows how functions and subroutines can make problem solving easier. We begin our discussion by illustrating limitations of single, large programs and indicating why such programs should be broken into smaller parts. Functions and subroutines are then introduced as program structures that can be used as components for constructing larger programs. Finally, we solve a number of problems that illustrate the use of functions and subroutines.

So far, complete algorithms have been used to solve problems. As problems become more difficult and involved, it is necessary to produce longer and more complicated algorithms. Let us begin our discussion of functions and subroutines by solving a problem that is best solved in parts. In so doing, we shall discover the limitations of writing single programs, and, at the same time, we shall illustrate how one realizes he should divide his solution into parts using functions and subroutines.

For the purpose of discussion, let us assume that we are required to calculate the ratio of the nth and mth terms of a Fibonacci sequence:

$$0, 1, 1, 2, 3, 5, 8, 13, 21, 34, \ldots$$

In this sequence, the first two terms are 0 and 1, and each following term is the sum of the two preceding terms. We are told that we shall be given integer values for n and m and are to produce a single value that is the ratio of the nth and mth terms. For example, if $n = 7$ and $m = 4$, we are to produce a value of 8/2 or 4.

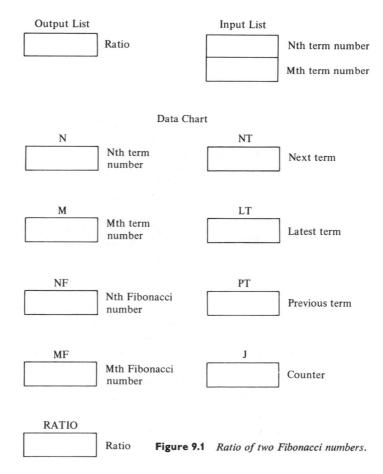

Figure 9.1 *Ratio of two Fibonacci numbers.*

Flow Chart

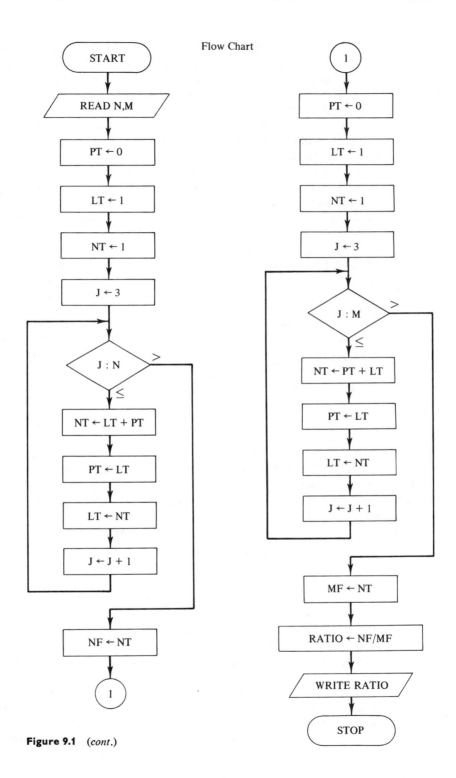

Figure 9.1 (*cont.*)

Actually, this problem involves no new techniques, so you should be able to follow its solution in Figure 9.1. Each Fibonacci number is the sum of the two previous values. In other words, the next term equals the latest plus the previous. Thus, a complete Fibonacci sequence can be calculated using just three values: next, latest, and previous. Since only the nth and the mth terms are required, there is no reason to save a complete sequence. Consequently, few data values need be retained in memory; therefore, single cells are suitable for this problem.

In Figure 9.1, the next, latest, and previous Fibonacci terms are saved in NT, LT, and PT, respectively, while NF and MF retain the nth and mth terms. After reading values for N and M, the flow chart uses separate loops to determine NF and MF. In both loops, J serves as a counter that terminates computations as soon as the desired terms are reached.

Study of this flow chart indicates that the two loops which calculate the Fibonacci numbers are quite similar. In fact, they have the same structure and are identical except for their test statements. The first loop terminates when J exceeds N; the second halts when J surpasses M. This duplication could be eliminated if we were able to predefine the operation of calculating a desired Fibonacci number. For example, we have already discussed and used the built-in function ABS(A), which calculates the absolute value of A. If we had a similar function, FIB(I), that determines the ith Fibonacci number, we could calculate the desired ratio in a single statement.

$$RATIO \leftarrow FIB(N)/FIB(M)$$

**9.2
The Function
and
Subroutine**

So far, we have discussed one type of flow chart. Since we are about to introduce two more, we shall henceforth refer to these earlier ones as *main* flow charts. Figure 9.2 shows the components of *function* and *subroutine* flow charts and compares them with those of main charts. Essentially, they are identical except for their terminals. Let us now consider functions in more detail.

9.2.1 Components of a function

Figure 9.3 shows an example of a function that finds the largest of three numbers. It begins with a single entry terminal that contains its name, MAX3, and its arguments, A, B, and C. As with built-in functions, arguments are separated by commas and enclosed with parentheses. An end of function is signaled by one or more *return* statements enclosed within exit terminals. Each return includes an expression whose value is returned as the value of the function. Here, MAX3 returns L.

Each function has its own set of totally separate data structures. It is as if an invisible barrier surrounds each function. Consequently, it is possible to select variable names for functions without fear of disturbing other structures. Since there is no connection between a function and other charts, there must

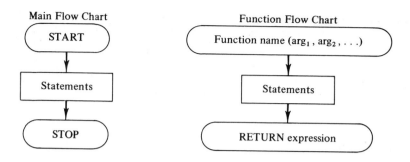

Main Flow Chart

Function Flow Chart

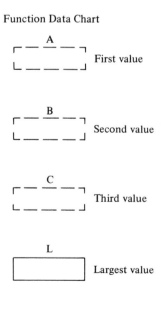

Subroutine Flow Chart

Figure 9.2
*Comparison of main, function,
and subroutine flow charts.*

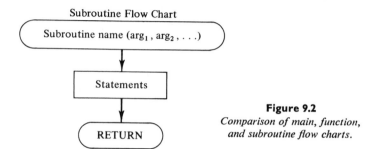

Function Data Chart

Function Flow Chart

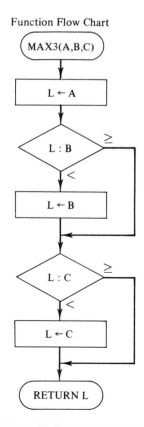

Figure 9.3
Function for finding the largest of three values.

be some way for it to receive its operands. This communication is provided by its arguments. When a function name is encountered in a flow-chart statement, that function is told the location of its arguments and then control is transferred to that function. The physical process of passing arguments to a function depends upon the actual computer and particular programming language. However, the effect can be visualized as follows.

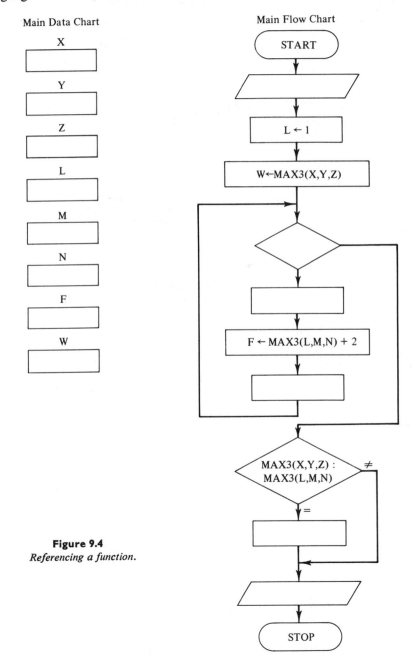

Figure 9.4
Referencing a function.

The main chart shown in Figure 9.4 employs MAX3 from three separate locations. As always, execution begins in the main chart at START and when the assignment statement

$$W \leftarrow MAX3(X,Y,Z)$$

is reached, MAX3 is asked to determine the largest of X, Y, and Z. The function flow chart is then performed as if X were its first argument, Y its second, and Z its third. In other words, throughout the function flow chart, X is substituted for A, Y for B, and Z for C. Note that the arguments are substituted in sequence in the same order as they appear in the following argument lists:

Main	MAX3(X,Y,Z)
	↓ ↓ ↓
Function	MAX3(A,B,C)

Arguments in a function entry can be considered as *dummy* variables that serve as stand-ins for actual variables, which are supplied each time a function is performed. Consequently, they do not require storage space and for this reason are drawn with dashed lines in function data charts to distinguish them from those that require space. For example, MAX3 requires only one single cell, L, since A, B, and C are arguments.

Since all communications are sent to a function via its arguments, great care must be taken to ensure that they are passed correctly. First, a function name must be followed by the proper number of arguments; e.g., MAX3 always requires three. Second, each argument that is passed should contain the same type of data, i.e., numeric, alphanumeric, etc., as is expected by its corresponding variable in the function. In MAX3, A has a numeric value and is replaced by X, also numeric. Third, corresponding arguments should have the same data structure. Here, X, Y, and Z are single cells and are substituted for single cells A, B, and C.

Generally, the results of a function are transmitted back to its requesting program via a return statement. In Figure 9.4, when the main flow-chart statement

$$W \leftarrow MAX3(X,Y,Z)$$

is performed, MAX3 uses its L to determine the largest of X, Y, and Z. When the return statement is reached, the contents of L are returned as the value of MAX3, and are then assigned to W. Later, in the same flow chart, the statement

$$F \leftarrow MAX3(L,M,N) + 2$$

is reached, and MAX3 uses the main chart L as A, M as B, and N as C. When the largest value is returned, it is added to the constant, 2, and the result is assigned to F. Here, it is important to appreciate that the L in the main chart is different and separate from the L in MAX3. Finally, MAX3 is used twice in the test statement

$$MAX3(X,Y,Z) : MAX3(L,M,N)$$

to compare the largest values from two sets of three numbers.

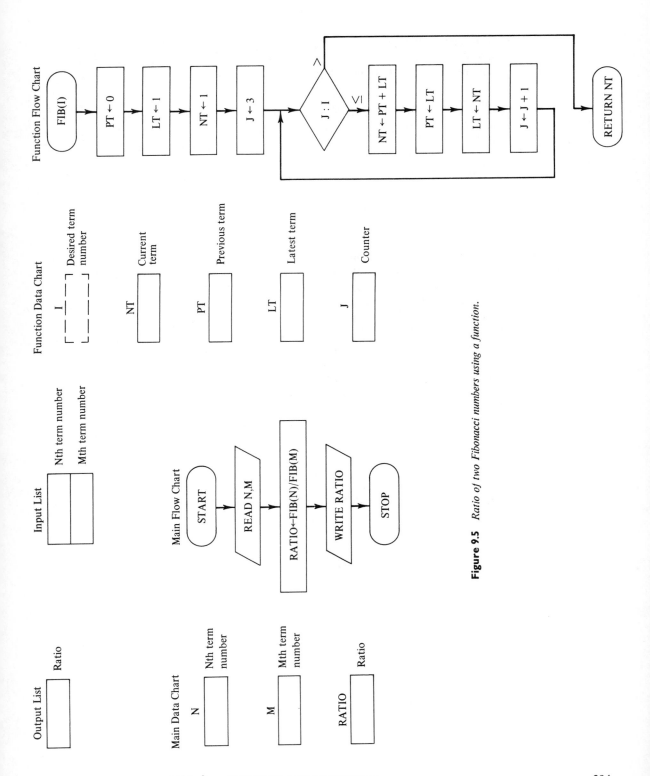

Figure 9.5 *Ratio of two Fibonacci numbers using a function.*

Now that we can define our own functions, let us rework the Fibonacci problem discussed in Section 9.1. Since we have already solved this problem, we know that our solution requires one output and two input values, as shown in Figure 9.5. Furthermore, we realize that we must calculate two Fibonacci numbers. Therefore, let us predefine a function, FIB(I) that returns the value of the *i*th Fibonacci number. The function flow chart in Figure 9.5 uses the same algorithm that was employed in Figure 9.1. In this case, I is used as an argument to pass the term number of the desired Fibonacci number. Consequently, I is shown with dashed lines in the function data chart, indicating that it is an argument.

9.2.2 Components of a subroutine

Now that we can predefine operations as functions, we can use them as building blocks to solve problems. Generally, functions are employed when single values are required. Let us now introduce subroutines as program structures that can also be predefined and yet produce multiple values.

Basically, subroutines and functions are quite similar. Figure 9.2 compares their components and shows that they are identical except for exit terminals. In the case of functions, an end is signaled by a return statement that includes an expression. In contrast, a subroutine end is indicated by a return without an expression. Consequently, all communications *to* and *from* subroutines must be transmitted via their arguments.

Subroutines also differ from functions in the way each is invoked. A function is simply mentioned by name in a flow-chart statement just as if it were a variable, and it is performed as part of the evaluation of that statement. Subroutines, on the other hand, are called into operation by a special flow-chart statement known as a *call* statement. A call statement has the form

$$\text{CALL subroutine name } (\text{arg}_1, \text{arg}_2, \ldots)$$

and is enclosed in a special flow-chart outline

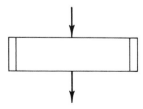

known as a *predefined operation* symbol.

As a simple introductory example, Figure 9.6 shows data and flow charts for a subroutine that exchanges the contents of two single cells. Its name is XCH, and it has two arguments, A and B. The main chart calls for XCH from two different locations. As always, execution begins in the main chart at START. When the statement

$$\text{CALL XCH}(X,Y)$$

is reached, the subroutine XCH is called upon to interchange the contents of X and Y.

At this point, execution of the main chart is suspended and control is transferred to XCH along with arguments X and Y. These arguments are then substituted for dummy arguments, A and B, just as if XCH were a function. When the return statement is executed, control is given back to the main chart and execution resumes with the statement following the subroutine call.

As an example of a problem where subroutines can be used to advantage, let us assume that we have the following situation. We are given two sets of numbers, each of which contains *n* values. We are asked to determine whether they both contain the same values, i.e., for each number in one set is there a corresponding value in the other.

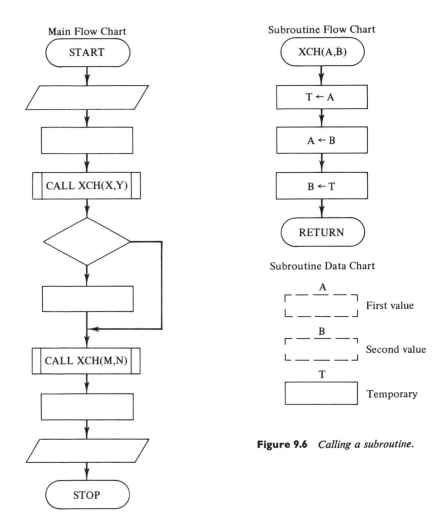

Figure 9.6 *Calling a subroutine.*

We can solve this problem if we can develop a means for checking or crossing off corresponding values. However, since breaking a problem into parts is an advisable procedure, let us subdivide this problem. For the moment, let us assume that the two sets have been sorted into ascending sequence before we receive them. If such is the case, we can determine whether they contain identical values by comparing numbers from each set in sequence. In other words, if linear lists X and Y contain the sorted sets, the sets are identical if X(I) equals Y(I) for I from 1 to N.

With this discussion in mind, it is logical to solve this problem in parts. First, the two input data sets are read into separate, linear lists—say, X and Y—and then sorted. Since we must perform the same operation on two different data sets, it is reasonable to predefine a sort subroutine that can be called twice, once for each input set. Once the sorts are complete, sequential comparisons can be performed in a single loop that varies I from 1 to N.

Figure 9.7 shows a solution to our problem that incorporates a sort subroutine. The actual routine has a name of SORT and two arguments: A and N. To sort a set of numbers, SORT must know the name and length of each particular set. In this case, A is that name and N is its length.

In the main chart, the subroutine is asked to sort the first input set by the statement

CALL SORT(X,N)

Here, X replaces the dummy argument, A, whereas N replaces dummy argument, N. As soon as the first set is in sequence, the subroutine is immediately called upon to sort the second. Finally, the chart enters a loop and compares X(I) with Y(I). If a mismatch is found, the output message is NO; otherwise it is YES.

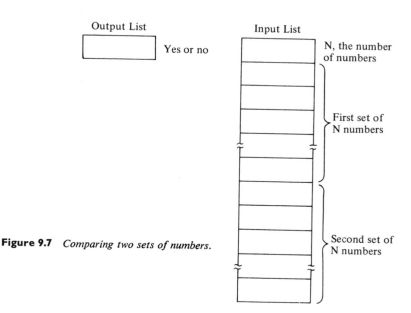

Figure 9.7 *Comparing two sets of numbers.*

Main Data Chart

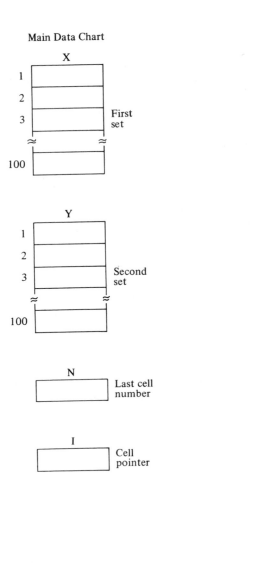

Figure 9.7 (*cont.*)

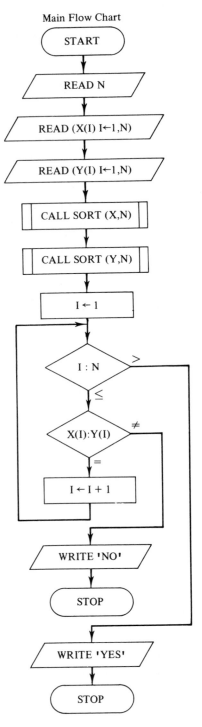

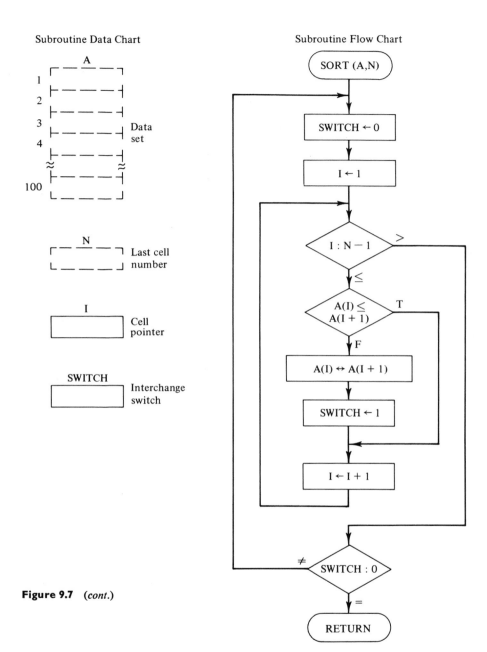

Subroutine Data Chart

Subroutine Flow Chart

Figure 9.7 (*cont.*)

Subroutine Flow Chart

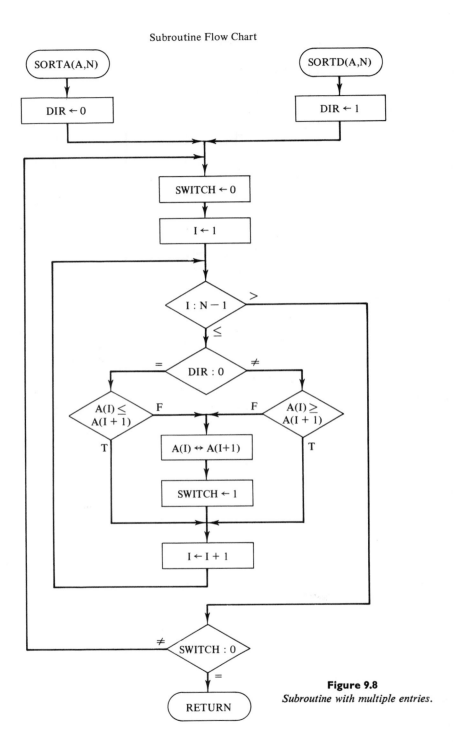

Figure 9.8
Subroutine with multiple entries.

9.2.3 Multiple entries and exits

So far, we have limited our discussion to functions and subroutines that have just one entry and exit terminal. One reason for using these predefined operations is to eliminate duplicate statements. Sometimes, this reduction can be carried even further by combining them together into one with multiple entries or exits.

As an example of multiple entries, let us suppose that we need to perform both ascending and descending sorts in the same problem, We can either develop two separate routines, say SORTA and SORTD, or we can combine them together into one, using multiple entries as in Figure 9.8. When an ascending sort is required, a call is made to SORTA, whereas SORTD is requested for a descending one. Here, a single cell, DIR, is used to remember the desired sort direction. In this case, the use of multiple entries eliminates statements that would be common to separate sort routines.

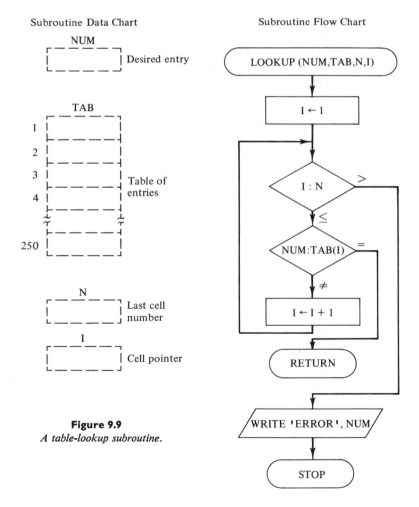

Subroutine Data Chart   Subroutine Flow Chart

Figure 9.9
A table-lookup subroutine.

When a return statement is executed in a subroutine, control is given back to its calling program and execution resumes with the statement following the subroutine call. Sometimes, it is desirable to allow a subroutine to return control to other statements, depending upon conditions encountered during execution. For example, Figure 9.9 shows data and flow charts for a subroutine, LOOKUP, that performs a table lookup in a manner similar to that discussed in Section 7.3.5. Here, this routine attempts to find a match for a value, NUM, in a table, TAB, that has N entries. When a match is found, I is returned as the location of NUM. If, by chance, LOOKUP cannot find a match, it halts execution after it outputs an appropriate message.

Now, let us suppose that we wish to permit a calling program to decide what should be done when LOOKUP fails to produce a match. In other words, we wish LOOKUP to return control to its calling program with some indication of its outcome. In general, this can be done in one of two ways. Either the routine returns this information via an additional argument or it returns control to different statements depending upon the outcome of its execution. Here, we shall discuss the first method, since it is applicable to all machines and languages.

In Figure 9.10, ERR has been added to LOOKUP as an argument. If a match is found, ERR is returned as 0; otherwise, it has a value of 1. The calling program can then interrogate this argument to determine if a match was found. The main chart in Figure 9.10 uses LOOKUP with this return parameter to solve the problem discussed in Section 7.3.5. Here, the main program outputs its own error message and then bypasses incorrect input values.

Figure 9.10   *A table-lookup using a return parameter.*

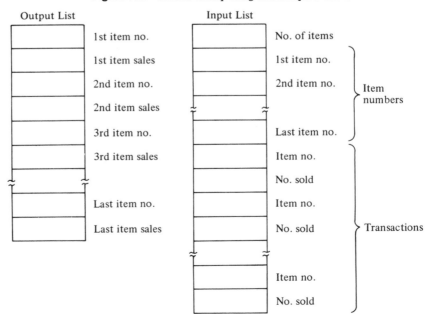

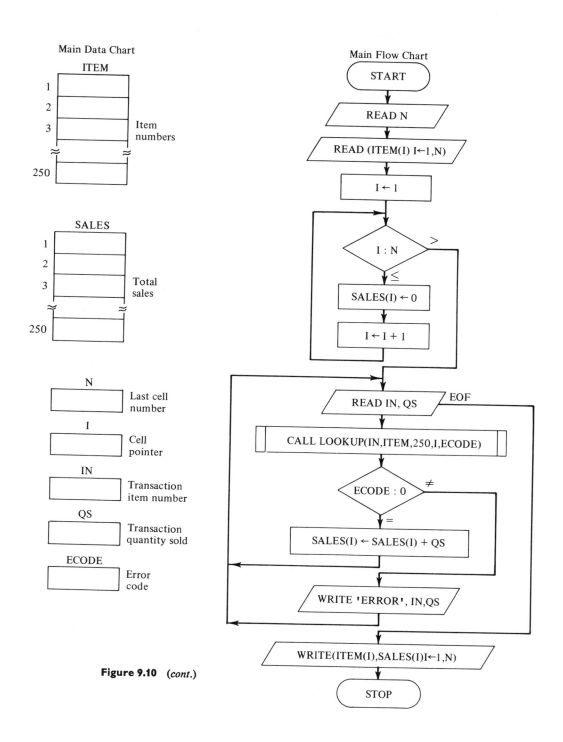

Main Data Chart

ITEM

1
2
3
≈
250

Item numbers

SALES

1
2
3
≈
250

Total sales

N — Last cell number

I — Cell pointer

IN — Transaction item number

QS — Transaction quantity sold

ECODE — Error code

Main Flow Chart

START

READ N

READ (ITEM(I) I←1,N)

I ← 1

I : N   >

≤

SALES(I) ← 0

I ← I + 1

READ IN, QS   EOF

CALL LOOKUP(IN,ITEM,250,I,ECODE)

ECODE : 0   ≠

=

SALES(I) ← SALES(I) + QS

WRITE 'ERROR', IN,QS

WRITE(ITEM(I),SALES(I)I←1,N)

STOP

Figure 9.10 (*cont.*)

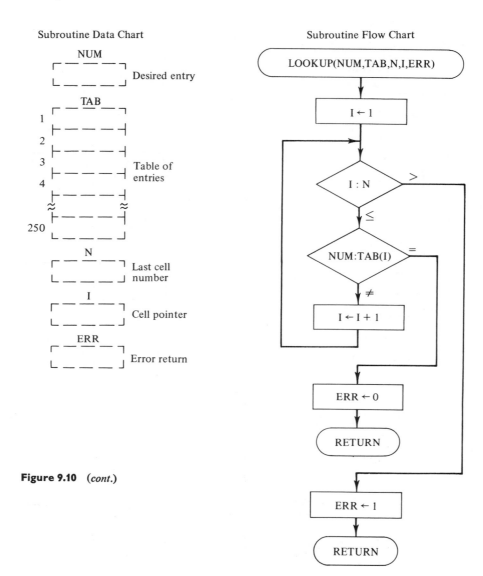

Subroutine Data Chart

NUM

Desired entry

TAB

1
2
3
4

250

Table of
entries

N

Last cell
number

I

Cell pointer

ERR

Error return

Subroutine Flow Chart

LOOKUP(NUM,TAB,N,I,ERR)

$I \leftarrow 1$

$I : N$ >

$\leq$

NUM:TAB(I)   =

$\neq$

$I \leftarrow I + 1$

$ERR \leftarrow 0$

RETURN

$ERR \leftarrow 1$

RETURN

Figure 9.10   *(cont.)*

9.3
Using
Functions and
Subroutines

Now that we have studied the construction of functions and subroutines, let us use them for problem solving. So far, we have talked of functions and subroutines as a means of eliminating duplicate statements. Of course, it is best if you can see in advance how to divide your problem so that these program structures can be used to advantage. Next best is to notice that your flow chart is beginning to contain duplicate or similar statement patterns. On the other hand, you may wish to develop a function or subroutine for a current solution because you foresee the need for the same operation in future ones. Finally, you may wish to use functions or subroutines because someone else has already predefined one that you need.

9.3.1 Calculating a binomial coefficient

As our first example of the use of predefined operations, let us assume that we are asked to calculate a *binomial coefficient*, which is prescribed by the relationship

$$\frac{n!}{m!(n-m)!} \quad \text{for} \quad n \geq m$$

The term $n!$ is read as *n factorial*, and is defined by the equation

$$n! = n(n-1)(n-2) \cdots (2)(1)$$

where

$$0! = 1$$

Basically, this problem involves the calculation of three factorials: $n!$, $m!$, and $(n-m)!$. In other words, if we had a function, FAC(N), which returns the value of $n!$, we could calculate a binomial coefficient in one statement

$$BIN \leftarrow FAC(N)/(FAC(M) \times FAC(N-M))$$

Figure 9.11 shows a complete solution that includes the function, FAC(N). When FAC receives its single argument, it first checks for the special condition of 0!. If such is the case, a value of 1 is returned immediately; otherwise, a single loop calculates the desired factorial.

Figure 9.11   *Calculating a binomial coefficient.*

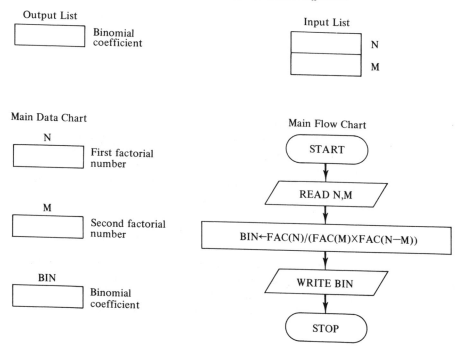

Output List

☐ Binomial coefficient

Input List

☐ N

☐ M

Main Data Chart

N ☐ First factorial number

M ☐ Second factorial number

BIN ☐ Binomial coefficient

Main Flow Chart

START

READ N,M

BIN←FAC(N)/(FAC(M)×FAC(N−M))

WRITE BIN

STOP

Function Data Chart

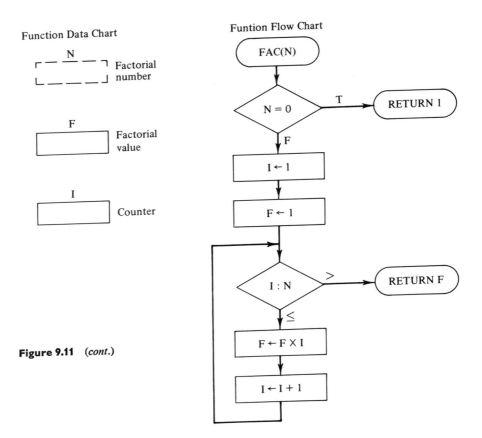

N
┌ ─ ─ ─ ─ ─ ┐ Factorial
└ ─ ─ ─ ─ ─ ┘ number

F
┌─────────────┐ Factorial
└─────────────┘ value

I
┌─────────────┐ Counter
└─────────────┘

Figure 9.11 (*cont.*)

Funtion Flow Chart

FAC(N)

N = 0 ──T──> RETURN 1

F

I ← 1

F ← 1

I : N ──>── RETURN F

≤

F ← F × I

I ← I + 1

9.3.2 Taylor's series

As our next example, let us develop a function, EXP(X), that returns a value of e^x. In fact, most languages include this function as a built-in; but as an example, let us predefine our own. In general, arithmetic and trigonometric functions, such as e^x, $\log_{10} x$, $\sin x$ and $\cos x$, can be expressed as the sum of an infinite number of terms, referred to as a *Taylor's series*. In this case, e^x is defined by the relationship

$$e^x = 1 + x + \frac{x^2}{2!} + \frac{x^3}{3!} + \cdots$$

Because an algorithm must be finite, we must have some method for truncating the preceding series after a limited number of terms. In this case, $n!$ always exceeds x^n for large n; thus, $x^n/n!$ approaches 0. Therefore, let us agree to terminate the series when the magnitude of its next term becomes less than 0.000001.

The function flow chart in Figure 9.12a displays a straightforward algorithm for this problem. Here, a single cell, SUM, is employed as a running total, and each term is calculated separately, assuming that FAC(N) is available as a predefined function. The summation process continues until a term magnitude drops below 10^{-6}.

Although the proceding algorithm produces a correct result, it fails to take advantage of the relationship between adjacent terms. In this case, the ratio of neighboring terms is x/n. In other words, the nth term, t_n, can be calculated from the $(n-1\text{th})$ term, t_{n-1}, by the relation

$$t_n = t_{n-1} \cdot \frac{x}{n}$$

The flow chart in Figure 9.12b uses this iterative relationship and thus avoids separate calculation of each factorial.

Figure 9.12 *Calculating e^x.*

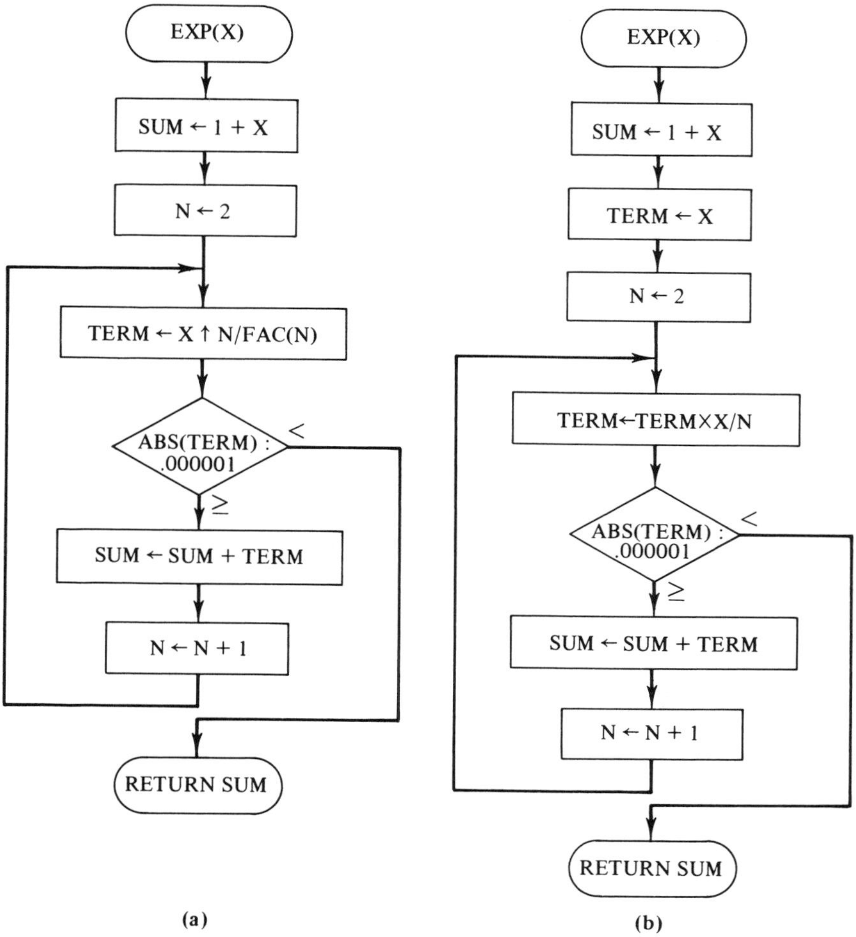

(a)   (b)

Subroutine Data Chart

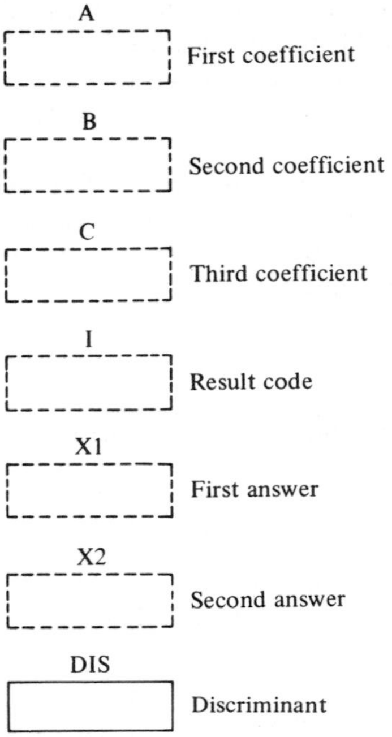

A

First coefficient

B

Second coefficient

C

Third coefficient

I

Result code

X1

First answer

X2

Second answer

DIS

Discriminant

Figure 9.13
Roots of a quadratic equation.

Subroutine Flow Chart

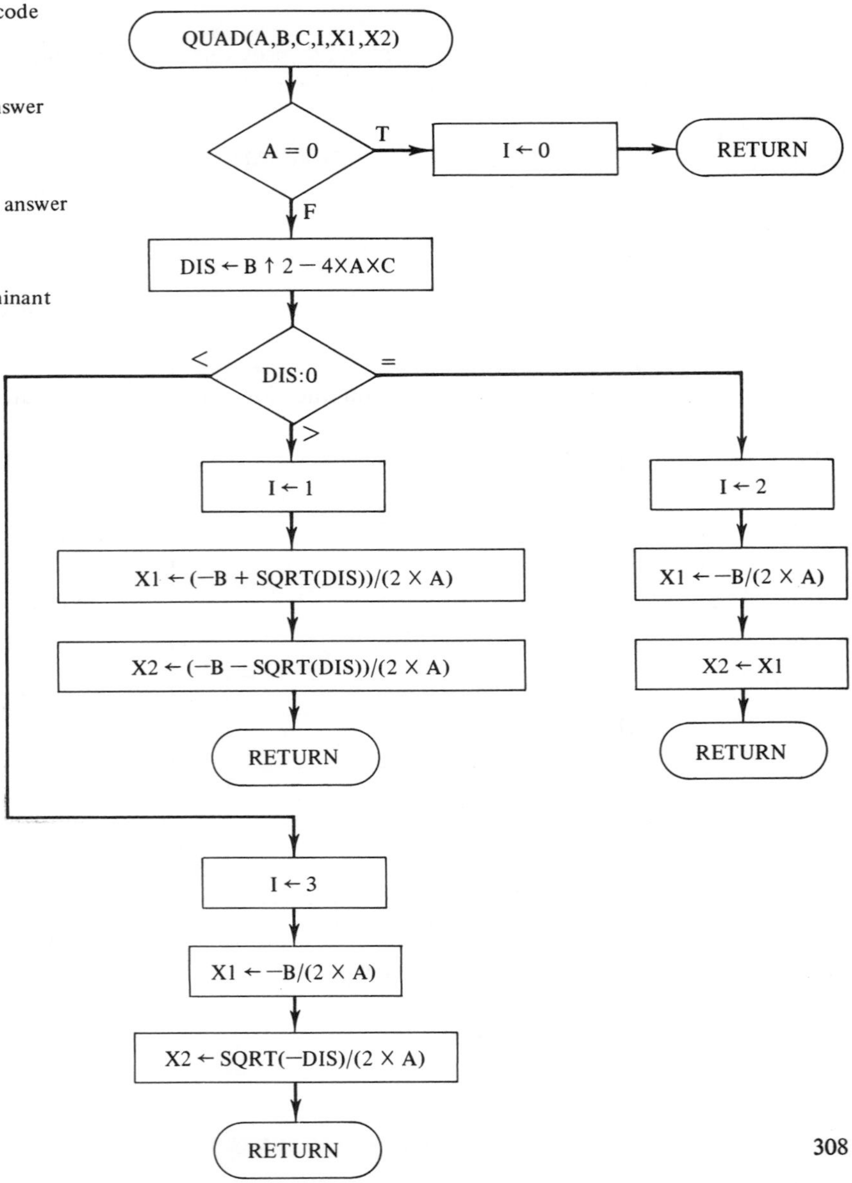

QUAD(A,B,C,I,X1,X2)

A = 0 — T → I ← 0 → RETURN

F

DIS ← B ↑ 2 − 4×A×C

DIS:0

I ← 1

X1 ← (−B + SQRT(DIS))/(2 × A)

X2 ← (−B − SQRT(DIS))/(2 × A)

RETURN

I ← 2

X1 ← −B/(2 × A)

X2 ← X1

RETURN

I ← 3

X1 ← −B/(2 × A)

X2 ← SQRT(−DIS)/(2 × A)

RETURN

308

9.3.3 Quadratic Equations

For purposes of discussion, let us assume that we are asked to develop a pre-defined process that finds the solution to a quadratic equation

$$ax^2 + bx + c = 0$$

using the well-known relationship

$$x = \frac{-b \pm \sqrt{b^2 - 4ac}}{2a}$$

In addition, we are told that the coefficients, a, b, and c, are real and that our predefined process must determine all values of x satisfying the preceding equation.

All quadratic equations have two roots, and the relation,

$$b^2 - 4ac$$

referred to as the *discriminant*, can be used to predict their form. If the discriminant is positive, they are both real; whenever it is 0, both are real and equal to each other; whenever it is negative, they are *complex conjugates*, i.e., their real parts are equal but their imaginary parts have opposite signs.

So far, we have limited our consideration to predefined operations that need to return a single value. In such situations, we can employ functions. In this case, we should use a subroutine because multiple values must be returned.

Figure 9.13 shows a data and flow chart for a subroutine, QUAD(A,B,C,I, X1,X2). It receives its coefficients through its first three arguments: A, B, and C; X1 and X2 are used to return its results, and I tells the calling program how to interpret them, as shown in the following table:

Value of I	Result
0	No solution (A = 0)
1	Two real roots
2	Two equal real roots
3	Two complex roots

For example, when I is returned as zero, then the calling program can tell that there was no solution. In contrast, if I is 3, X1 and X2 contain the real and imaginary parts of the first root. The real part of the second root equals X1 while its imaginary part has a value of $-X2$.

9.3.4 More text editing

As a final example of the use of functions and subroutines, let us expand the text editing problem discussed in Section 7.3.6. In that situation, we were given a character string that represented a paragraph and were asked to subdivide it into lines, given a maximum line length. In this case, we are to edit the string to ensure that it is in usual paragraph form. Specifically, we are to indent the first line five spaces and to remove multiple blanks that may occur between words. Furthermore, we are to assume that a period followed by at least one space is an end of sentence and must be succeeded by two and only two spaces.

Obviously, this problem is similar to the earlier one; therefore, we can borrow from its solution. In both problems, it is necessary to input the paragraph; consequently, we can use the same read loop as in Figure 7.27. In addition, once the text has been edited for proper spacing, the output procedure is the same as before. Now that we see how this problem differs from the previous one, let us subdivide it even further.

Here, text editing can be broken into at least three operations. First, we must be able to scan down a character string until a given character is found. Second, we need be able to delete a character at a given location. Third, we should be able to insert a character at a specific position. For this problem, we need to locate blanks and then insert or delete extra ones as required. Since we know in advance that these three operations are necessary, let us predefine them.

Figure 9.14 shows data and flow charts for these three operations as subroutines. For example, the subroutine, FIND, looks for a character, CHAR, in a string, STRING, of length, LENG, starting at position, INIT. When it finds the desired character, it returns the location of that character in LOC. If by chance the desired character is not found, LOC is returned as zero; thus, the calling program can determine whether FIND was successful. The routines, DELETE and INSERT, delete and insert a character, CHAR, at position, LOC. In both cases, the length, LENG, of string, STRING, is decreased or increased by 1, as appropriate. You should now stop and study the operation of these three subroutines so that you can understand their use in the main chart.

Finally, Figure 9.15 shows a main chart that performs text editing by calling these three subroutines. It starts by reading the complete paragraph into a linear list, PAR, and then uses the subroutine, INSERT, to add five blanks at the beginning of the paragraph. Next, it enters a loop which checks the input character string for correct paragraph format. The subroutine, FIND, scans down the string starting at P, and returns a new value of P that points to the next blank. If FIND returns a value of 0, the end of paragraph was reached before the next blank was found. When this happens, the edit is complete and the character string is ready for output, using the procedure in Figure 7.27.

If FIND returns a nonzero P, the character at $PAR(P-1)$ must be checked for a period. If it is a period, it must be followed by two blanks; therefore, $PAR(P+1)$ must also be a blank. If it is not, one must be inserted at $P+1$. If $PAR(P-1)$ is not a period, $PAR(P+1)$ must not be a blank. If it is, it must be deleted. At this point, P is adjusted to point to the next nonblank character, and the chart loops back to find the next blank.

Subroutine Data Chart

Subroutine Flow Chart

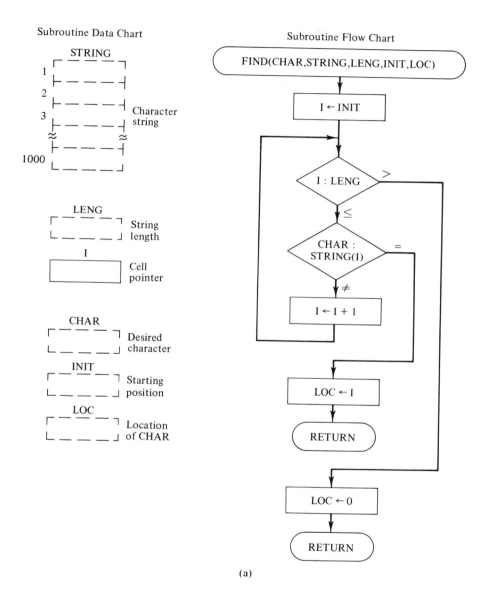

(a)

Figure 9.14 *Text editing subroutines:*
(a) find subroutine; (b) delete subroutine; (c) insert subroutine.

Subroutine Data Chart

STRING

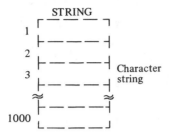

1
2
3

Character string

1000

LENG

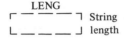

String length

I

Cell pointer

LOC

Location of CHAR

Subroutine Flow Chart

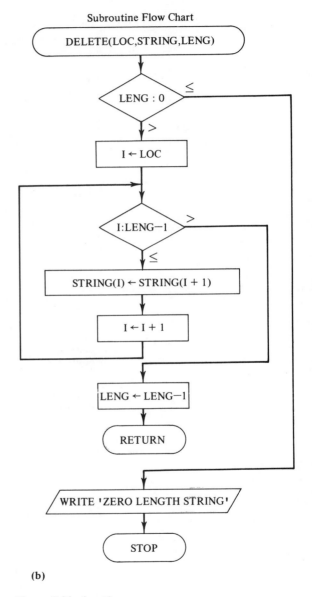

(b)

Figure 9.14 (*cont.*)

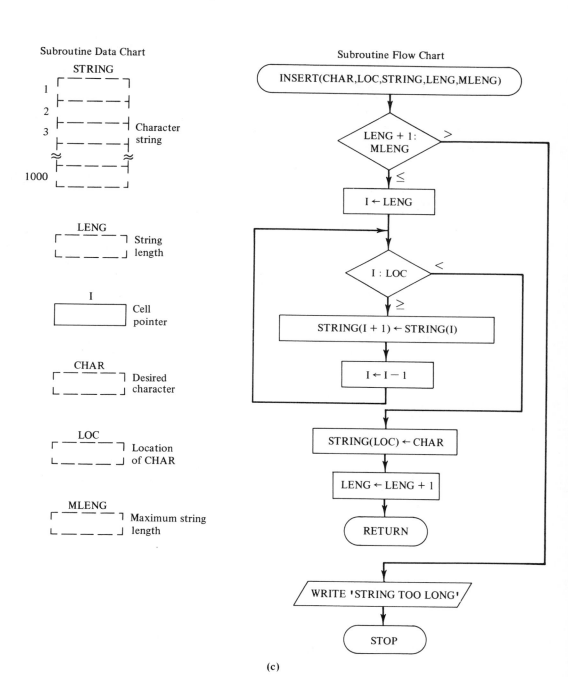

Subroutine Data Chart

STRING

Character string

LENG   String length

I   Cell pointer

CHAR   Desired character

LOC   Location of CHAR

MLENG   Maximum string length

Subroutine Flow Chart

INSERT(CHAR,LOC,STRING,LENG,MLENG)

LENG + 1 : MLENG

≤

I ← LENG

I : LOC

≥

STRING(I + 1) ← STRING(I)

I ← I − 1

STRING(LOC) ← CHAR

LENG ← LENG + 1

RETURN

WRITE 'STRING TOO LONG'

STOP

(c)

Figure 9.14 *(cont.)*

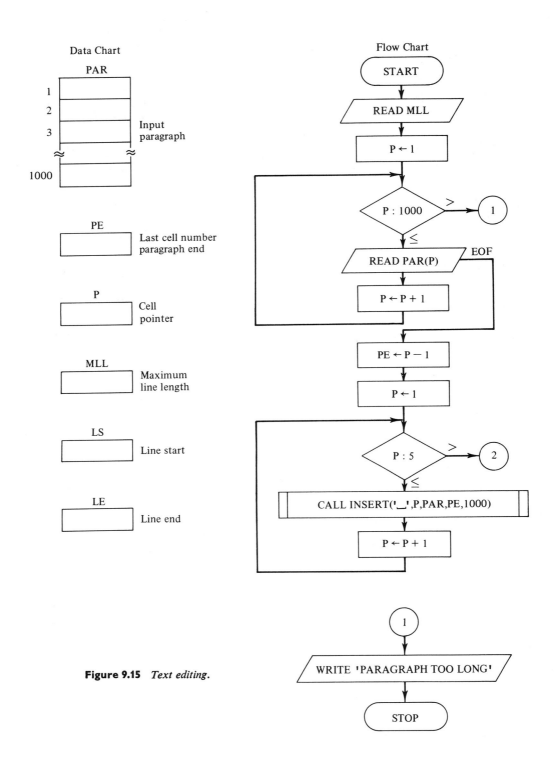

Data Chart

PAR

1
2
3

≈   ≈

1000

Input
paragraph

PE   Last cell number
            paragraph end

P   Cell
            pointer

MLL   Maximum
            line length

LS   Line start

LE   Line end

Figure 9.15 *Text editing.*

Flow Chart

START

READ MLL

P ← 1

P : 1000   >   ①

≤

READ PAR(P)   EOF

P ← P + 1

PE ← P − 1

P ← 1

P : 5   >   ②

≤

CALL INSERT('⌴',P,PAR,PE,1000)

P ← P + 1

①

WRITE 'PARAGRAPH TOO LONG'

STOP

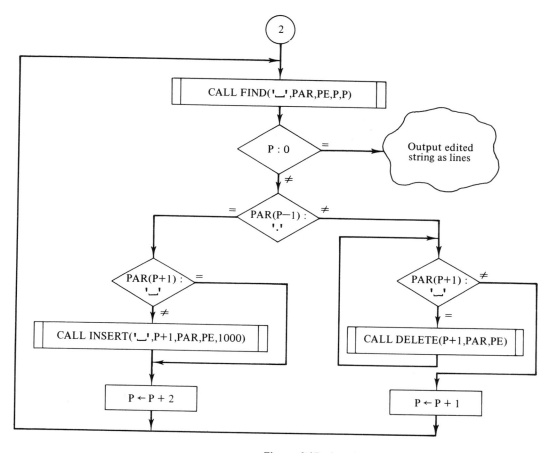

Figure 9.15 *(cont.)*

9.4
Summary
Basically, there are four reasons why functions and subroutines can make problem solving easier. *First*, you can use them to eliminate flow-chart duplication, as in the Fibonacci sequence example. *Second*, you may wish to develop a function or subroutine for a current problem because you foresee its need in future ones. For example, once a factorial function was developed for binomial coefficients, it could then be used for Taylor's series. *Third*, you may wish to employ functions and subroutines because someone else has already predefined them. We have already discussed built-in functions, such as ABS. Furthermore, most computer operating systems include a set of predefined subroutines, any of which can be invoked by a call with suitable arguments. Such routines are said to comprise the *subroutine library*. *Fourth*, you may wish to subdivide a large or complicated problem into parts and then solve each one separately. In the case of text editing, find, insert and delete operations were predefined as subroutines, which were then used as components for constructing a main program.

SELECTED REFERENCES

1. FORSYTHE, ALEXANDRA I., *et al.*, *Computer Science: A First Course*, John Wiley & Sons, Inc., New York, 1969.

2. HASTINGS, CECIL, *Approximations for Digital Computers*, Princeton University Press, Princeton, N. J., 1955.

3. SHERMAN, PHILIP M., *Techniques in Computer Programming*, Prentice-Hall, Inc., Englewood Cliffs, N. J., 1970.

PROBLEMS

9.1 Develop a function, SIGN(X), that returns a value of

$$\begin{matrix} 1 & \text{if} & X > 0 \\ 0 & \text{if} & X = 0 \\ -1 & \text{if} & X < 0 \end{matrix}$$

9.2 Write a function, SUM(X,N), that calculates

$$\sum_{i=1}^{n} x_i = x_1 + x_2 + x_3 + \cdots + x_n$$

9.3 Develop a function, DIAG(X,N), that returns a value of

$$\sum_{i=1}^{n} x_i^2$$

9.4 Write a function, PROD(X,N), that calculates

$$\prod_{i=1}^{n} x_i = x_1 \cdot x_2 \cdot x_3 \cdots x_n$$

9.5 The dot, inner, or scalar product of two vectors of length n is defined as

$$a_1 \cdot b_1 + a_2 \cdot b_2 + \cdots + a_n \cdot b_n = \sum_{i=1}^{n} a_i \cdot b_i$$

Write a function, DOT(A,B,N), that returns the dot product of two vectors, A and B, of length N.

9.6 Produce a function, TRUNC(X), that returns a value of

$$\begin{matrix} \text{FLOOR(X)} & \text{if} & X \geq 0 \\ \text{CEIL(X)} & \text{if} & X < 0 \end{matrix}$$

9.7 Write a function, IPOWER(X,N), that calculates x^n without using the exponentiation operator; N can have any integer value.

9.8 Write a subroutine, ZERO(LIST,LENG), that zeros a linear list, LIST, of length, LENG.

9.9 In Figure 9.5, the function FIB(I) does not produce the correct result for $i = 1$. Modify the subroutine to handle this case. How does this affect the main chart in that figure?

9.10 Develop a function, Y(X), that returns a value according to the graph shown.

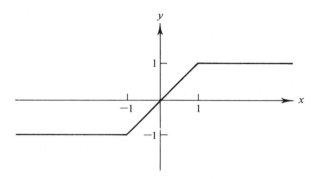

9.11 Given the relationship shown, develop a function, I(T).

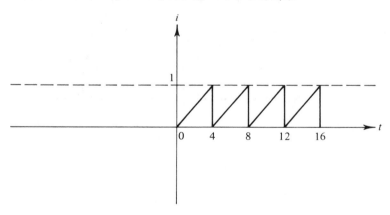

9.12 Develop a subroutine, MSUB(A,B,C,N,M), that finds the difference of two matrices, such that

$$c_{ij} = a_{ij} - b_{ij} \quad \text{for} \quad \begin{matrix} i = 1, n \\ j = 1, m \end{matrix}$$

9.13 Sometimes, it is desirable to smooth or filter a set of experimental data. A simple smoothing algorithm consists of replacing each value, d_i, by the value

$$d_i = \frac{d_{i-1} + d_i + d_{i+1}}{3}$$

Develop a subroutine, SMOOTH(D,N), that uses the preceding relationship to smooth the contents of a linear list, D, of length, N.

9.14 In Section 9.2.1, a binomial coefficient was defined as

$$\frac{n!}{m!(n-m)!} \quad \text{for} \quad n \geq m$$

Since n is greater than or equal to m, it can also be written as

$$\frac{n(n-1)\,(n-2)\cdots(n-m+1)}{m(m-1)\,(m-2)\cdots(1)}$$

Develop a function that can be used to evaluate each of the preceding products.

9.15 Develop a function, SINE(X), that calculates the trigonometric sine of x using its Taylor's series.

$$\sin x = x - \frac{x^3}{3!} + \frac{x^5}{5!} - \frac{x^7}{7!} + \cdots$$

Terminate the series when the next term is less than 10^{-6}.

9.16 (a) Develop a subroutine, RSUM(A,N,S), that calculates the sums, S, of the rows of an N × N matrix A.
(b) Develop a similar routine, CSUM(A,N,S), that sums its columns.
(c) Combine RSUM and CSUM into a multiple-entry subroutine.

9.17 In the game of chess, a knight makes L-shaped moves on a board that has eight rows and eight columns. More exactly, it must move two spaces forward, backward, or sideways, and then an extra square to either side. In the diagram, x's indicate all legal moves from the blackened square. Develop a subroutine that determines all legal moves for a knight, given its original location. *Hint:* Remember that a playing board has edges.

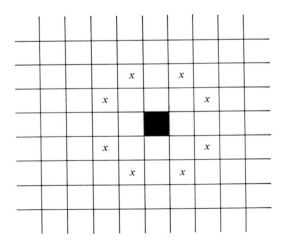

9.18 Develop a subroutine, CONCAT(A,LA,B,LB,C,LC), that concatenates two strings, A and B, of lengths, LA and LB, into a single string, C, of length, LC.

9.19 Write a main program that uses the subroutine FIND to count the number of occurrences of a given character in a character string.

9.20 Write a subroutine, EXTRACT(A,LA,INIT,B,LB), that produces a substring, B, of length, LB, by copying from the string, A, of length, LA, starting at position, INIT.

9.21 Write a subroutine, PFIND(STRING,LENG,INIT,LOC,TYPE), that searches for parentheses in a string, STRING, of length, LENG, starting at position, INIT. When PFIND detects a parenthesis, it is to return its position in LOC. If an open parenthesis is found, TYPE is returned as one; if it is a closed parenthesis, TYPE is minus one. If a parenthesis is not found, LOC is returned as zero.

9.22 Use PFIND from Problem 9.21 to determine whether an expression exhibits proper use of parentheses.

10 Sequential and Random Files

So far, we have discussed one family of data structures. These structures include single cells, linear lists, and arrays and retain their data relationships via physical cell arrangement. Throughout our discussions, we have assumed that memory is large enough to accommodate any and all structures no matter how many cells are required. Unfortunately, such is not always the case.

The purpose of this chapter is to show how auxiliary storage can be used to solve problems. It begins by illustrating the need for auxiliary storage and then introduces the concepts of *sequential* and *random* processing. Next, the characteristics of sequential and random access devices are described; then, their use is illustrated by example problems.

10.1
Need for
Auxiliary
Storage
For purposes of discussion, let us assume that we have the following problem. We are asked to develop a computerized procedure that rearranges a set of numbers such that positive values precede all negative ones. For the time being, let us restrict the input to no more than 1000 values.

Certainly, this problem is similar to ones we have already solved. For example, sorting the input into descending sequence would produce the desired output since all positive values would appear before any negative ones. However, such a procedure would involve more processing than necessary. Here, we need only separate values, not sequence them. Consequently, let us devise a simpler algorithm.

This problem statement tells us to output all positive numbers followed by negative ones. Therefore, let us input values one at a time. If a value is positive, it can be transmitted as output immediately. Otherwise, if it is negative, it can be saved temporarily in a linear list. When the last input value is processed, it is a simple matter to output the negative values. The solution in Figure 10.1 incorporates this procedure.

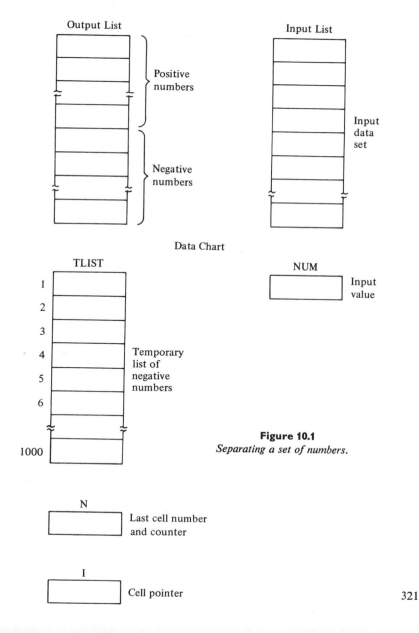

Figure 10.1
Separating a set of numbers.

Figure 10.1 *(cont.)*

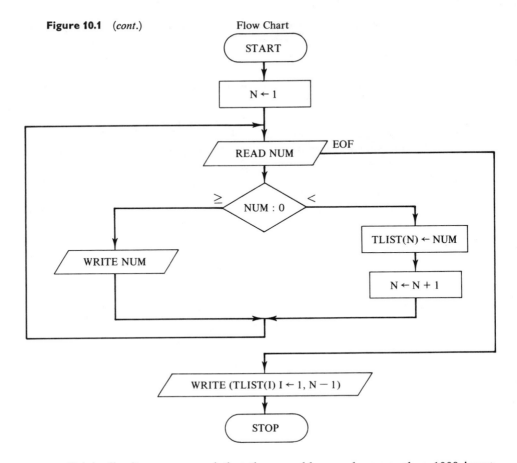

Flow Chart

Originally, it was assumed that there could never be more than 1000 input values. Thus, it is impossible to exceed the size of the temporary list, TLIST, even if all input values are negative. In contrast, if this input restriction is removed, our solution must be modified, as shown in Figure 10.2, to ensure that TLIST does not overflow. Here, TLIST has been enlarged and now contains 10,000 cells. Nevertheless, it is possible for some input set to contain more than 10,000 negative values or even to exceed the capacity of memory. Consequently, auxiliary storage is required if this problem is to be solved in general.

10.2
Sequential
and
Random
Processing

Before we proceed, we should introduce several concepts concerning auxiliary storage. One such concept is the *file*. A file is a set of related *records*. An everyday example is an inventory file that contains one record for each different inventory item. Let us now introduce the concepts of *sequential* and *random* *processing*.

For purposes of discussion, let us assume that we are asked to keep track of the inventory of a small store. We are told that each different item has its own unique item number and that the store inventory is kept on a deck of 3 × 5 cards. Each card contains an item number and quantity on hand for that item. Here, each inventory card is considered a record and the card deck is a file. Furthermore, the inventory file is said to contain master data, and consequently, is referred to as a *master file* consisting of *master records.*

As sales are made during the day, sales slips describing items and quantity sold are prepared. For simplicity, let us assume that one slip is generated for each different item. At closing time, the day's transactions will have produced a stack of sales slips. This stack could be referred to as a *transaction file* and each slip a *transaction record.*

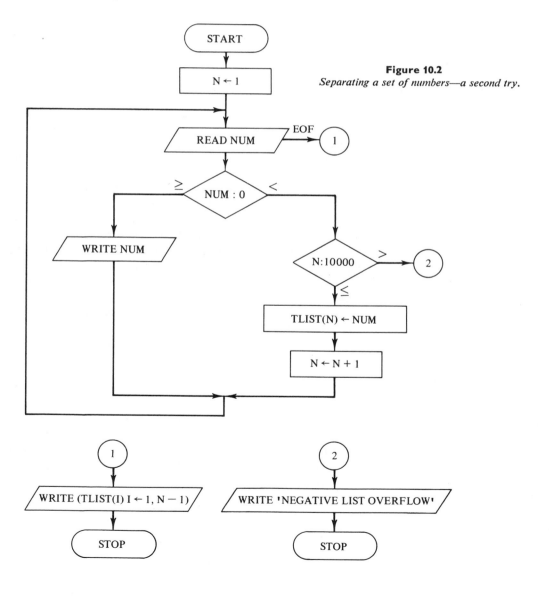

Figure 10.2
Separating a set of numbers—a second try.

Our problem is to process the transaction file (sales slips) against the master file (inventory deck). In other words, we must take each sales slip and reduce the quantity on hand on its associated inventory card. Essentially, we can do this in two ways. First, we take the top sales slip, hunt through the inventory deck one card at a time until we find the desired one, and then reduce its quantity on hand by the quantity sold. This process could be continued for the second sales slip, and then the third, and so on, until the last one has been processed.

In this case, sales occur at random, and, consequently, the transaction file has no particular order. In addition, the master file has not been prearranged. Since no effort has been made to control transaction and master file sequence, and since transactions are applied to the master at random, this procedure is an example of *random processing*.

No doubt, updating a master inventory file using this random process would be tedious and time consuming because we cannot immediately access inventory records by item number. Rather, we are forced to hunt through them until the desired one is found. One way to improve this process is to keep the master file in some known order, such as ascending sequential order by item number. This would facilitate locating individual master records, but would still require processing transactions at random.

The alternative to random processing is *sequential processing*. In this case, both master and transaction files are in sequential order. This implies that the master be maintained in sequence while transactions are sorted into that sequence before processing begins.

If both inventory cards and sales slips are in sequence by item number, we can take the top sales slip and begin searching for its corresponding inventory record. When we find it, we can reduce its quantity on hand and then go to the next transaction. Since they have been sorted, the second transaction refers either to the inventory card just updated or to one further into the inventory file. Thus, we do not have to start our second search from the beginning but can continue from where we are. In other words, once we have passed an inventory record, we need not examine it again. Consequently, with one scan or pass through the master file, we can process all transactions. Figure 10.3 illustrates this process.

10.3 Sequential Files The choice of whether one uses random or sequential processing depends upon what type of equipment is available for reading and writing files. Auxiliary storage units, such as magnetic tapes and disks, were introduced in Chapter 2. In general, these devices are classified by the manner in which they access and store data. If a unit must process data serially, it is said to be a *sequential* storage device; data sets stored on such devices are referred to as *sequential files*. On the other hand, if a unit can access data in any order it is known as a *random* storage or *direct* access device and is said to contain *random files*. Let us now consider sequential files in more detail.

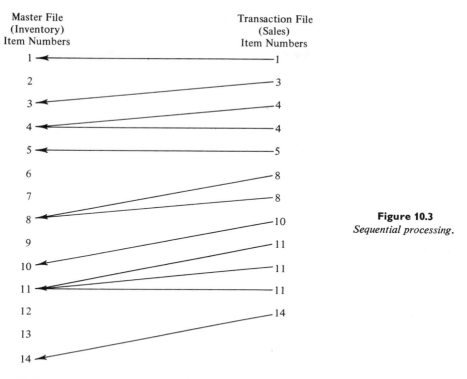

Master File
(Inventory)
Item Numbers

Transaction File
(Sales)
Item Numbers

Figure 10.3
Sequential processing.

10.3.1 Sequential file operations

Usually, there are five operations that can be performed with sequential files. First, we can output information onto a sequential file; but since most computer systems have more than one sequential storage device, it is necessary to specify the particular file along with the values to be placed onto that file. Consequently, we shall use the flow-chart statement

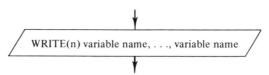

WRITE(n) variable name, . . ., variable name

to write onto a sequential file where *n* specifies the number of a particular file. Here, *n* can be either the actual file number or the variable name of a single cell which contains that number.

When a write statement is executed, the contents of its data structures are retrieved from memory and written onto the particular file. The information placed onto a sequential file by each write statement is referred to as a *record*. The number and sequence of values in any one record are the same as the number and sequence of variables specified in the write statement which generated the particular record. For example, the statement

WRITE (1) A,B,C

produces a record on file 1 that contains three values where A is the first value, B is second, and C is last. In contrast, the statement

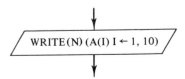

WRITE(N) (A(I) I ← 1, 10)

generates a record on the file specified by the contents of N which consists of ten values: A(1), A(2), ..., A(10).

Figure 10.4 shows a simplified picture of a sequential file, assuming it is stored on magnetic tape. Here, record size varies depending upon the number of values specified when it was written. Note that each record is followed by some space that separates it from the record that trails it. This space is referred to as an *inter-record gap*. These gaps indicate the end of a record and are automatically inserted by the tape drive after the execution of each write statement. Finally, records previously written on tape may at any time be destroyed by over-writing with new data, i.e. magnetic tapes can be used more than once.

Figure 10.4 *A sequential file.*

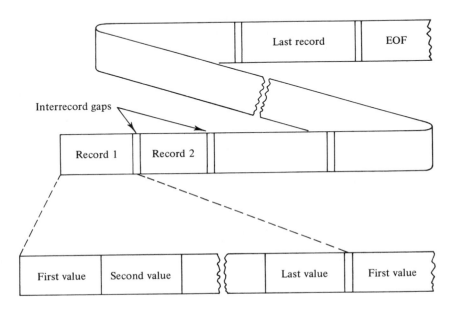

Once a sequential file has been loaded with data, we may want to access some of its information. Before we do so, we should mark its end so that we can recognize when we have read its last data value. This is done by writing a special record, known as an *end of file* (EOF) or *tape mark*, after the last data record. We shall use the flow-chart statement

to write an EOF. Once again, *n* specifies the particular file. For example, the statement WRITE EOF(2) places an end-of-file mark of file 2.

Now that we can write information onto a sequential file, we are ready to read that information back into memory. This we do by the flow-chart statement

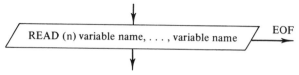

This statement reads the next record into memory and assigns its values to the data structures. For example, the statement

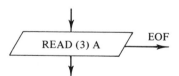

inputs a record that contains a single value from file 3. In contrast, the statement

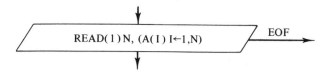

reads the next record from file 1 and uses the first value in the record to determine how many more values must be read in that record. In most computer systems, if the record just read does not contain the same number of values as in the read statement, an error occurs stopping the program. If the record just read is an end of file, the next flow-chart statement is found by following the arrow labeled EOF. Otherwise, the nonlabeled arrow is followed.

Generally, sequential files are processed from beginning to end. It is therefore necessary to be able to reposition a file at its start. This is done by the flow-chart statement

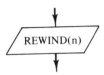

For example, the statement REWIND(4) rewinds file 4 back to its starting point. In general, it is a good practice to rewind all sequential files before using them for the first time. This ensures that all files are in fact at their starting points. If by chance a file is already positioned at the beginning, it simply remains there. Some tape drives do allow for reading a tape backwards. When this is possible, the need for waiting for a tape to be rewound is eliminated.

Finally, it is sometimes necessary to retrieve a record that has been processed earlier. This can be accomplished in two ways. Either the file is rewound and then read one record at a time looking for the desired record, or the file can be backed up until that record is reached. This latter procedure is performed by the flow-chart statement

This statement causes the selected file to backspace one complete record. Repeated application of this statement takes a file back to its start. If a file is already at the beginning, this instruction has no effect. In general, backspacing is slow and should be avoided.

Now that we have discussed sequential file operations, let us use a sequential file to solve the problem of separating a set of numbers. From the previous section, we know that we can read input values one at a time as shown in Figure 10.5. If a value is positive, it is written directly onto the output list. Otherwise, it is placed at the end of sequential file 1. After the last input value has been processed, an end of file is written onto file 1, and file 1 is rewound. The negative values are then read one at a time and written onto the output list. This process continues until an end of file is detected on file 1. When this occurs, file 1 is rewound.

10.3.2 Updating a sequential file

As a first example of the use of sequential files, consider the following problem. We work in the checking account department of a bank and are asked to develop a computerized check processing system. We are told that each customer is assigned a unique customer number and that each *transaction*, which in this case is either a withdrawal or deposit, is identified by that number. Given the current or old balances of all customers, we must process these transactions by making appropriate changes in customer balances. Such a procedure is generally referred to as *updating*.

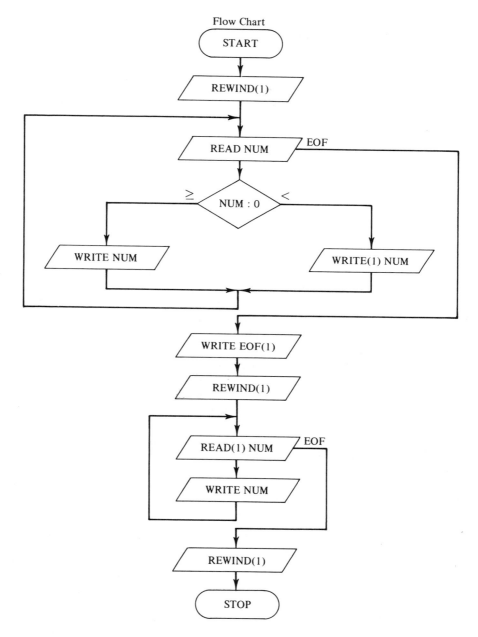

Figure 10.5
Separating a set of numbers using a sequential file.

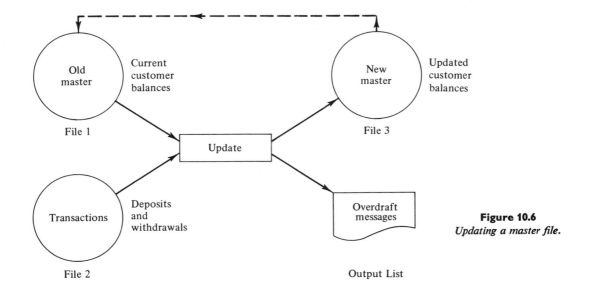

Figure 10.6
Updating a master file.

The diagram in Figure 10.6 specifies an update process. Here, a complete update algorithm is compressed into a single process box, and input and output are represented by appropriate media symbols. Since this diagram shows an overview of a process without any algorithmic details, it is referred to as a *system* flow chart. In this situation, there are two input data sets: the old master file (current customer balances) and the transaction file (deposits and withdrawals). Both appear as sequential or tape files and are arbitrarily assigned to files 1 and 2, respectively. Likewise, there are two outputs: overdraft messages and the new master file (updated or new customer balances). Here, overdraft warnings appear as printed messages, whereas updated customer balances are written on file 3. The dashed arrow that leads from the new master file to the old one indicates that the output file of the latest update becomes input for the next update.

Now that this problem is defined, we are ready to begin our solution process. In this case, we know that we must produce two output data sets, as shown in Figure 10.7. The output list contains attempted overdraft messages. If in any transaction a customer attempts to withdraw more than his current balance, an appropriate message is printed, including customer number, transaction amount, and current balance. The new master file contains one record per customer where each record consists of two entries: a customer number and updated balance. As input, the transaction file contains one record per transaction consisting of three entries: a customer number, a transaction code, and a transaction amount. Here, let us use a transaction code of 0 to indicate a deposit and a 1 for a withdrawal. Finally, the old master file has the same format as the new one. Notice that a customer number acts as an identifier for each transaction and master record. Such an identifier is frequently referred to as the record *key*. A key can be numeric, such as a social security number, or alphabetic, such as a name.

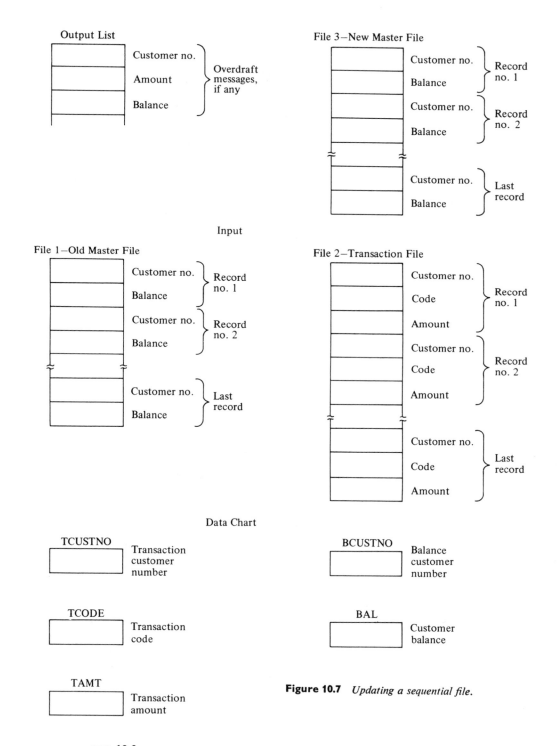

Output List

Customer no.

Amount } Overdraft messages, if any

Balance

File 3—New Master File

Customer no. } Record no. 1
Balance

Customer no. } Record no. 2
Balance

Customer no. } Last record
Balance

Input

File 1—Old Master File

Customer no. } Record no. 1
Balance

Customer no. } Record no. 2
Balance

Customer no. } Last record
Balance

File 2—Transaction File

Customer no.
Code } Record no. 1
Amount

Customer no.
Code } Record no. 2
Amount

Customer no.
Code } Last record
Amount

Data Chart

TCUSTNO — Transaction customer number

TCODE — Transaction code

TAMT — Transaction amount

BCUSTNO — Balance customer number

BAL — Customer balance

Figure 10.7 *Updating a sequential file.*

Flow Chart

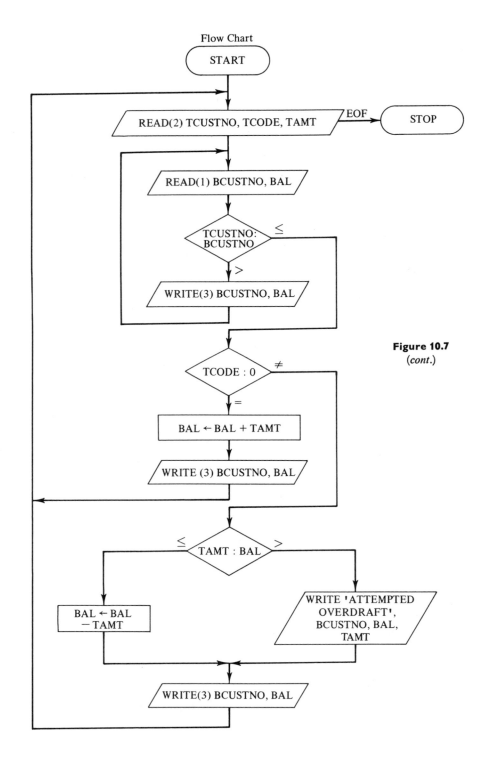

Figure 10.7
(cont.)

Now that the output and input are determined, let us decide what data should be retained in memory and how those data should be stored. From problems in previous chapters, we might be tempted to read the complete master file into memory before any transactions are processed; however, since the number of customers has not been specified, it is best to develop an algorithm that processes one customer at a time. In other words, we would like to read a single transaction and retrieve its associated customer balance from the old master file. Unfortunately, this file is accessed by a sequential storage device, and such a search procedure involves repetitive scans. Consequently, it is desirable to process all transactions with one pass of the old master, as was described in Section 10.2.

If the old master is not to be rewound except at the end of a run, both it and the transaction file must be in the same order. For the time being, let us assume that master files are maintained in ascending order by key (customer number) and that the transaction file is sorted into that sequence before an update is performed. With both files in the same order, given a transaction customer number, it should be possible to find the corresponding balance by reading down the old master file one record at a time. If the master record just read does not contain the desired key, that record does not need updating and can be copied directly onto the new master file. When a matching key is finally found, its balance can be adjusted, provided there is no overdraft, and then the updated record can be written onto the new master. At this point, the next record is read from the transaction file, and the preceding search process is repeated. With this procedure, five data values need be in memory at any one time: a transaction customer number, code, and amount, plus an old master customer number and balance.

The flow chart in Figure 10.7 incorporates this update algorithm. Careful study of the diagram reveals that a number of situations have not been anticipated. For example, when the end of transaction file is reached, might there not be more records on the old master file? In other words, when the last transaction is processed, the remainder of the old master file should be copied directly onto the new one. Also, the end of the transaction file must always be reached before the end of the old master, even when the last transaction matches the last master record. Furthermore, no provision has been made for missing input balances or incorrect transaction customer numbers. When this occurs, one or more records in either file are out of order. This situation is detected when a transaction key is smaller than an old master key.

Finally, the algorithm in Figure 10.7 contains one grave assumption. It presumes that there is no more than a single transaction for any one master record during one update run. In other words, after it locates a matching master record, it updates the customer's balance and then immediately outputs the modified master record. Rather, it should input the next transaction to see if its key matches the master presently in memory. If it does, the customer's balance can be further updated. This continues until a transaction is found that no longer matches the current master. When this occurs, this master is ready for output. The flow chart in Figure 10.8 corrects these omissions.

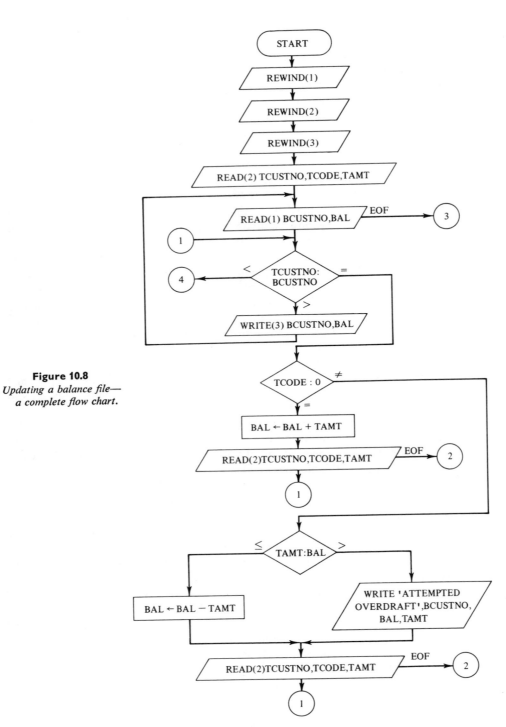

Figure 10.8
*Updating a balance file—
a complete flow chart.*

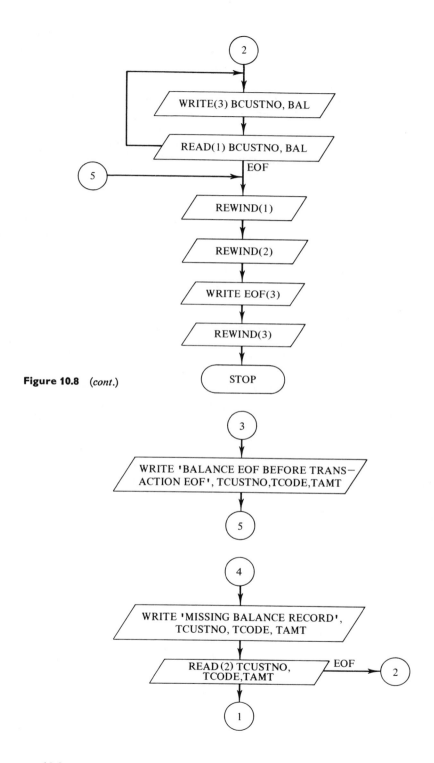

Figure 10.8 (*cont.*)

As a last aspect of this problem, let us consider the sequence of the transaction file. Here, it has been assumed that this file is sorted by customer number. This implies that records are grouped by customer but says nothing about transaction order for the same customer. In other words, it is possible for deposits to follow withdrawals and vice versa. Consequently, a customer can overdraw his account even though a sufficient deposit follows the withdrawal that exhausts his balance. Needless to say, this is a poor *system design*.

This problem can be eliminated if a customer's deposits precede his withdrawals. Thus, the transaction file should be sorted by customer number and then within each customer by transaction type. In this case, customer number is said to be the *major sort field* and transaction type is the *minor sort field*. In contrast, since deposits have a code of 0 and withdrawals a 1, customer number and transaction code can be combined into one sort field, thereby simplifying the sort procedure and yet producing the same desired sequence.

10.3.3 Merging two sequential files

In the previous example, great care was taken to ensure that no new records were added to the updated master file. In fact, if a transaction could not be matched with an existing record, it was bypassed as an error. By so doing, the possibility of losing transactions is reduced. Nevertheless, we are left with the problem of adding new customers to a master file. Let us now consider that problem.

In this case, we wish to insert new records into an existing file. Generally, this process is referred to as *merging*, and Figure 10.9 shows its system flow chart. Here, a merge algorithm is compressed into a single process box; as before, there are two input data sets: transactions (additions) and an old master file. However, now there is a single output—a merged master file. As before, the dashed line indicates that the output is intended as input to the next merge. Furthermore, this merged file must be usable as input to an update.

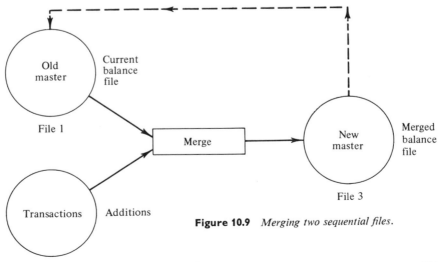

Figure 10.9 *Merging two sequential files.*

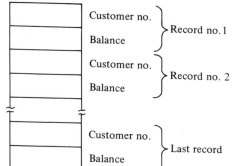

Figure 10.10 *Merging two sequential files.*

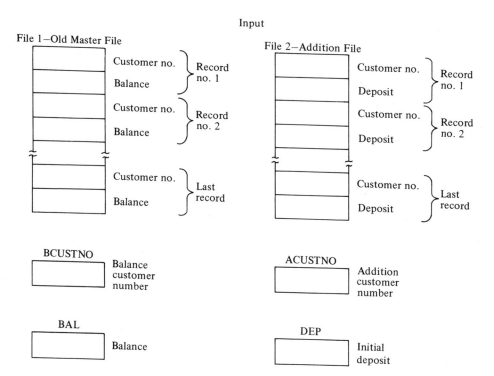

This problem discussion has completely specified both output and input master files; they must have the same form as an updated master file from the previous section, i.e., one record per customer where each record contains two entries and records are arranged in ascending order by customer number. Similarly, addition transactions need two entries per customer. Here, each initial deposit is identified by a new customer number that does not appear on the master file. As before, customer number acts as a record key.

As in an update, it is desirable to minimize the number of data values in memory at any one time, implying that additions be processed one at a time. Likewise, a merge should require one pass, which necessitates that both input files be in the same relative order. Consequently, an addition transaction file, like an update transaction file, must be sorted as a separate operation prior to the start of a merge.

Basically, a merge algorithm must insert addition records into a master file, keeping the master in sequence. This can be done by reading one record from the addition file and one from the master. The two keys (customer

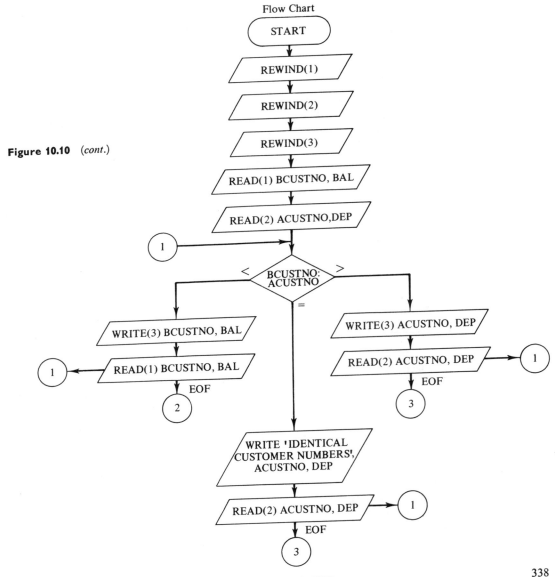

Figure 10.10 (*cont.*)

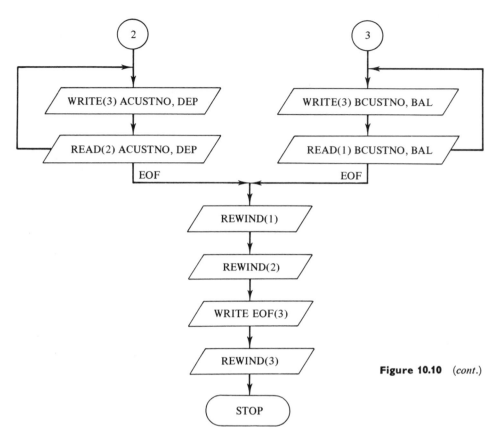

Figure 10.10 (*cont.*)

numbers) are then compared, and the record with the smaller key is written onto the merged master. If the master were smaller, the next master record would be read; if the addition were smaller, the next addition record would be read. If, by chance, the keys were equal, the addition record would be incorrect, because its customer number already appears on the master file. When this happens, an error message should be written and the duplicate addition record bypassed for later correction. The flow chart in Figure 10.10 incorporates this algorithm. Note that when an end of file occurs on one file, the remainder of the other file is copied directly onto the merged master.

10.3.4 Sorting a sequential file

In the previous examples, it was assumed that all files were maintained in customer number sequence. By so doing, it was possible to complete an update or merge in a single pass. In addition, memory requirements were minimized because only two records, one from each input file, were needed in memory at any one time. However, when update or addition transaction files are actually generated, they undoubtedly will not be in proper sequence. Consequently, it is necessary to have a sorting procedure that arranges these files into customer number order. Generally, each computer manufacturer includes a sort package along with his machine. Since sorting is such an important aspect of sequential processing, let us discuss it briefly.

Usually, a file to be sorted contains more values than can be stored in memory at one time. Therefore, a sorting procedure must be developed that utilizes sequential files. Since such files are best processed serially, the procedure should not involve searching for specific data values or require a large number of file passes.

The most common method of sorting sequential files involves two phases. During the first phase, the input file is broken into small pieces that can be sorted internally in memory. In the second phase, these small sequences are merged to form longer sequences, and then these are merged to form even longer ones. These merges are repeated until a single sequence remains. The technique is referred to as a *sort merge*, and requires a minimum of four tapes, two for input and two for output.

Let us now illustrate this sort procedure in more detail by using the list of numbers shown in Figure 10.11a as a sample input set. For simplicity, let us assume that these data values have previously been copied onto file 1 and that our computer is quite limited in memory and can sort just three values at one time.

File 1	File 3	File 4	File 1	File 2	File 3
3	1	2	1	4	1
1	3	5	2	7	2
11	11	10	3	8	3
2	4	7	5	9	4
10	9	8	10	12	5
5	12		11		7
4					8
12					9
9					10
8					11
7					12
(a)	**(b)**		**(c)**		**(d)**

Figure 10.11 *Example of a sort-merge: (a) before; (b) after phase 1; (c) after first merge; (d) after second merge.*

During phase one, input values are read from file 1 until memory is filled, in this case with three values. These values are sorted and then written onto file 3. This done, the next three values are read, sorted, and then written onto file 4. This process is continued until all values on the original file have been read, internally sorted, and written alternately onto files 3 and 4. Figure 10.11b shows data arrangement on the two output files after completion of the first phase.

To start the second phase, all files are rewound and files 3 and 4 are designated as input and 1 and 2 are switched to output. One record from file 3 and one record from file 4 are then read. The smaller value is then written onto file 1 and the next record is read from whichever file contained the smaller record. The current values from 3 and 4 are compared and again the smaller value is placed on 1. This read, compare, write process is repeated until all values from the first sequences on 3 and 4 have been merged into a single sequence on 1. The output is switched to file 2, and the preceding merge process is then repeated for the next two input sequences. The first merge pass ends when all sequences have been transferred from files 3 and 4 to 1 and 2. Figure 10.11c shows our sample after a single merge pass.

Since the input is still split between two files, a second merge pass is begun by rewinding all files. The input and output files are switched, so that files 1 and 2 are input and 3 and 4 are output. The preceding merge procedure is then repeated with this new file arrangement. During this pass, only one sequence is produced, so file 4 is never used, and the sort is complete. Figure 10.11d shows our sample input after a second merge.

Before we develop a complete sort algorithm, let us consider the merging process in further detail. A merge can be accomplished by a series of comparisons among the value just read from one input file, the value read from the second input file, and the last value just placed on the output file. Values are written in ascending sequence on one output tape until both input values are smaller than the last output value. At this point, a new sequence is started on the other output file. The diagram in Figure 10.12 displays a basic algorithm for a single merge pass. Here, ACC1 represents the last value read from the first input file, ACC2 represents the last value read from the second input file, L represents the value last written onto the output file, and OF indicates the output file number.

Finally, Figure 10.13 shows a complete solution to our problem of sorting a sequential file. It expects the unsorted input on file 1 and begins by reading and sorting that file into sequences of 1000 records alternately onto files 3 and 4. Here, ISORT(ACCNO,AMOUNT,N) is assumed to be a subroutine that internally sorts N input records by account number.

The merge phase begins by writing end-of-file marks on both output files, rewinding all files, and switching the output to input and vice versa. Here, SWITCH is used to remember whether a merge pass has used more than one output file. The input records are then merged as discussed earlier. If it is necessary to change output files, SWITCH is set to 1, indicating that both output files have been used. When an end of file is detected during a read, the remainder of the other input file is copied directly onto the output. At this point, if SWITCH is 0, the sort is complete and the sorted file is on OF. Otherwise, another merge pass is required.

In this procedure, the total number of output sequences is cut in half during each merge pass. Working backward from the last pass, which has only one sequence, we see that the preceding pass has two sequences, the one before that has four, the one before that has eight, and so on. Thus, at the start of a

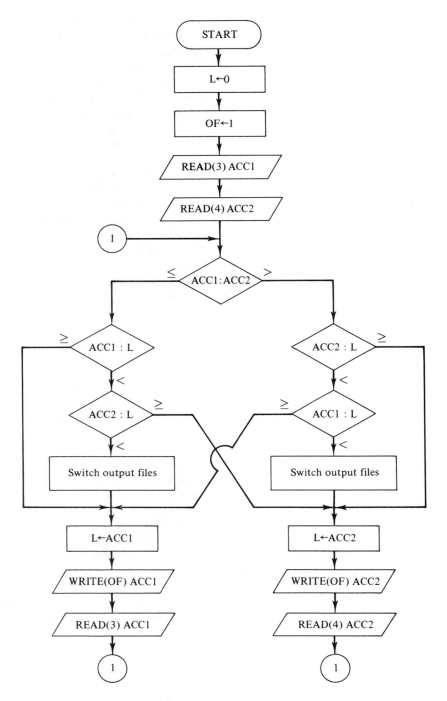

Figure 10.12 *A single merge.*

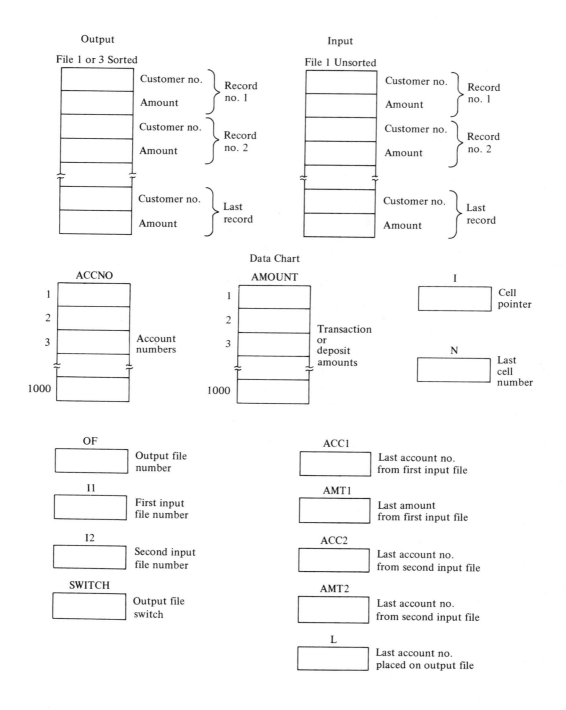

Figure 10.13 *Sorting a sequential file.*

Flow Chart

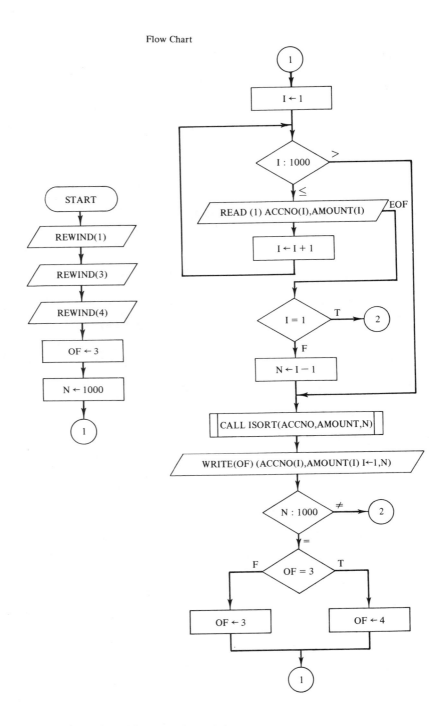

Figure 10.13 (*cont.*)

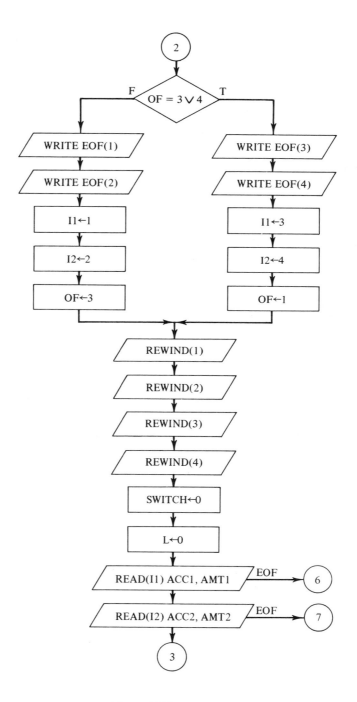

Figure 10.13 (cont.)

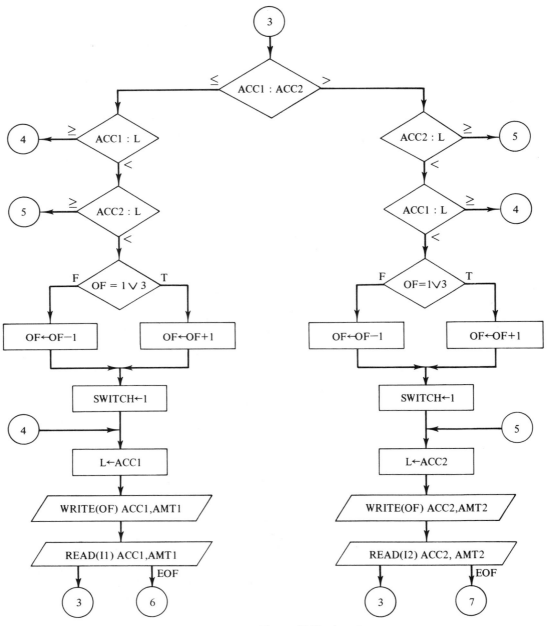

Figure 10.13 (*cont.*)

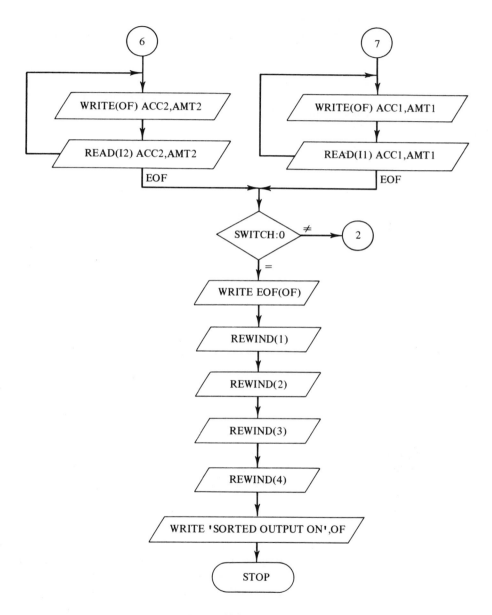

Figure 10.13 (*cont.*)

merge phase requiring p passes, there are a maximum of 2^p sequences. Conversely, if there are 2^p sequences or less evenly divided between two files, the sort can be completed in p passes at most.

Suppose we wish to know how many merge passes are required to complete the sorting of a file. If we know the number of sequences, s, on the two input files at the beginning of the merge phase, we can determine the number of additional passes, p, required to complete the sort by choosing p as the smallest whole number satisfying the relationship $2^p \geq s$.

If during phase 1 the input records are sorted internally into sequences of length l, and if there are r input records, then $s \geq r/l$. Thus, p satisfies the relation

$$2^p \geq \frac{r}{l}$$

or

$$p \geq \log_2 \frac{r}{l}$$

The merge process described is referred to as a *two-way merge* because it uses two input files. It is possible to use three input files and three output files and obtain a *three-way merge*; corresponding higher-order merges may be devised. If we let m represent the number of input files used, the corresponding formula obtained is

$$m^p \geq \frac{r}{l}$$

or

$$p \geq \log_m \frac{r}{l}$$

10.4 Random Files

If a storage unit can access its data in any order, it is known as a *random* storage device; data sets stored on such devices are referred to as *random* files. Since disks have characteristics similar to all random storage or direct access devices, let us concentrate our attention on disks.

10.4.1 Random file operations

Since the physical construction of a disk unit affects the manner in which its files are processed, let us briefly review the structure of such a device and determine how its records are accessed. Basically, a magnetic disk is a flat circular plate coated with ferromagnetic oxide. A disk is divided into a set of concentric *tracks*, each of which stores information as magnetic bits in a manner similar to magnetic tape. In turn, each track is subdivided into *sectors*, as shown in Figure 10.14a.

A number of disks are stacked on top of each other and rotated by a motor at a high, constant speed. The individual disks are separated by sufficient space

Figure 10.14
Disk construction:
(a) disk surface; (b) disk unit.

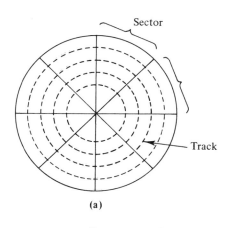

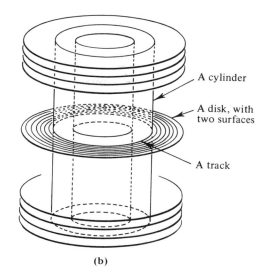

A cylinder

A disk, with two surfaces

A track

(a)

(b)

to allow a set of read-write heads to move between them and access any particular track or sector on any surface. The read-write heads are physically mounted on arms in such a way that they move in and out together at the same radius. Thus, if there are n disks, there are $2n$ disk surfaces. Usually, the upper surface of the top disk and the lower surface of the bottom one are not used. Consequently, $2n-2$ tracks, one on each surface, can be accessed without head movement.

A set of tracks which can be accessed without arm movement is known as a *cylinder*. This name is derived from its physical appearance as shown in Figure 10.14b. In general, it takes about 100 to 750 milliseconds (ms), depending upon the particular disk and distance moved, to switch the heads from one cylinder to another. This head movement is referred to as *seeking*, and it results in an access delay known as *seek time*. On the other hand, it takes much less time to access a track if both it and the previously accessed track are in the same cylinder. In this latter case, the track can be accessed as soon as its starting point rotates around to the read-write heads. On the average, this *rotational delay* equals the time for one half of a revolution. For a disk rotating at 2500 revolutions per minute, 40 ms are required per revolution, resulting in an average access time of 20 ms.

To facilitate access, cylinders, tracks, and sector are numbered. For example, an average disk might consist of 200 cylinders numbered from 1 to 200. Each cylinder might contain 20 tracks numbered from 1 to 20 with each track subdivided into 8 sectors numbered from 1 to 8. By so doing, any sector can be identified, and thus accessed by three values: its cylinder number, the track number within that cylinder, and the sector number within that track.

For simplicity, let us assume that each sector can store one record. Consequently, if we wish to access a record, we must be able to specify its sector. To do so we must know (1) its cylinder number so that the read-write heads can be moved into correct position, (2) its track number so that the proper head can be activated; (3) its sector number so that the desired record is accessed.

In general, there are three operations that can be performed with random files. First, we can output information; but since a record can be placed anywhere within a file, we must specify which sector is to be used. Consequently, we shall use the flow-chart statement

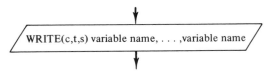

to write a random file where c, t, and s specify the cylinder, track, and sector numbers of the output record. Here, c, t, and s can either be the actual numbers or the variable names of cells that contain those numbers. For example, the statement

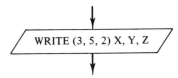

writes a record consisting of three values in the third cylinder, in the fifth track of the cylinder, in the second sector of that track.

Now that we can write information onto a random file, we are ready to read that information back into memory. This is done by the flow-chart statement

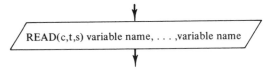

As above, c, t, and s specify the cylinder, track, and sector numbers of the desired record. For example,

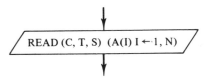

inputs N values from the record whose cylinder, track, and sector numbers are contained in C, T, and S.

In each of the above instructions, execution is suspended while the read-write heads are moved to the desired cylinder. Sometimes, the number of that cylinder is known in advance. In such cases, it is desirable to *seek* that cylinder, i.e. to start the heads moving, while the CPU finishes processing the current record. This operation is performed by the flow-chart statement

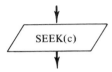

where *c* specifies the desired cylinder. For example, the statement, SEEK(7) causes the disk drive to move the read-write heads to the seventh cylinder.

10.4.2 Using random files

As an example of the use of random files, let us assume that we work in the credit approval section of a large department store and are asked to develop a computerized credit-checking system. We are told that each new customer is assigned an account number and credit limit that must not be exceeded. Furthermore, we are told that all sales personnel must telephone our section for approval of any credit sale over a specified amount. Thus, our system must input a customer number and charge amount and then output an approval or rejection message.

Implicit within this problem statement is a requirement for speed. Undoubtedly, a customer is waiting whenever a sales clerk requests credit approval. Consequently, our system must handle each inquiry separately and must also produce a quick response. This means that we must have rapid access to the credit record of any customer. In other words, we do not have time to search a sequential file; we must use a random file so that we can retrieve any record immediately.

Figure 10.15 shows a basic credit-checking system. Here, each customer number is divided into three parts, which specify the cylinder, track, and sector number of its record. The flow chart begins by reading a three-part customer number and charge amount. In this application, all input and output might be by typewriter console or visual display unit. A customer number is then used to access the desired credit record, which includes the customer's balance and credit limit. If the new charge amount plus the customer's current balance exceeds his credit limit, the charge is rejected; otherwise, the balance is increased by the charge amount, and the updated record is rewritten at its previous location.

Although sufficient, this credit-checking procedure does not take advantage of the power of a computer, especially one with direct access storage. For example, it does not check for an unusual number of charges or for large credit purchases within a brief period of time. Such activity might indicate a stolen credit card.

Figure 10.16 incorporates these additional features. Here, each customer record is expanded to include a list of charges made this period along with their dates. As before, a customer number is used to access the desired record.

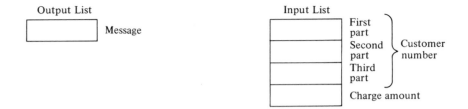

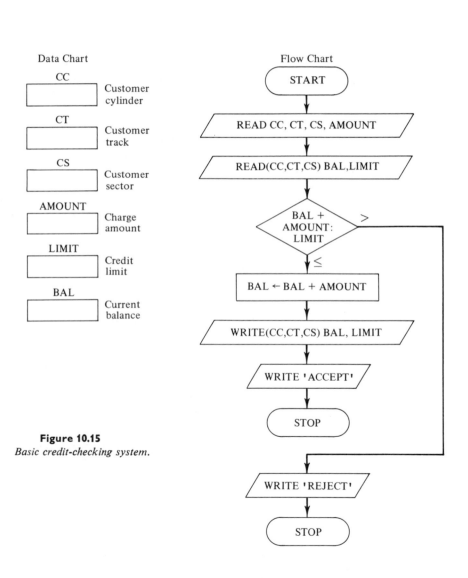

Figure 10.15
Basic credit-checking system.

If the latest charge increases the current balance past the credit limit, the charge is refused. Otherwise, the algorithm checks to see if there have been more than 10 charges this period. If there have, a warning message is printed so that appropriate action can be taken. Finally, charges within the last five days are totaled to see if they exceed half the credit limit. Here, DAY is assumed to be a subroutine that returns today's date. If the total exceeds half the limit, a warning message is printed. In this example, the choices of 10 days and one-half the credit limit in five days are arbitrary, and can be adjusted to fit actual operating conditions.

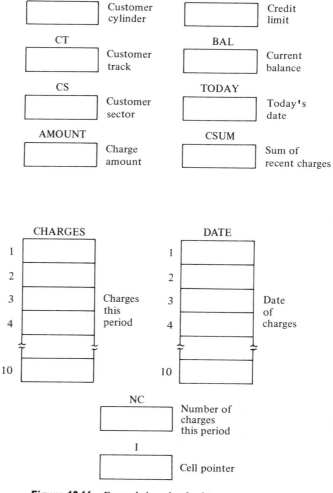

Figure 10.16 *Expanded credit-checking system.*

Flow Chart

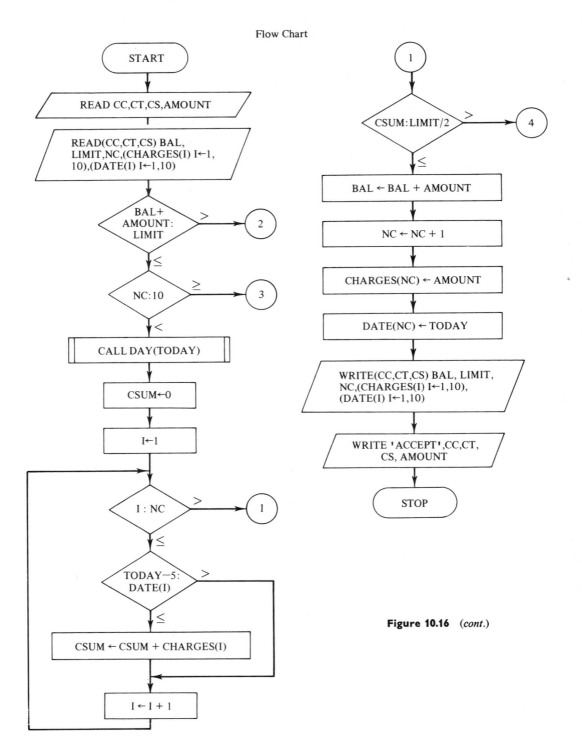

Figure 10.16   (cont.)

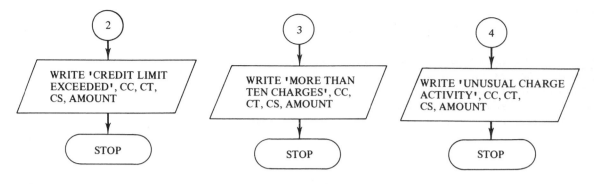

Figure 10.16 (*cont.*)

10.4.3 Random file organization

As can be seen from the previous example, the major problem with random processing is identifiying the address (cylinder, track, and sector numbers) of desired records. This was not a problem with sequential files because records were stored in sequence by key. In that case, if a given record were desired, we had no other choice but to search a file one record at a time until the one with the desired key was located.

Basically, random files can be organized in four ways so that their individual records can be located:

1. Sequential;
2. Direct;
3. Calculated;
4. Indexed.

In *sequential* organization, records of a random file are arranged in sequence just as they would be if they were stored on a sequential file. Consequently, this method does not take advantage of direct accessing capabilities of random storage devices. On the other hand, some random devices, such as disks and drums, generally have faster transfer rates than tape drives, and therefore can actually input and output sequential files faster than tapes. Furthermore, random access devices need not waste time rewinding their files.

In *direct* organization, the file address of a record equals its identifying number or key, as in the previous section. Here, a key might consist of three parts: the first portion could indicate the cylinder number of the desired record, the second its track number, and the third its sector number. Although straight-forward, this method is usually not feasible because keys are generally not suited for addresses. In addition, purging obsolete records leaves unused file locations. This problem can be illustrated by credit account numbers. To avoid confusion, a customer should not be assigned the account number belonging to another, even though the first is no longer a store customer.

In *calculated* organization, the file address of a record is calculated from its key. Here, routine arithmetic operations are performed upon a key producing a derived storage address. The difficulty with this method is that the calculation algorithm may produce the same identical address for two or more keys. When this happens, one of these records is stored at this location and a pointer is added to this record to indicate the *overflow* location of the second record, termed a *synonym*. If there is more than one synonym, additional overflow locations are required, each having a pointer to the next one. With this file organization, we locate a record by first deriving its address from its key. If the record at this location does not have the desired key, we use its pointer to find the overflow location.

In *indexed* organization, a table is used to find addresses. This table contains all keys along with the addresses of where their records are stored. Any record can be found by doing a table lookup on its key. Here, a hierarchy of tables can be used to reduce lookup time. For example, the first table might give the number of a smaller table that gives the location of the desired record.

Finally, these four organizational methods can be combined to produce others. For example, a table can be used in conjunction with a sequentially organized random file. Here, records are arranged by key, whereas a table contains the addresses of selected records throughout the file. A record is located first by using this table to find an approximate address for the desired record and then by searching the file sequentially from that point. As an example, Figure 10.17 shows that the record whose key is 20,199 is located somewhere between file addresses 10,2,1 and 10,3,7. Thus, our search begins at 10,2,1. Consequently, we need examine fewer records and access delay is greatly reduced. This storage method is referred to as *indexed sequential*.

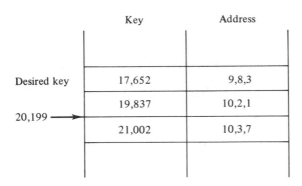

Figure 10.17 *Indexed-sequential table.*

10.5 Summary This chapter has shown how we can use auxiliary storage to solve problems having cell requirements exceeding available memory. We began by illustrating the need for auxiliary storage. Next, we introduced the concepts of sequential and random processing. We defined sequential file operations and described standard sequential file procedures of updating, merging, and sorting. Finally, we specified random file operations, illustrated the use of a random file, and discussed random file organizations.

SELECTED REFERENCES

1. GILDERSLEEVE, T. R., *Design of Sequential File Systems*, John Wiley & Sons, Inc., New York, 1971.

2. GRUENBERGER, FREDERICK, ed., *Critical Factors in Data Management*, Prentice-Hall, Inc., Englewood Cliffs, N. J., 1969.

3. *Introduction to IBM System/360 Direct Access Storage Devices and Organizational Methods*, Student Text, IBM Corp., Form C20–1649, October 1967.

4. IVERSON, KENNETH E., *A Programming Language*, John Wiley & Sons, Inc., New York, 1962.

5. LADEN, H. N., and T. R. GILDERSLEEVE, *System Design for Computer Applications*, John Wiley & Sons, Inc., New York, 1963.

6. LEFKOVITZ, D., *File Structures for On-Line Systems*, Spartan Books, Washington, D. C., 1969.

7. SALTON, GERALD, *Automatic Information Organization and Retrieval*, McGraw-Hill Book Company, New York, 1968.

PROBLEMS

For each of the following problems, develop a computerized solution, including an output list, input list, data chart, and flow chart.

10.1 Modify the update in Figure 10.8 so that it outputs a trace showing all changes made to the master file. Include customer numbers, new and old balances, and transaction information.

10.2 Modify the update in Figure 10.8 so that it calculates and outputs three batch totals: sum of all withdrawals, sum of all deposits, and sum of updated balances.

10.3 Sometimes it is desirable to be able to add new records to a master file during an update run. Expand Figure 10.8 so that this is possible. Give careful consideration to the choice of transaction codes.

10.4 Assume that in Section 10.3.1 it is now the bank's policy to permit selected customers to overdraw their accounts to prearranged limits. Assume that each master file record contains this value and expand Figure 10.8 to include this feature. In this case, there must be two different types of warning messages: overdrafts below the overdraft limit, and attempted withdrawals above the limit.

10.5 Assume that a sequential file contains one value per record. Develop a computerized procedure that copies this file onto a second sequential file.

10.6 Assume that two sequential files each containing one value per record have previously been sorted into ascending sequence. Develop a computerized procedure that outputs those values which occur on one file but not on the other.

10.7 Assume that a sequential file contains one value per record. Develop a computerized procedure which inputs this file and outputs one that contains N values per record, where N is specified before each computer run; N is known not to exceed 1000. This operation is known as *blocking*, the output is referred to as a *blocked* file, and N is the *blocking* factor.

10.8 Repeat Problem 10.5, using two blocked files having the same blocking factor, N, known in advance of each computer run; N never exceeds 100.

10.9 Repeat Problem 10.5, using two blocked files having different blocking factors, N and M, which are known in advance of each computer run; N and M never exceed 500.

10.10 Repeat Problem 10.7, but in this case *deblock* a file from N values per record. down to one value per record; N is never more than 250.

10.11 Develop a computerized procedure that inverts a sequential file end-to-end. In other words, its last value becomes its first, and its first becomes its last.

10.12 Assume that you are in charge of processing student records. The master file contains one record for each course taken by a student and each record consists of four values: student number, course number, course credits, and course grade. This file is maintained in ascending student number sequence. Develop a computerized procedure which:
(a) Adds new course records;
(b) Corrects grades in specific courses;
(c) Deletes course records.

10.13 Can a two-way sort merge be performed using just three sequential files? If so, explain.

10.14 Modify the sorting algorithm in Figure 10.13 so that it performs a three-way merge. Assume that six sequential files are available.

10.15 Modify the sorting algorithm in Figure 10.13 so that it performs an M-way merge. Assume that 2M sequential files are available.

10.16 A disk contains 200 cylinders, 10 tracks per cylinder, and 6 sectors per track. It stores a file, one record per sector. Each record contains one value, and these records are organized sequentially. Develop a computerized procedure that inputs one value, X, and then outputs the disk address of this value by searching this file sequentially, starting at disk address 1,1,1.

10.17 Repeat Problem 10.16, but now insert X into its proper place in the sequential file.

10.18 Assume that a random file contains 10,000 records and has indexed organization. Develop a subroutine INDEX(ID,C,T,S) that determines the disk address; C, T, S, of a record whose key is ID. Explain how your index table is organized and how its contents are retained in memory.

10.19 A subroutine, DADD(ID,C,T,S), is available that calculates the disk address of a record whose key is ID. Show how this subroutine would be used in Figure 10.16, assuming the credit account master file has a calculated organization.

10.20 Assume that each record of the credit account master file in Figure 10.15 is expanded to six entries: a customer account number, customer balance, change limit, and cylinder, track, and sector numbers of an overflow record. These last three values are 0 if there is no synonym for this record key. Develop a subroutine, RADD(ID,C,T,S), that returns the disk address, C, T, S, for a record whose key is ID. Use the subroutine, DADD, from 10.19 and be sure to handle the problem of multiple synonyms.

10.21 Develop a subroutine, ISADD(ID,TAB,N,C,T,S), that determines the disk address, C, T, S, of a record whose key is ID. Assume that the file has an indexed-sequential organization and that its indexed table is TAB and contains N entries. Assume the disk contains 200 cylinders each having 20 tracks with 4 sectors per track.

11 List Structures

So far, we have discussed three data structures: single cells, linear lists, and arrays. *Single cells* are suitable for problems involving limited data or requiring few values in memory simultaneously. *Linear lists* can be employed when many values must be in memory at the same time or when a single data relationship need be retained. Finally, *arrays* can be utilized for data sets that possess multiple relationships.

Actually, these structures are quite similar. In fact, their cell layouts form a geometric progression when single cells are considered as points, linear lists as line segments, and arrays as squares, rectangles, cubes, etc. As a group, these structures are sometimes referred to as *regular* or *orthogonal* data structures. In addition, such structures retain data relationships via the physical configuration of their cells. For example, a linear list maintains data order through its cell sequence. In other words, these structures contain no explicit information about data relationships; rather, such information is implicit in the structure itself. For this reason, these structures are sometimes said to be *implicit* data structures.

This chapter introduces the *list structure* as a data structure that can be used for solving problems unsuitable for orthogonal or regular structures. It begins by illustrating the limitations of orthogonal structures and then shows how list structures can overcome such drawbacks. Once the data- and flow-chart representations of list structures are presented, examples and techniques for using simple list structures are considered. Finally, more complex list structures are introduced and more involved problems are solved.

**11.1
Need
for List
Structures**

In solving any problem, it is necessary to decide which data structure is best suited for each data set. Therefore, let us begin our discussion by using orthogonal structures to solve a problem that is inappropriate for such structures. By so doing, we shall uncover the limitations of orthogonal structures and shall further illustrate how one recognizes that he has selected the wrong structure.

For purposes of discussion, let us suppose that we have the following problem. We are asked to develop a computerized procedure that sorts a set of names and addresses into ascending zip-code sequence. We are told that each name and address always contains 75 characters followed by a zip code at the seventy-sixth position. In addition, we are told that we shall always know how many names and addresses are in any one set.

Since sorting has already been discussed, you should be able to follow the solution shown in Figure 11.1. Basically, A is a two-dimension array whose first dimension represents address and whose second indicates position within address. Here, each row stores a separate name and address, one character per cell. Because these addresses must be sorted by zip, zip codes are saved in the same column, cell 76. Since A contains 1000 rows, it can store a maximum of 1000 names and addresses. The flow chart reads the input into A and then orders its rows by an interchange sort. Since zip codes are located in column 76, adjacent codes can be checked for sequence by the test statement

$$A(I,76) : A(I+1,76)$$

When an inversion is detected, the out-of-sequence addresses must be switched, cell-by-cell, for all 76 cells. Comparisons continue until all addresses are in sequence and no further interchanges are required.

In previous sorting examples, linear lists with their sequential cell arrangement were employed to retain data order. Here, each name and address consists of more than one value; thus, a second dimension is required for these additional values. Nevertheless, the rows of the array can be used to retain data order; since row order implies data order, it is necessary to interchange out-of-sequence addresses continually until proper order is achieved. In this case, these cell-by-cell exchanges are the most time-consuming operation in the algorithm.

Figure 11.2 shows a method for reducing these interchanges. Here, the array, A, stores names and addresses; once they have been read, they are not disturbed. In this case, a linear list, P, stores a set of cell pointers that are used to indicate the relative order of addresses in A. Initially, P contains a sequence of numbers, 1, 2, 3, ... , N, where each value represents the row number in A of its corresponding name and address. Since P(I) contains the

Output List

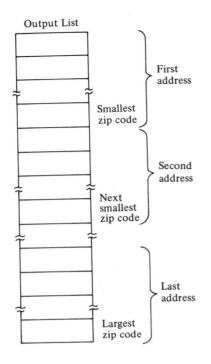

Input List

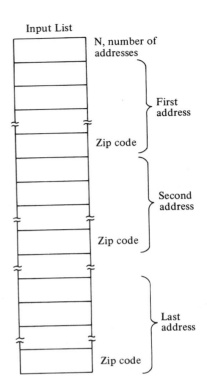

Data Chart

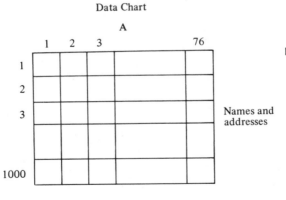

Figure 11.1 *Sorting addresses.*

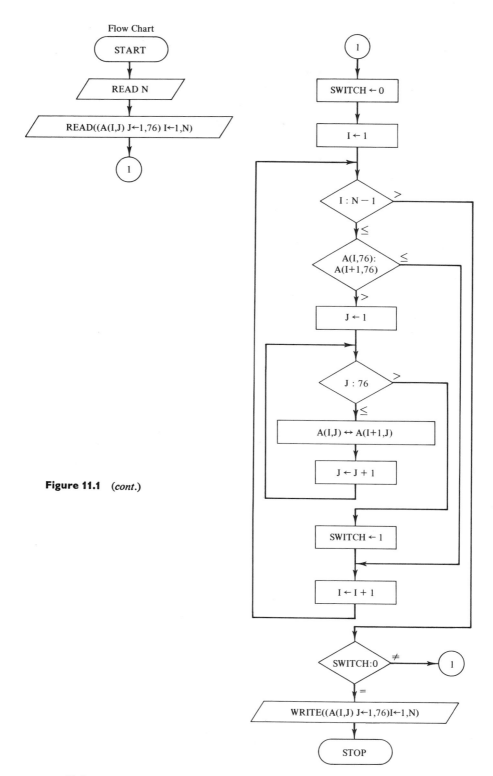

Flow Chart

Figure 11.1 (*cont.*)

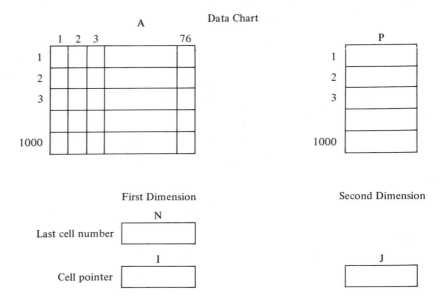

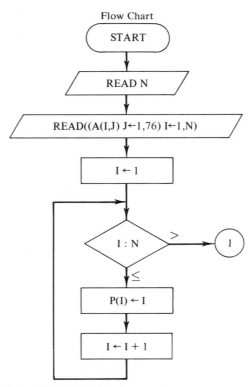

Figure 11.2 *Sorting addresses using pointers.*

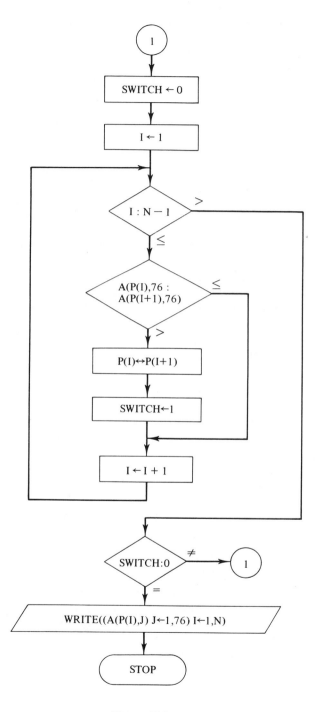

Figure 11.2 *(cont.)*

cell number of the ith address whereas $P(I+1)$ points to the $(i+1)$th, the test statement

$$A(P(I),76) : A(P(I+1),76)$$

can be used to compare zip codes of adjacent addresses. If they are out of sequence, we reverse their order by simply interchanging $P(I)$ and $P(I+1)$. Thus, the use of pointers to indicate relative data order reduces the number of cell exchanges per inversion from 228 to 3. Incidently, this same technique can be used to eliminate row interchanges during a Gauss partial-pivoting operation, as discussed in Section 8.3.3.

The difficulties encountered in our initial solution are caused by our choice of data structures. Since arrays do not contain explicit information as to the location of succeeding data, data arrangement was expressed by row order. In the second solution, we overcome this restriction by explicitly storing data order in a separate linear list. Orthogonal structures are also limited by the way they are allocated memory space. In general, they are assigned a specific amount of memory space in advance; once assigned, they are trapped between other structures and cannot be expanded or contracted conveniently. If a data structure is overassigned, its excess cells are left vacant and cannot be used by other structures; if underassigned, it cannot be expanded if a larger-than-expected data set exceeds its original allocation. Consequently, there is a need for data structures that explicitly retain data relationships and also permit dynamic storage allocation.

11.2 Single-Linked Lists

As in the case of orthogonal structures, list structures form a family of similar data structures. Therefore, let us first discuss the components of the simplest one, the *single-linked list*, and show how it is represented and used in data and flow charts. With this background, we can then generalize to more sophisticated list structures.

11.2.1 Components of single-linked lists

Examples of single-linked lists are displayed in Figure 11.3. The basic component, shown in Figure 11.3a, is referred to as an *element* and consists of two parts. The *datum* stores data values and the *link* points to the datum of the next element. For the time being, we shall assume that a datum consists of a single cell; thus, each element contains two cells, one datum and one link.

Figure 11.3b shows how links are used to chain together individual elements. Each link points to the next element, and since each element has a single link, it can be connected to one and only one element. Consequently, this structure is known as a *single-linked list*. Likewise, it is sometimes referred to as a *one-way list*, since there is only one path or direction through its elements. In addition, a separate pointer indicates the first element or *head* of a list, whereas a link of 0 signals its last or *tail* element.

(a)

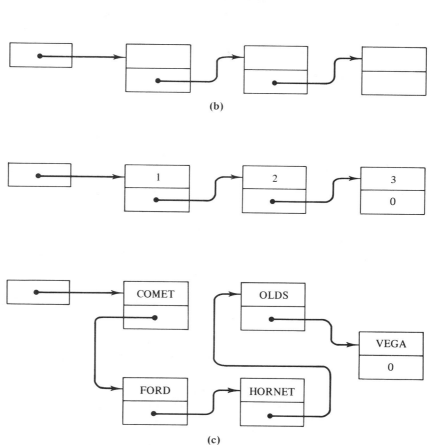

(b)

(c)

Figure 11.3 *Components of single-linked lists: (a) element; (b) single-linked list;*
(c) examples of single-linked lists.

Figure 11.3c shows two examples of single-linked lists. In the first case, the head points to an element whose datum contains a value of 1. The link of this element points to an element containing a 2, which in turn points to a 3. At this point, a link of 0 indicates end of list. In the second case, a single-linked list retains a set of automobile names in alphabetical order. Here, the datum of each element contains a car name and its link points to the next one. This example emphasizes that data sequence is indicated by link, not physical arrangement.

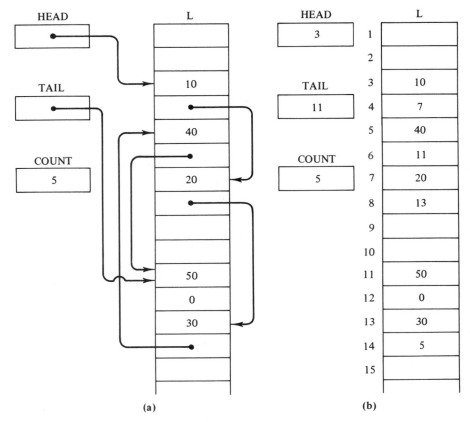

Figure 11.4 *Data chart of a single-linked list: (a) pointers represented by arrows; (b) pointers represented by cell numbers.*

The data chart representation of a single-linked list is shown in Figure 11.4. For simplicity, its elements are considered as being stored in a linear list whose odd numbered cells contain data followed by links in its even ones. In Figure 11.4a, links are represented by arrows, whereas actual cell numbers are used in Figure 11.4b. The single cell, HEAD, indicates that the datum of the first element is located at the third cell of L. Thus, the first element contains a data value of 10, followed by a link of 7. By tracing links through this list, we see that it contains the sequence 10, 20, 30, 40, 50. Note that this is the case even though list elements are not physically arranged in this order. At times, it is convenient to know the location of the last element and also the number of elements in a list. Here, single cells, TAIL and COUNT, perform these functions.

Figure 11.5 shows how two separate single-linked lists can coexist in memory. Here, HEAD1 indicates the beginning of one list and HEAD2 points to the other. Even when two lists coexist in the same area, it is quite probable that

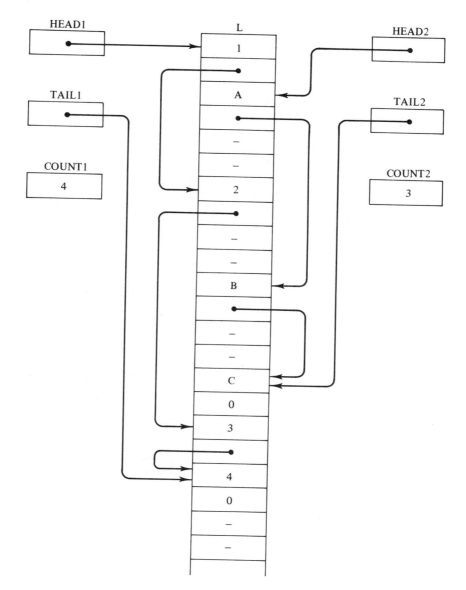

Figure 11.5 *Coexisting single-linked lists.*

there will still be unused elements. Furthermore, in later examples, we shall wish to expand and contract lists. Therefore, it is useful, as shown in Figure 11.6, to have yet another one, known as the *free list*, that ties all unused elements together. When an additional element is required, one is simply removed from the free list. Likewise, elements that are no longer needed are attached to the free list for later use.

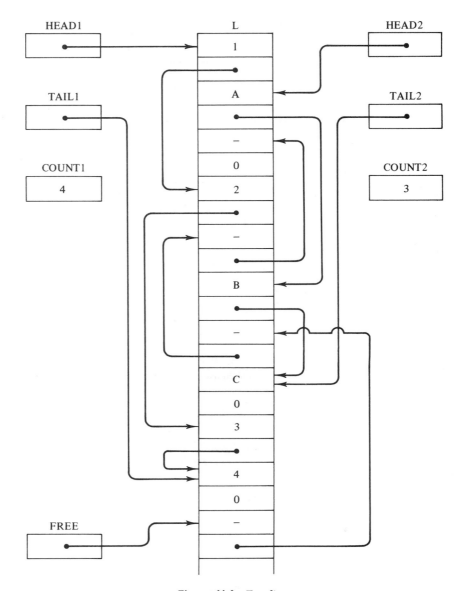

Figure 11.6 *Free list.*

Before we discuss basic list operations, let us review the components of single-linked lists by considering a brief example. In Figure 11.7, a previously sorted list is checked for ascending sequence. The first input value points to the head element; the second indicates the number of list elements that follow. A linear list, L, is used to store the linked list. Since L contains 1000 cells and each element has two values, the input must be no more than 500 elements.

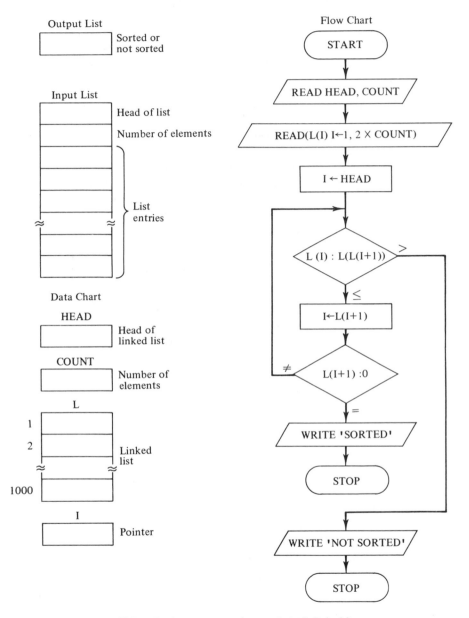

Figure 11.7 *Checking a previously sorted single-linked list.*

Once the linked list is in memory, I is initialized to point to the head element, and then the sequence of the list is checked, one element at a time. If I points to the datum of an element, then L(I) is the data value of that element. Likewise, I+1 points to the link of that element; therefore, L(I+1) points to the datum of the following element. Consequently, L(L(I+1)) is the data value of the next element. Thus, the test statement

$$L(I) : L(L(I+1))$$

can be used to compare adjacent data values.

11.2.2 Basic list operations

If data values are to be added and deleted from linked lists, there must be some method for maintaining a source of unused elements. As we said earlier, such elements are linked together in a separate list, referred to as the free list. However, this list must be generated at the beginning of an algorithm before any list operations are performed. Basically, this involves (1) linking to-

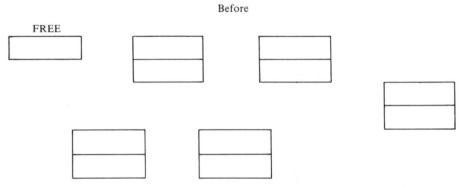

Before

FREE

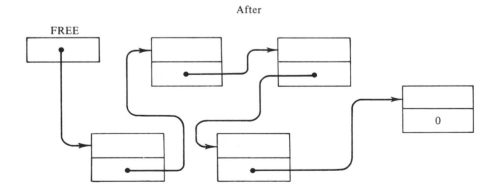

Figure 11.8 *Generating a free list.*

After

FREE

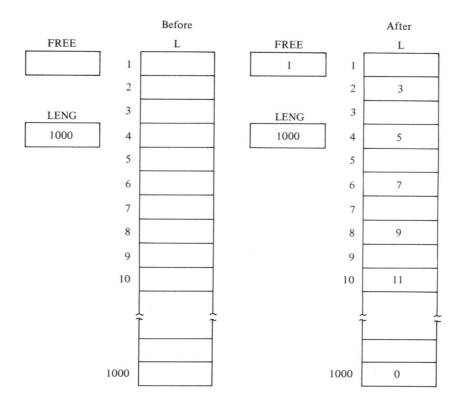

Figure 11.9 *Generating a free list in memory.*

gether a set of available elements, (2) setting the link of the last element to 0, and (3) saving a pointer that indicates the beginning of the free list. Figure 11.8 shows a set of unused elements before and after they have been connected to form a free list. Here, a single cell, FREE, acts as head of this list.

Figure 11.9 shows how a free list is generated in memory. Here, L is assumed to be a set of cells available for linked memory, whereas LENG specifies the number of cells in L and FREE indicates the head of the free list. Initially, all cells in L are unused; therefore, they belong on the free list. Consequently, FREE is initialized to 1 while each even-numbered cell is set to point to the odd-numbered cell that follows it. When the last element is reached, its link is given a value of 0. The subroutine, GEN(L,LENG,FREE) shown in Figure 11.10, incorporates this procedure to generate a free list in L consisting of LENG cells starting with FREE at 1. Here, the test statement,

$$I : 2 \times FLOOR(LENG/2)$$

insures that the upper boundary of L is not exceeded if LENG is by chance an odd number.

Subroutine Data Chart

Subroutine Flow Chart

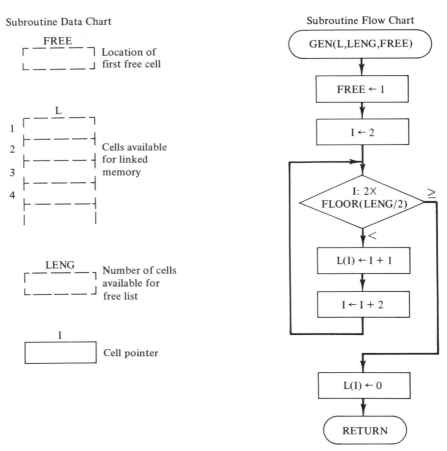

Figure 11.10 (*Above*) *Subroutine for generating a free list.*

Figure 11.11 (*Below*) *Inserting a value at the tail of a single-linked list.*

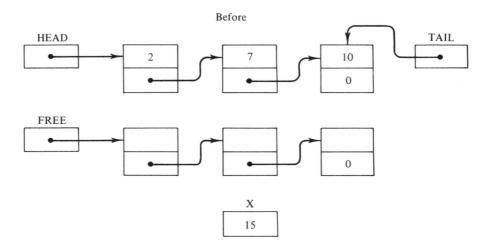

Now that we have a source of free elements, let us predefine the operation of inserting or appending a value to the tail of a single-linked list. Figure 11.11 shows an example before and after this operation is performed. Here, a linked list consists of three elements, and its head and tail are indicated by single cells, HEAD and TAIL. FREE points to the first element on the free list, and X contains the value to be appended to the end of this list.

Figure 11.12 shows the effect of this operation on a linked list stored in L. Essentially, the head element is unlinked from the free list and relinked to the tail of L. Careful study of this figure reveals that four links, numbered from 1 to 4, are altered in that sequence, as shown.

Link	Operation	Flow-Chart Statement
1	Free element linked to tail of L	L(TAIL+1)←FREE
2	TAIL revised to indicate new tail of L	TAIL←FREE
3	FREE revised to indicate next element	FREE←L(FREE+1)
4	New tail link set to 0	L(TAIL+1)←0

This procedure assumes that there is at least one free element. Unfortunately it is possible for the free list to be exhausted; therefore, we must allow for this situation. Further study of Figure 11.12 reveals that when an element is removed from the free list, its link is used to revise FREE. If, by chance, that element is the last available one, its link is 0; thus, FREE is set to 0 when the last element is removed from the free list. Consequently, FREE must be checked for 0 before an attempt is made to remove an element from the free list.

Figure 11.11 (*cont.*)

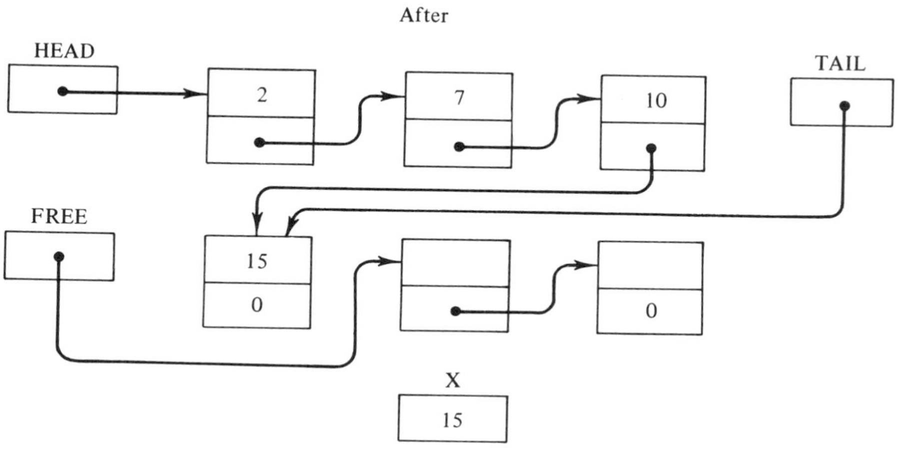

After

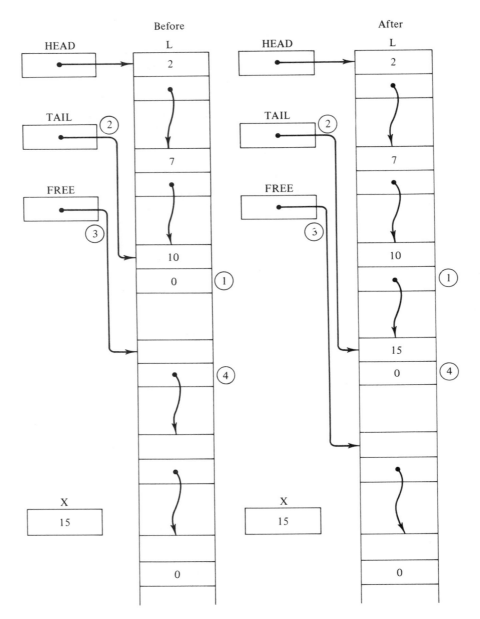

Figure 11.12 *Inserting a value at the tail of a single-linked list in memory.*

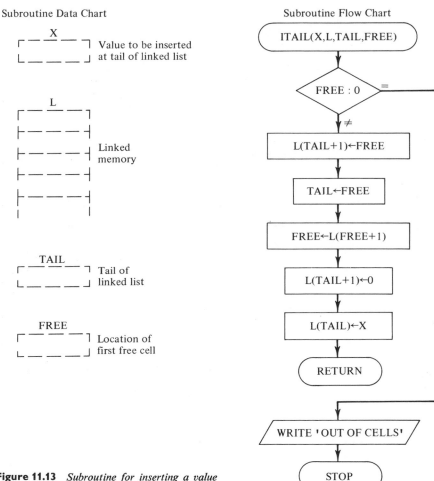

Subroutine Data Chart

X
Value to be inserted
at tail of linked list

L
Linked
memory

TAIL
Tail of
linked list

FREE
Location of
first free cell

Subroutine Flow Chart

ITAIL(X,L,TAIL,FREE)

FREE : 0 =

≠

L(TAIL+1)←FREE

TAIL←FREE

FREE←L(FREE+1)

L(TAIL+1)←0

L(TAIL)←X

RETURN

WRITE 'OUT OF CELLS'

STOP

Figure 11.13 *Subroutine for inserting a value at the tail of a single-linked list.*

Figure 11.13 shows a subroutine, ITAIL(X,L,TAIL,FREE), that inserts the contents of X at the tail of the list, L. The routine begins by checking for an exhausted free list; if FREE is 0, it terminates with an appropriate message. If there is at least one free element, it is unlinked and appended to the tail of L, as discussed previously. Finally, the contents of X are stored in the new tail element and control is returned to the calling program.

Inserting a value at the top of a single-linked list is quite similar to the previous example. Figure 11.14 shows a list, L, before and after an insertion is made. Here, the first free element is unlinked and relinked as the head of L.

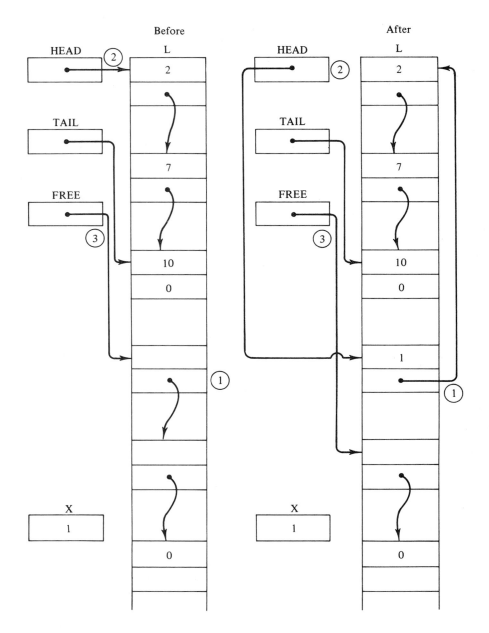

Figure 11.14 *Inserting a value at the head of a single-linked list in memory.*

Study of the figure indicates that three links must be altered in a cyclic permutation

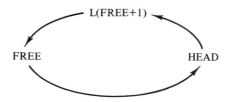

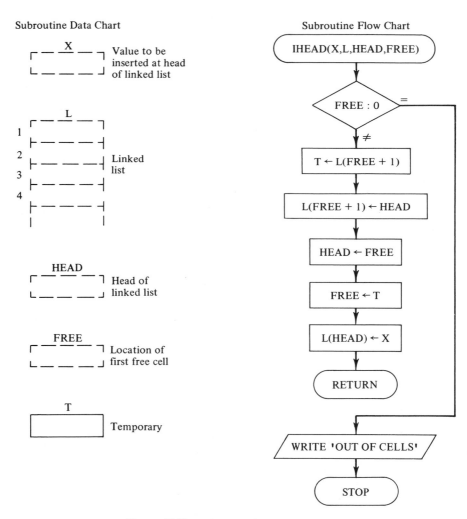

Figure 11.15 *Subroutine for inserting a value as the head of a single-linked list.*

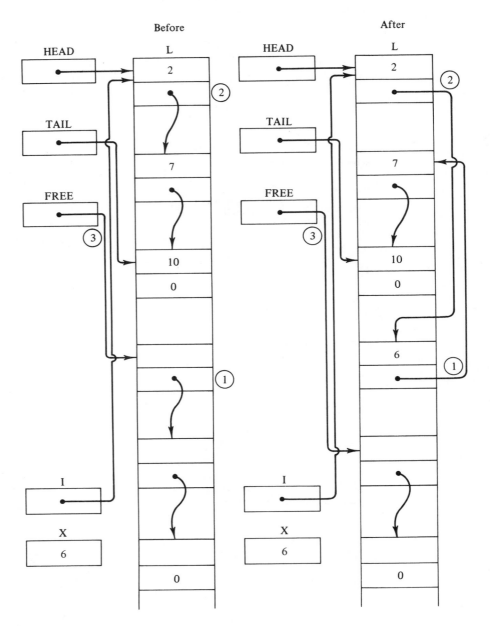

Figure 11.16 *Inserting a value in the middle of a single-linked list in memory.*

In this case, HEAD goes into L(FREE+1), which goes into FREE, which goes into HEAD. This requires that one link be saved in a temporary cell, T, as follows:

Link	Operation	Flow-Chart Statement
	Save link to next free element	T←L(FREE+1)
1	Free element linked as head of L	L(FREE+1)←HEAD
2	HEAD revised to indicate new head element	HEAD←FREE
3	FREE revised to indicate next free element	FREE←T

The subroutine, IHEAD(X,L,HEAD,FREE), shown in Figure 11.15, incorporates this procedure to insert the contents of X as the head of a list, L.

Inserting a value somewhere in the middle of a single-linked list follows directly from the previous example. Figure 11.16 shows a list, L, before and after an insertion. As before, the first element is unlinked from the free list; but now, it is relinked into L. In this case, I points to an element in L, and the insertion is made *after* that element. This requires that three links be altered in a cyclic permutation

in the following sequence

Link	Operation	Flow-Chart Statement
	Save link to next free element	T←L(FREE+1)
1	Free element linked to L	L(FREE+1)←L(I+1)
2	L linked to free element	L(I+1)←FREE
3	FREE revised to indicate next free element	FREE←T

The subroutine, IMID(X,L,I,FREE) shown in Figure 11.17, incorporates this procedure.

Deleting a value from a single-linked list is simply the inverse of insertion. Therefore, let us consider only one case, removal from the middle. Figure 11.18 shows a list, L, before and after deletion. Here, an element is unlinked from L and then relinked at the head of the free list. As above, I points to an element in L, and the deletion is made after that element. In this case, the direction of link permutation is reversed

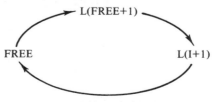

Subroutine Data Chart

Subroutine Flow Chart

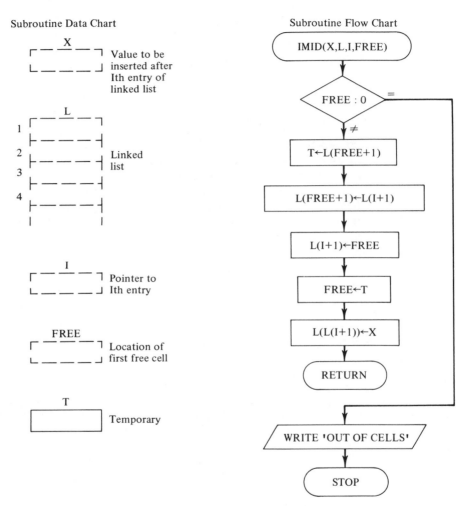

Figure 11.17 *Subroutine for inserting a value in the middle of a single-linked list.*

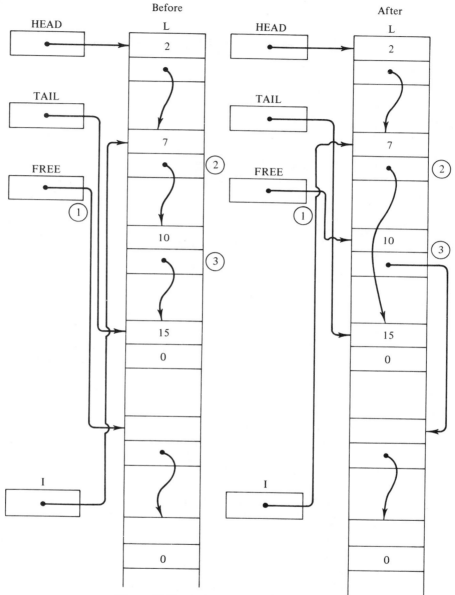

Before HEAD L

After HEAD L

Figure 11.18 *Deleting a value from the middle of a single-linked list.*

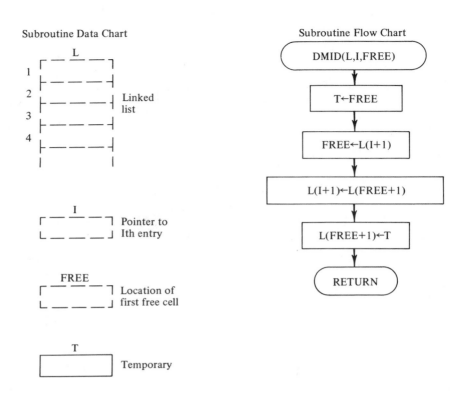

Subroutine Data Chart

L

1

2 — Linked
list

3

4

I
Pointer to
Ith entry

FREE
Location of
first free cell

T
Temporary

Subroutine Flow Chart

DMID(L,I,FREE)

T←FREE

FREE←L(I+1)

L(I+1)←L(FREE+1)

L(FREE+1)←T

RETURN

Figure 11.19 *Subroutine for deleting a value from the middle of a single-linked list.*

and is performed as follows:

Link	Operation	Flow-Chart Statement
	Save link to first free element	T←FREE
1	FREE points to deleted element	FREE←L(I+1)
2	Element unlinked from L	L(I+1)←L(FREE+1)
3	Deleted element linked to free list	L(FREE+1)←T

The subroutine, DMID(L,I,FREE) shown in Figure 11.19 incorporates this procedure.

Finally, it is useful to have a predefined operation that locates the kth entry in a single-linked list. In a linear list, k itself points to the desired entry; however, in a single-linked list, it is necessary to trace through the list counting element by element until the kth is reached. The function, LOCATE(L,HEAD, K), shown in Figure 11.20, returns a value that points to the kth element of L beginning at HEAD. If, by chance, L does not contain k elements, it returns a value of 0.

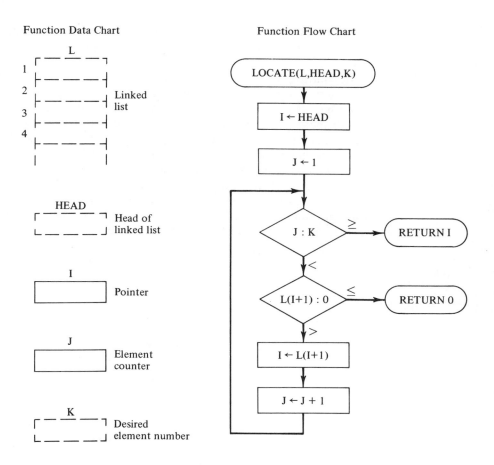

Function Data Chart

Function Flow Chart

Figure 11.20 *Function for locating the kth element of single-linked list.*

Now that we have a set of predefined operations for manipulating single-linked lists, let us use them to solve problems. As always, we should pay particular attention to the choice of data structures and how these choices affect algorithmic design.

11.3.1 Sorting by insertion

As a first example, let us repeat the sorting problem discussed in Section 7.3.3. In that situation, a linear list with its sequential cell arrangement was used to retain data order. All input values were read and then adjacent number pairs were interchanged until an ascending sequence was achieved. Although straightforward, this procedure requires many data exchanges. For example, if a set contains 1000 values and if, by chance, its largest value initially appears first, it takes 3000 data movements for that value to reach its proper location at the end.

In contrast, values can be sorted as they are read. This involves inputing one at a time and comparing it with numbers that are already stored in a linear list. When its proper position is determined, the value already at that location and all those below it must be moved down one cell to make room for this latest value. This procedure is referred to as *sorting by insertion*, and, when used with a linear list, still requires many data movements.

Single-linked lists are ideally suited for sorting by insertion, and Figure 11.21 shows a solution that uses this technique. Here, L is reserved for linked memory; since it contains 1000 cells, it can be divided into 500 single-linked elements. Single cells, HEAD and TAIL, indicate the head and tail of L, whereas FREE points to the first free element.

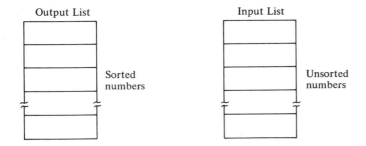

Data Chart

Figure 11.21 *Sorting by insertion.*

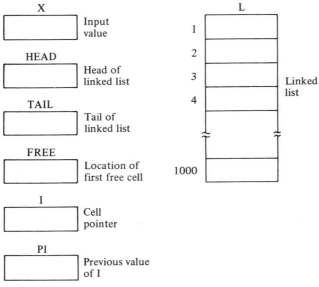

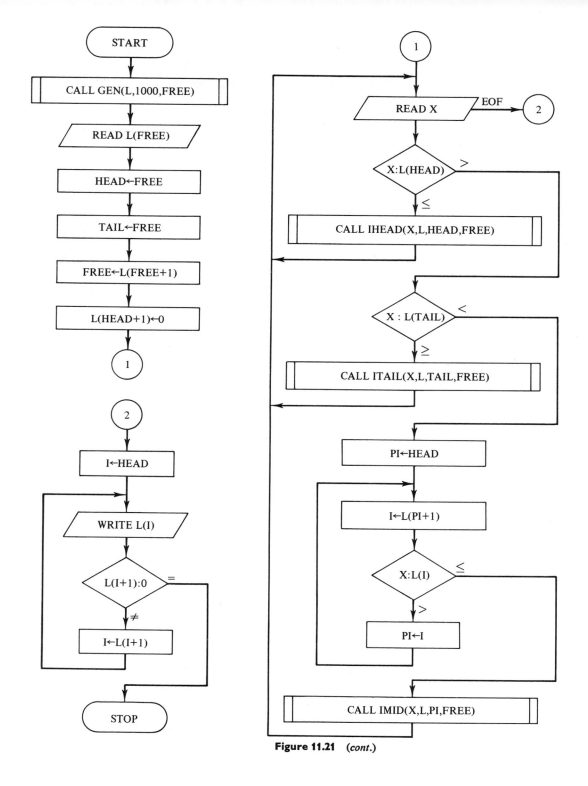

Figure 11.21 *(cont.)*

The flow chart begins by using the subroutine, GEN(L,1000,FREE), to generate a free list of 500 elements. It then reads the first input value directly into the first free element. This is done because subroutines, IHEAD, IMID, and ITAIL, expect a linked list that already contains at least one entry. Note that the initial value of FREE is determined by subroutine, GEN, when it sets up the free list. Next, HEAD and TAIL are initialized and FREE adjusted to point to the next free element. Finally, the link of the first element is set to 0.

Remaining input values are then read one at a time into X. If $X \leq L(HEAD)$, it belongs at the head of L; if $X \geq L(TAIL)$, it goes at the tail; otherwise, it must be inserted somewhere in the middle. In this case, I is used as a pointer to trace through the list one element at a time. As long as $X > L(I)$, I is advanced to the next element. As soon as $X < L(I)$, X must be inserted between $L(I)$ and the element preceding it. Since single-linked lists are chained in only one direction, there is no direct way to return to the previous element once I has been advanced. Consequently, it is necessary to remember the previous value of I; here, PI performs that function.

11.3.2 Text editing

As a second example of single-linked lists, let us repeat the solution to the text editing problem discussed in Section 9.3.4. In that case, a paragraph was edited such that its first line was indented by five spaces and multiple blanks were removed. In addition, a period followed by at least one space was considered an end of sentence to be succeeded by two and only two spaces.

In that situation, a linear list was used to save text order. A complete paragraph was read and then examined character-by-character in sequence. When an addition was required, all characters below the point of insertion were moved down one position. Likewise, when a deletion was necessary, characters were shifted up one place. These data movements were required because data relationships were implied by data order in a linear list. These movements can be eliminated by the use of a single-linked list.

The flow chart in Figure 11.22 performs the same text editing, assuming that a paragraph is already contained in a single-linked list, L. It begins by inserting five blanks at the head of L and then uses the function, LOCATE, to return a value for I that points to the sixth data element. Characters are then examined one at a time. In this case, insertions and deletions are made using appropriate subroutines; data relationships are altered by link changes rather than data movements.

11.3.3 Airline reservations

As a third example of the use of single-linked lists, let us assume that we are asked to develop a computerized airline reservation system. For this discussion, we shall greatly reduce system requirements to define a reasonable problem. Nevertheless, this simplified example exhibits the usefulness of list structures.

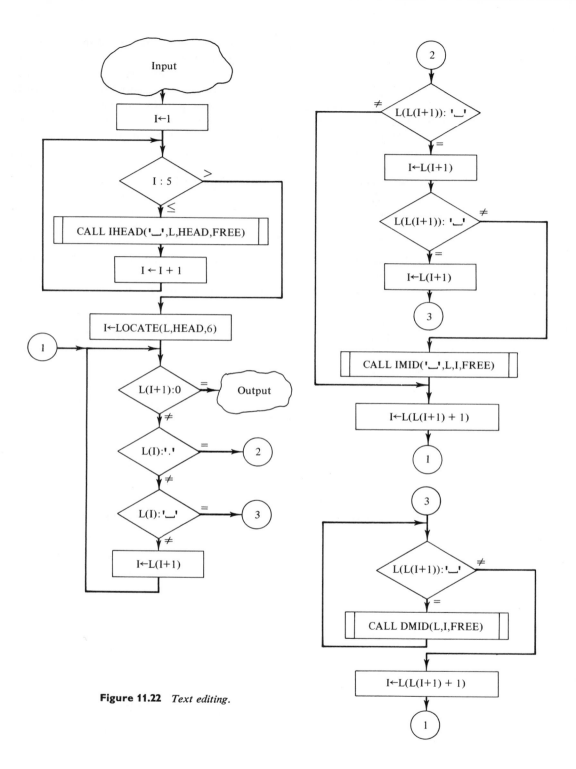

Figure 11.22 *Text editing.*

We are told that our airline has 100 different flights, numbered from 1 to 100. Each particular flight may be assigned an airplane that carries from 1 to 250 passengers, but aircraft size is always known in advance. Our system must be able to maintain a record of the number of seats still available on each flight, add passengers to and remove them from a flight, and switch them from one flight to another. Finally, for simplicity, let us assume that we need only retain passenger last names and that our records are for a single day of operation.

As output, our solution should produce messages in response to input inquiries. For example, suppose we wish to know how many seats are still available on flight number 17. We might input via a remote console an inquiry or request code followed by flight number. Our system should respond with a suitable message, such as

23 SEATS AVAILABLE ON FLIGHT 17

Note that inclusion of the flight number as output allows us to verify that we typed the correct flight number. Figure 11.23 shows a table of possible inputs and outputs for this problem. In each case, the first input value is an inquiry or request code. Note that output can vary for the same input code. For example, there are three possible responses for a switch request: switch completed, no space on desired flight, and passenger name not found on current flight.

Request	Input Data	Output Message
Space available	1 Flight no.	No. of seats available on flight no.
Add passenger	2 Flight no. Passenger name	Passenger name added to flight no. or No space available on flight no.
Remove passenger	3 Flight no. Passenger name	Passenger name removed from flight no. or Passenger name not found on flight no.
Switch passenger	4 From flight no. to flight no. Passenger name	Passenger name switched from flight no. to flight no. or No space available on flight no. or Passenger name not found on flight no.

Figure 11.23 *Airline reservation responses.*

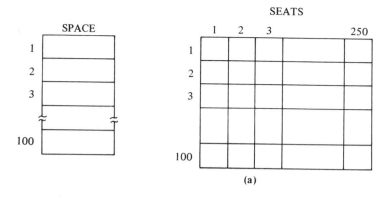

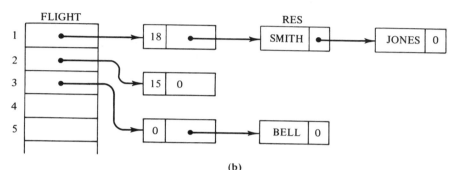

Figure 11.24 *Airline reservation data structures:*
(a) orthogonal structures; (b) single-linked lists.

Now that output and input are specified, let us consider what data must be retained in memory and how those data should be stored. Let us begin by seeing how this might be done with orthogonal structures. First, we need to keep track of the number of seats still available on each flight. Since there are 100 flights, this can be done with a 100-cell linear list, SPACE, as shown in Figure 11.24a. Second, we must maintain a list of passengers currently holding space on each flight. Each flight can be assigned an airplane with up to 250 seats. Therefore, let us use a 100 × 250 array, SEATS, whose first dimension represents flight and whose second indicates seat. This method requires 25,100 cells. In reality, not all airplanes would have a 250-seat capacity, but, because we are using orthogonal structures, we must reserve enough cells to handle the largest possible data set. Consequently, this method wastes much memory space.

Figure 11.24b shows how this same information can be stored via single-linked lists. Here, a 100-cell linear list, FLIGHT, is used to save the head pointer for each of 100 single-linked lists stored in RES. The first element of each list specifies the number of seats still available, whereas following elements maintain passenger names, one name per element. For example, flight number 1 has 18 seats still available while holding space for passengers SMITH and

Flow Chart

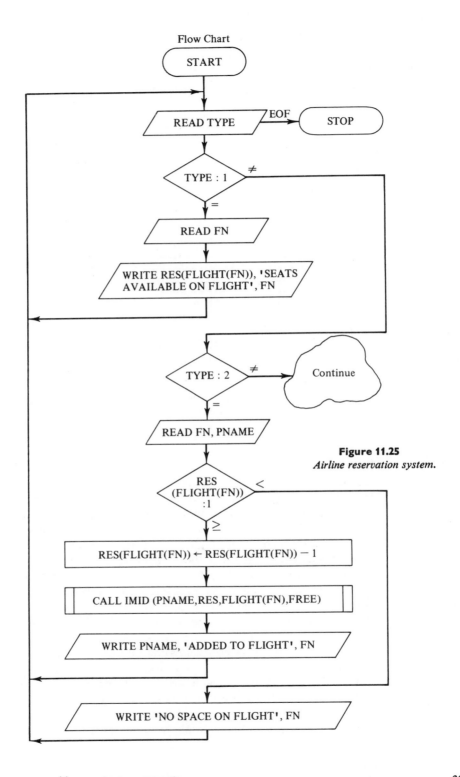

Figure 11.25
Airline reservation system.

JONES. In contrast, flight 2 is empty with 15 unused seats and flight 3 is booked to capacity. This storage method requires 3 cells per flight plus 2 per reservation, or $300 + 2n$ cells for n customers.

It should be noted that these two methods require the same memory space when

$$300 + 2n = 25,100$$

$$2n = 24,800$$

$$n = 12,400$$

In other words, linked lists require less memory space as long as there are fewer than 12,400 passengers or an average of 124 passengers per flight. This is true even though linked lists require two cells per passenger reservation, whereas orthogonal structures require just one.

Finally, we can develop an algorithm and draw its flow chart. Basically, we must process inquiries one at a time. Here, each inquiry contains a code that specifies how it is to be handled. If this code is 1, we are to read a flight number, FN, and then access the datum of the first element in its particular single-linked list in RES. Since FLIGHT(FN) points to the datum of the desired element, we can answer this inquiry by accessing RES(FLIGHT(FN)).

In contrast, if the inquiry code is 2, we are to read a flight number, FN, and passenger name, PNAME. Before this passenger can be added to this flight, we must ensure that it still contains at least one unassigned seat. If it does, this passenger name can be added to the end of the proper linked list. If the flight is completely booked, our system must respond with a "no space" message. The flow chart in Figure 11.25 handles these two inquiry codes. Others are left to you as problems at the end of the chapter.

11.4 Other Single-Linked List Structures

For simplicity, we have so far limited our consideration to single-linked lists whose elements contain a single data cell. Actually, the form of a list structure should be dictated by its data. For example, Figure 11.26 illustrates three variations. In the first case, each element contains a single link followed by a fixed or constant number of data cells. In the second one, elements are comprised of a variable number of data cells where the second cell of each element contains a data count. Finally, in the last one, each element consists of two pointers, one to the next element and one to the data values of this element.

Figure 11.27 shows an example of a single-linked list with variable-length elements containing the phrase A CRAZY FOX. As before, unused elements are retained as a free list. Here, elements have variable lengths; therefore, when an additional element is required, the free list must be searched for one that contains enough cells. For example, suppose we wish to insert the word, RED, between CRAZY and FOX. Since RED has three letters, it is necessary to find an element with three data cells. If we select one with more, we must be able to return unused cells to the free list.

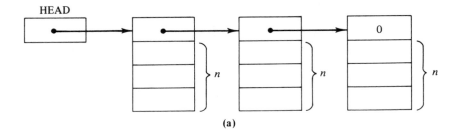

(a)

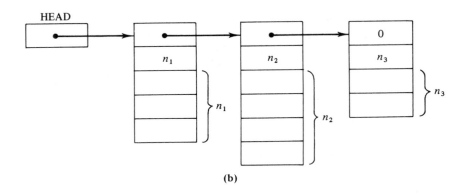

(b)

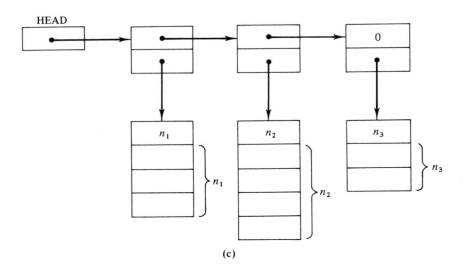

(c)

Figure 11.26 *Other forms of single-linked lists: (a) fixed-length data;*
(b) variable-length data; (c) remote data.

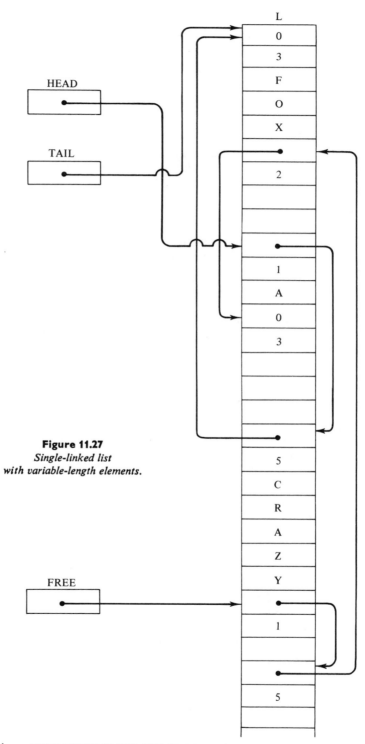

Figure 11.27
*Single-linked list
with variable-length elements.*

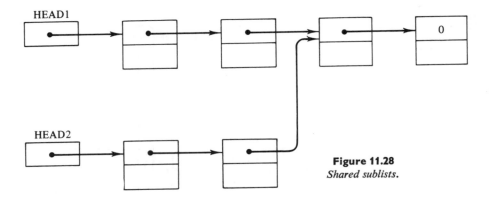

HEAD1

HEAD2

Figure 11.28
Shared sublists.

Sometimes, lists have common data values. If such is the case, duplicate entries can be eliminated by sharing common elements, as shown in Figure 11.28. Here, two single-linked lists share a common sublist. On the other hand, a data set may not have a beginning or an end, but may be circular, as in the *single-linked ring* shown in Figure 11.29. Here, the zero link of a tail element is replaced by a link connecting the tail to the head. Consequently, every element is followed by another element, and this structure has no end.

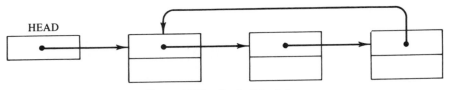

HEAD

Figure 11.29 *Single-linked ring.*

11.5
Multilinked
Structures

So far, we have limited our consideration to single-linked structures. Because elements of these structures contain a single link, each element is followed by one and only one element; therefore, there is just one path through such structures. Let us now consider list structures with elements containing multiple links.

11.5.1 Double-linked lists

As in the case of single-linked structures, there are a variety of multilinked structures. Therefore, let us first discuss the components of the simplest one, the *double-linked list*, and show how it is represented in data and flow charts. We can then generalize to other multilinked structures.

Figure 11.30 displays an example of a double-linked list. As before, the basic component, shown in Figure 11.30a, is referred to as an element. In

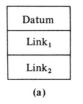

(a)

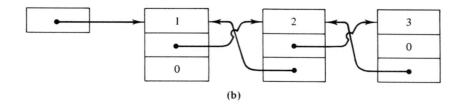

(b)

Figure 11.30 *Components of a double-linked list:*
(a) element; (b) double-linked list.

this case each element consists of three parts: a datum and two links. For simplicity and ease of discussion, each datum is comprised of a single cell.

Figure 11.30b shows how individual elements of a double-linked list are chained together. Here, one link of each element points forward to the next one, and the other points backward to the previous one. Since elements are connected in sequence by two links, this structure is known as a double-linked

Figure 11.31 *Data chart of a double-linked list:*
(a) pointers represented by arrows; (b) pointers represented by cell numbers.

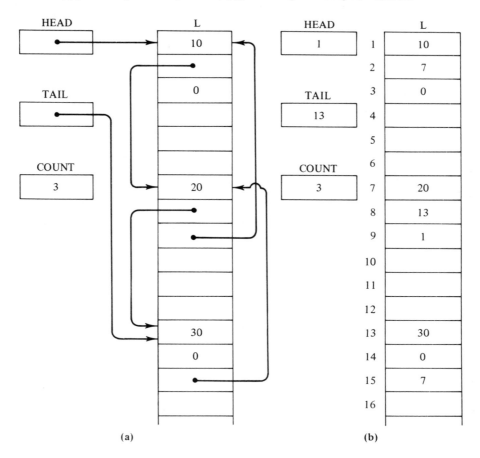

(a)   (b)

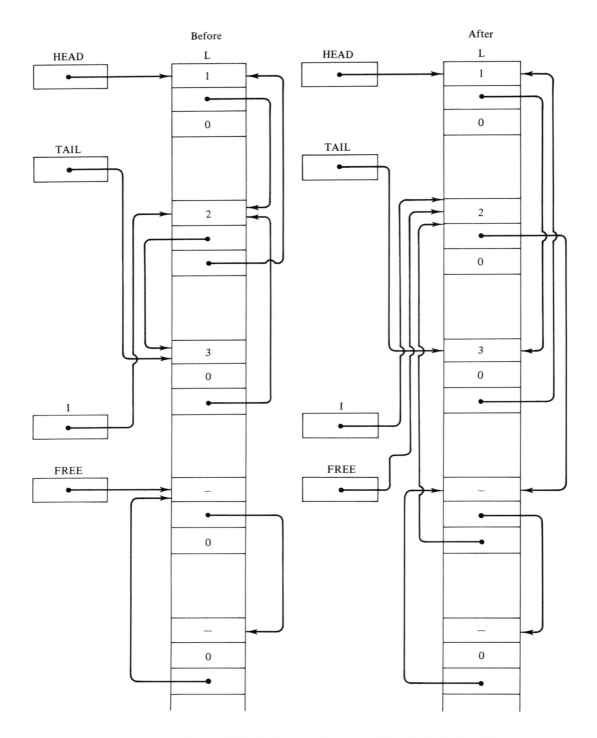

Figure 11.32 *Deleting a value in the middle of a double-linked list.*

list. Similarly, it is referred to as a *two-way list*, since there are two paths or directions through its elements. As before, a separate pointer indicates the head element, but, in this case, a zero link signals end of list in both directions.

The data chart representation of a double-linked list is shown in Figure 11.31. In one case, links are represented by arrows; cell numbers are used in the other. Here, single cells, HEAD and TAIL, point to the datum of the first and last elements, whereas COUNT specifies the number of elements. A trace of the links starting at HEAD reveals that this list contains the sequence 10, 20, 30.

As with single-linked lists, it is possible to predefine a set of operations for manipulating double-linked structures. Since procedures are similar, let us consider just one in detail—that of deleting an element from the middle of a list. Figure 11.32 shows a list, L, before and after a deletion is completed. Here, I points to the element that is to be unlinked from L and relinked as the head of the free list. In the case of a single-linked list in Figure 11.19, I pointed to the element preceding the one to be removed. This was necessary because we cannot delete an element without knowing which element precedes it and is to be relinked to the element that follows it. Here, the second link provides that information. The subroutine DMID(L,I,FREE) shown in Figure 11.33, performs this operation.

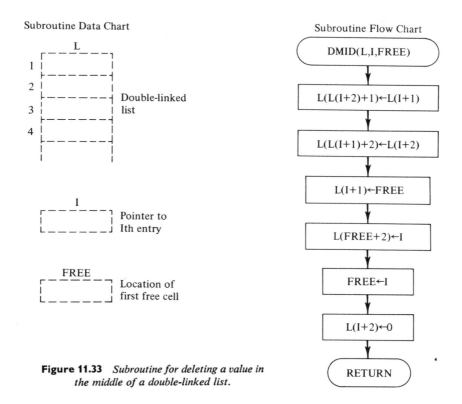

Figure 11.33 *Subroutine for deleting a value in the middle of a double-linked list.*

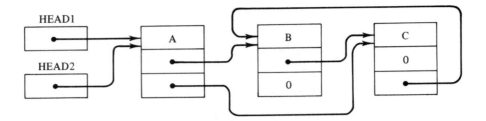

Figure 11.34 *Entwined lists.*

Double-linked lists form a basis for other structures. For example, Figure 11.34 illustrates a structure that might be referred to as an *entwined list*. Here, elements are connected in two different sequences, one for each set of links. For example, a trace of the first link produces a sequence A, B, C, whereas the other is A, C, B. Such a structure would be useful for retaining an address file in both alphabetic and zip-code order without duplicating data entries. Finally, Figure 11.35 displays *entwined rings*.

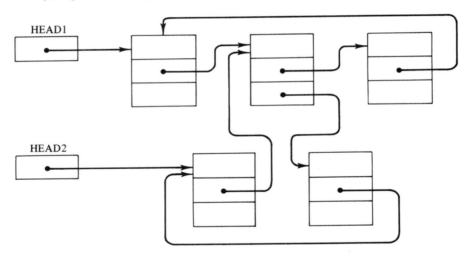

Figure 11.35 *Entwined rings.*

11.5.2 Trees and tree searching

Now that multilinked elements have been introduced, let us use them to construct the most interesting of all list structures, *trees*. Actually, these structures are quite similar to those in nature. Figure 11.36a shows the conventional abstraction of a tree. Here, branches are represented by directed arrows, whereas branch points are known as *nodes*. A node with only outgoing branches is referred to as a *root*; those with only incoming ones are classified as *terminals*.

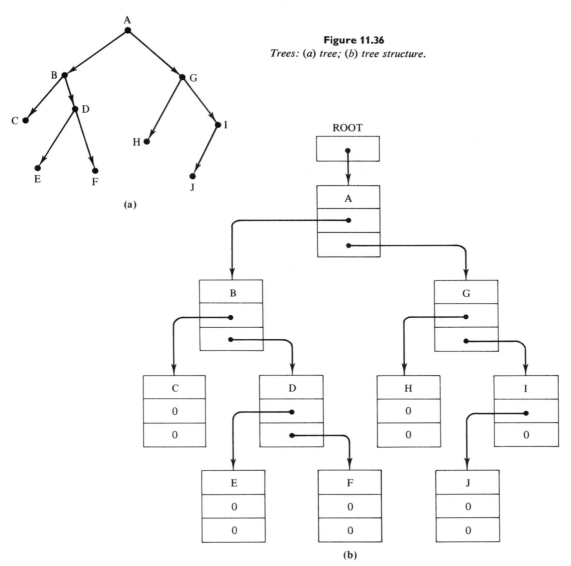

Figure 11.36
Trees: (a) tree; (b) tree structure.

(a)

(b)

Trees are limited to a single root and to one incoming branch per node. This latter restriction implies that there is only one path from a node to any other node. Finally, it is by convention that trees are drawn with their root pointing upward, whereas their branches "grow" downward.

Figure 11.36b shows how double-linked elements are used to construct a tree. Here, a separate element represents a node and its branches are specified by links. In this case, elements are limited to two links; therefore, nodes can have no more than two outgoing branches. Such trees are referred to as *binary trees*. As always, a single cell is used to indicate the start of a list structure. Here, ROOT points to the root element. Finally, terminal elements contain two zero links.

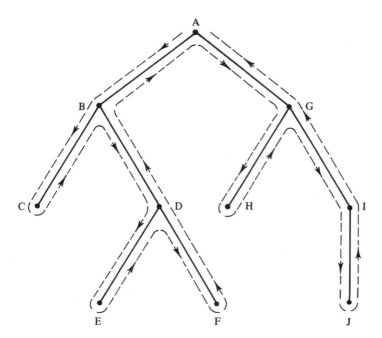

Figure 11.37 *Left-order search.*

As a data structure, trees exhibit precedence or branching relationships. In Chapter 4, a genealogical diagram was used as an example of a data set possessing a tree structure. In Figure 4.7, father-son relationships were indicated by vertical arrangement and husband-wife, brother-sister, and cousin relationships were represented by horizontal placement. In contrast, the tree in Figure 11.36 might represent airline routes originating from some city. In this case, cities B through J can be reached from A, but only B and G have nonstop service. This diagram indicates that, for example, C can be reached by stopping at B, whereas service to both H and I includes landing at G.

Because trees contain branch points, additional techniques are required if one wishes to search these structures. Suppose that we are asked to find all terminals in a given tree. To do so involves tracing through the structure one link at a time, examining each element to determine if it has two zero links. Since we must ensure that we reach every node, let us follow the path shown in Figure 11.37.

Basically, this path can be described as follows. Each time we reach a node, we attempt to exit downward via the left-most untried branch. Whenever we reach a terminal or a node that has no more untried branches, we exit upward and repeat the process on the previous node. If that node has an untried branch, we move downward. Otherwise, we continue upward. Eventually, having started out at the root, we return to that root and terminate the search for lack of untried branches. Because this procedure traverses branches from left to right, it is referred to as a *left-order search*. Similarly, a *right-order search* can also be used.

Although straightforward, a left- or right-order search does have one drawback. In the tree structure illustrated in Figure 11.36, all links point down the tree; thus, there is no way to move back up in the structure once a terminal is reached. Consequently, if we intend to search a tree for all terminals, we must save information about the path currently being traced. Obviously, we can keep a list of names of nodes traversed. In Figure 11.38a, the search has reached terminal C, and LIST indicates that B was the previous node. However, there is no relation between the name of a node and the location of its element in memory. Consequently, we should instead store pointers to traversed nodes as shown in Figure 11.38b. However, when we reach a terminal we would prefer to know the location of the next node, not the previous one.

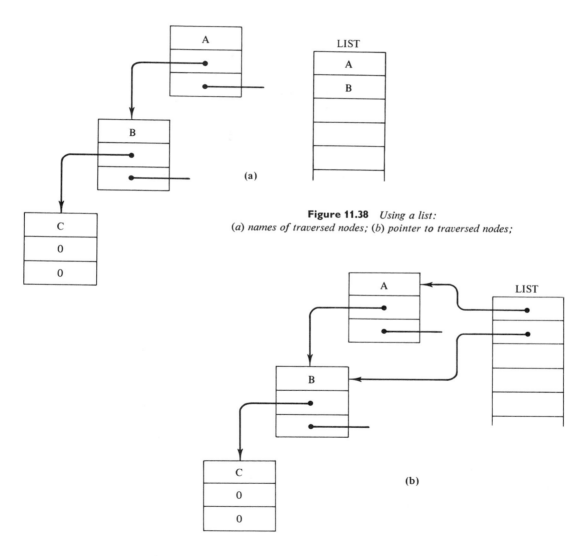

Figure 11.38 *Using a list:*
(a) names of traversed nodes; (b) pointer to traversed nodes;

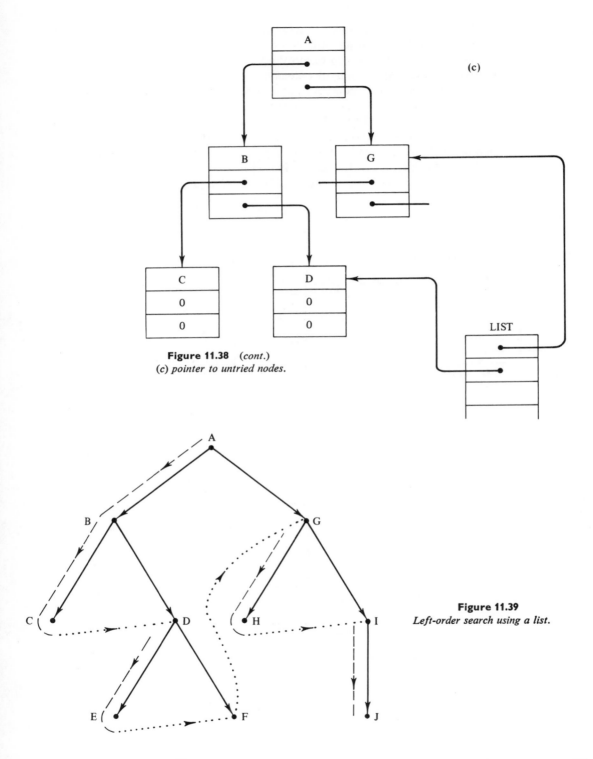

Figure 11.38 *(cont.)*
(c) pointer to untried nodes.

Figure 11.39
Left-order search using a list.

Rather than saving pointers to traversed elements, we should retain untried links, as shown in Figure 11.38c.

Before we develop an algorithm for finding all terminals of a tree, let us consider how a list of untried links affects our tree search. As before, we begin at the root; but now each time we reach a node, we save its right-hand link at the end of LIST and then use its left-hand one to locate the next node. When we reach a terminal, we remove the last entry from LIST and use it as a link to the next element. If, by chance, that element is also a terminal, we return to LIST to locate the next element. Otherwise, we save the right-hand link and continue down the tree via the left-hand one. Figure 11.39 shows the path of a left-order search using such a list. Here, dashes indicate the use of left-hand links, whereas dots indicate links from that list.

The list described in this example is known as a *push-down list*. Entries are stored at one end and, as used, are removed from that end. In other words, the last entry on is the first entry off, i.e., last in-first out or LI-FO. Such lists can be compared to a tray holder in a cafeteria. As the top tray is removed, the next tray pops up to take its place. Likewise, when the holder is filled, it pushes down, leaving access to the top tray. In a similar manner, a push-down list provides access to its last entry via a pointer to that entry.

Finally, Figure 11.40 shows data and flow charts that find all tree terminals. Here, the tree is stored in T and PDL functions as the push-down list. This procedure begins by initializing PDL with a link to the root element. The chart then follows a left-order search through T. This algorithm assumes that if a node has only one outgoing branch, that branch is stored in the first link position. This implies that if a first link is 0, its second link must also be 0, therefore, the element represents a terminal.

Now that we can perform tree searches, let us assume that we have the following problem. We are given a map that indicates road connections between two cities, and we are asked to determine the lengths of all routes between those cities. The diagram in Figure 11.41a illustrates sample input for this problem. Here, cities are represented by nodes, whereas road connections and distances are specified by branches. The figure indicates that G can be reached from A via four different routes, two of which pass through D. For this sample, our problem is to find the lengths of these routes from A to G.

Previously, we said that trees are limited to one incoming branch per node, and that this restriction implies only one path from one node to another. Thus, the diagram in Figure 11.41a is not a tree because nodes D and G have more than one incoming branch. In general, a set of connected nodes is referred to as a *graph*. Here, we note that there can be parallel paths between nodes but that a node cannot be reached along a path starting at itself. Consequently, this graph is said not to contain *loops* or *cycles*.

In the previous example, data values were associated with nodes; in this case, branches also have values. Therefore, it is necessary to represent both nodes and branches by elements, as shown in Figure 11.41b. Here, node elements consist of three cells, one datum and two links, whereas branch elements contain two, one datum and one link.

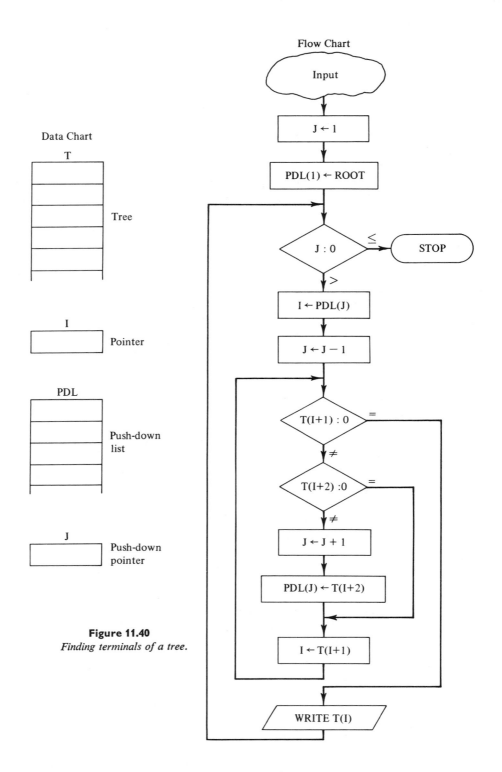

Data Chart

T

Tree

I   Pointer

PDL

Push-down
list

J   Push-down
           pointer

Figure 11.40
Finding terminals of a tree.

Flow Chart

Input

J ← 1

PDL(1) ← ROOT

J : 0   ≤   STOP

>

I ← PDL(J)

J ← J − 1

T(I+1) : 0   =

≠

T(I+2) :0   =

≠

J ← J + 1

PDL(J) ← T(I+2)

I ← T(I+1)

WRITE T(I)

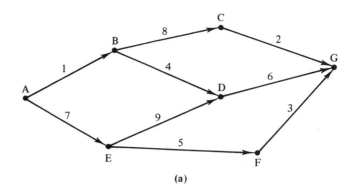

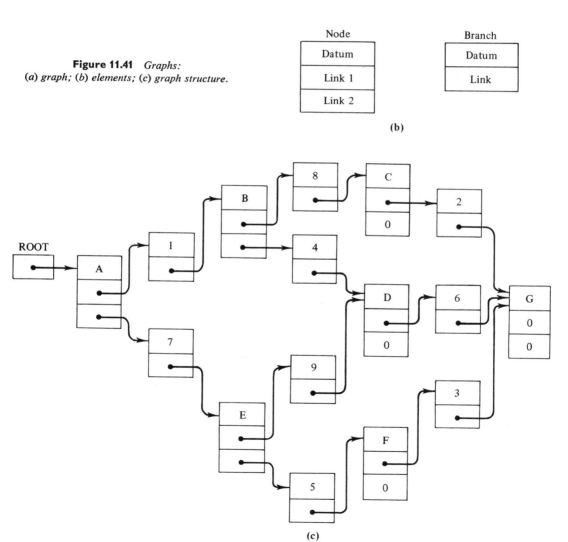

Figure 11.41 *Graphs:*
(a) graph; (b) elements; (c) graph structure.

(a)

(b)

(c)

Figure 11.41c shows how node and branch elements are chained together to construct a graph. As before, a single cell points to the root element; but here, each node element is followed by a branch element, which, in turn, is followed by another node element. In other words, nodes are always separated by branches.

Now that we have a structure that retains the relationships of our data, we are ready to develop an algorithm. Actually, this problem is quite similar to the previous one, but here we must remember the length of paths as we trace through the graph. In the previous solution, a push-down list was used to indicate untried nodes. Here, an additional list can be used to remember path lengths to those nodes.

Figure 11.42 shows a data and flow chart for finding the lengths of paths between beginning and ending nodes. Here, the graph is stored in G, whereas I points to the current node and LENG indicates the path length to that node. NPDL is a node push-down list that saves pointers to untried nodes; LPDL is a length push-down list that indicates the path length to those nodes. In other words, LPDL(1) specifies the path length to NPDL(1), etc.

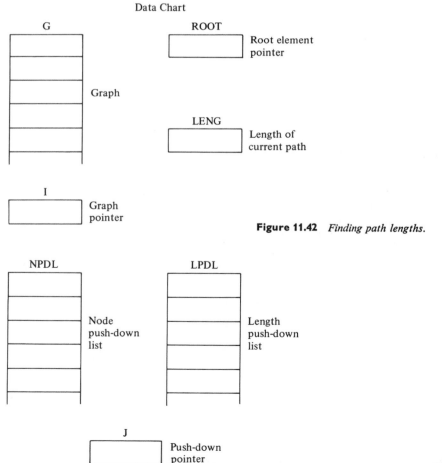

Data Chart

G

Graph

ROOT

Root element pointer

LENG

Length of current path

I

Graph pointer

Figure 11.42 *Finding path lengths.*

NPDL

Node push-down list

LPDL

Length push-down list

J

Push-down pointer

408

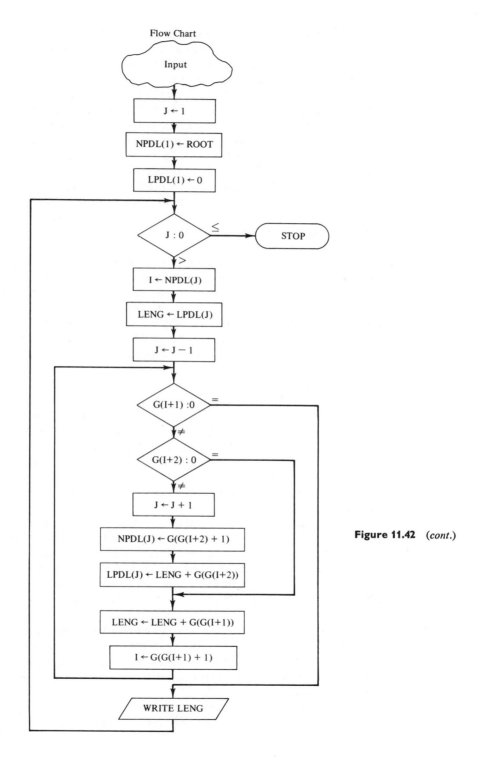

Figure 11.42 (*cont.*)

The flow chart begins by initializing NPDL(1) with a link to the root element and sets its path length LPDL(1) equal to zero. The chart then follows a left-order search through G. As before, this algorithm assumes that if a node has only one outgoing branch, that branch is stored in the first link position of its node element. Consequently, if the first link in a node element is 0, it represents a terminal element, and its path length, LENG, is ready for output.

On the other hand, if the first link is not 0, the second one must then be checked for 0 to determine if there is more than one branch leaving the current node. If it is nonzero, entries must be made to both push-down lists. Since I points to the datum of the current node element, I+2 points to the second list. Therefore, G(I+2) indicates the datum of the following branch element, and G(I+2)+1 specifies the link of that branch. Finally, G(G(I+2)+1) accesses the link that locates the node element which follows the current node. Likewise, since LENG is the length to the current node, LENG + G(G(I+2)) is the path length to that node.

Once necessary entries have been made to the push-down lists, I and LENG must be advanced to the next node down the current path. Since G(I+1) points to the length of the branch that separates the current node from the next one, the length of that branch is G(G(I+1)). Therefore, the length from the root to that node is LENG + G(G(I+1)). Similarly, the location of that node is G(G(I+1)+1). Once I and LENG have been advanced, the chart loops back to see if the next node is terminal.

11.6 Summary

Comparisons have been made between list and orthogonal data structures. Perhaps the most obvious is that list structures consume more memory space because of their links. In previous examples, each data value was accompanied by one or more links; therefore, list structures require at least twice as much memory as orthogonal ones. However, storage efficiency improves when there is more than one data value per element, as suggested in Figures 11.26 and 11.27.

In contrast, orthogonal structures are allocated a fixed amount of storage in advance and cannot be contracted or expanded. This can be wasteful because a large number of cells must be left vacant in each structure just in case a larger than normal data set is encountered. On the other hand, list structures can coexist in the same memory area and each can take advantage of cells freed by the others. Furthermore, such structures can save storage by sharing common entries.

Generally, list structures are easier to manipulate than orthogonal ones. For example, we can insert items into or delete them from linked lists simply by altering a few links. On the other hand, such operations on linear lists require many data movements. Furthermore, it is easier to join two linked lists and to break one apart.

Finally, references to random entries are much faster in orthogonal structures. For example, the ith entry in a linear list, A, is accessed by the notation, A(I).

In contrast, the ith entry of a linked list is found by tracing links and counting elements one at a time. Consequently, orthogonal structures lend themselves to random processing, whereas list structures are best used when values can be processed one at a time in sequence.

SELECTED REFERENCES

1. BERGE, CLAUDE, *The Theory of Graphs and Its Applications*, John Wiley & Sons, Inc., New York, 1962.

2. BERZTISS, ALFS T., *Data Structures: Theory and Practice*, Academic Press, Inc., New York, 1971.

3. DODD, GEORGE G., "Elements of Data Management Systems," *Computing Surveys*, Vol. 1, No. 2, June 1969, pp. 117–33.

4. FLORES, IVAN, *Data Structure and Management*, Prentice-Hall, Inc., Englewood Cliffs, N. J., 1970.

5. GAUTHIER, RICHARD, and STEPHEN D. PRONTO, *Designing Systems Programs*, Prentice-Hall, Inc., Englewood Cliffs, N. J., 1970.

6. KNUTH, DONALD E., *The Art of Computer Programming*, Vol. 1, "Fundamental Algorithms," Addison-Wesley Publishing Co., Inc., Reading, Mass., 1968.

7. STONE, HAROLD S., *Introduction to Computer Organization and Data Structures*, McGraw-Hill Book Company, New York, 1972.

8. VAN DAM, ANDRIES, and DAVID E. RICE, "On-Line Text Editing: A Survey," *Computing Surveys*, Vol. 3, No. 3, September 1971, pp. 93–114.

PROBLEMS

11.1 Develop a function, TAIL(L,HEAD), that returns a pointer to the tail of a single-linked list, L, which starts at HEAD.

11.2 Write a function, FIND(L,HEAD,CHAR), that returns a pointer to an element which contains CHAR in a single-linked list, L, starting at HEAD. If no match is found, return a value of 0.

11.3 Develop a subroutine, CONNECT(L,HEAD1,HEAD2), that connects two single-linked lists one after another. *Hint:* Use the function TAIL(L,HEAD) developed in Problem 11.1.

11.4 Draw a diagram that shows how double-linked elements can be used to construct a two-dimension array.

11.5 Assume that I points to an entry of a single-linked list, L. Develop a subroutine, EXCHANGE(L,I), that interchanges that element with the one that follows. Produce two solutions: one that moves data and one that alters links.

11.6 Develop a subroutine, INVERT(L,HEAD,TAIL), that inverts a single-linked list, L, via link alterations such that its data values appear in opposite order. HEAD and TAIL specify the head and tail elements of L.

11.7 Expand the airline reservation system in Figure 11.25 to handle the "remove passenger" option.

11.8 Expand the airline reservation system in Figure 11.25 to handle the "switch passenger" option.

11.9 Expand the airline reservation system in Figure 11.25 to handle reservations for more than one day.

11.10 Expand the airline reservation system in Figure 11.25 so that flights can be added and removed.

11.11 Revise the flow chart in Figure 11.40 so that it performs a right-order trace.

11.12 Modify the structure shown in Figure 11.36 so that it is possible to move upward in a tree without the need of a push-down list.

11.13 Develop a function, TRACE(T,ROOT,DATUM), that searches a tree similar to the one shown in Figure 11.36, looking for a datum that equals DATUM. When a match is found, return a pointer to that datum. Otherwise, return 0. The tree is stored in T and ROOT points to its root.

11.14 Assume that T represents a tree and that I points to a node that has at least one unused link position. Develop a subroutine, ATTACH(T,I,X,FREE), that fastens a terminal node to T via that unused link and then saves X in that new node. Finally, FREE specifies the head of an unused element list.

11.15 Write a function, VTREE(L,ROOT), that verifies whether a structure is a tree. This structure is stored in L and ROOT points to its first element. Return a value of 1 if it is a tree and 0 if not.

11.16 Modify Figure 11.42 so that it outputs the length of the longest path.

11.17 Expand Figure 11.42 so that it outputs the nodes on the longest path.

Index

Branch structure, in flow chart, 122
Bubble sort, algorithm for, 206
Bug, in a flow chart, 132
Built-in function, 131

Calculated disk organization, 355
Calculating a binomial coefficient, algorithm for, 305
Calculating a grade-point average, algorithm for, 171
Calculating an average and above average count, algorithm for, 200
Calculating simple interest, algorithm for, 142
Calculating the average of a set of numbers, algorithm for, 184, 194, 200
Call statement, 295
Card, punch, 20
CRAM storage unit, 40
Card reader, 20
Cathode ray tube (CRT), 28
Cell, definition of, 81
  number, 186
  pointer, 187
    hazards of using, 191, 243
Central processing unit (CPU), 16
Character machine, 93
Chain printer, 25
Channel, 20, 33
  on magnetic tape, 33
  on paper tape, 20
Character printer, 25
Checking a set of numbers for numerical sequence, algorithm for, 156
COBOL, 42
Coincident-current core memory, 29
Colon, comparison operator, 117
Column, in a data structure, 234
Column order, in data input, 239, 241
Comparison operator, 117
Compiler, 42
Complex calculator, 12
Complex conjugates, in quadratic equations, 309
Computerized procedure, 122
Computer model, 45–72
  analysis of, 60–66
    data-instruction coordination problem, 62–63
    instruction sequence problem, 63–66
  block diagram of, 46
  components of, 46–54
    accumulator (AC), 49
    arithmetic unit (AU), 48–49
    control unit (CU), 46
    input unit, 47–48
    instruction address register (IAR), 49
    instruction unit (IU), 49–52
    memory unit, 46–47
    output unit, 48
  instruction cycle, 52–57
    execute phase, 53
    fetch phase, 53
    examples of, 54–57
  instructions, 49–52
    format, 49
    ADD (add), 50
    BMI (branch if minus), 51
    BPL (branch if plus), 51, 55

Computer model (*cont.*)
    BRA (branch absolutely), 51, 55
    BZE (branch if zero), 52
    DIV (divide), 51
    LOAD (load accumulator), 50, 54
    MPY (multiply), 50
    READ (read), 52, 57
    STOP (stop), 52, 59
    STORE (store accumulator), 50
    SUB (subtract), 50
    WRITE (write), 52, 58
  purpose of, 45
  using the model, 57–60
Connector outline, in a flow chart, 147
Console typewriter, 22
Constants, 97–98
  alphanumeric, 97
  floating point, 97
  integer, 97
Control unit (CU), 46
Core plane, memory, 29
Counting a set of positive numbers, algorithm for, 149
Credit checking system, algorithm for, 351
Cross tabulation, algorithm for, 270, 277
Cycle, in a graph, 405
Cycle, instruction, 53
Cylinder, disk, 349

Data cell, 40
Data chart, definition of, 80
  for different data structures
    array, 83, 235–238
    double-linked list, 397
    entwined ring, 400
    linear list, 81, 186
    multidimension, 83, 235–238
    single cell, 81
    single dimension, 81, 186
    single-linked list, 366–368, 393–395
    single-linked ring, 400
    tree, 83, 401
  with data values, 96
Data-instruction coordination problem, 62
Data representation, 93–97
  forms of data, 93–96
    alphanumeric, 95
    integer, 93
    floating point, 94
  variables and constants, 96–97
Data structure, definition of, 80
  array, 83, 235–238
  double-linked list, 397
  entwined ring, 400
  linear list, 81, 186
  multidimension, 83, 235–238
  single cell, 81
  single dimension, 81, 186
  single-linked list, 366–368, 393–395
  single-linked ring, 400
  tree, 83, 401
Datum, of a list structure, 366
Debugging, 132
Decision outline, in a flow chart, 86, 116
Deque, definition of, 190
Descending sequence, sorting into, 204
Desk checking, 132
Destructive readout, memory, 29
Difference engine, 9